About the author

Dr Gerhart von Westerman, who died early in
1963, was a prominent figure in German
musical life and was particularly connected
with the Berlin Philharmonic Orchestra, of
which he was the director for many years. He
compiled both his *Opera Guide* and *Concert
Guide* in order to provide the layman with
a 'deeper understanding and increased
enjoyment of the great forms of music' and
to provide the experienced concert-goer,
record-collector and amateur musician with
an invaluable reference book.

Also by Gerhart von Westerman
and available in Sphere Books

OPERA GUIDE

Concert Guide

A Handbook for Music-Lovers

by
GERHART VON WESTERMAN

Preface by
JOHN RUSSELL

Foreword by
WILHELM FURTWÄNGLER

Translated and edited by
CORNELIUS CARDEW

SPHERE BOOKS LIMITED
30/32 Gray's Inn Road, London WC1X 8JL

First published in Great Britain
by Thames and Hudson 1963
Copyright © Thames and Hudson 1963
Adapted from *Knaurs Konzertführer*
Copyright © Droemersche Verlagsanstalt, Munich 1951
Copyright © Th. Knaur Nachf. Verlag, Munich 1956
First Sphere Books edition 1968
Reprinted May 1970, October 1973

TRADE
MARK

Set in Bembo

Printed in Great Britain by
Hazell Watson & Viney Ltd
Aylesbury, Bucks

ISBN 0 7221 9003 4

CONTENTS

PREFACE

The author of this book, Dr Gerhart von Westerman, died in Berlin on 17 February 1963 at the age of sixty-eight. Since 1951 he had been the artistic director and governing spirit of the Berlin Festival. For three weeks in September and October of each year, West Berlin welcomed the best that the world had to offer in the way of music, drama and art. Our hosts had, of course, great resources of their own in all these fields: a better singer than Fischer-Dieskau, a better orchestra than the Berlin Philharmonic, a better repertory theatre than the Schiller-Theater and a greater museum than the one in Dahlem would be hard to find anywhere. Dr von Westerman knew how to show all these off to their best advantage; but as the *Berliner Festwochen* are addressed in large part to the beleaguered city itself he busied himself with a particularly devoted ingenuity to the task of getting the very best from other countries. When he succeeded, and when Glyndebourne, the Comédie-Française, Callas, Stravinsky, or the Vienna Philharmonic were on hand, his delight was touching to see. When hopes were disappointed, on the other hand, and the imported attraction was rather less good than it had promised to be, his was never the face that made its disappointment manifest. In such matters he had the diplomacy of the heart, not of the protocol-book. Whether his fellow-Berliners were as grateful to him as they should have been, I cannot tell; but I do know that many a foreign guest marvelled at the felicity with which the classic German repertory was intermingled with standard international attractions, and it was possible, for instance, for an English visitor to duck the Royal Ballet, if he so wished, and see the plays of Kleist and Barlach and Hauptmann, for which our theatres never find room. But although Dr von Westerman took pride in his foreign guests and was always available to hear what they had to say, he was, I think, proudest of all on the occasions on which, thanks to him, the ordinary Berliner could feel himself once again at the heart of great events.

There are many efficient festival directors who know only the names, only the outward aspects, of what is being put on the programme. But Dr von Westerman was not at all like that, and the immense popularity of his *Konzertführer* in its original edition comes in part from the evident enthusiasm with which he explores the concert repertoire, and in part from his readiness to do the right homework before putting pen to paper. He never lost the feeling that every performance, every act of listening, was important; he was a natural teacher, but he was also a natural enjoyer, and in the anglicized *Concert Guide* both sides of his nature shine out, it seems to me, and remind his friends of one who was an ideal audience for music of every sort.

Designed for a German-speaking and German-listening public, the original book included a number of works which no English or American audience is ever likely to hear, and omitted others of which the English-speaking concert public would expect such a book to give an account. The text was, therefore, extensively revised and enlarged; and in particular a long section on twentieth-century music was contributed by Mr Cornelius Cardew. Himself a composer of outstanding promise, Mr Cardew has the best of all reasons to know what he is talking about. He has also been responsible for a large number of new entries about older music.

As a result of these amendments, the Westerman *Konzertführer* has become more than a concert guide of the kind pioneered in this country by Rosa Newmarch. It is a guide to the whole evolution of orchestral and choral music; and, as such, it will be as invaluable to the gramophone public as to the concert-goer.

JOHN RUSSELL

FOREWORD

I have been asked by my colleague of long standing, Gerhart von Westerman, to write a few introductory words to his *Concert Guide*.

I am very happy to comply with this request. Dr von Westerman has been my righthand man for years as director of the Berlin Philharmonic Orchestra, and has always introduced the broadcasts of the Philharmonic concerts. Besides, the subject of this book is a spiritual possession essential to Europe: the world of the great symphonists, which seems, as do all spiritual traditions at the present time, to be in a situation of imminent peril.

The last war saw the breakdown of the economic structure of Europe and the mass-murder of youthful talent. Nowadays it is often said that the world of the great symphonists is obsolete, exhausted, and holds nothing for the present generation; that performances of a Beethoven symphony, for example, are quite superfluous. This view is flatly contradicted by the experience of musicians, organizers of concerts, and sellers of tickets. The work of Bach, Mozart, Brahms, Schubert, Bruckner—to name but a few—still fills our concert halls, providing the audiences with the communal experience of great art, lifting them above the everyday world, and proving itself an unquenchable source of spiritual strength.

Here the function of this book becomes clear. Full enjoyment of great works is only possible when the strength of their form is seen as clearly as their more readily appreciable content. This book is not addressed to the musical expert, but to the open-minded, unprejudiced, anonymous audience at our concert halls, who all have a need for musical culture, and who are essential for its preservation and development.

WILHELM FURTWÄNGLER

INTRODUCTION

This concert guide is for those who love music, especially symphonic music, without possessing expert knowledge of the subject. My aim and purpose is to deepen understanding and increase enjoyment of the great forms of our music.

Many concert guides have been written for the connoisseur and the professional musician. They presuppose specialized knowledge of music: analyses, for instance, depend on musical examples, which are unlikely to increase the layman's appreciation of the music heard in a concert hall, even if he is able to pick the examples out on a piano. In this book I have been careful always to explain the theme of a musical example in words: written music, whenever it appears in the book, is additional to verbal explanation.

I believe that anyone genuinely interested in instrumental music has a feeling for the elemental themes of musical form: tension and relaxation, symmetry and change, repetition and contrast, statement and answer. I hope to make this feeling for form articulate, and in this way bring about a real understanding of music. It is my main concern to describe the formal structure of individual works of music, and the book begins with a brief discussion of musical form which, attentively read, should clarify the rest of the book. Music, on the whole, is so formal that any method of elucidation should be welcome, and I have not hesitated to talk historically, or in terms of instrumentation, or about themes, rhythms and tunes in the music. This type of explanation is useful especially with programme music, which by its nature is based on an extra-musical subject; but even here formal qualities are of the first importance.

When I write about my own musical experience, I do so only to stimulate the reader, so that he may make such experience his own. The spiritual nature of music is a matter which must be individually and personally created by the imagination.

G. v. W.

MUSICAL FORM

If architecture is frozen music, then music is architecture in flux. Music is formally bonded: without architectonic shape, only sound, not music, is possible. Understanding of music requires a spontaneous, unconsidered grasp of the formal regularities that inhabit it. Melody, rhythm, harmony, metre, tonality, all the basic elements of music, are formal qualities, regularized by formal laws.

The music of the classical composers—Haydn, Mozart, Beethoven—achieves an unconditional structural clarity, the zenith of closed formality. I shall keep these composers in mind while trying to give an outline of the great schools of music. Pre-classical, romantic and modern forms can all easily be derived from the concepts of classical music.

Music is wonderfully rich, complex and varied, yet analysis always reveals the same few basic laws. Revolutionary spirits have believed that their music possessed new fundamental formal structure. They have always been wrong: cool analysis has always demonstrated that music is articulated by the same concepts of variation and unity, symmetry and change, repetition and contrast, tension and relaxation.

There are two basic types of musical structure: successive form and development form. *Successive form* is a succession of equally important parts, as in songs and rondos, for example. In a *development form* the structure is evolved from the cell of a motif or a theme. Examples of this form are the fugue, canon, passacaglia, chaconne, toccata, and the first movement of a sonata.

All composed music can be divided into *periods*. These periods need not be regular, nor follow each other symmetrically, but symmetry is present to a high degree in classical music. All classical music can be analysed as a succession of even periods, almost always eight bars long, and containing two balancing four-bar phrases. The phrase itself contains a two-bar germinal cell, which is known as the *motif*. The melodies or themes of classical music are built up by the successive combination of two two-bar motifs, then two four-bar phrases, and so on.

Successions of two eight-bar periods constitute the independent musical form of folk songs, chorales, small art songs or *lieder*, and also traditional dances. The themes of variation movements are often of this form, known as *binary form*, in which a period A, the verse, is followed by a period B, the refrain. B is thematically related to A, but its content is new; B never contains even a partial repetition of A. This sixteen-bar framework is often extended by short repetitions within the period, little preludes and extensions. It is even found extended to cover two sixteen-bar periods. Almost all verse songs take this form.

Ternary form consists of a succession of three periods; the last is generally a repetition of the first. The repetition of the main idea is called the *reprise* or *recapitulation*. Most folk songs and many *lieder* and dances are in this form, which is usually designated by the schema A–B–A (main section, middle section, repetition of the main section).

Occasionally a song consists of a succession of three different periods, A–B–C.

Though it is relatively rare to find short ternary forms made up of eight-bar periods, extended versions of ternary form—in periods of sixteen bars or more—account for about two-thirds of all pieces of music. Ternary form is further extended by taking in little preludes or introductions, cadential figures at the end, and short repetitions and insertions within the periods. By these and similar devices ternary form can easily assume quite considerable proportions. All sorts of dances, character pieces and almost all entertainment music is in ternary form of the A–B–A type.

Compound ternary form has come to have great significance in symphonic music. It consists of three parts, each of which is in ternary form. The third part is an exact repetition of the first part. Thus, the first part runs A–B–A, the second part offers new themes and ideas, but arranged in the same form, and the third part duplicates the first part exactly.

I	II	III
A–B–A	C–D–C	A–B–A

All the minuets and most of the scherzos in symphonic music are in this compound ternary form, and the middle section is generally known as the *trio*, because in the older forms of the dances the middle section was usually played by only three instruments, as opposed to the full orchestra involved in the main section and its recapitulation. Though the habit of using only three instruments in the middle section fell into disuse the name 'trio' has been retained. The third section, being an exact repetition of the first, is not written out a second time, but is indicated by the expression *da capo*, Italian for 'from the beginning', that is 'repeat', after the trio. At the end, after the repeated sections, there may be a *coda*, an Italian word meaning 'tail', which is a little appendage of eight or sixteen bars which often refers fleetingly back to some idea from the trio.

The *rondo* is really an extended ternary form. It developed from the idea of a round or rondelay, in which the refrain is continually repeated. The refrain—the main or rondo theme—frames the most diverse episodes, after which it always makes a fresh appearance. The rondo theme may sometimes be decorated or perhaps slightly altered, but it is always easy to recognize it. It remains in the same key, whereas the episodes are generally in a closely related key. The following is a schematic rendering of classical rondo form: A–B–A, C, A–B–A, A being the rondo theme, B a subsidiary group that reappears shortly before the end, and C a completely self-sufficient middle section. This has an obvious similarity with compound ternary form, the middle section C representing the trio. One of the main differences between ternary and rondo forms is that in the rondo the transitions are made more smoothly and gradually than they are in the ternary form, which is clearly demarcated.

Most of the finales in Mozart and Haydn symphonies are in rondo form. The masters do not, of course, feel obliged to respect such schemata too strictly: their rondos are enriched by endless little deviations and slight variations. But they choose as memorable a main idea as possible to facilitate its recognition when it is repeated.

The forms that we have been considering—binary, ternary, rondo—are all based on the principle of the successive juxtaposition of different themes or groups of themes. But with development forms the basic idea is to develop the movement, that is, the form, out of a single motif or theme. One of the commonest features of motivic structure is imitation. *Free imitation* involves approximate, but recognizable imitation of a motif. *Strict imitation* involves note-for-note repetition of the phrase by another voice entering shortly afterwards. This sort of strict imitation is called *canonic*. Canons can be written in unison, at the octave, at the third, fourth or fifth, or at any interval. They can be two-part, three-part or any number of parts; they can proceed by contrary motion, or by inversion, or the second voice can be in augmentation or diminution (that is, the note-values can be lengthened or shortened). Before the era of classical music it was quite common practice to write a whole movement as a canon; even the classical and romantic composers were not above applying the canon to effect still greater climaxes. In modern times, the canon has once more come into occasional use as an independent form.

The strict imitational form of the fugue has proved itself much more readily applicable and richer in significance than the canon. A *fugue* (derived from the Latin *fuga* meaning 'flight') is a piece of music in which the theme is worked in two or more voices according to strict rules of imitation. The peculiar feature of the fugue is that it is built on a single theme, and the whole form is derived from it. This inevitably gives a unified, concise, closed form.

As a rule, a fugue begins with a single voice playing the theme. This first entry of the theme is called the *subject*. When the theme is over, it is repeated by a second voice, but in the dominant key— a fifth higher or a fourth lower. This second entry is called the *answer*. While the second entry is going on, the first voice spins out a contrasted counterpoint against it (which is called the *counter-subject*). If the fugue is in three or four parts, the third and fourth voices now enter successively, alternating between the tonic and the dominant, while the first voices continue to develop additional countersubjects in free counterpoint. When all the voices have played the theme the first section—called the *exposition*—is over.

Fugues are built in three sections. The exposition is followed by the *middle entry section*, in which the theme appears in the various voices, either in its subject form or as the answer. In the middle entry section the entries are not subject to such strict rules as in the exposition, and it is not essential that all the voices engage in any particular group of entries. The middle entry section generally steers clear of the tonic key, and modulates to related keys. A large-scale fugue can have three or four or even more of these groups of middle entries: no fugue should have less than two. The introduction of the tonic key begins the final section, which is a sort of reprise. Various technical gimmicks can be used to emphasize the air of finality of the final section, the most common being the *stretto* (several voices entering with the subject in quick succession) and the introduction of the theme in augmentation.

The individual groups of middle entries are connected by free episodes, that generally derive either from the subject or the countersubject, and thus maintain the unity of the form. The theme and the countersubject are often written in *double counterpoint*, a contrapuntal device by means of which the melodies are so devised that either can serve as the bass.

Johann Sebastian Bach was the greatest master of the fugue. The most perfect examples of this form are to be found both in his instrumental and his vocal works. In subsequent generations the interest in fugal form has never flagged; Mozart, Beethoven, Brahms, Reger, Strauss and Bartók have often turned their attention to the fugue, though not always with such strictness as is to be found in the exemplary fugues of Bach. The term *fugato* refers to a style of writing in which the fugue does not get much further than the first characteristic set of entries, the exposition. Fugatos are often used within a thematic framework for purposes of intensification. A double fugue is a fugue with two themes, and a triple fugue has three themes.

A form that has been a particular favourite with composers has been the *variation form*, a technique of changing and modifying a chosen theme. At first—in the early eighteenth century—these variations were little more than embellishments or decorations of the melody, unconcerned with the rhythm or the harmony. In classical music, variations affect both rhythm and harmony, but the theme always remains clearly recognizable.

The variation technique of Beethoven and the romantic composers goes much further. Both the melody and the rhythm change greatly; often only the harmonic scaffolding remains, providing a basis for free improvisation. The metre is also changed occasionally for individual variations, and the tempo too. In a classical set of variations a change of key was still out of the question; the only change allowed was into the tonic major or minor, for example from C major into C minor. (An excursion of a minor theme into a major key was generally announced by the word *maggiore*, and one in the other direction, *minore*.) Schumann overrode this principle, and Reger is the composer who carries variation technique to its extreme limits; his variations are really free fantasias, stimulated in one way or another by the theme.

The theme of a set of variations is always in *lied* form, either binary or ternary. It may be written by the composer himself or be a borrowed melody, perhaps a folk song. Often composers prefer to use very familiar, popular melodies. The variations are generally arranged to contrast with one another, or form groups like individual movements within the set. The final variation is often extended, so as to achieve a stronger air of finality. The larger sets of variations are sometimes crowned by a final fugue.

Almost all classical sets of variations are *harmonic variations*, in which the unchanging harmony forms the basis for the alterations. In *contrapuntal* variations, such as those by Bach, it is the contrapuntal devices that count, and besides free melodic counterpoint, these include the stricter contrapuntal forms such as the canon and the fugato.

The *chaconne* and the *passacaglia* can also be classed as contrapuntal variations. Both of these forms are built over an unchanging bass figure, or *basso ostinato* ('obstinate bass-line'), sometimes abbreviated to *ostinato*. The theme in the bass—usually four or eight bars—is repeated again and again, and the other voices build up progressively over this ostinato, forming a long chain of short variations. Both the chaconne and the passacaglia were originally slow dances in $3/4$, and both are characterized by this build-up of variations over the basso ostinato.

Of all forms, whether or not development form, *sonata first movement form* has become the most important. (This form is sometimes misleadingly called 'sonata form'.) A *sonata* is an instrumental piece in several movements, and may be for piano, violin or some other instrument. The characteristic of the sonata, as opposed to the suite, which also has several movements, is the richly developed form of its first movement, which was extended and established by the classical composers. In fact, the first movement (allegro) of all sonatas, trios, quartets and symphonies employs first movement form, besides most overtures, and also a few of the finales and several of the slow movements of sonatas, symphonies and so on.

The secret of the dramatic and expressive strength of first movement form lies in the contrast between the two themes. The first theme, virile and rhythmically accented, opposes the second theme, characterized by femininity and cantabile. The structure of the movement emerges from this contrast; in the middle section, the development, the two themes argue it out together, until in the final section, the recapitulation, the first section is repeated with its successive juxtaposition of the two. Sonata form, with its layout in three sections—exposition, development, recapitulation—seems similar to ternary form. But in ternary form the exposition consists of only one theme, and the contrast is provided in the middle section, which in sonata form is devoted to the long dramatic development. Sonata form is very much richer; its extraordinarily varied possibilities of development have made it the most important form in instrumental music.

The *development section* consists of the working-out of the themes exposed in the first section, and the most diverse methods are applied. The themes can be broken down into their individual motivic components, the motifs can be combined, or played off one against the other; in the process their rhythm and harmony may be altered to make room for their contrapuntal exploitation. Imitation is an important factor here, and also the fugato, which is used to build up climaxes. Occasionally a new theme is introduced in the development, and this then confronts the already existing themes and is worked over in conjunction with them.

The *tonal framework* is very important in the structure of classical and romantic sonata movements. The main theme is in the tonic key, as opposed to the second theme, which is in the dominant. The development modulates freely amongst the closely related keys, generally avoiding the tonic, which is only introduced when the time comes for the main theme to be repeated in the recapitulation. In the recapitulation the second theme is also in the tonic key, so this key dominates the whole of the final section. Naturally, one can find many types of variations from this norm, but the basic features of this tonal scheme are generally retained for the sake of unity. The tonal framework can be presented schematically as follows:

Exposition	First theme	Tonic key
	Second theme	Dominant key
Development	Freely modulating	
Recapitulation	First theme	Tonic key
	Second theme	Tonic key

Classical composers generally indicated a repeat for the exposition before going on to the development, probably to enable the listener to get a better grip on the thematic material. But this repetition was discarded by Beethoven in his later works. The exposition was considerably enriched at about the same time: themes are enlarged into thematic groups, and there is often an abbreviated version of the main theme at the end of the exposition. Occasionally the exposition even embraces a third theme. This filling-out of the exposition naturally resulted in a great enlargement of the whole form. It became a favourite habit to add a coda at the end, in which one of the main themes is developed once more; when this is combined with an increase in tempo, it is called a *stretto*.

The application of developmental technique to binary, ternary and rondo forms resulted in significant enrichment of these forms, which were actually simpler and more primitive. The combination of sonata form with rondo form is known as *extended rondo form*, or *sonata rondo*, and big finales are often in this form.

The forms that we have treated so far are 'abstract' forms, formal types which were applied to all the great genres of instrumental music.

In this book I am mainly concerned with orchestral music. I shall concentrate on the three most important forms of orchestral music: the suite, the symphony and the concerto. Other forms, such as the overture, serenade and symphonic poem, cannot compare in significance with these three forms.

The *suite* is the oldest of the cyclic forms for instrumental music. Even in the seventeenth century composers were writing orchestral suites, which at that time usually consisted of four dances. The normal sequence of dances in these suites was pavane, galliarde, allemande, courante; then, later, allemande, courante, sarabande, gigue. In the eighteenth century other dances, such as the minuet, gavotte and bourrée, became popular. At this stage the overture, sometimes called a sinfonia, was added as an introductory movement. The suite, still the decisive orchestral form for Bach and Handel, was almost entirely neglected by the classical composers, in favour of the symphony. The late romantic composers took it up once more, and included more modern dance forms, such as the march, mazurka, polonaise and waltz. Another popular form of the suite is that consisting of movements taken from larger works, somewhat in the manner of ballet music or incidental music for plays.

But the characteristic rhythm and forms of the individual dances had a significant effect even outside the realm of the suite. The *minuet*, for example, had been included in the symphony in its original form, but was exchanged by Beethoven for the scherzo. In baroque music the minuet is a worthy, respectable stepping dance in $3/4$, but by the end of the eighteenth century it had acquired a charming and graceful character, accompanied by an increase in tempo. The *courante* and *sarabande* are also in $3/4$ but the tempo is slower. The *siciliano*, sometimes called pastorale, is in $6/8$;

this is a shepherd dance, often used for Christmas music. An important fast dance in compound time is the gaily animated *gigue*. Of the newer dances in ³/₄, the *waltz* is the one that springs to mind, with its rocking rhythm ♩ ♩ | ♩ ♩ and its typical accompaniment figure

The *ländler*, ancestor to the waltz, is quieter and more rustic. It was included in the symphony by Schubert, and later by Bruckner and Mahler. The *mazurka*, a Polish national dance, is characterized by its staccato rhythm, the strong accent being on the heavy part of the bar: ♫♩ ♩ | ♫♩ ♩.

The *polonaise* is also in ³/₄, but in slow tempo, with the striking rhythm ♫♫ ♫ ♫, that is also peculiar to the Spanish *bolero*. The most animated dance in compound time is the *tarantella*, a Neapolitan dance in a swift ⁶/₈.

Of the simple-time dance forms, the grave *pavane* springs to mind and the animated *gavotte*, usually written *alla breve* with the characteristic two crotchet up-beat: ♩ ♩ | ♩ ♩ ♩ | ♩ ♩. The *musette* is often used as a trio to the gavotte. The characteristic peculiarity of the musette—which is French for 'bagpipe'—is the organ-point or pedal-point in open fifths, intended as an imitation of the bagpipes. The *march* is a very common example of a dance in simple time, and one finds it in the most diverse forms. The quiet funeral march is particularly significant, with its main section always in the minor key.

We have already encountered the *symphony* in the word 'sinfonia', the overture or introductory movement to the suite. The operatic overtures of the seventeenth century were called sinfonias, and at that time there was also a distinction between Italian and French overtures or sinfonias. Alessandro Scarlatti's Italian overtures consisted of three movements in the order fast–slow–fast, whereas Lully's French overtures start with a solemn slow movement to accompany the entry of the court, followed by a fugal allegro as the middle section, and closing with another solemn grave. This gives us the schema slow–fast–slow.

Both these forms of the sinfonia are predecessors of the classical symphony. In the middle of the eighteenth century, the Mannheim

school added the minuet, thus increasing the number of movements from three to four, and this determined the basic form
of the classical symphony as we know it in the work of Mozart
and Haydn. The main movement of the symphony, the first
allegro, is always in sonata form. This allegro is very often preceded
by a solemn introduction in the style of a French overture. The
second or slow movement is usually in ternary form in Haydn and
Mozart, though sometimes a set of variations is substituted. In
Beethoven, and later in Brahms and Bruckner, the adagio movements are almost always in large-scale sonata form. The third
movement, the minuet or scherzo, is, of course, in the compound
ternary form, with the trio forming the middle section. Haydn's
and Mozart's finales are laid out in the rondo form. Beethoven and
the romantic composers, however, laid extraordinary emphasis
on the finale: being an antipode to the first allegro, it too acquires
the character of a dramatic movement. The cross-referencing of
ideas and thematic material between these two outside movements
underlines the unity and closed form of the symphonic structure.

The *serenade* is a hybrid between the suite and the symphony.
The word 'serenade' means 'evening music'; in Mozart's day serenades were played at open-air sessions, like street music. But the
serenade soon found its way into the concert hall. A smaller instrumental ensemble, treated as a collection of soloists, is typical for
the serenade. Like the suite, it is a series of short movements, but
by no means restricted to dances. The overture, which is often in
sonata form, and one or two long, slow movements, tend to tip
the scales towards the symphony. But on the other hand it is clearly
differentiated from the symphony by the larger number of movements, and the slighter orchestral apparatus.

The *divertimento* is very closely related to the serenade. Mozart,
in particular, favoured this description for little series of pieces with
the character of a serenade.

The *overture*, as an independent form, connected neither with the
suite nor with opera, is generally described as the *concert overture*.
It is generally thought of as a small-scale symphonic poem, and is
always in first movement form, as are all operatic overtures. But
Italian opera tends to prefer a potpourri type of overture, a sort of
medley of melodies from the opera formed into a loose chain,
without any further attempt at development or exploitation.

The *symphonic poem*, favourite form of composers of programme
music, employs the same forms as the larger movements of ab-

solute music. However important a part the programmatic idea may play in the structure of a symphonic poem, it is always the absolute musical forms that are decisive for the formal layout. First movement form is naturally the one most frequently employed, often greatly extended to accommodate several subsidiary themes. Even in Richard Strauss, who uses variation forms (*Don Quixote*) and variants of rondo form (*Till Eulenspiegel*), developmental technique is always firmly embedded in these forms.

A *concerto* is a large-scale piece of music for one or more solo instruments with orchestra. The result is a prizefight (*concertare* means 'to compete') which gives the soloist the opportunity to show off his artistic abilities to their best advantage. The typical distinguishing mark of concerto form is the contrast of soloists and *tutti* (full orchestra) which crops up again and again. The *concerto grosso* of baroque music is already a clear example of concerto form: the sound of the full orchestra always sets off the *concertino*, or small body of soloists, usually three in number. Alongside the concerto grosso, there evolved the solo concerto (Vivaldi) and later the harpsichord concerto (J.S. Bach). The concerto grosso disappeared entirely during the classical era, whereas the solo concerto, with the symphony, became the great form of orchestral music. Solo concertos are restricted to three movements: fast–slow–fast. The first allegro is always in sonata form, the slow middle movement in extended *lied* form, and the finale is usually laid out as a large-scale rondo. In accordance with the concerto character, the soloist's part is laid out as effectively as possible for the instrument. Towards the end of the first movement, and also the third, the player is given the opportunity to show off his technical skill as brilliantly as possible in a long solo, or *cadenza*. The cadenza was originally improvised at the discretion of the player, but in more recent times all cadenzas have been written out in full by the composers.

Further developments of the concerto form have given it a strong resemblance to the symphony. Sometimes the clear contrast between soloist and orchestra is obscured for long stretches at a time; the soloist sacrifices his independence and the orchestra takes the upper hand.

Finally, I should like to say a few words about the formal concepts that govern *vocal music*. The most important form of solo song both in opera and oratorio is the *aria*. The baroque aria in three sections is usually called the *da capo aria*: the first section is repeated after a contrasted middle section. The short instrumental preludes and interludes in arias are called *ritornelli*. The later form of the aria is generally in two sections: an andante is followed by an allegro section that is effectively written for the voice.

Arias are usually preceded by a *recitative*. Whereas the aria is in a lyrical, reflective style, the recitative can be dramatically treated; it is a sort of spoken singing. There is a distinction between the *recitativo secco*, in which the voice is accompanied only by short chords, and the *recitativo accompagnato*, in which the orchestral accompaniment underlines the dramatic content of the words. The style of expression peculiar to the recitative is sometimes to be found in instrumental music, and similarly, the word 'aria' is sometimes used to describe particularly expressive pieces of a calm cantabile feeling.

A HISTORY OF THE CONCERT

The first European concert society—the Concerts Spirituels—was founded in Paris in 1725. At the time no one would have dreamt what a significant place this institution would assume in European cultural life. In the seventeenth and early eighteenth centuries the nearest approach to concerts took place in the courts and great houses of the aristocracy, and probably served only as entertainment music for particularly festive occasions. This sort of music was not usually considered worth serious consideration; the musical interest of the higher circles of society was almost entirely devoted to opera.

Monstrous sums of money were spent on operatic performances—scenery, stage machinery, and not least the singers and the orchestra. The body of court musicians, which formerly consisted chiefly of a large church choir, was now extended instrumentally in order to perform opera; every sort of instrumentalist was added to the trumpeters, but the chief addition was the strings.

Louis XIV's orchestra, the Violons du Roi, conducted by Lully, was the most celebrated orchestra of the seventeenth century. The chief form of French instrumental music, the suite, derives from the extended ballet interludes in the French operas of the period and from the solemn introits and overtures that accompanied the entries of the court. The suite was later to have a decisive influence on the general development of European instrumental music. The reason for the foundation of the Concerts Spirituels was probably the fact that operatic productions were forbidden during Lent. Someone had the idea of providing the musical public with biblical operas without any dramatic action. The intervals between the acts of these oratorios were then filled with instrumental pieces, in which soloists and singers could display their skill. These concerts soon began to enjoy such a high reputation that even foreign artists considered it an honour to be allowed to participate in them. In 1778, Mozart played his own compositions at one of these concerts.

The first subscription concerts took place in Leipzig in 1743. They were the forerunners of the world-famous Gewandhauskonzerte, so called after the hall in which they took place (*Gewandhaus* is German for 'cloth hall') after 1781. They establish Leipzig as having the oldest musical tradition in Germany. Collegia Musica, regular meetings of professional musicians, had long assembled in Leipzig, and had become a significant institution in the musical world. There had been musical societies on the student level since the beginning of the eighteenth century; the Telemann Society, which later produced some important performances when Bach became its director, is an example. But these organizations were put in the shade by the concert society. The twenty-four concerts produced each year by the society were on a sound economic basis, thanks to the subscription system, and had a considerable reputation in artistic circles. The programmes consisted chiefly of vocal music, but instrumental pieces and occasionally whole suites were also performed. It is amazing that Johann Sebastian Bach, who was working in Leipzig at the time of the founding of the subscription concerts, never appears in connection with them. It is the singspiel composer Johann Adam Hiller, whose name is always associated with the heyday of Leipzig's concert life. For decades he was at the head of the subscription concerts, and can legitimately be regarded as the founder of the later Gewandhaus concerts.

Handel carried out most of the pioneering work in England. The first public concert performances of his oratorios took place in London in 1731, and later in many provincial towns, where the choral societies were even then backed by a fairly lengthy tradition. The ground was well prepared for Johann Christian Bach, the composer's youngest son, when he founded his Bach-Abel concerts in London in 1746. The concerts were a great success.

The founding of the Royal Philharmonic Society in 1813 was an event of great importance in the history of English concert life. The Society's intention was to encourage orchestral and instrumental music in England. The concerts rapidly became very popular and it was difficult even for subscribers to get seats on some occasions. Particularly in its early days the Society promoted many first performances, and even commissioned works from the great composers on the continent.

From 1894 onwards the Society's concerts were given in the Queen's Hall, until its destruction in the Second World War. Sir Thomas Beecham, who had governed the Society's affairs during the First War, returned as its conductor in 1927, at which time the Society's position, artistically and financially, was rather low. Sir Thomas Beecham imbued it with fresh life, and 1932 saw the formation of a new orchestra, the London Philharmonic Orchestra, under his baton. The number of concerts each season increased, and many special occasions were commemorated (Delius 1929, Sibelius 1938), but new music came to be rather neglected.

The Henry Wood Promenade Concerts were instituted in 1895. The idea of 'promenade concerts' had originally come from France and in the years following 1840 numerous speculators founded series that were more or less successful. The 'proms' took place in the Queen's Hall up until 1940, and after the war they were resumed at the Royal Albert Hall. Sir Henry Wood, the original conductor of the concerts, was a voracious musician who wanted to play almost everything he could lay hands on. Consequently, the 'proms' came to be the largest testing-ground for new works, both English and continental. Schönberg's *Five Orchestral Pieces*, opus 16, had their English première at a promenade concert in 1915.

In 1927 the concerts were taken over by the BBC, and the BBC Symphony Orchestra began to come into prominence. The British Broadcasting Corporation had been founded in 1922, and since that date its influence on English musical life has never ceased to grow. Sir Adrian Boult became director of BBC music in 1930 and in 1932 the corporation moved to Broadcasting House, which boasted a small studio concert hall. Concerts of modern music were given in this studio, but were not well supported. With the establishment of the Third Programme—purely for culture—in 1946, modern music came to be a regular feature of BBC music, and the recent Thursday invitation concerts instituted by the present director of music, William Glock, concentrate on a juxtaposition of old and new, and those interested can actually go to the BBC's Maida Vale Studios and hear 'what this modern stuff is all about' with their own ears.

Besides this growth in specialization, there has been a large increase in the scale of the BBC's operations. Besides the BBC Symphony Orchestra, seven regional and supplementary orchestras are maintained (each with their own conductors) and three vocal bodies, the BBC Choral Society, the BBC Chorus, and the BBC Singers. The amount of music thus 'placed on the market' in England—and a great deal of it is serious symphonic music—is now seen to be phenomenal and probably unparalleled; which does not prevent the English from complaining that their favourite pieces are neglected.

Thanks to the academies, Italy could boast a relatively lively concert life even in the seventeenth century, independent of court music. The academies were gatherings of artists, scientists and interested laymen that had sprung up in all the leading towns of Italy at the time of the Renaissance. They were forcing-houses of art and science, and, as such, a constant spur to the newer developments in music. Opera came into being at the Florentine academy, and the first oratorio performances took place in the academies. Touring instrumentalists and singers were always honoured to participate in the concerts, despite the fact that their accompaniments must have been of variable quality. They often performed in the churches, by no means confining themselves to sacred music. But the academies played the decisive rôle in the formation of Italian concert life; and this very aristocratic institution remains the model in the Italian concert world.

In Vienna and Paris, concert performances did not, for many years, rival opera, which was staged in the grandest style and held sway over the entire population. The concerts were, for the most part, organized in court circles, and no one was admitted without an invitation. The founding of the Viennese Tonkünstler Society in 1771 marks the start of regular public concerts in Vienna. At first it was intended to give only four concerts each year, two in Advent and two in Lent. The receipts from these concerts went to make a fund for the widows and orphans of Austrian musicians. This worthy end was the inspiration of the founder of the Tonkünstler Society, the venerable court conductor and composer Florian Gassmann.

The first Viennese concert programmes consisted of oratorios and biblical histories—operas without scenery. But here, too, the practice of introducing soloists in the intermissions gradually gained momentum. Mozart and many of his celebrated contemporaries were featured as performers in the Society's concerts. The next step was the inclusion of the larger forms of orchestral music—symphonies, suites and concertos—and, this achieved, the typical concert programme already resembled its nineteenth-century form.

The music-loving Austrian aristocracy had a considerable share in the development of Viennese concert life. Music was practised very seriously in the great houses, and many lords retained excellent private orchestras, so that symphonies and concertos could easily be performed. Chamber music was very popular, and soloists of note were engaged to take part in the concerts. Although these concerts were of a strictly private nature, they served as the model for the public concerts of chamber music that established themselves during the early nineteenth century.

Johann Friedrich Reichardt tried, in 1771, to institute a series of subscription concerts in Berlin, in the style of the Parisian Concerts Spirituels. But the first event to have any significance for the musical life of Berlin was the foundation of the Singing Academy in 1790 by Johann Friedrich Fasch, one-time harpsichordist to Frederick the Great. The society rehearsed industriously under his leadership; they studied *a cappella* works to begin with, until they felt sufficiently confident to undertake an oratorio performance in 1794. This choral society soon became a model for similar foundations in all the larger German cities; by the beginning of the nineteenth century, concert organizations and choral societies were springing up all over Europe, and even in Russia (St Petersburg, 1802, for example). This closed the initial phase of public concert life. It was now to be enlarged and glorified.

Concerts in the eighteenth century, like opera, were a purely aristocratic institution. An artist's primary concern was always to perform before the reigning prince, then, if he were successful, he could move into the leading houses of the nobility. His fee generally took the form of a present, or—what was probably more sought after—a commission to write something, for those were still the days when almost every virtuoso was also a composer and vice versa. The end of the eighteenth century saw a gradual but complete reversal of this system, brought about by the growing interest of the rising bourgeoisie in music, and the foundation of the various concert societies. Thus, it is the bourgeois that were the real driving force behind the concert life of the nineteenth century, which was rapidly evolving into concert life as we know it today. Besides the choral societies, amateur orchestras were formed in all the sizeable cities in Germany, Italy, France, England and Scandinavia, and these played a prominent part in their cities' musical life. The touring virtuosi, both singers and instrumentalists, had no other alternative than to work with these bodies of amateur musicians, for the conventions of the period forbade the appearance of a virtuoso in any other context but an orchestral concert. So the artist had first to make sure of the collaboration of an amateur orchestra, and it was their business to make the town concert hall—usually one of the larger hotels—available to him.

The local people of importance had a great influence on the success or failure of this sort of concert; the artist's first job was to display his talents to them in their homes, and he often had to endure his public concert being poorly received by a meagre audience. These concerts were arranged roughly as follows: after an introductory orchestral piece, the virtuoso was obliged to play a concerto accompanied by the amateur orchestra. Only then was he allowed to play his solo pieces, and these were expected to display as much virtuosity as possible. The concert always ended with some free improvisation on well-known popular themes.

Liszt and Paganini were the first to break with this tradition of always playing with an orchestra, and then only at the peak of their success, when they began to play solo for the whole evening, and so initiated the recital as we know it today. Liszt even played sonatas in his recitals, which had previously not been the done thing at all. (Sonatas were chamber music, and at the close of the eighteenth century, chamber music was only played in the salon.)

Most of the pioneering work for the introduction of chamber music into public concert life went on in Vienna, and the credit goes to the great Viennese violinist and string quartet player, Ignaz Schuppanzigh. He was the first to organize public quartet recitals, in Vienna in the winter of 1804–05. He sustained his subscription concerts, consisting mainly of Beethoven quartets, for over a decade. This achievement firmly inculcated the idea of chamber music concerts (it was perfectly natural that the idea should have originated in Vienna, the birthplace of classical chamber music) and the practice spread slowly throughout Europe.

Schubert, Schumann and Mendelssohn made great use of the German *lied*, and it appeared in concerts around the middle of the nineteenth century; *lieder* recitals, almost unknown at the beginning of the century, were widespread at the end, at least in German cities. Before then concert halls had been dominated by Italian *bel canto*: coloratura singing of bravura arias.

The end of the nineteenth century saw the introduction of the conductor in the rôle of virtuoso, and he rapidly became the controlling figure of musical life. The first modern conductor able to concentrate the audience's whole attention on himself was Hans von Bülow. In the 1880's he undertook concert tours with the Meininger Orchestra through all the important musical centres in Germany, a quite remarkable undertaking for that time. The playing of the orchestra achieved a standard of discipline and finish that was previously unheard-of, and the credit for this went, quite rightly, to the conductor, whose powerful personality was the cause of his astonishing success. Hans von Bülow stands at the beginning of the great series of virtuosi of the baton who have made their decisive mark on modern concert life.

The climax in the evolution of European concert life was reached in the first decade of the twentieth century. All the great cities were rich in concerts of every description; Berlin and Paris were the centres of the musical world. Even the provinces were drawn into this activity. In all the towns the subscription series of big orchestral and choral concerts formed the main pillar of concert life, and the leading pianists, violinists and singers could be heard. Around this central block of concerts were grouped piano recitals, violin recitals, 'cello recitals, string quartet concerts, piano trios, *lieder* recitals, church concerts with *a cappella* choral works, organ recitals, recitals given by singers accompanying themselves upon the lute, guitarists, concertante harpists, and many more. This abundance of concerts and concert artists was organized and directed by a host of concert agents and artists' impresarios, some of whom had a great influence upon the concert life that they were running.

This development was interrupted by the 1914–18 war in Europe. After the war a new generation had grown up, and people felt differently about the world. Concert life in the sense that it had existed at the beginning of the century was dead. Concerts were plentiful in the 1920's, but the love and enthusiasm with which they had been previously received was gone. Only big orchestral and choral concerts attracted big audiences; the small concerts that had given the musical life of the beginning of the century such diversity and colour were finished.

Radio and the gramophone were invented. At first, they were regarded as mechanical twittering, but very soon their potential became obvious. They now have a rôle complementary to that of live concerts, rather like the relationship of the cinema and the theatre. But the concert life of the bourgeois nineteenth century seems gradually to be dying out. Composers of new music are trying to come to terms with radio and the gramophone, and concert life has changed greatly. But it is certain that as long as the great music of the last two hundred years is appreciated, and fills, as it does now, millions of people with enthusiasm and inspiration, we need have no fear for its continued existence.

SYMPHONIES AND ORATORIOS

The symphony, the chief form of orchestral music, is only two hundred years old, and the beginning of public concert life is no older. Haydn's early symphonies were actually court music, written for the orchestra of the prince in whose service he worked. The same applies to the symphonies written by Haydn's direct predecessors, the composers of the Mannheim school. It was only at the beginning of the nineteenth century that concert music in the sense in which we know it today really got under way, and it was then, too, that the tremendous developments in symphonic music began.

Haydn represents the beginnings of modern orchestral music, bringing together the scattered ideas of his predecessors. Bach and Handel represent the completion and perfection of the polyphonic style that had dominated the music of the preceding centuries; they stand at the far side of an enormous bridge that comes to earth again in the polyphonic music of our times. In between, the classical period, which reached its peak in the year 1800 or thereabouts, is represented by the great Viennese trio: Haydn, Mozart and Beethoven. The nineteenth century is the century of romantic music. The first half of the century gives us the early romantic composers, Schubert and Weber, Schumann and Mendelssohn; late romanticism, as represented by Wagner, Berlioz, Liszt, Brahms and Bruckner, takes us right up to the last decade of the century. This musical direction spread its innumerable ramifications

throughout Europe, and these form the transition to the music of
the twentieth century, which proceeded to free itself from romanticism and look for possibilities of a new style and a new spirit.

JOHANN SEBASTIAN BACH

born Eisenach 21 March 1685
died Leipzig 28 July 1750

Bach came from a family in which the profession of music was a
tradition. When only eighteen, he took the post of organist at
Arnstadt, and later at Mühlhausen. In 1708 he was called to Weimar
to take up the post of court organist, and in 1717 he became Kapellmeister in Cöthen. In 1723 he went to Leipzig where he remained
until his death in 1750. Bach hardly ever left his home province of
Thuringia-Saxony; even the effect of his work hardly penetrated
any further during his lifetime. His enormous productivity was
always devoted to whatever post he held at the time.

Bach was extremely happy as regards his family life; he married
twice and had twenty children, ten of whom survived him. He
walked to Lübeck when he was eighteen to hear the great organist
Buxtehude, and he met Marchand, the French virtuoso of the
organ and harpsichord, in Dresden in 1717. Bach challenged Marchand to a contest; the Frenchman, knowing defeat to be inevitable,
refused to compete. In 1747 Bach visited Frederick the Great in
Potsdam, and amazed all who heard him when he played for the
King, to whom he later dedicated his contrapuntal masterpiece
The Musical Offering, in which he cleverly manipulated the theme
that the King had played him in Potsdam. Late in life Bach suffered
from acute disorders of his eyes and shortly before his death he
became totally blind.

In his music he combined, with consummate mastery, the old
polyphonic style and the new harmonic style of writing. His most
significant works are the Passions and oratorios, several hundred
sacred and secular cantatas, the works for organ (for example, the
powerful *Toccata in D minor*), and his harpsichord works, of which
the most important is *The Well-tempered Clavier*, containing two
sets of twenty-four preludes and fugues in all the keys, the first of
which appeared in 1722, the second in 1744.

Bach's purely orchestral works consist of the four big suites and the six *Brandenburg Concertos*. Bach called the suites 'overtures', in accordance with the practice of the time, because the first and most important movement of the suite, the overture, was always grandly laid out in the French style. Dance movements like the gavotte, bourrée, minuet and gigue followed the overture, just as they did in the keyboard suites of the period. The title 'overture' is misleading today; 'orchestral suite' is less ambiguous.

The four suites are very similar in character and style of execution; the first is in the key of C major, the second in B minor, and both the third and fourth in D major. *Suite No. 3 in D major* is the one most played in our concert halls. It is performed by a string orchestra, with continuo played by a harpsichord, and in addition two oboes, three trumpets and timpani. The bright sound of the high trumpets gives the suite its special gaiety and resplendence. The grand introduction is laid out in the style of the French overture; the majestic processional grave is followed by a spun-out fugal allegro which leads back to a version of the solemn grave. The second movement of the *D major Suite* is the famous air,

probably one of Bach's best-known melodies. With calm solemnity the bass progresses downwards by slow steps, while above, the violins extend the arching lines of their melody. This wonderfully solemn movement is played by the strings alone, and this makes the fresh entrance of the high trumpets in the gavotte all the more pleasing. The happy rhythmic melody, an extremely charming idea, is not easy to get out of your head once you have heard and

grasped it. It is no easy matter for the bourrée to hold its own against such a particularly pretty piece. The cheerfully flowing gigue, full of elegance and grace, closes the suite.

The other three suites are similar to the *D major Suite* in character and layout, though they use different dance movements and slightly different orchestras. The *Suite No. 1 in C major* uses only two oboes and bassoon besides the strings and continuo. After the three sections of the opulent and festive introduction, come the courante,

gavotte, forlana, minuet, bourrée and passepied, and most of these
dances have two forms. The second version is more transparent; a
delicate contrast to the powerful first version, which is repeated
afterwards. This makes a ternary form with the trio—which later
passed into general usage—as a contrast in the middle section. Bach
sticks to the rule for the trios, writing them for only three instruments, or at least only three voices. The trio of the bourrée is
played by the three wind instruments, *piano* and in the minor key,
as opposed to the energetically striving strings of the first bourrée,
in C major. The trio of the passepied is particularly charming: the
strings repeat the theme of the first passepied, softly, while the
oboes spin their delicate counterpoint above it.

In the *Suite No. 2 in B minor* the usual festive overture is followed
by a rondo that is very effective, particularly the main tune. The

polonaise is an original piece: a virtuoso variant by the flute soloist,
over the tune of the polonaise in the continuo part, forms the trio
for the formal main section in five voices. Ending the suite is a
swift cascading little piece called a badinerie.

The final *Suite No. 4 in D major* is not so much played. It consists of five movements: overture, bourrées I and II, gavotte,
minuets I and II, and a final piece entitled 'Réjouissance', which is
in a similar vein to the badinerie in the second suite. The second
bourrée and the second minuet both constitute trios, with a repetition of the first bourrée and minuet to finish off. The *Suite No. 4*
is scored for three trumpets, three oboes, bassoon and strings.

Around 1721, Bach wrote *Six Concerti Grossi* for the youngest son
of the Great Elector, the Margrave Christian Ludwig von Brandenburg, who maintained his own orchestra. The name by which the
works are generally known today, the *Brandenburg Concertos*,
springs from Bach's dedication of the concertos to this music-loving
Margrave. Bach himself called them 'Six Concertos for divers
instruments'. They were concerti grossi in the seventeenth-century
sense: the concertante solo instruments, playing in a purely personal
fashion, are set against the ensemble of the other instruments, either
solo or played by an orchestra. Both methods of playing, either as
chamber music or as orchestral music, are quite justified, and both

are to be heard in our concert halls. Each of the concertos is a masterpiece, and as a group they form the high point of the early orchestral heritage in Europe. The first, second and sixth concertos are rarely played in concerts, not because they are considered unworthy, but because they require instruments which are now rarely found.

All the *Brandenburgs* are in three movements, and in this Bach is making a decisive break with previous usage, where dance movements were needed even in the concerto grosso, just as we have seen in the suites. The layout of the three movements anticipates the layout which later became the general rule for all instrumental concertos: an expressive slow movement is sandwiched between two allegros, the first of which has a striving character, and the other a much more playful vein. An exception to the rule, the *Brandenburg No. 1 in F major* has a minuet and a polonaise at the end. Actually these two movements form a whole, since the polonaise takes the place of a second trio and is followed by a restatement of the minuet-trio-minuet I combination. This whole 'fourth movement' is sometimes omitted, which is excusable, for the solo violin (originally a violino piccolo, tuned a third higher than usual) does not play a leading part in this group. The first three movements follow the general plan mentioned above. In the first movement there is something approaching a cadenza for the solo violin just before the return of the theme.

The *Brandenburg No. 2 in F major* is scored for a concertino consisting of trumpet, oboe, flute and violin and the usual ripieno strings with continuo. The trumpet part goes so high that the work is not often played. Richard Strauss was reduced to the expedient of using a piccolo heckelphone when he conducted the work in 1909. However, recent research into the building of small trumpets similar to those used by Bach himself in his performances has done much to obviate this difficulty, and the work justifies its rediscovery. The trumpet is absent in the andante, which is scored for flute, oboe, violin, 'cello and continuo.

The *Brandenburg No. 3 in G major* is a concerto for strings alone, scored for three violins, three violas, three 'cellos and continuo, and when it is played orchestrally there are usually a great many strings to each part, which can produce an overwhelming body of sound. The first allegro opens with the main theme, in a broad and powerful exposition of eight bars, ending in self-satisfied unison. The whole movement, which is laid out on a large scale, is derived from

this extremely memorable tune. Sometimes polyphonally and sometimes in unison, the individual groups are constantly kept in play, fastening on to new motifs and figurations from the main theme and developing them. The atmosphere is full of gaiety and *joie de vivre*; even towards the end, where the argument takes on a more excited character, the raised voices soon unite into a peaceful unanimity. The usual adagio is missing in this concerto; two long chords take its place, giving the listener time to regain his composure before being completely captivated by the dancing grace of the last movement. This finale also shines with the joy of living, but in a more playful, dancing mood.

There is no sign in the first and third concertos of the basic principle of the concerto grosso: the contrast between the individual soloists and the full orchestra. Bach makes up for this in the second and fifth concertos, where he makes significant play with the principle. In the *Brandenburg No. 4 in G major*, he plays the solo violin and two flutes against the ripieno, or ensemble, of strings. The last movement is very gripping: a marvellous fugue, with a swinging

current full of surprising new twists, strongly thought out and magnificent in form construction. Because of its virtuoso violin part, this concerto can almost be regarded as a violin concerto, and it is equally possible to see a harpsichord concerto in the *Brandenburg No. 5 in D major*. There are solo parts for flute and violin also, but it is the harpsichord part that dominates the work. Festivity and enthusiasm are the basic characteristics of the *Fifth Brandenburg*, particularly in the outside movements. The middle movement is of a more reflective nature; it dispenses with the accompanying instruments, and is thus a harpsichord trio. A melancholy theme is announced, and the three instruments spin it out in canonic

imitation. But despite this elegaic interlude, it is the fiery swing of
the first movement and graceful mood of the finale that determine
the character of the work as a whole. All three solo instruments have
full and important parts, but the harpsichord takes most of the
limelight, particularly in the cadenza of the first movement, whose
strangely magical sound is full of an almost romantic poetic quality.

The *Brandenburg No. 6 in B-flat major* is a concerto for two violas,
with an orchestra consisting of two violas, 'cello and continuo. In
Bach's time the ripieno violas were distinguished from the solo
violas in that the former were violas da gamba, played like the
'cello. The sonority of this concerto is perhaps the most remarkable
of all the *Brandenburgs*. The first allegro opens with canonic imi-

tation between the two soloists accompanied by reiterated thick
chords of B-flat major in the orchestra. The acres of time that are
devoured by this constantly recurring B-flat major throb create
an almost obsessive atmosphere, heightened by the richness and
darkness of the sound. It was a happy decision to write the adagio
in E-flat major, as a relief from the B-flat major tonality. The
ripieno violas are silent in this movement. The last movement is
again in B-flat major, and considerable drive is developed by the
two soloists, who are constantly spurring each other on by treading
on each other's tails.

The *Triple Concerto in A minor* is scored for the same orchestra
as the *Fifth Brandenburg*, and also uses the harpsichord, violin and
flute as solo instruments. The harpsichord is dominant here too,
which is understandable since both the allegro movements of this
concerto are arrangements of big preludes and fugues for harpsichord. These two movements, enriched still further by the themes

for the *tutti* entries, are among the liveliest and richest in ideas in the music even of a giant like Bach. Fiery strength and a never-failing drive pulsate throughout both fast movements. The orchestra is silent during the serious, soulful andante; this gentle lament is played by the trio of soloists.

The practice of substituting a modern piano for the harpsichord in performances of Bach's orchestral works has been much debated. This question is closely connected with the problem of the size of the string orchestra in Bach. It is obvious that the harpsichord can be used for all correctly styled chamber music performances, for example of the *Brandenburg Concertos*, when the strings have one player to each part. But when there are several strings to each part, the sound of the harpsichord can hardly penetrate, which is the reason generally put forward for using the piano. Some conductors dispense with the continuo altogether. This dispute was an inevitable consequence of the habit, fashionable for a time, of playing Bach's suites and *Brandenburg Concertos* with a full string orchestra.

Bach certainly deserves the credit for being the first composer to give a keyboard instrument a concertante function; he is the founder of the piano concerto. Before Bach's time the violin had already become a solo instrument, and concertos existed for two violins, and later for one violin. But the harpsichord remained an accompanying instrument. Bach, however, favoured the harpsichord and made for it numerous arrangements of his own works and of the works of other composers. Perhaps he intended these primarily for home use, for besides himself, his two eldest sons were both exceptional players. He was, too, in dire need of concert pieces for the performances given by the Telemann Music Society in Leipzig, which he organized, and this also accounts for the large number of different harpsichord compositions and arrangements.

Modern research has revealed that all the seven harpsichord concertos that have survived are arrangements of earlier pieces, mostly violin concertos; Bach has filled out the solo violin part very richly in keyboard terms, while copying the *tutti* almost note for note. He arranged two of his own violin concertos (the two best-known ones in E major and A minor), transposing them into D major and G minor respectively, presumably to get a fuller sound on the harpsichord. Only two of his harpsichord concertos are played at all frequently now: the one in D minor and the one in F minor. The other five are hardly ever heard. Surprisingly, the two popular concertos do not seem to be arrangements of Bach's own pieces,

but of works by other masters. But they are both real masterpieces, and should on no account be missed.

The basic character of the *D minor Concerto* is solemn, almost
tragic. The main idea of the first allegro, played in powerful unison,
lays the foundations of the work's seriousness, which is maintained
throughout all three movements. The adagio, a sort of chaconne,
is most effective. In this movement, too, the characteristic main
theme is played in unison at the beginning, and then retained
throughout as a basso ostinato. Above this, plaintive and sometimes passionate, the harpsichord part is heard, and the violins play
a quiet balancing melody against it. The last movement with its
richness of figuration is very rewarding for the soloist.

The *F minor Concerto* has a playful, carefree atmosphere. The
elegant little echo at the end of each phrase is characteristic of the
main theme of both this movement and the presto finale: an extremely charming and typical harpsichord effect. The middle
movement, on the other hand—the adagio—is charged with sublime grandeur; the delicate improvisatory melodic line sways along
over the regularity of the accompaniment, and gives expression
to an infinite peace and final harmony.

Of the concertos for two harpsichords, the *C major Concerto* is
the one that is best known. It is an effective work, and rewarding
for both soloists. In the first movement the two soloists outbid
each other in a lively duel, taking turns with an assertive trill motif;
the orchestra has little to say in this enjoyable musical wrangle. In
the middle movement, a wistful adagio, the orchestra is completely
quiet. The finale is a fugue with a lengthy subject; the fugue itself
is executed by the soloists. The orchestra comes forward only
in the transitional episodes, thus clearly underlining the formal layout.

The other concertos for two harpsichords are both in C minor,
and both are arrangements of double violin concertos. One, an
arrangement surviving in its original form of the wonderful *Double
Violin Concerto in D minor*, is hardly ever played. The other, of
which the original has been lost, is occasionally included in concert
programmes. It has a beautiful adagio; a magnificent canon played
by the two harpsichords over the delicate backcloth of the orchestra's *pizzicato*.

The *Concerto in C major* is the more significant of the two concertos for three harpsichords. The opposition of the harpsichords,
all of which have equally rewarding parts, is a mine of new and

absorbing combinations. The first movement is extremely powerful, and sets out characteristically with the three harpsichords in
unison. The fascinating adagio is characterized by a certain melancholy, whereas the finale, with its opulent polyphony, evolves into
a display of colour magnificent even for Bach.

The *Concerto for four harpsichords in A minor* is an arrangement of
Vivaldi's concerto for four violins. The original version, composed
by Vivaldi, seems to me preferable; the magical sound of the four
violins can hardly be bettered, however artfully engineered the
sound of the four harpsichords may be.

Bach arranged a whole series of Vivaldi's violin concertos for
harpsichord and for organ. There is no doubt that Vivaldi had a
great influence on Bach, who then exceeded and outshone him in
every way. Even today Vivaldi's violin concertos are still occasionally included in concert programmes. Extremely violinistic
and musically effective, these works contain many interesting
melodic ideas, but their main interest is rhythmic. Formally, Vivaldi's concertos are the link between the concerto grosso (which was
the real point of departure for the solo concerto) and the Bach
concerto, from which it is but a short distance to the fully developed structure of the Mozart concerto.

Two of Bach's violin concertos have survived, of great and equal
merit. They are both basic in the repertoire of all leading concert
violinists. The *A minor Concerto* has a restrained air, and is built up
into austere grandeur by the dramatic contrast of solo and orchestra. The slow movement of this concerto is marvellous: a lengthy,
spun-out duet between the soloist and the bass. The solo violin
raises its voice in recitative-like song, with passionately excited
figurations, above the obstinately repeated motif, fateful and
threatening, in the bass. The last movement is in the form of a
gigue and abounds in concertante brilliance.

With its equal brilliance of sound, pulsating with an uncommon
affirmation of life, the *E major Concerto for violin* is perhaps even more
directly telling. Not only the first movement, laid out on a grand
symphonic scale, exudes this feeling of life (despite its middle section in the minor key), but also the almost insolent last movement,
with its happy orchestral dance melody that constantly recurs as a
sort of refrain. Between these gay, mobile allegros Bach inserts a
breathtakingly beautiful adagio, a melody of rare spirituality and
expressive strength, a most moving lament.

The *Concerto in D minor for two violins* and orchestra is quite exceptional in the literature for the violin. The aural magic of this concerto is indescribable; the two solo violins play not so much *against* each other in a dramatic contest, but rather inextricably *with* one another, constantly complementing one another. He spins a wonderful web of counterpoint among the solo parts and those of the orchestra, full of artful intertwinings that never fail to sound natural. The eternal beauty of classical balance smiles through the three movements of this extraordinarily finished work; the middle movement, the justly famed 'largo ma non tanto', is particularly satisfying.

The greatness of Bach's genius is still more apparent in his vocal works. His untiring industry and never-failing creative strength in this field is almost unbelievable. Besides the Masses, Passions, oratorios, motets, and other vocal works, he produced nearly two hundred church cantatas. Everything that the previous centuries could produce in these various fields is realized once more in the work of Johann Sebastian Bach.

In Bach's Passions we admire a consummation of the musical tradition of centuries. In the Middle Ages it was the custom to relate the story of the Passion in musical terms in church, during Holy Week. A priest would sing the narrative parts in psalmodic style, another would sing the words of Christ, and the chorus would represent the multitude. This custom was carried over into the Protestant Church; there are numerous Passions in a psalmodic style with German words dating from the second half of the sixteenth century, but musically they are still remarkably uniform. Parallel with this, there emerged a sort of motet form of the Passion, springing from the tradition of unaccompanied choral music in several parts. This form was also accepted by the Protestant Church, and in the ensuing years a natural mixture of the two forms resulted. The Evangelist's story and Christ's words were sung by individual singers, still in a psalmodic style, while the exclamations of the multitude came from a multi-part chorus. The music was unaccompanied throughout; no additional instruments were used. But when the new monodic style reached Germany from Italy, the music of the Passion was also shaken by the stylistic change. Free dramatic recitatives with instrumental accompaniment, arias devoted to commentaries of a lyrical kind, and the introduction of purely instrumental movements were the most significant innovations introduced by the monodic style. After making their appearance in the newly evolved forms of opera and oratorio, they were incorporated into the music of the Passion.

This mingling of old and new is seen in the sacred choral works of HEINRICH SCHÜTZ (1585–1672), the most significant German composer of the seventeenth century. Four Passions by Schütz have survived, and his *Matthew Passion* is still performed occasionally. Despite the fact that Schütz wrote his *Matthew Passion* as an unaccompanied work, closer observation discloses distinct traits of the new Italian musical spirit. The Evangelist and the actors in the drama— Jesus, Peter, Judas, Pilate—are dramatically characterized, and the unbroken psalmody has disappeared completely, to make room for firm musical progression; the choruses, too, are sensitively individualized in a most lively manner. There are contemplative choruses at the beginning and end of the work. At the outset, he places a free setting of the announcement 'The Passion of our Lord Jesus Christ, as described by the Evangelist St Matthew', and the final chorus is a composition in the form of a motet, using the hymn 'Glory be to thee, O Christ', and ending with the words 'Kyrie Eleison, Christe Eleison'.

Schütz's smaller choral work, *The Seven Words from the Cross*, written in 1645, requires instrumental accompaniment, and what is more, there are little instrumental 'symphonies' after the first chorus and before the last. He also prescribes instrumental accompaniment, with careful differentiation according to the various situations, for his *Christmas Oratorio*. Thus, the strings accompany the six-part chorus of angels, 'Glory be to God on high', and woodwind are added for the accompaniment of the shepherds' scene. Hefty nine-part choruses are placed at the opening and at the close. The style that Schütz evolved from the mixture of powerful polyphony with the new monodic form of expression had a fundamental significance for the development of Protestant church music, and also for the music of the Passion.

The chorale had long been the basis of Protestant church music. It was the custom for the congregation to sing the appropriate chorale at the beginning and at the end of the Passion; to refresh them, intervals were often inserted in the middle of the Passion, and the congregation would again sing an appropriate hymn. Thus, the chorale gradually came to have a firm place in the Passion; but the congregation's participation in these fell off considerably, and they became considered rather as contemplative lyric components

of the Passion, sung either by a soloist, as a sort of aria, or by the
chorus in several parts. German oratorio at the beginning of the
eighteenth century was, then, composed of a wide variety of elements, some surviving from the German tradition, and some taken
over from the new Italian style. The texts, or libretti, produced for
this crossbred form by German poets tended also to follow Italian
models, which completely divorced them from the German spirit.
'Dying Jesus', by the Hamburg councillor Berthold Heinrich
Brockes, was the most admired of these texts, and was set to music
by several composers, including Telemann and Handel. Bach
deserves a lot of credit for not simply accepting these fashionable
texts for his Passions; guided by his unshakeable artistic instinct, he
declined these turgid versifications of the Evangelists' stories, and
re-inserted the original texts into his compositions. He used some
sacred poetry for the arias; in the *St John Passion* he even took texts
for individual arias from Brockes' version; but he sought to change
and simplify these, guided by his own sound intuition. For the
chorales he revived the ancient hymn texts, matching the appropriate stanzas to each situation.

Bach is supposed to have written five Passions; only the *St John
Passion* and the *St Matthew Passion* have survived. A third Passion,
according to St Luke, has been doubtfully ascribed to Bach. If it
is really by him, it is a work of his earlier period, published by his
biographer, Philipp Spitta, in his Weimar days. But compared with
other works from that period, it seems improbable that Bach could
have written it. The recitatives are primitively fashioned, and the
whole is extremely uneven: there are undoubtedly significant passages, but also stretches which are undistinguished and dull. Yet a
sympathetic performance of the *St Luke Passion* is not without
effect, even today. It is short, simple and often touching; and the
few arias and the chorales are certainly graceful.

The *St John Passion* is the earlier of the two main Passions. It can
be fairly assumed that Bach wrote it in 1723 when he was still in
Cöthen, and then reworked it and undertook important alterations
in 1727. The character of the whole, due largely to the text, is
somewhat austere and reserved. St John's report of Christ's suffering is relatively brief and limits itself to the scene of the arrest and
the various interrogations, and this imperceptibly heightens the
drama, at the same time making it possible to achieve a positively
overwhelming unity in the giant work.

Bach chose the following words for the opening chorus:

> Lord our redeemer, Thou whose name
> In all the world is glorious,
> Show us in this thy Passion
> That Thou, the true and only Son
> For ever more
> E'en from humiliation sore
> Dost rise victorious.

He unfolds a magnificent tone-painting to these words, leading straight into the drama, and immediately capturing the listener's attention. The ideas behind the opening chorus express simultaneously the suffering and the glorification, and these two aspects are musically delineated too: the flute and oboe parts overlap in syncopations, lamenting with bitter dissonances, while the strings sustain the solemn, quiet semiquaver movement. The voice-leading of the chorus is broad and powerful, and also engages in the semiquaver movement; it descends to depict Christ's 'sore humiliation', and then ascends steeply to stress the rejoicing victory. This introductory chorus is filled with the dark secrecy of sublime majesty; as a prologue to the coming drama it sets the atmosphere with uncanny accuracy.

The action commences with Jesus' arrest, the Evangelist's narration alternating with short dramatic choruses. In accordance with tradition, the Evangelist is sung by a tenor, and Jesus by a bass. In the *St John Passion* these recitatives are accompanied only by the organ. The words of Christ express passionless sovereignty. The biblical drama of the solo recitatives and dramatically excited choruses is contrasted with the thoughtful lyrical contemplation expressed in the chorales and arias. In the deeply-moving chorales, all sung in four-part harmony and accompanied by organ and strings, the whole congregation define their attitude to the Passion. For the words, Bach chooses the appropriate stanzas from old hymns and sets them with extreme simplicity to their original melodies.

The arias consist of observations on details of the described events, so they, too, like the chorales, are musical resting-places. The texts for the arias, written in the richly figurative language of the time, sound dated to modern ears, but Bach's symbolical musical language draws out their implicit meaning and enables us to forget the words themselves, which are often trivial. Directly following the gloom of the first alto aria comes the gay mobility

of the soprano aria 'I follow Thee also, my Saviour, with gladness';
the fluid movement of the constant melodic imitation represents
the happy hurrying of the text.

The first part closes with Peter's three-fold denial of Christ. At
the words 'and wept bitterly' the recitative, which has so far remained a calm, prosaic report by the Evangelist, rises in a passionate
lament, and this prepares the listener for the confused suffering of
the tenor aria 'Ah my soul, ah whither wilt thou fly?'. The chorale

which ends the first part on a note of consolation is an old Passion
hymn, 'Jesus' Suffering, Pain and Death', which will recur twice in
the work and can be regarded as a sort of theme tune of the *St John
Passion*.

The second part is much longer than the first. In the centre are
the passionate and excited people's choruses during the scene before
Pilate; each remark from the crowd, no matter how short, is
oratorially extended. The first dramatic climax is reached when
the chorus cries out 'Not this man, but Barabbas', and following
this the Evangelist reports the scourging of Jesus in painfully vivid
melismas. Two peaceful songs of a beauty that is utterly detached
follow this wild excitement; the first is the arioso for bass, 'Come
ponder O my soul', and the second is the lengthy aria for tenor,
with its visionary promises of the signs of God's grace; two violas
d'amore sway above the vocal line, coming together in passages
in thirds and sixths, restrained both in sound and expression.

The people's choruses rise again to even wilder passion, and the
excitement reaches its climax in the two big 'Crucify' choruses.
'Crucify' is hacked out in semiquaver cries against the long, howling calls; irrevocably the action marches forward with unbridled
passion. Pilate has handed Jesus over to the Jews and they lead him
away to Golgotha. A bass aria calls to all Christianity to come to
Golgotha, constantly interrupted by the timid query of the chorus:
'Come where?'

It is surprising how much space is given to the argument of the
soldiers under the Cross about the division of Jesus' robe, and it is
also surprising that though there were really only a few soldiers
dicing for the possession of the coat, the whole chorus takes part in
this extremely artistic episode. Then the contralto takes up Jesus'

last words, 'It is finished', and the aria, which also takes over the
musical sequence of notes for these words, is worked up into a
touching song of consolation to form a moving climax. The lively
middle section, 'See! Juda's hero triumphs now', sounds magnificent as the accompanying strings break out into rejoicing fanfares.
After this flowing promise, the reappearance of the consolatory
mood from the beginning of the aria has a still more calming effect;
the delicate melody of the accompanying 'cello plays lightly around
the voice part. With the bass aria in the words of the Evangelist,
'He bowed his head and departed', the chorus sings the melody of
the Passion chorale 'Jesus' Suffering, Pain and Death' for the third
time in the course of the Passion. The second time was as Jesus
spoke to John from the Cross, saying 'Behold, thy mother'.

The final chorus is a burial chorus as the Christian congregation
stands by Jesus' grave, mourning and lamenting; the delicate
middle section, which is played twice, thus giving the chorus a
form in five sections, promises consolation and deliverance. The
gentle, resigned chorale, 'Ah! Lord, when my last end is come',

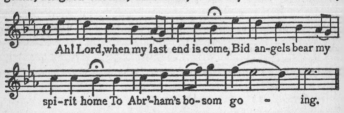

follows immediately after this long burial song, a really magical
close to the whole work; its simplicity and childlike piety is most
moving, and it lends a melancholy but hopeful closing touch to
all the terrible events of the Passion.

The circumstances surrounding the composition of the *St Matthew
Passion* in 1729 were much more favourable than they were for the
St John Passion, for Bach had at his disposal a poet who, though by
no means significant, was at least experienced. This was the poet
Picander. With his help Bach could avoid all the mistakes which
had crept into the earlier work with its lack of suitable texts. The
St Matthew text in itself offers more diversity, simply because it
includes the episodes of the Last Supper and the Garden of Gethsemane. Besides this, Bach introduced numerous resting-places in
the form of contemplative arias and recitatives, and Picander fol-

lowed his instructions in setting their moods. Some of these texts, particularly in the accompanying recitatives, are quite successful poetically. The words of the Passion no longer prevented Bach's work from being a perfect masterpiece.

Because of the broader textual layout here, Bach uses much larger musical forces than usual: two choruses are required, each accompanied by its own orchestra and organ, and they are used together in the big dramatic chorale movements. In the introductory chorus a third chorus in unison is added, in an opening chorus that is overwhelming in every respect. The first chorus sings with painful excitement, 'Come ye daughters, share my mourning; see him, The bridegroom Christ, a spotless lamb', and the second chorus interrupts excitedly with its questions: 'Whom? What? How?'. The waves of sound advance and retreat continually, calling and questioning, and they break on the cantus firmus of the unison chorus, 'O Lamb of God most holy', creating a tone-painting of infinite richness and grandeur. It became the practice to regard this vast double chorus as an intensely heightened expression of pain, and accordingly to perform it at a dragging pace. But Albert Schweitzer, the great authority on Bach, regards this tone-painting as a vision of a mass of people pushing through the streets of Jerusalem, exchanging excited shouts. This realistic interpretation is extraordinarily convincing; a deep excitement is expressed, which effects the appropriate turbulent impact.

Whereas the *St John Passion* opened with Jesus' arrest, the beginning of the *St Matthew Passion* consists of the quiet propitious images of Jesus' anointment and the Last Supper. The short chorus of the pharisees and the news of Judas' treachery are inserted into the drama and sound like gloomy presages of inexorable fate. The arias, lyrical points of rest interrupting the action, pursue the ideas arising out of the story and comment on them, expressing suffering and confusion, remorse and repentance, grief and consolation. Lighter, happier aspects are almost entirely absent. There is an infinite variety of expressive possibilities in these reiterated emotions. The form of the arias is always da capo: the first section of the aria is repeated after a short middle section; generally with a somewhat contrasted atmosphere. The big arias are frequently introduced by a recitative accompanied by the same combination of instruments that will accompany the aria; the recitative and aria have a similar textual content, and Bach often preserves the same thematic line in the music. They exude the same mildness and virtue that gives the whole work its encouraging character. The one or more accompanying solo instruments give each aria its particular colour; melody, timbre and expression merge into an unforgettable unity. Just as in the *St John Passion*, the Evangelist's recitatives and those of the subsidiary characters are accompanied only by the organ; but each time Jesus speaks, a four-part string group illuminates his words with a silvery clarity. Schweitzer wonderfully describes this as a halo playing around his head. The accompaniments are extremely simple, and correspondingly direct in their effect. Every receptive listener is bound to retain a happy memory of, for example, the opening words of the Last Supper, where the strings delicately pick up the motion of the solo voice and prolong it with complete calmness. This consecrated atmosphere leads into the soprano aria 'Jesu Saviour, I am thine', one of the few pieces that gives expression to happier emotions; in a bright G major and accompanied by a duet of oboes d'amore, the aria is an expression of childlike surrender. In the next scene on the Mount of Olives, the chorale with the melody 'O sacred head, sore wounded' is sung twice. The melody is the theme of this enormous work; Bach repeats it constantly on the most significant occasions throughout.

The arias for the scenes in the garden of Gethsemane are particularly noteworthy. Jesus' words, 'My soul is exceedingly sorrowful, even unto death', are taken by the tenor soloist. The 'heavy-laden breast' is filled with impassioned suffering; the chorus puts its questions, in the tone of a chorale, with timid concern, and the whole excited recitative is charged with tremulous disquiet. This is balanced by the more placid aria, 'I would beside my Lord be watching'. Confidence flows into the hearts of the believers; the chorus takes part in this too, softly re-echoing and reflecting the emotions of the soloist.

The first part closes with Jesus' arrest. This part of the action is accompanied by two marvellous pieces of music: the duet with chorus, 'Behold, my Saviour now is taken', and the chorus at the end, 'O man, thy heavy sin lament'. The chorus's perplexed cries of 'Loose him! Leave him! Bind him not!' constantly interrupt the triste lament of the two soloists who follow the procession at the

head of which Jesus is under arrest. Finally, both choruses burst
out, passionate and outraged, and call down thunder and lightning
to destroy the filthy traitor. This chorus is laid out as a vivace
constantly gaining in intensity. The two choruses cry out to one
another and unite at the end in an impassioned avowal. This final
chorus of part one is a choral fantasia on the Passion chorale, 'O
man, thy heavy sin lament'. The cantus firmus is sung by the

O man, thy hea - vy sin la - ment!

sopranos and the other voices take up the lament with plaintive
figurations, while the orchestra complements this with its own
weeping and sighing sounds. This impressive chorus was originally
the introduction to the *St John Passion*; but its noble lamenting
tone is much better suited as the placating aftermath of mighty
experiences rather than as their solemn prologue. Bach, with his
usual sureness of touch, finally decided to place it here, where it
fulfils its function ideally.

In the second part of the *St Matthew Passion*, which tells of the
interrogations with the high priests and Pilate, it happens quite
naturally that the people's choruses come to the foreground. But
they are treated with extreme brevity and are very strongly characterized, without a great deal of verbal repetition. Even the passionate crucifixion chorus, which is quite extended in the *St John
Passion*, is limited to a few bars, but these few bars are immensely
effective: the first chorus repeats them exactly, but a whole tone
higher, which intensifies the excitement and passion. The cry
'Barabbas', which has a whole chorus in other Passions and in the
St John Passion has four lengthy bars, is reduced to a single long
drawn-out cry on a diminished seventh chord. The lyrical sections
in the second part form a wonderfully balanced contrast to these
dramatic climaxes, among which must also be numbered the marvellous description, using the most primitive means, of the earthquake, in the Evangelist's narrative. Indeed the formal equilibrium
of this giant opus always fills one with admiration and amazement;
the most heterogeneous elements—on the one hand, the dramatic
report of the Passion and the people's passionate choruses, and on
the other hand, the lyrical transfiguration of the arias and chorales,
and the grandiose choral movements—become a beautifully unified

whole. The representation of these terrible events is unsparing and passionate; yet Bach spreads over the whole a veil of mildness, virtue and consolation that determines the character of the work. Among the lyrical sections of the second part, two of the most beautifully inspired are the aria for contralto, 'Have mercy, Lord, on me', with the expressive violin obligato, and the soprano aria, 'For love my Saviour now is dying', which shines out like a luminous apparition between the passionate crucifixion choruses. The placing of the chorales in the second part is, perhaps, even more important for the distribution of light and shade, particularly the melody 'O sacred head, sore wounded' which Bach inserts three times in the second part. The first time, he uses Paul Gerhart's well-known words, 'Commit thy way to Jesus', after Jesus has silently submitted himself to Pilate. Directly after Jesus has been spat upon and scourged by the soldiers it recurs with the first two verses of the original chorale text, and finally it comes after the Evangelist's words, 'Jesus, when he had cried again with a loud voice, yielded up the ghost'. Here the chorale is sung *pianissimo* to the words, 'Be near me, Lord, when dying'—one of the most moving moments in this score, so laden with shattering experiences.

I would like to draw attention to two particularly beautiful musical climaxes which occur towards the end of this mighty work. Particularly effective as a light contrast after the gloomy burial song 'O Golgotha', is the contralto aria, 'See ye, see the Saviour's outstretched hands', which reaches us like a vision of bliss, interrupted by questioning cries from the faithful. Then there is the wonderfully healing atmosphere, achieved by the simplest of means, of the bass arioso, 'At evening, hour of calm and peace'. The quietly flowing violins and violas against the long notes of the bass perfectly succeed in evoking the twilight atmosphere of an evening in nature; the impressionists, with the most skilful orchestral devices in the world, could not have done better.

The final chorus, a long burial lament, is built in the form of a large *da capo* aria. Even the introductory recitative is there; each of the soloists bids farewell to the Redeemer, and the chorus sings 'Lord Jesus, fare thee well' in the most delicate *pianissimo*. At last comes the actual burial song, when the two choruses sing sometimes alternately, sometimes together. Quietude and gentleness are the hopeful and reassuring concepts that underlie this mourning song, typical of the placating atmosphere that pervades the whole of the *St Matthew Passion*.

The first performance of the *St Matthew Passion* probably took place on Good Friday, 1729, in the church of St Thomas in Leipzig. Despite the extraordinary difficulties involved in presenting such a mighty work, it was repeatedly performed there, even after Bach's death. But it then lapsed into obscurity. The credit goes to the young Felix Mendelssohn for reviving the work exactly one hundred years after its first performance. His revival in the Vocal Academy in Berlin, using four hundred singers, created an enormous impression. Soon afterwards it was performed in various larger German towns, and gradually won its present place in the musical heritage of Europe.

Besides his Passions Bach wrote music for other chief feasts of the church, Christmas, Easter and Whitsun. The *Christmas Oratorio* has become very popular, but the other two are rarely performed. The *Christmas Oratorio* consists of six cantatas, to be played on the three holidays of Christmas, New Year's Day, the Sunday after New Year's Day and at the feast of the Epiphany: this was the way Bach had it first performed in 1734. Thereafter he collected all six cantatas together under the title of the *Christmas Oratorio*, which is perfectly justified by the unity of line that connects the six parts. But it is hardly possible to perform the whole in one evening without badly tiring the listener, so one usually hears only a selection, particularly the first two sections, which certainly contain the most beautiful music in the work. The *Christmas Oratorio* is largely unoriginal writing. 'Parodying' his own compositions, Bach took several of the arias and also choruses from his earlier secular cantatas. The marvellous opening number, 'Christians be joyful', was originally in a birthday cantata in honour of the Queen, to the words 'Beat the drums and sound the trumpets', and the solo use of the kettledrum at the beginning of the instrumental prelude only really makes sense with the original text. But usually the transplanted arias and choruses fit the Christmas texts so beautifully that it is difficult to believe they were composed to other words. The form of the *Christmas Oratorio* is similar to that of the Passion; the Evangelist's narrative is framed by commentaries in the form of recitatives, arias and choruses. An innovation in the *Christmas Oratorio* is the independent accompaniment sometimes given to the chorales. The festive introductory chorus is followed by the Evangelist's report that Joseph and Mary are moving to Bethlehem where Mary is to bear a child. The famous contralto aria, 'Prepare thyself, Zion', takes up the idea that Christ was born for our redemption. This aria, with its popular melodic style, sets the tone for the whole work, one of gentle gaiety and devotion. The following chorale, 'How shall I fitly meet thee', sounds like a serious warning, sung to the melody of 'O sacred head, sore wounded', but the Evangelist's relation of the birth of Christ disperses all the shadows. The bass recitative, leading to the festive aria and finally to the radiant chorus at the end of the first part, is filled with joy. The last chorus is the greeting chorale to the wonderful festive melody, 'From heaven above I hither come', interrupted by flourishes of trumpets.

A long instrumental symphony introduces the second part: strings and oboes vie with one another, each group developing its own theme. This represents, according to Schweitzer, communal music-making among the angels and shepherds; the shepherds in the fields blow their shawms, while the angels in the air above them execute heavenly string music. With its swung melodic style and quietly flowing $12/8$ rhythms, this Christmas symphony has tremendous charm. The second part is devoted to the notification of the shepherds; the familiar words of the Evangelist and of the angel are complemented by the aria for tenor, 'Haste, ye shepherds, haste to meet Him', and by the solo contralto's wonderful lullaby. This lullaby, 'Slumber, beloved', is one of Bach's most beautiful tunes, and it is difficult to see why he places it in this shepherd scene rather than in the third part, where the shepherds find the Child in the crib. But the choruses of angels are the really big climaxes of the second part: the jubilant 'Glory to God', and at the end, 'With all thy hosts, O Lord, we sing', where the wonderful chorale melody, 'From heaven above I hither come', sounds out again in all its solemn grandeur.

The *Christmas Oratorio* would have to be performed on two evenings to avoid extensive cutting. The first three cantatas form a closed group and include all the essential elements of the Christmas story, but it is a great pity to perform only the first half of the oratorio and miss the many musical treasures in the last cantatas. The last three cantatas tell of the three kings and their audience with the Child. Particularly remarkable is the wonderfully characteristic chorus, 'Where is the new-born King of the Jews?', with its soulful contralto recitative. Once more, at the end of the oratorio, the solemn warning implicit in the chorale melody 'O sacred head, sore wounded' returns, but this time it is clothed in a bright orchestral cloak bringing the work to a festive close.

Bach's *Easter Oratorio* of 1736—subtitled 'Cantata Festo Pas-
chali'—is quite moderate in its proportions. It is laid out in eleven
sections, the first two of which, sinfonia and adagio, are purely
instrumental. The sinfonia is scored for a powerful orchestra with
trumpets, drums and organ, and the adagio only for oboe, strings
and continuo, in a long, flowing line over a slow dotted rhythm
accompaniment. The 3/8 rhythm of the sinfonia returns with the
full orchestra in the third section. After an orchestral introduction,
there is a long duet for tenor and bass to the words 'Now come let
us hasten' which are subsequently developed amongst the four solo
voices: 'Oh unbelieving hearts.' This is followed by a slow, gracious soprano aria, 'Sorrow shall no longer vex me' with flute
obbligato. The next recitative is shared by alto, tenor and bass and
relates the discovery of the empty sepulchre after Jesus' resurrection,
and the following beautiful tenor aria with two flutes, two violins,
bassoons and continuo expresses the feeling that after Jesus' resurrection death can hold no more terrors: 'Calmly I await my ending.' Section eight begins with a recitative for soprano and alto,
'With patient hearts we await the appointed hour', which leads
straight into the arioso duet 'Ah! May we soon behold in glory the
Saviour who for us hath died'. An alto aria, 'Tell me where I shall
find Jesus, whom my soul would fain adore', and a bass recitative,
'Rejoice, rejoice, for now we know our Saviour liveth', bring us
to the final movement, the chorus 'Praise and thanks, Father, unto
thee we raise'. This exciting movement with its characteristic juxtaposition of dotted rhythms and triplets ends at the words 'All his
work on earth is done', and then breaks into a fast 3/8 section with
fugal entries for the chorus that recall the rhythm of the opening
of the work. The chorus has no dramatic rôle in this work: it is
rather the audience—it debates on what the story will be about at
the beginning, and at the end expresses its enthusiasm for, and
enjoyment of the tale told.

Bach's *Cantata No. 11* (1735 or 1736) is subtitled 'Oratorio for
the feast of the Ascension'. It is on a larger scale than most of his
church cantatas, and is subdivided into two separate parts, the first
with six movements and the second with five. The text was probably provided by Picander, and tells the story of Jesus' ascension
poetically, and without any dramatic dialogue. The first chorus,
'Praise to God on high', is vigorously scored for trumpets, drums,
woodwind and leaping strings. A sizable instrumental introduction
precedes the chorus entry. The choral writing is in Bach's best

incisive—almost instrumental—vocal style. After this joyful and substantial curtain-raiser the soloists commence the narrative: the tenor describes Jesus blessing the children, the bass realizes most movingly that His departure is near, and the alto pleads that He remain. The material for this aria was later incorporated into the Agnus Dei of the *B minor Mass*, and the fact that Bach considered it suitable for inclusion in that great work is some indication of its value. A tenor recitative announces Jesus' ascension, and to end the first part the chorus comments 'Now ruler art thou of earth and sky' in a chorale. The second part is headed 'After the sermon'. It consists of three recitatives, a soprano aria and a final chorus, the first recitative being remarkable for the wonderful canon that develops between the tenor and bass soloists.

The final chorus is a grand chorale-fantasia with the theme in long notes in the soprano part. The instrumental interludes are again scored for full orchestra with trumpets, and the mood is more solemn but no less joyful than the opening chorus.

Bach probably wrote his great *Magnificat*, the holy Virgin Mary's song of praise, for Christmas in 1723. In the church of St Thomas in Leipzig it was the custom to sing the *Magnificat* in Latin after evensong on the first day of the feast. Originally, so as to underline the Christmas aspect of his *Magnificat*, Bach inserted four numbers on Christmas texts which were partly in German and partly in Latin, but these he abandoned when he revised the work later. In its final form the *Magnificat* takes little more than half an hour, and this compression brings out with great clarity the extraordinary beauties of the score. On a festive scale, the orchestral prelude, brightened by three high trumpets, opens with the main theme, which is taken up later by the chorus. The first five-part chorus uses only the words 'Magnificat anima mea dominum' (My soul doth magnify the Lord). The idea in the text is marvellously described by the upward striving of the vocal parts, which are handled almost instrumentally. The vocal lines pile jubilantly one on top of the other, and a big build-up leads to the orchestral postlude, closing the rejoicing chorus with a brilliant flourish. The two arias following this are in a delicate and exceedingly fervent mood, particularly the second one, 'Quia respexit', which depicts Our Lady's meekness: an oboe d'amore plays a counterpoint against the submissive figuration of the strongly expressive vocal line. The final words, 'Omnes generationes', are taken up by the chorus, which extends the modest, humbly expressed idea, 'All generations shall call me blessed'. This chorus is very powerfully built, as though the whole of Christendom were uniting in a magnificent manifestation of faith. The chorus 'Fecit potentiam' has a similar proud grandeur; the masterful intervals of the chorus entry are answered with equal strength by the orchestra, symbolizing the impossibility of escape from God's power. The sudden adagio at the end of this passionately excited chorus is strange; it opens with the words 'In the imagination of their hearts' (which is a little obscure, for it concerns their pride: 'He hath scattered the proud in the imagination of their hearts'). But this sudden restraint is extraordinarily effective on a purely musical level. The strange and impressive interpretation of the concept of compassion is worthy of particular note: the trio of women's voices in delicate imitation forms itself around the chorale melody intoned by the oboes in unison. After this, the chorus basses enter firmly with 'Sicut lucutus est', which develops into a powerful fugato. The short final chorus is a gripping Gloria; after an impetuous lead-in, the theme of the opening chorus is taken up and leads the work through, with brilliant jubilation, to its Amen.

The *Mass in B minor* is the only complete Mass that Bach wrote. The first two movements, the Kyrie and the Gloria, were written in 1733 after the death of the Elector Friedrich Augustus II, and Bach intended them as an expression of his veneration and loyalty to the Elector's successor. The subsequent movements of the *Mass in B minor* were written separately at later dates, and the whole work was in existence probably not later than 1738.

Naturally Bach took the fixed forms of the individual sections of the Mass as they were used in the Catholic church. He also makes use of the general practice, stemming from Italian opera, of subdividing the long sections into choruses, arias and duets. But Bach's own spirit is unmistakable in the *B minor Mass*, even if some of his commentators find Catholic traits in the grandiosity of the Gloria, or Protestant feeling in the formal economy of the Agnus Dei. All one can do is uphold the all-inclusive greatness of Bach's world, unlimited by any particular confession of faith. Schweitzer, for instance, sees Catholic traits in the *B minor Mass*, but the fact is that Catholic grandeur and Protestant fervency co-exist in Bach, and the Mass, as Schweitzer goes on to say, is indeed both Catholic and Protestant at the same time.

The *B minor Mass* is constructed in four big sections, in accordance with the Catholic liturgy: the Kyrie, the Gloria, the Credo, and the Sanctus coupled with the Agnus Dei. The fundamental ideas contained in these sections are as follows: consciousness of guilt and the plea for compassion in the Kyrie Eleison (Lord have mercy upon us); the glorification of God in the 'Gloria in excelsis Deo' (Glory be to God on high); Christ's work of redemption and the confession of faith in the Credo (I believe); the beatification of God in the Sanctus (Holy) and 'Christi, Agnus Dei' (Lamb of God), ending with the words 'Dona nobis pacem'. Bach subdivides the Mass into twenty-four pieces of music, mostly sung by the chorus. The grandeur and strength of these choruses and the effect produced by them is indescribable and unique; even with a first hearing they make an exceedingly forceful impression. Devoted study of the score is necessary for even an approximate grasp of the beauties of this work, which is surely the most sublime manifestation of Bach's spirit. His clever, balancing, reflective mind is traceable in a thousand details within the marvellous conception of the whole.

The Kyrie has five parts. The powerful statement by the chorus introduces the work, setting the elevated tone of the whole. Then a considerable orchestral prelude gives a foretaste of the gloomy theme, which is to become the first giant fugue of the Kyrie. This expressive theme, full of painful emotion, goes through a process of unimaginable intensification in the five-part fugue; this is no mere prayer but passionate and urgent entreaty, a confession and a demand that becomes ever more insistent in proportion to the ever more acute intensity of its expression. The call to Christ (Christe Eleison) is a duet between the two female soloists; the music has an air of quiet confidence and faith in the compassion of our Saviour, mediator between God and man. After this the closing Kyrie has quieter contours; it grows like an enormous lament, but one through which some hope always shines.

The Gloria opens with jubilant flourishes from the three trumpets: 'Glory be to God on high, peace on earth, good will among men.' The contralto solo 'Laudamus te' is followed by the solemn grandeur of the chorus of gratitude, 'Gratias agimus tibi'. These three sections are addressed to God the Father; the following section rather to his Son, the Redeemer. The musical climax comes with the chorus entry, 'Qui tollis peccata mundi, miserere nobis'; the humble devotional prayer sounds out in a secret *pianissimo*, in an aura of delicate string figurations. The stormy progress of the triumphant chorus, 'Cum Sancto Spiritu', constitutes the festive and brilliant close of the Gloria.

The Credo of the *B minor Mass* is the highest expression of the original and eternal secret of the confession of faith, the mystery of the Holy Trinity. The medieval chorale intonation of the 'Credo in unum Deum' emerges as from the mysterious twilight of a cathedral. The five-part fugue, in which, besides the voice parts, the violins also take part, builds up with ever-increasing strength. The continuo and the basses march on irresistibly in majestic crotchets, while the fugue attains to ever more powerful formations, until the grandiose ecclesiastical theme in the bass, using doubled note-values, broadens the piece out into its final intensity. The dramatic and musical climax of the Credo in the all-surpassing crucifixion chorus; the imploring voices of the chorus are raised above the rigid, chromatically descending basso ostinato (repeated thirteen times) with the delicate colourations of hopeless suffering, and finally, on the words 'Sepultus est' (and was buried), they fade away into *pianissimo*. At the end, the basso ostinato line modulates soothingly into the relative major key. Then comes the bright rejoicing of 'et resurrexit', the instrumental interludes continually take up the chorus's exultant shouts and intensify their gladness with flourishes of trumpets. As in the introductory chorus, Bach uses the Gregorian chorale melody of 'Confiteor unum Baptisma' in the grandly laid out final chorus of the Credo. This ancient intoned melody was not suited to the polyphonic construction of a choral movement, so Bach builds up the chorus in big lines over a freely invented theme, and only later introduces the Gregorian theme, very tellingly and with great intensity.

The choruses in the fourth part are also displayed in luminous colours: the great sublime Sanctus with the jubilant fugue, 'Pleni sunt coeli et terra gloria ejus' (Heaven and earth are full of His glory) and the lively powerful double chorus, 'Osanna in excelsis'. The most moving solo in the *Mass in B minor* is the contralto aria, 'Agnus Dei, qui tollis peccata mundi'. The suffering contained in this song of entreaty is as though transfigured into calm confidence; it is softened by the quiet certainty that this plea will be granted. The final chorus, 'Dona nobis pacem' is a note-for-note repetition of the chorus of gratitude in the Gloria. And so this prayer for peace can also be understood as a pious and devoted prayer of gratitude, ending the mighty work like a long and solemn 'Amen'.

GEORGE FREDERICK HANDEL

born Halle 23 February 1685
died London 14 April 1759

Handel was the son of a surgeon. He went to Hamburg as early as
1703, where, with Reinhard Keiser, he was able to maintain a position as a successful composer of opera. In the years 1706–09 his
operas and oratorios enjoyed tremendous success in Italy, and it
was after this that he took the post of Master of the court orchestra
in Hanover. Then, in 1712, Handel went to London, where he
stayed until his death. In London, too, he started off as a composer
almost entirely of opera, and it was only after the collapse of his
operatic undertakings that he finally turned his attention to oratorio. As it turned out, it was in this field that Handel reached the
peak of his achievement; the oratorios can be viewed as the crowning glory of his life's work.

In some circles it is fashionable to belittle Handel's significance
as a composer; people compare him disparagingly with Bach.
Certainly the temptation to compare the two is all too appealing:
they were born in the same year, and both grew up in reduced circumstances in provincial towns. But since the sequels of their lives
followed such different courses, is it not inevitable that the art of
each of them should also have developed quite differently? On the
one hand we see Bach, living with his large family almost exclusively in the provincial world of his home town, and on the other,
Handel, the bachelor, accustomed to rich takings, like a courtier in
the big business of the world. It was not chance that made Handel
devote two-thirds of his life to opera, whereas Bach never even
thought of writing one. It is natural, then, that Handel's music
should show a tendency towards grandeur, worldly breadth and
opulence, as opposed to the depth and intensity of Bach's. The
bold, clear lines of his music lead one to call it homophonic, as
compared with the variegated forms of Bach's polyphony. The
work of both men is great and masterful in its own way, and the
Germans have good reason to be proud that two such gigantic
figures occur right at the beginning of the musical history of
Germany.

Handel's most famous work is the oratorio, the *Messiah*, and this
one work alone would have been sufficient to carry his fame, un-
diminished, through the centuries. Most of Handel's operas are

now forgotten; even the great beauty of some of the music cannot blind us to the defects of their completely undramatic texts. Of his instrumental works, the trio sonatas for two violins and continuo can still be heard in the concert hall, as well as the organ concertos and the occasional concerto grosso.

The *Twelve Concerti Grossi* are scored for strings and continuo only, and were published by Handel in 1739 as his opus 6. When a large orchestra is used, as is usually the case—and quite rightly so—the continuo part is played on a modern grand piano, or omitted altogether. Handel took the title 'Concerto Grosso' from the Italian master, Corelli, who brought the concerto grosso to its final form. As I remarked earlier in connection with the *Brandenburg Concertos* of Bach, the characteristic thing about the concerto grosso is the grouping of the instruments. There are the concertante instruments, which are used in a solo manner, and the ripieno instruments, which are used orchestrally. The group of solo instruments is referred to as the concertino, or 'little orchestra', as opposed to the full orchestra, the 'concerto grosso'. In Handel's concertos the concertino usually consists of two solo violins and a solo 'cello.

There is something extremely festive, joyful and affirmative about Handel's concertos; their magnificent and pleasurable character is ideally suited to any sort of festive musical function, and, used as overtures, they set the mood perfectly for a symphony concert. Besides this, all of Handel's music has the additional recommendation of being marvellously accessible; he deliberately aimed at breadth of effect. His music is addressed to a large public, to the musical layman; there is something artless about the clear simplicity of his forms. His themes are easy to remember and have a strong rhythmic profile; they are quite short, often only one bar. When he writes a fugato it is usually only in two voices, so that even an untrained ear is capable of following the voices. But the music is so rich in ideas and brims with such strength of personality that it would be madness to deny oneself the directness and effectiveness of its content.

The *Concerti Grossi* are all in the form of the suite, with between four and six movements. Each one opens with a majestic grave. The *Concerto No. 1 in G major* begins with a masterful *tutti*, followed by the concertino's timorous plea as a contrast. Then an allegro presents a variant of the powerful orchestral theme, which the solo parts now take up like an echo. Gravity is the keynote of the adagio; the movement exudes grandeur and strength, rather than

the mourning and lamenting that so often characterizes Bach's slow movements. The next allegro opens energetically with a fugato duet for the two solo violins, but this is abandoned when the orchestra enters and reappears only in the reprise, in its inverted form. At the end, Handel appends a lively dance in a fluid 6/8.

The *Concerto No. 2 in F major* is distinguished by its idyllic quality. The first andante runs through a series of exchanges between *tutti* and soloists. This is quite uncomplicated, but the D minor allegro that follows displays great virtuosity. A neat game of question and answer develops out of the short themes in constant imitation, and this builds up with great liveliness, only to die away again rather timidly. The third movement is a solemn largo. The crowning glory of the work is certainly the magnificent finale, in which a tugging theme is introduced and developed fugally,

but the fugal form is abandoned with the entry of the second theme, *pianissimo*. An extremely charming opposition between these two contrasted themes is set up, until in the end they are combined: the fugue theme in the bass alternates with the slow flowing counter-theme in the violins, and vice versa, and all this with such artful naturalness that the listener, if he is not careful, will be caught quietly smiling to himself.

The *Concerto No. 3 in E minor* is much quieter. The polonaise is particularly charming: a simple melody, memorable on account of its peculiar rhythmic articulation, unfurls itself over an unruffled bass. Handel follows this with an attractive little dance movement which ends the work.

The *Concerto No. 5 in D major* is in six movements. The opening maestoso introduces the solo violins in cadenza style and the powerful theme is delivered by the full string chorus. The allegro follows, a lively fugato with a charming opposition of soloists and *tutti*. This

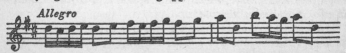

allegro makes great technical demands on the players, but the
following presto requires a really consummate virtuosity. The
light, scurrying theme, which appears sometimes in the solo instruments and sometimes, with a great rushing sound, in the full

orchestra, is interrupted to great effect by striking *forte* passages or
pianissimo pizzicato. This is followed by a largo in which the solo
instruments predominate, and which has a marvellous ending: the
bright sound of the full orchestra dies away gradually, and then,
out of this almost inaudible *pianissimo*, out of nothingness, the
graceful minuet emerges, clothed in the most delicate colours. The

contours of the reserved and flowing melodies are lit up by Handel's subtlest instrumentation. The final movement is in a wanton
mood; the gay trills are answered again and again, with a perverse
insistence on the repetitions, by a highly characterized figuration.
The concerto ends on this festive note.

The *Concerto No. 7 in B-flat major* dispenses with the concertino.
After a few bars of largo introduction there enters a skilful fugal
allegro with a theme that is like a caricature: one bar of minims,
one of crotchets, and finally one of quavers, all on the same note!
But, as is frequently the case in Handel's fugal movements, the
fugue is abandoned after four voices have entered and a free fantasia develops, the amusing theme now in one voice, now in
another, with little regard for the form or rules of fugue. The
bridge to the idyllic andante is formed by a short largo with an
expressive duet between the two groups of violins. Handel uses
a hornpipe for his finale, which with its syncopated rhythms forms
an effective close for the concerto.

The *Concerto No. 12 in B minor* is laid out like a symphony in
three movements. The two allegro movements, each introduced

by a short largo, enclose a simple slow movement, a larghetto whose peculiar charm lies in the natural delicacy, the artlessness with which the touching and delicate theme is handled. The fiery finale has the character of a gigue. Besides the main idea, which is treated fugally, there are several charming subsidiary themes; these sometimes join up with the main theme and then again separate, leading the dance on their own, only to be overtaken ever and again by the fiery fugato theme.

Better known than the *Concerti Grossi* are Handel's two 'occasional' pieces, the *Water Music* and the *Firework Music*. Handel wrote his *Water Music* in 1717 on the occasion of the King's summer trip on the Thames. Besides the royal boat there was another, which accommodated a large orchestra consisting of over fifty musicians. The score requires flutes, horns and trumpets in addition to the usual strings and oboes, and these instruments lend their particular character to the movements in which they are used. The long overture is followed by diverse dance movements. This music was not intended to be anything more than light music, but it is light music of the very highest quality.

The *Firework Music* is also light music in the best sense of that expression; the structure of the music is clear and the melodic style popular and memorable. Handel wrote it for a firework display that was organized to celebrate the Aix Peace Treaty of 1749. The orchestra consists of wind instruments alone, but a large quantity of these—about fifty. Handel achieved his greatest successes with his open air music, and the only reason that these pieces are not played more often than they are is that it is difficult and expensive to muster an orchestra of the size and composition required.

Most of Handel's organ concertos are arrangements of earlier pieces. Since he did not write a separate line for the pedals of the organ, it would be possible to play them as piano concertos; it seems a pity that these great works should be so seldom performed simply because the proper organ is not available in most concert halls. Handel himself was an excellent organist who knew no limitations of technique, and consequently some of the movements in his concertos require an almost frightening virtuosity. But the lines of his music are always broad and clear, and his outside movements especially are always powerful and energetic. The two *Concertos in B-flat major* are the best known; one comes from opus 4, and the other, which includes a powerful chaconne, from opus 7.

Handel's work in the field of vocal music is even greater than his instrumental pieces. He devoted more than thirty years of his life to Italian opera and wrote countless operas in the Neapolitan style; he can even be considered the most outstanding representative of this school. But his work in oratorio is incomparably more significant; he was really the originator of the people's oratorio. And whereas his operas are almost entirely forgotten, his big choral works are as much alive today as they were two hundred years ago.

The addiction to choral societies has always been a peculiarity of the English musical tradition. In the thirteenth century, England was a hotbed of polyphonic singing and the rich development of polyphony in the school of the Netherlands was a direct result of this. The love of choral singing survived in England despite all distracting fashionable trends and took the form of numerous singing clubs for canons, catches and glees. Thus it was that Handel found a choral tradition in England capable of affording him considerable stimulus. His first oratorios, commissioned by the Duke of Chandos, were *Esther,* based on Racine's play, and the pastoral *Acis and Galatea,* first performed in 1718–20. But a full decade was to elapse before he turned his undivided attention to oratorio. In 1732 Handel arranged both *Esther* and *Acis and Galatea* for the theatre and produced them with décor, costumes and all the machinery of the stage, but without any dramatic action, like living tableaux. These arrangements were to determine the fundamental form of the great number of oratorios he was to write in following years.

Recognizing clearly the peculiar laws of oratorio, Handel gave the lion's share of the action to the chorus, unlike in opera, where the chorus is always somewhat subordinate. The arias, and even more the recitatives, receded into the background, since there was no dramatic treatment. Contrary to his general practice in his operas of using Italian texts, he set his oratorios to English texts, which played a considerable part in making his oratorios the popular institution they have become. Handel used the Old Testament almost exclusively for his material. God, with the fate of the Children of Israel in his hands, is always the central figure in the oratorios, and the Children of Israel carry most of the action, which results quite naturally in the chorus taking the leading rôle. If we think of opera as dominated by the heroic character, oratorio is dominated by the sublime, and this is the fundamental character of the genre in Handel's hands.

Of Handel's oratorios, the *Messiah* is the best-known and most performed right up to the present day. The reason for this preference is to be found in the choice of material; the figure of the Messiah was closer to the hearts of Handel and his public than were the characters in the Old Testament. The familiar story of Jesus' childhood, growth and suffering would naturally provide the composer with a totally different inspiration to that of the fate of the Children of Israel.

Like all Handel's oratorios, the *Messiah* is written in three parts. The first part tells of the birth of Christ, the second of His passion and resurrection, and the third celebrates the redemption of all mortal souls. The orchestra consists almost exclusively of strings and harpsichord; it is only occasionally that the oboes and bassoons join in, or the trumpets and drums for the particularly brilliant choruses, like the famous Hallelujah Chorus. This orchestral simplicity has given rise to numerous later orchestrations, aimed at adapting the work to the changing demands of fashion. Mozart's orchestration towers high above all other attempts; for the most part he restricts himself to using additional wind instruments, filling out the strings, and rewriting the passages where the trumpets go too high.

Nevertheless, even Mozart's arrangement is played less and less as time goes on. The strange magic and charm of the original orchestration has gradually come into its own. Nowadays nothing is added to the performance, but great efforts are made to present the orchestra as colourfully and as richly as possible by using a large body of strings, doubling or tripling the wind instruments and using several harpsichords wherever possible, and, of course, bringing in a large and opulent organ to support the big choral movements. For magnificence of sound there is little to choose between a typical Handelian orchestra like this and the orchestra of the romantic composers.

The overture—Handel calls it 'Sinfonia'—opens with a solemn grave, followed by a lively allegro which sets off like a fugue. The

strict fugal form is abandoned after the first few entries, and the
fugal idea is pursued only in free imitation. After the E minor
astringency of the overture, the E major string group introducing
the first recitative has a lovely promising sound. The tenor solo
announces that the Redeemer will soon be here, and the chorus
takes up the happy message in a big allegro movement, 'And the
glory of the Lord shall be revealed'. The bass soloist's proclamation
in the recitative, 'Yet once a little while and I will shake the heavens
and the earth', is longer and more impassioned, and in the aria the
question 'But who may abide the day of His coming?' is pressed
with ever-increasing ardour. The following alto solo, 'O thou that
tellest good tidings to Zion', communicates a mood of cheerful
confidence, and this is joyfully substantiated by the chorus. The
strange bass aria, 'The people that walked in darkness', with its
uncanny unison passages for the strings, prepares the way for the
great event of the first part, the chorus 'For unto us a child is born'.
This chorus builds up with majestic grandeur: 'He is a mighty
God, the Everlasting Father, the Prince of Peace, this child that is
born to save us'. The shepherd scene is delightfully created: the
episode is introduced by a delicate orchestral pastorale scored not
for woodwind as one might have imagined, but for strings alone.
The solo soprano, raising her voice for the first time, now takes
the lead in the rôle of the Angel of the Annunciation. The following
arias are also entrusted to her; the gay and lively song of jubilation,
'Rejoice greatly', and the lovely aria, 'He shall feed His flock',
which must be one of the most beautiful pieces in the whole score.
The first part ends with a long, gaily excited choral fugue.

Chorus and soloists are steeped in dark, painful colours at the
beginning of the second part, as choruses and arias tell of Christ's
suffering. The alto aria, 'He was despised', is particularly impressive, with its fervent declamatory style. The extreme plasticity of
the fugue theme of the chorus, 'And with His stripes we are healed',
seems distorted and coloured by an interior glow. The tenor soloist
tells of the death of the Saviour, but proclaims at the same time
that God will not suffer him to putrefy in the grave. After this
comes the first resurrection chorus; the darkness of the Passion is
dispersed, and the Lord of Hosts appears in all the brightness of
His glory. The powerful choruses are interrupted by the soprano
solo, 'How beautiful are the feet', which, with its delectable melody,
is surely one of Handel's most beautiful inspirations. But the hosts
of the heathen raise their voices against this joyful message; the

grandiose aria for bass, 'Why do the nations so furiously rage together?', paints their impotent anger in striking colours. The tenor responds to this picture of anger with the words, 'Thou shalt break them with a rod of iron', and this is where the climax of the work occurs, the Hallelujah Chorus, which, with its irresistible tide of jubilation at the resurrection, makes a glowing finale to the second part.

The third part opens on a note of transfigured peace. The soprano aria, 'I know that my Redeemer liveth', is set in a mood of resigned humility, lit by the confidence of the faithful. The rejoicing 'By man came also the resurrection' follows, with its steeply rising melodic figure. And this resurrection brings redemption to all men, as is proclaimed in the antiphony between the solemn question and the blessed freedom of the chorus's answer. 'The trumpet shall sound' and 'The dead shall be raised incorruptible' sings the bass soloist with conviction, and the trumpets flourish happily. The final chorus sounds out with solemn grandeur. Its middle section builds up powerfully with a fugato, 'Blessing and honour, glory and power be unto Him', and reaches its climax with the words, 'For ever and ever', which form the bridge to the final Amen. This majestic final fugue crowns and transfigures an incomparable work.

The *Messiah* was first performed in April 1742 in Dublin, where Handel was spending the winter. The performance was a charity concert, and all subsequent performances in Handel's lifetime were for the benefit of the London Foundling Hospital. Handel at the peak of his fame could afford to give such truly royal presents.

In London, February 1743, Handel produced the oratorio *Samson*. The textual plan alone demands a very much more dramatic treatment here. However, Samson himself is not introduced as a celebrated war hero, but at the time of his downfall and misery. The hero of the Israelites, who has spent his life successfully fighting off the Philistines, succumbs to the seductions of the Philistine Delilah and betrays the secret of his strength to her—the hair of his head has never known the shears. Delilah then proceeds to cut his hair while he is asleep, and delivers him, defenceless, to his enemies, who blind him and throw him into chains. The oratorio opens with a jubilant chorus of Philistines, who are celebrating the festival of their god, Dagon. The chorus of Israelites is cloaked in gloomy colours as they entreat God's grace; it is only when they think of Samson that a ray of hope pierces their depression. The argument between Samson and Delilah is handled in an almost operatic manner. She begs him to forgive her and take up their love anew (aria with chorus), he declines brusquely (recitative), she swears vengeance on him (duet) and hurries away. The opposition of the choruses after this operatic scene is a piece of real oratorio: the chorus of Israelites begs God's protection with simple grandeur, while the Philistines celebrate their god, Dagon, in dazzling coloratura; then the two worlds are brought together in a mighty double chorus.

The third part of the work describes the catastrophe. The Israelites cry for help; Samson is to be taken to the idol's feast and, if he regains his strength, he will give the enemy another lesson about respecting the power of Jehovah. Samson sings a song of praise to the new dawn in an aria that conjures up a vision of better times—a wonderful piece of music with great expressive strength. Delilah's aria with chorus introduces the final scene, in which Manoah (bass), the Israelite who has followed Samson, witnesses the catastrophe that now breaks over the Philistines: Samson breaks down the pillars that hold up the roof of the temple, which collapses, burying the chiefs of the Philistines under the debris. Crying for help and begging for mercy, the Philistines (chorus) are overcome, but with them, the hero Samson. The short chorus bewailing his death, *pianissimo*, is very moving, followed by a solemn funeral march. But this heroic death is not celebrated by lamentations alone, and a rejoicing chorus closes the work: 'Let their celestial concerts all unite, Ever to sound his praise in endless morn of light.'

Judas Maccabaeus has always been the next most frequently performed oratorio after the *Messiah*, and its extraordinary popularity can be explained by the heroic character of the work. Handel wrote *Judas Maccabaeus* in honour of the Duke of Cumberland, who suppressed the Scottish uprising of 1746. The first performance, in April 1747, was thus also a celebration of victory. Long-suffering and lamenting choruses introduce the work: Israel weeps for its lost freedom, but there is a man, Judas Maccabaeus, who will rise up and liberate them from the foreign yoke. The people rejoice and all are ready to follow him into battle. Battle songs and choruses of victory follow, songs to the glory of the heroes, and expressions of thanks to God. Soloists and chorus alternate with one another, but the chorus is entrusted with the most important parts. 'Fallen is the foe' makes a tremendous elemental impact with its dramatic double fugue, and the gripping victorious chorus, 'See the conquering hero comes', must be one of the most popular melodies that Handel ever wrote.

Handel's few secular choral works are much less significant than his biblical oratorios. His first work of this kind, the pastoral *Acis and Galatea*, which, as we have already mentioned, he revised for its performance in London, has remained the best loved of his works in this genre. It is frequently presented in the concert hall and sometimes on the operatic stage. The story-content is based on an ancient legend: Galatea, a nymph, loves a young shepherd, Acis. When Polyphemus, the uncouth cyclops, wishes to woo her, Galatea scornfully repulses him. Polyphemus resolves to take a terrible revenge. Raging, he strikes Acis with a boulder, but Galatea changes her dead lover into a 'gentle murmuring stream'. This relatively small-scale work is laden with musical treasures. Galatea's aria of longing, with the twittering of birds in the orchestra, is an enchanting piece, but it is perhaps even surpassed by the delicate pastel shades of the lovely aria, 'As when the dove laments her love'. The characterization of Polyphemus is masterly, particularly in his first recitative with its aria, 'O ruddier than the cherry', where the monster's essential uncouthness and madcap quality is tellingly pictured in the short, broken phrases followed by exhaustive melismas. But the most amazing thing about this work is Handel's unique faculty for unerringly setting the atmosphere. He communicates a real sense of the antique in this work, though naturally it is an antiquity in baroque clothing.

Handel wrote his eleven *Chandos Anthems* when he was staying at the country house of the Duke of Chandos between 1717 and 1720. Not all of these Anthems are frequently sung, but they are sizable works and should not be forgotten. The *Chandos Anthem No. 4* is a setting of Psalm 96 for soloists, chorus and orchestra in seven movements. The *Chandos Anthem No. 8* is entitled 'O come let us sing unto the Lord' and is scored for chorus and orchestra with solos for soprano, alto and tenor. The first chorus is preceded by a weighty orchestral overture. The fugal chorus 'Tell it out among the heathen', which is preceded by an accompanied setting of the subject for alto solo, is remarkable for the peculiar rhythm of its word-setting. The final chorus, introduced by a motto for altos and orchestra in octaves, is in Handel's most rejoicing vein, with many of the semiquaver runs that are characteristic of his choral style.

The *Chandos Anthem No. 9*, 'O Praise the Lord with one consent', starts with a marvellous chorus that juxtaposes a square melodic statement of rigid crotchets with jumpy themes composed of arpeggios in the orchestra, and fugato running passages in the chorus. The lucidity and strength of this long chorus is really gratifying. Solos for alto, tenor and bass follow and the fifth movement is again a cheerful chorus in $3/2$ to the words 'With cheerful notes let all the world to heaven their voices raise' with operatic pedal point *tremolos* to end. A solo for soprano leads to the final pair of choruses, 'Ye boundless realms of joy, exalt your maker's fame', which for some reason chooses to make great play with the difficult word 'exalt', and 'Your voices raise, ye Cherubim and Seraphim, to sing his praise', which evolves into a lesser Allelujah chorus, with ejaculated quavers and runs.

The *Chandos Anthems Nos. 6 and 7* are settings of the 42nd and 89th Psalms respectively: 'As pants the hart for cooling streams' (no relation to the hymn-tune), and 'My song shall be alway of the loving kindness of the Lord'. Both are scored for soprano, tenor and bass soloists, mixed chorus, and an orchestra of strings with oboe, bassoon and organ continuo.

There is no end to the rewarding anthems by Handel; *Zadok the Priest*, for example, is a hot cathedral favourite for coronations and so forth. It consists of three short movements: maestoso—'Zadok the priest and Nathan the prophet anointed Solomon King'—for seven-part chorus and an orchestral accompaniment that builds up from *piano* to *fortissimo* in majestic steps. The chorus enters when *ff* is reached for the second time, and states the words in powerful, simple chords. The next movement is a $3/4$ allegro, 'And all the people rejoiced, and said' (this is a five-part chorus); in the last movement comes a six-part chorus: 'God save the King, long live the King. May the King live for ever. Allelujah. Amen.' The weight and power of this brief work create a marvellous mood of excitement. *Zadok the Priest* is in fact one of four coronation anthems that Handel wrote in 1727 for George II. The others are 'The King shall rejoice', 'My heart is inditing' and 'Let thy hand be strength-

ened'. One further choral work of Handel's which it would be
drastic to omit altogether is the Te Deum he wrote in 1743, to
celebrate an English victory, the *Dettingen Te Deum*. This score is
full of trumpets and drums, and falls into eighteen movements, the
majority of which are for chorus. However, there are two lyrical
movements for a trio of soloists or semichorus, and a number of
solo arias.

Finally, there is one other small choral work that is worthy of
mention: the *Ode for St Cecilia's Day*. Handel wrote this charming work, a setting of Dryden's poem, whose title refers to the
patron saint of music, in 1739, in honour of the art of music. The
Ode is more like a solo cantata than a choral work; Handel emp-
tied a veritable cornucopia of brilliant ideas over the arias. The
earnest query of the first melody, 'What passion cannot music
raise?', provides its own answer. The following arias are devoted
to the sounds of the different instruments. The tenor sings of the
trumpet's battle-cry, while the trumpets blaze away accompanied
by the 'Double double double beat of the thundering drum'. The
chorus takes up this aria very powerfully, and the warlike episode
ends with a march. The flute's lament tells of 'The woes of hopeless
lovers' (aria for soprano), and the violins 'Proclaim their jealous
pangs and desperation' (aria for tenor). But the brilliance of the
holy organ outshines all these, joined by the angels of heaven. A
chorus of rejoicing closes this festive work.

CHRISTOPH WILLIBALD GLUCK

born Erasbach, Oberpfalz 2 July 1714
died Vienna 15 November 1787

Gluck was the great reformer of eighteenth-century opera and the
decisive predecessor of Richard Wagner. With their innovations,
both Gluck and Wagner created epoch-making revolutions. Gluck
turned away from Italian opera, which till then had held total
sway, and created a new musico-dramatic style based on the
assertion that the poetic idea should take precedence in opera. Educated in Italy, where he had his first successes as a composer of
opera, in 1754 Gluck took the post of Kapellmeister at the Court
Opera in Vienna. From Vienna he made several trips for perform-

ances of his works in other places. Paris was particularly important in his career, and it was there that he found the proper springboard for his reforms. With *Orpheus*, *Alceste* and *Paris and Helena*, Gluck created a new type of opera, a foundation for a Mozart to build upon, develop and extend.

In the preface to *Alceste* (1776), Gluck requires that the overture 'should prepare the listener for the action which is to follow; the overture is thus a sort of Table of Contents for the action'. His overture certainly does fulfil these requirements, which was unheard-of at the time. The plan of the opera is as follows: Alceste sacrifices herself for her husband, Admet, who is mortally ill, so as to save his life, and also so that the people should not lose their leader. She dies, but Heracles snatches her from the gods of death and takes her back to her husband. The solemn seriousness of this story, in which the love of both parties is subjected to the bitterest tests, is expressed in the overture. Alongside the solemn, almost rigid monumental quality, is the most delicate sensitivity of feeling; the gloomy character of the minor key is sustained throughout. In the overture to *Alceste* it is as though the classical perfection of an ancient building were dissolved into musical lines.

The overture to the opera *Iphigenia in Aulis* (1774) comes still nearer perhaps to meeting Gluck's demand for dramatic verisimilitude. Richard Wagner was so impressed with this piece that he made a concert arrangement of the work; this entailed composing a concert ending, for in the original the overture led directly into the first act. Wagner recognized in the work a 'cry born of the painful, gnawing suffering of the heart'. Agamemnon suffers deeply under the gods' command that he sacrifice Iphigenia, but in the allegro the divine imperative, to the sound of the whole body of

strings in unison, is overwhelming and unavoidable. A delicate idea expressing Iphigenia's virginal grace is contrasted with the

main theme of the allegro. A third theme, with the recurrent sobbing of the oboe, begs sympathy for the innocent victim. The

great drama of the soul develops out of the argument between
these themes; in a very real sense, this presages the content of heroic
opera.

JOSEPH HAYDN

born Rohrau 1 April 1732
died Vienna 31 May 1809

Haydn, the son of a poor wheelwright, went to Vienna as a choirboy in 1740. There, besides singing, he learnt both the violin and
the piano. In 1749 he had to leave the choir and earn a living by
taking private pupils, and at the same time he eagerly began to
compose. In 1759 Haydn at last got a post as composer and conductor with Count Marzin, and then in 1761 with Esterhazy, first
at Eisenstadt and later at the castle of Esterhazy. He made journeys
to London in 1791–92 and 1794–95, and it was there that he achieved
his greatest successes. He spent the evening of his life in Vienna,
honoured and celebrated throughout the civilized world.

Haydn may be regarded as the founder of the symphony, for
his life's work is the first great landmark in the development of
symphonic music. The early eighteenth century was particularly
rich in stimuli; there were forces at work in all quarters provoking
new musical development. The masters of northern Germany, with
Carl Philipp Emanuel Bach at their head, had evolved the sonata
form which was to be the basis of the large symphonic movements;
under the leadership of that genial master, Stamitz, the Mannheim
school had created a new orchestral language; the Viennese symphonists, who usually constructed their movements according to
the strictest rules, had seen their way to incorporating popular and
national elements into their music; the French, with the strict
division of the French overture into a two-part form, also made
their contribution; and the Italian symphonists (Sammartini) were
beginning to include vocally derived melodic lines—the influence
of opera—in their symphonic work. Haydn responded to all these
stimuli; his genius sensed the way to mould them and extend them,

gradually evolving the new style which was to introduce the classical period in music. This is not to say that the new style came abruptly into existence in the work of Haydn; on the contrary, Haydn worked on this style and digested the influences of his contemporaries right up to the end of his long and industrious life, and in this way laid the firm foundations on which Mozart, Beethoven and Schubert were to build.

The symphony, which was the most important form of the new style, with the string quartet running a close second, had four movements in Haydn's time: two fast movements enclosing a slow movement and a dance movement (minuet). This norm was finally established by Haydn, and its basic features have survived up to the present day, which testifies to its solidity and balance. The first allegro is in sonata form, with two contrasted themes, a development section and a reprise. Probably the foremost hallmark of the new style is the extended theme, as opposed to the short motif which was the dominating factor in the polyphonic epoch directly preceding Haydn. It is self-evident that the polyphonic type of form receded in proportion as the accent was laid more on melody and harmony. The vertical principle or harmonic feeling supplanted the horizontal or linear principle.

Haydn wrote more than one hundred and twenty symphonies, which is amazing when one considers that he took up this form only relatively late in his career. He wrote his first symphonies for the Marzin orchestra that he directed from 1759–61, when he was not yet thirty years old. These first symphonies, forgotten today, were partly programmatic in character. He wrote a cycle of symphonies with the heading 'The Times of Day'. The *Morning Symphony*, No. 6 in D major, offers some charming descriptions of nature: sunrise and the twittering of birds, and the second movement introduces us to a lesson in school—the jocular parody was much in favour—in which the wrong notes played by the violin class are corrected by the solo violin. The *Noon Symphony*, No. 7 in C major, is largely a matter of meal-time music. In the *Evening Symphony*, No. 8 in G major, he begins with gay dance tunes and ends with a tone-painting of bad weather. The *Night Symphony* is not available; it probably got mislaid.

The *Farewell Symphony*, No. 45 in F-sharp minor, has become the best-known of Haydn's early symphonies. Its exceptional popularity is probably due to the original circumstances surrounding its composition, though these were very typical of the times and par-

ticularly of Haydn's spirited and cunning way of combining fun
and seriousness. The story runs that Esterhazy, giving no particular
reason, did not want the musicians of his orchestra to have their
holiday in the summer of 1772. But Haydn, determined to get his
leave, decided to present the urgent pleas of the musicians to their
sovereign in the form of a symphony. The four movements retain
the appearance of normality: allegro, adagio, minuet and presto.
The outside movements in F-sharp minor are relatively short, particularly the finale, which has a sort of annoyed and stubborn
character with its recurrent unison passages. But before this gets as
far as a proper development, the movement breaks off abruptly,
and Haydn strikes up a lamenting adagio. The prince must have
been considerably astonished alone by this departure from all
previous practice, but how much greater was his amazement when,
in the middle of the piece, the second horn shut up his music, extinguished the candles on his stand, and left the hall. At short intervals, the first oboist, the bassoonist, the second oboist, the double
bass, and so on, went through the same routine, until finally, in a
hall plunged in almost total darkness, only two violinists remained,
who carefully, in a complaining tone, their instruments muted,
carried the adagio through to its close.

The symphony directly preceding the *Farewell Symphony*, No. 44
in E minor, known as the *Mourning Symphony*, is a rewarding
work, full of emotional intensity. The minuet and trio movement
comes second, the minuet being a strict canon at the octave. The
trio is in E major, and Haydn returns to that key for the third
movement, the adagio, that is perhaps the most beautiful piece that
Haydn wrote around this time. After a statement in the strings,

the movement seems to blossom when the oboes and horns enter
with a marvellously sustained phrase, promptly imitated by the
first violins. This standard of warmth is maintained throughout
the movement. The first and last movements both have fairly conventional unison openings, and the finale exploits to the full the
characteristic colour of E minor.

The *Imperial Symphony*, No. 53 in D major, composed around

1775, deserves to be heard more often, despite the obscurity concerning its finale. Haydn was not satisfied with his original finale, and later substituted an overture to an opera of which we know nothing. Apparently the first aria of this opera was in C major, for the overture, after reaching a perfect cadence in the key of D, quickly modulates to end on a strong dominant G, but for the purposes of this symphony Haydn drew a firm double bar before this modulation, and in this form it is admirably fitted to increase the scope and weight of the *Imperial Symphony*. The first movement is preceded by a maestoso introduction and the vivace is characterized by a smooth swift theme on the notes of the D major triad. And then Haydn immediately hacks it out staccato in an orchestral *tutti* in octaves. The appearances of a gently two-part second theme are brief and the triad theme and its counterpoints carry the movement, now smooth and swift, now hard and staccato, to its end.

The slow movement is an andante set of gracious variations and the minuet and trio is characterized by the surprise pause on an interrupted cadence just before the end of the minuet. The ensuing coda passage is a master stroke of original orchestration for that time, with *pianissimo* chromatic wind chords over a pedal in the basses later supplemented by the horns. An octave statement of the melody cuts the piece off. After the trio this procedure is repeated. If Haydn had written nothing but minuets and trios his whole life long, we would still revere him today. This simple form provided him with a very special inspiration.

The *Imperial Symphony* was extremely popular and widely known; in the 1789's it was printed and performed several times in Berlin, Amsterdam, Paris and London, and it was certainly instrumental in preparing the ground for Haydn's successes in 1791 and after.

The Symphony No. 55 in E-flat major, subtitled the *Schoolmaster*, was written a little earlier, in 1774. There is something touching about this work, with its fresh, childlike themes. The adagio is the most popular movement of this little symphony, and it must have been the gravity implicit in its walking theme that gave rise to the programmatic title. Haydn writes the most perfectly naïve variations on his droll theme, and they are bewitching, by very dint of their naïvety.

Meanwhile, Haydn had become a famous man and copies of the symphonies written for his orchestra in Eisenstadt were circulated throughout Europe. Commissions for new symphonies streamed in from all sides, but mostly from Paris, the emancipated musical metropolis of those days. Haydn wrote the six of his most important symphonies of this period for Paris, which is why they have come to be known under the collective title of the 'Paris Symphonies'. This collection includes the symphonies known as *La Poule, La Reine* and *L'Ours*. But the fact that most of these titles sound so programmatic is the result of pure chance, for Haydn had completely withdrawn from his earlier practice of writing programmatic symphonies. At this stage he is not too far away from the style of first symphonies, though the contrapuntal work is more differentiated and the instrumentation more careful. One external hallmark of the new style is the abandonment of the harpsichord, which had really become superfluous with an orchestra so rich in harmonic possibilities. We seldom hear the 'Paris Symphonies' these days; most people know the titles but have never heard the works. One reason for this is to be found in the uneven quality of the individual movements, and another is the fact that we can lay hands on incomparably greater masterpieces in the later Haydn symphonies, which are the ones that represent for us today the real Haydn.

The Symphony No. 83 in G, *La Poule*, was written in 1785. The main theme of the first movement, allegro spirituoso, is a strong rising minim motif followed by brusque descending dotted rhythms. The second theme is stated by violins alone in the relative major, and is characterized by the acciaccaturas at a semitone below

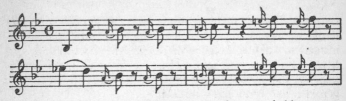

each note of the melody. This coloristic effect is probably responsible for the nickname that the Parisians gave the symphony. Viewed conventionally, 'the Duck' would have been more appropriate: over the restatement of the second theme, the dotted rhythms of the first theme are reintroduced by a quacking oboe as an inverted pedal point of five bars. The development section is shared by the two themes, but the first theme undergoes more extensive treatment, especially in counterpoint with material from the bridge passage. The leadback is effected by this strong theme

stripped of its orchestral backing, running smoothly and quietly
into the recapitulation, which is again brusquely *ff*. The key changes
to the major for the bridge and second theme, and after further
work on the main theme, the movement ends in G major.

The andante opens with a lovely ³/₄ melody in E-flat major for
strings. The repeated quavers of the melody's first bar are subtly
relegated to the accompaniment in the second bar; this is one instance of that gentle interpenetration of melody and harmony that
lends the appearance of counterpoint to music that genuinely
derives from the *lied,* or song.

The minuet, in G major, derives its bounce from the cunning
rhythm of the melody:  The trio
interlude is provided by a decorative melody for flute and violin,
from whom the limelight is stolen only once, briefly and artfully
by 'cellos and basses. The finale, vivace, is an exciting ¹²/₈ movement with a great deal of chromaticism to illuminate its rhythmic
drive. A generous sense of fulfilment is achieved at the end by a
series of anticipatory pauses, and a contrary motion build-up before
the final flourish.

In the Symphony No. 85 in B-flat major, 1785–86, entitled *La
Reine*, it is the variations that still retain their brightness. Even in the
variation in the minor key, Haydn hardly varies the theme, which

is traceable back to a French Romanza; he restricts himself to the
simple melody, casting new light on it with fresh twists of instrumentation. The title 'La Reine' derives from the fact that the queen,
Marie-Antoinette, took a special fancy to the work, and the populace took this up to such an extent that the symphony came to be
generally known by this nickname.

In the Symphony No. 82 in C major, 1786, entitled *L'Ours*, the
finale is in a totally different class from all the other movements,
and the amusing title also derives from this finale. Over the drone
of the basses, Haydn sets a happy dance tune which, for the Parisians, was evocative of the dancing bears that used to perform their
clumsy antics to the accompaniment of fairground music. An instrumental effect like this, taken straight from popular music, was
an unheard-of novelty, and was considered very daring. Haydn
proceeds to exploit the effect in a charming way: he shifts the drone

into the top part, while the basses are put through their paces, and
finally reintroduces the open fifths in the bass, with bassoon, horns
and violas, thus achieving a typical bagpipe effect.

An earlier symphony, No. 73 in D major, 1781, *La Chasse*, also
got its title from the last movement. This finale is a hunting piece,
full of horns and fanfares, and in the development section a real
chase is set in motion. The second movement is also remarkable:
its theme is an anticipation of the well-known theme of the variations in the *Surprise Symphony*.

There are two symphonies, both in G major, that follow the
Paris group. They are the *Symphony No. 88* and the *Oxford Symphony*, No. 92, which represent the culmination of this creative
epoch. The ideas and execution, the tensity and contrapuntal refinement of the thematic work (this last is one of the chief hallmarks
of late Haydn) put these symphonies in a class far above the previous ones, and they point quite clearly to the coming masterpieces
of Haydn's final period. They should be considered rather as a
transition to this final period than as belonging among the symphonies of the Paris group.

The *Symphony No. 88 in G major* is one of Haydn's most beautiful works. The fact that it is not so widely known as the *Military
Symphony* or the *Surprise Symphony* can only be attributed to its
lack of any such programmatic title; so far as its beauty and refinement are concerned it ranks no lower than the better-known symphonies. After a short slow introduction, the allegro opens with a
gay, exuberant theme that dominates the whole movement, in

countless tiny derivations. The secondary idea, particularly ingenious harmonically, modestly steps aside in the face of this bumptious main theme.

The second movement too, a largo, has only one theme, but it

is a particularly fervent and sensitive one, which recurs seven times
in the course of the movement with hardly any changes. In the
variations Haydn limits himself to simply changing the contrapuntal accompaniment figures, and yet the tension is maintained

right to the end. That is because of the wonderful basic mood or aura surrounding this theme; it permits only of peaceful thoughts and happy memories. The minuet is also a charming piece, with a slightly rough, countrified air. This peasant character is delightfully underlined in the static open fifths in the bass in the trio. The finale takes up the gay and easy atmosphere of the first movement, and the symphony ends on the gayest of notes.

The *Oxford Symphony*, No. 92 in G major (*c.* 1788), is one of Haydn's most popular works. Haydn's own high opinion of it is shown by the fact that he took the manuscript with him when he went to Oxford for his doctorate in 1791. The symphony was played there on this solemn occasion, instead of the work that was originally programmed, and that is the origin of its title. In contrast to the sunny *Symphony No. 88*, the *Oxford Symphony* is of a serious disposition. The introductory adagio is quiet and reserved, like a *pianissimo* question. Hesitantly, the strings take up this question in the following allegro, but the energetic answer follows hard on its heels with the *forte tutti*. The first theme plays itself out in this game of question and answer, sometimes weighty and annoyed, sometimes coy and careful. The second theme, with its friendly,

calming effect, is played down considerably at this stage; it is only in the grand reprise, when the waves of excitement are already subsiding, that the gay, childlike idea keeps on coming to the fore, in its reconciliatory rôle. This movement is extremely rich in counterpoint; both themes are treated in the most charming ways: played off one against the other, and combined with one another. However skilful this game may be, its effect is one of simplicity, achieved so naturally that it is immediately appreciable by any listener with open ears. The theme of the adagio is of a perfect quietness. The melody unfolds in an unbroken flow of form and sensitivity. The variation in the minor key in the middle section is like an intruding evil spirit, but demons can do nothing against the beauty and equilibrium of the main idea. The minuet is brusque and self-willed; its energetic buckings are far removed from the dancer's grace, but the trio, with its voluptuous horn sounds, lets in a little peace. And there is something headstrong and obstinate hidden in the charming theme of the rondo finale. Though it

hurries on with apparent ease, it contains some sharp corners. But when all is said and done, the gay mood carries the whole to a happily animated ending.

The crown of Haydn's symphonic achievement is the group of twelve symphonies written by the master for the concerts conducted by himself in London in 1791–92 and 1794–95. These symphonies are known as the 'Salomon Set'. They are the most perfect embodiment of Haydn's genius; each one is a masterpiece in its own right, and although their reception by the public has always been uneven, the only way to do them justice is to discuss them all, and in their right order.

The *Symphony No. 93 in D major* opens with an adagio with *fortissimo* orchestral chords interspersed between two melodic phrases for strings. The following allegro assai is probably the most familiar-sounding movement in the symphony, since its main

theme has been slowed down and used as a hymn-tune to the words 'Come, my soul, thou must be waking'. However, the main bulk of the movement is concerned with the second theme, introduced by the strings, and the first theme returns only briefly in the recapitulation.

Of the remaining three movements the minuet is the most remarkable: the minuet itself is a straightforward statement by the full orchestra, but in the trio each little phrase is preceded by a flourish in the winds. The finale is a typically witty Haydn rondo.

The best-known of these symphonies, and probably the best-loved of all Haydn's symphonies, is the *Surprise Symphony*, No. 94. The nickname derives from the joke Haydn permitted himself in the second movement: after unfolding the theme in *piano* and *pianissimo*, there is an unexpectedly loud bang on the drum, intended—or so the story goes—to awaken the audience from their little nap and encourage them to listen harder. This symphony, like three other favourite Haydn symphonies, the *Military*, the *Oxford*, and the *Symphony No. 88*, is in G major. Each movement is better than the last; Haydn surpasses himself in invention and atmosphere, and yet there is hardly a contrast in the four movements. The theme of the first allegro, a delicately animated four-

bar melody played first by the two violin groups and then taken up by the *tutti*, dominates the whole movement; a second theme that can hardly be called a contrast plays itself out at its first appearance. The development section and extended reprise are both dominated by this one main theme, which occurs in constantly new variants, now exposed, now concealed, now in the bass, now in the middle parts, taking all the smaller subsidiary ideas under its wing. The andante with the unexpected drumbeat is naturally the most famous movement of the symphony. The charming theme is like a children's song; there is a special charm in the

simple sequence of notes, a magic that captures the listener in spite of himself, quickening his pulse imperceptibly.

The variations consist of simple versions of the theme, with hardly any variation; the theme reappears constantly in its original form. After a powerful upsurge, the movement ends *pianissimo*. The minuet is very animated, and the trio is more of a complement than a contrast to the main melody of the minuet. The finale begins in a mood of exuberant gaiety, and here, too, the main theme dominates the whole of the broadly executed movement,

the timid secondary ideas hardly getting a word in edgeways. Just when the movement has apparently reached home, an unexpected twist towards E-flat interrupts the formal flow. But this is a red herring, and the movement rolls to its close with an extremely effective climax.

The *Symphony No. 95 in C minor* was first performed in London in 1791. The first movement starts straight in with the allegro moderato: first an energetic octave phrase with dramatic decorations of the dominant, then, after a whole bar of silence, a quiet climbing phrase for strings that takes six bars to reach a restatement of the energetic octave motif. This begins to develop contrapuntally before we reach the second theme, in the relative major, for violins and horns. The descending scale in triplets that ends this statement is thoroughly developed before the development section proper. The themes are well balanced in the development; noteworthy in the recapitulation are the omissions of the energetic motif, and the maggiore statement of the second theme over staccato quavers. This motion gives place soon enough, however, to the expected triplets, and these bear the movement to its end.

The second movement is an andante set of variations. The first variation opens with a lovely cantilena for 'cello, and the violins

answer with triplets that link this movement with the preceding allegro. The 'cello's cantering triplets may have been intended as an opportunity for the player to warm up for his hair-raising solo passage in the trio of the minuet. Thus the movements of Haydn's symphonies are bound together effortlessly and indissolubly. There is no formula for this sort of consistency; each device is an inspiration.

The minuet requires no explanation; we can only express our amazement at the range of musical feeling expressed in this concise movement. For example, the combination of the up-beat gracenote with the smooth chromaticism of the first few bars of the second half of the minuet, and the delayed return to C minor after the powerful dominant seventh before the final statement of the melody: this delay is a striking instance of Haydn's ability to think a long way ahead of his audience—that is why they loved him.

The finale begins with four bars of smooth melody and four bars of staccato. This is repeated and then the motifs begin to

develop immediately. The straightforward counterpoint of this
finale is one of the purest satisfactions that music has to offer.

In the Symphony No. 96 in D major, the *Miracle*, Haydn reverts
to his usual practice of beginning with a solemn introduction. A
strange triplet figure for the oboe leads into the allegro. As long as
one is not too pedantic and conscientious about trying to identify
and follow a second theme proper, this movement presents no
problems. The andante is more remarkable, not only for the fact
that at one performance, during an encore of the movement, a
chandelier fell on the audience—luckily not hurting anyone, hence
the symphony's nickname—but for the concertante character of
the end. Two solo violins, oboe, flute and bassoon all participate in a
communal cadenza, and the movement ends with only a brief *tutti*.

Again (the commentator is forced to repeat himself, which
Haydn never does in his minuets), expect anything in Haydn's
minuets. Their freshness and originality are proverbial. This gem
is like a microcosm of a sonata movement.

The restless quaver theme of the finale follows beautifully on the
heels of the minuet; a D minor passage intervenes after the exposition, but D major is soon reinstated. Shortly before the end, a pause
introduces a short delicate passage between winds and brass.

The *Symphony No. 97 in C major* (1792) opens enigmatically
with an open octave C followed by a diminished seventh on the
chromatic subdominant (F-sharp); this presents E-flat strongly,
thus leaving us in doubt as to whether the key is C minor or
C major—before sliding graciously on to the second inversion of
C major. The contrast between this subtle adagio and the following vivace is positively rude.

The simple string theme of the 'adagio ma non troppo' is
solemnly punctuated by repeated wind chords. The motion increases to triplets and finally to running semiquavers. The minuet
theme is characterized by some cross accents, while the trio affords
a lovely folk-like melody that falls strongly within the bar.

The tune of the finale is in two parts: four bars of light climbing strings, and four bars of hard orchestral descending scale. With a motif of repeated notes to mediate, Haydn modulates freely in the development. The brief coda is preceded by quiet repeated note interjections from the first violins and pauses on dominant and tonic.

The *Symphony No. 98 in B-flat major* (1792) opens with a solemn emphatic adagio in the minor key with dramatic pauses. The

allegro is based on a derivative of the adagio theme, and this runs through the whole movement, now in its original form, now varied, now segmented, now counterpointed. The interest never flags, and it never occurs to the listener to question the formal flow of the movement.

The stately theme of the adagio has a tripping tailpiece of sextuplet semiquavers which comes more and more into prominence as the music progresses. The marked rhythm of the minuet gives place to some subtle contrapuntal part-writing, and the trio presents a bassoon solo with a characteristic rocking quaver motion.

The finale has a soft, graceful and sprightly theme for violin, restated immediately by the oboe. A remarkable feature of this finale is the harpsichord part that Haydn played himself near the end. This was omitted from most editions, but has now been rediscovered and inserted at the proper place. The tempo has been slightly slackened to accommodate the rushing semiquavers of the strings and this impulsiveness sets off the keyboard's rippling figurations.

The *Symphony No. 99 in E-flat major* (1793) opens with an unusually richly orchestrated and extended adagio. The symphony is scored for double winds (including clarinets), two each of horn and trumpets, timpani and strings. By means of a pregnant enharmonic change Haydn brings his sighing introduction to a close in G major.

An unmitigated B-flat seventh for winds then leads us back to E-flat for the vivace assai. As we have come to expect, the first theme is developed so extensively that the appearance of a new theme comes almost as a surprise! Though brief, this second theme

is strongly characterized, scored for violins and clarinet, and plays
a large part in the development section, after two hesitant attempts
at the first theme have been abandoned. In the reprise it makes its
appearance earlier and comes in for more development. The accompaniment of this theme contains a charming irritant chromatic
mediant sliding from the last beat of each bar to the first of the
next.

The adagio contains a large variety of figurations, of which a
pulsating string accompaniment is memorable. An intensification
of the rhythmic movement into sextuplet semiquavers—however
much we may have come to expect it in these adagios—arises as a
natural consequence of these figurations. Although there is no
imitative counterpoint in this movement, the voice-leading is exceptionally beautiful, and contributes substantially to the movement's solemn and intense propriety.

The clarinets figure prominently in the minuet; they open with
a descent over the E-flat arpeggio, together with strings. In the trio
the oboes are given the solo work: they introduce it unaccompanied with five repeated Gs—the mediant of E-flat major (the key
of the minuet) and the dominant of C major (the key of the trio).

The finale (vivace) is one of Haydn's most spirited rondos in $^2/_4$.
The second idea is unusually complex: repeated staccato thirds
form the clarinets—a broken chord figure for flute—repeated
chords for oboes and horns—and a passing note figure for 'cellos—
two bars of accented appoggiaturas for the violins, and a tailpiece.
Each member of this string of elements is presented separately, and
yet the juxtaposition is so happy that no continuity is lost. The
variant that follows is an excellent example of the inexhaustible
fertility of Haydn's imagination. A central section shows the main
theme in counterpoint with itself. Near the end the theme is
slowed down—adagio—pause: and a brisk reprise with happy
scales rounds off the work.

The *Military Symphony*, No. 100 in G major (1794), enjoys great
popularity. It is difficult to say which of the four movements is the
best. Each has its own charm and embodies that musical magic by
means of which Haydn conferred immortality on the musical expression of his day. The short adagio that introduces the first allegro
is characterized by its grace and dignity. Its adjoining allegro is full
of carefree happiness; gay marching tunes dominate the movement.
The main theme, first heard in the flutes and oboes, played as if by
military band musicians, is contrasted with a quick march with a

swift melody that is genuinely Austrian and anticipates the *Radetzky March*.

The second movement also has a military nature. Such a large force of percussion is unusual in Haydn; besides the timpani, he uses triangle, cymbals and bass drum to emphasize the warlike tone of the *forte* passages. The theme is a gracious march melody which

is continually repeated with numerous slight deviations, now triflingly gay, now smilingly melancholy, then again powerful and intense in the minor key, leading back with a delicate twist in the rising, sustained notes of the violins, to the friendlier major key. The graceful march reappears, and this time reaches a climax with the horns and trumpets carrying the theme, and finally dying away with the melody *pianissimo*, creating a mood of farewell that borders on melancholy. But an energetic trumpet recalls the rococo soldiers disappearing in the distance. Tremendous unrest in the orchestra! Everyone hurries to reassemble for a last march past, waving goodbye.

The minuet is a countrified peasant dance of a pristine freshness; now slightly clumsy, now delicate and reserved. The dainty trio is effective in contrast. The final movement, a presto of the greatest imaginable liveliness, has only one short theme to offer, which Haydn presents over and over again in the most diverse guises. Originally so gay and careless, it undergoes various changes of character; here it has a mysterious sound, there it reappears as its old, excited self. Slight stumblings and general pauses create real suspense, but the gay side of the theme's character comes through again and again and the animated movement ends on a festive note.

No. 101 in D major (1794) is generally known by its nickname, the *Clock Symphony*. This name derives from the accompaniment of *pizzicato* strings with bassoons under the melody of the andante. The first movement begins with a slow ascending scale of D minor to the sixth over a sustained D, and then to a pause on the dominant via Haydn's beloved chromatic supertonic seventh. A descent from

G in similar style is begun but dissolves in sequential chromaticism. Another pause, this time on F major, and Haydn works through to the dominant with some dramatic *sforzati*. Now the presto begins: a run up for strings, *staccato*, in $^6/_8$ and the scene is set for one of Haydn's most inspired games. The ascending scale is paired with a descending scale (as in the introduction) and so we are not shocked to find the theme inverted *in toto* later in the development. The second theme is rhythmically similar to the first, but characteristically phrased.

The tick-tock rhythm of the andante enables Haydn to undertake extreme refinements of rhythmic articulation. Each particle of the melody is rhythmically exploited: the double dotted rhythm of the first two notes, the four demisemiquavers of the second bar

and the dotted semiquavers of the third bar. Then, in the reprise, the theme—so clear-cut and precise—is accompanied by triplet figuration! One endearing detail just after the exposition is the syncopated tocking of oboes and bassoons between the regular ticks of the strings.

The minuet is lusty and festive, with a lovely flute solo in the trio, over a rhythmic string accompaniment that recalls the D-flat trio in Beethoven's Piano Sonata No. 2, opus 10.

The vigorous finale is full of incident. The contrapuntal suitability of the theme strikes the musician immediately, but this does not lessen the effect when—after an exciting and powerful passage in the tonic minor ending on a dominant pause—the strings strike up a delicate fugato, *pianissimo*.

In the *Symphony No. 102 in B-flat major* (1794-95) the first movement is the most important. The secondary theme is introduced right at the outset by the full orchestra, like a brusque 'Who goes there?' challenging the exuberant drive of the main theme. The juxtaposition and combination of two ideas that are so sharply contrasted results in a highly dramatic development section. The end of the movement is also very impressive: the main theme dies

away in the distance and the orchestra holds its breath in one more
general pause, and then, *fortissimo*, and full of gusto, there follows
a short coda, forming a radiant conclusion to the allegro. The
relatively short adagio, with its wonderfully delicate colours, radiates harmony and peace. The minuet and finale offer no problems; they maintain, of course, the same high level of construction
and execution and, with their animation and unworried charm,
they are in no sense a disappointment after the first two movements.

The Symphony No. 103 in E-flat major, known as the *Drumroll
Symphony*, is no less significant than the *Surprise Symphony*, though
it is not quite so popular. The introductory adagio opens with a
pianissimo roll of the drums. Most of Haydn's symphonies begin
with a slow introduction, but elsewhere this never achieves the
importance attached to it in this E-flat symphony. When the drumroll dies away, the basses in unison announce a mysterious walking
motif; the first violins, accompanied by the second violins in syncopation, take up the motif and extend it upwards chromatically.
The air of mystery is preserved. In the course of the movement,
Haydn often returns to this strange motif from the introduction.
The main theme of the 'allegro con spirito' is reasonably spirited,

but by no means as gay as usual. Even the second theme, melodically particularly telling, carries an undertone of melancholy, for all

its grace of movement. Gaiety is never allowed to emerge in this
movement. The fugatos in the development section always slide
off into a *pianissimo* or die away on a pause. And then, after the first
of these pauses in the development section, the serious theme from
the introduction crops up in the basses like a warning, and this
gives a reflective air to the subsequent developments. It is only with
an effort that the main theme can swing out of this gloomy mood;
the second melodic theme comes to its assistance and forms the
bridge to the reprise. To begin with, this reprise proceeds according to the rules; but after the second theme has been played in the

tonic, the orchestra suddenly breaks out into threatening strokes.
Quickly this powerful uprising simmers down into a timid query.
The drum rolls and the lonely steps from the slow introduction are
heard again. The coda takes over this walking motif and transforms
it into lively mobility. Finally, the main theme is played once more
by the horns, and the movement ends *fortissimo*.

The andante opens with a gloomy theme of twenty-six bars in
C minor, followed by a bright transposition into the major key.
This antithesis occurs twice more; the themes remain unchanged,
but their instrumental clothing is more and more elaborated. After
the final variation there is a small reflective postlude in which the
main ideas of the movement are displayed once more, like a melancholy souvenir. The strange movement ends with four powerful
chords. The minuet is full of life; although reflective traits are
always creeping in, it is the element of dance that carries the day.
The finale is built on a single theme, and moreover on a short-
winded one. Here Haydn proves himself a master of contrapuntal

technique; there is no bar that does not bear reference to this theme,
that does not derive from it, yet at the same time the listener is
overwhelmed with an incredible multiplicity of ideas. There is
little here of the gaiety, or even relaxation, of most of Haydn's
final movements; the finale carries features of grandeur, as do all
the other movements of this symphony, and this marks it off as
one of the most illustrious forebears of Beethoven's early symphonies.

Health and joy are the fundamental characteristics of Haydn's
last symphony, Symphony No. 104 in D major, generally known as
the *London Symphony*, and these qualities pervade all four movements equally. The warning sound of the introduction to the first
allegro, the occasional stormy or demonic twist in the andante,
fail to contradict the gay foundation of the symphony. The finale
is the most effective movement of the symphony. It begins with

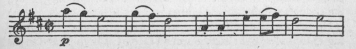

the theme of a popular song, played over a static bass, and the relaxed mood of a national holiday, already presaged in the minuet, takes hold of the movement.

This relaxation is significantly interrupted by the second theme: when the violins initiate their quietly descending and yet expressive melody it is like taking a deep breath, like a reflective siesta in the midst of general gaiety. This quiet thought occurs twice more in the course of the movement—it takes quite an extended form in the development section—and each time it effects a most happy respite; the renewed gaiety immediately after it serves only to enhance its effect.

Though Haydn's work in the field of symphonic music was decisive, he contributed very little to the evolution of the solo concerto. All his works in this genre were written in his first period, and, though laid out with a light touch, one feels the lack of any really dedicated working. None of Haydn's violin concertos have survived, and only one of his piano concertos is ever heard in our concerts, namely the *Piano Concerto in D major*. The neglect of this piece is quite unjustified; it is genuine and lovable Haydn. The finale particularly, a 'Rondo all'Ongharese', is an enchanting piece of virtuosity, extremely rewarding for the pianist, and anyone playing it can be sure of success.

Of all the concertos, the best known is the *'Cello Concerto* (1783), which has always enjoyed the favour of great 'cellists right up to the present day, and is indeed the only classical concerto for this instrument that can claim as much. And it deserves its favour, for the melodic invention has extraordinary charm. Musicological objections have sometimes been raised against this concerto, casting doubt on Haydn's authorship of the work. These, however, pale into insignificance in the light of the exquisite charm of the music, and the grace of the concerto speaks eloquently in its defence, testifying that it was certainly written by a master of Haydn's stature, if not by Haydn himself. (However, it is often played in a later, debased arrangement that is neither Haydn nor even in Haydn's spirit.) The sequence of movements is usual: fast—slow—fast. It is difficult to choose between the three movements: the first allegro has an infectingly elegant virtuosity, the adagio a fervent and simple expressiveness, while the final movement has a captivating and irresistible dancing grace.

Haydn was always highly celebrated as an instrumental composer, but his vocal works never received anything approaching the enthusiastic acclaim that was accorded his instrumental works. How many people have ever heard Haydn's operas? His Masses are performed only rarely, with the possible exception of the *Nelson Mass*.

Haydn in fact wrote fourteen Masses, and some of these should be mentioned specifically, but first let us look at his other large-scale, less-known choral work, the *Seven Last Words*, a work that passed through many stages between its inception and its emergence as an oratorio for soloists, chorus and orchestra. Haydn reports that he started work on it around 1785, at the request of a clergyman in Cadiz who wished for intervals of devotional music between his seven addresses on the seven words from the Cross. Haydn does not deny that the stipulations were not easy to keep to, and that it was no joke writing seven adagios each of ten minutes' duration without boring your audience.

In its final version, the oratorio opens with an orchestral prelude. Then we hear the separate treatments of the seven sentences, using related texts from the Bible, each (with the exception of No. 5, 'I thirst', which is preceded by an orchestral movement) preceded by a chorale statement of Jesus' words: 'Father, forgive them; for they know not what they do' (No. 1), 'Verily I say unto thee, this day thou shalt be with me in Paradise' (No. 2), 'Woman, behold thy son. Son, behold thy mother' (No. 3), 'Eli, Eli, Lama sabacthani?' (No. 4), 'It is finished' (No. 6), and 'Father, into Thy hands I commend my spirit' (No. 7). To end the work Haydn appends an earthquake chorus—an exciting presto movement to the words 'The veil of the temple was rent in twain'.

Haydn's first Mass, one of his earliest pieces probably written when he was seventeen, is scored for two sopranos, chorus and string orchestra. It is known as the *Missa Brevis in F*, and is remembered for its touching innocence. In 1957, the Haydn authority H. C. Robbins Landon had the good fortune to stumble on another juvenile *Missa Brevis*, hitherto believed lost, and dating from 1750 or thereabouts, in the archives of Göttweig Abbey in Lower Austria. This one is very brief, but shows a stylistic consistency remarkable in a composer so young. No solo voices are employed.

Of the larger Masses—the *Great Organ Mass in E-flat*, the *Saint Cecilia Mass*, the *Missa in Tempore Belli* or 'Kettledrum' Mass, the *Theresianmesse*—the *Nelson Mass* (Missa Solemnis) of 1798 is probably the best known. Sometimes also referred to as the 'Imperial Mass', it is at any rate supposed to have been inspired by Nelson's victory over the French fleet in the Bay of Abukir, although Haydn had already started work on the Mass when he heard the news. The martial (rather than maritime) overtones are unmistakable in the music, and not only in the writing for trumpets and timpani. The key of the work is D minor, and the Kyrie opens with a firm descent over an arpeggio of D minor which is implemented when the chorus enters in octaves with a downward leap of an octave. The brevity of the 'Christe' episode, introduced near the beginning by the solo soprano does not diminish its effect, and when the Kyrie returns it is accompanied by *staccato* figurations which carry the music forward into an extended development.

The Gloria again juxtaposes the solo soprano with the chorus, and the key changes to the tonic major. The slow movement 'Qui tollis' is in B-flat major and opens with a bass solo. The chorus enter later with psalmodic 'Misereres'. The movement rises to a climax on a strong dominant chord of A major, and the 'Quoniam tu solus' sets out firmly in D major. This sort of continuity is maintained throughout the work, and very forcefully. The degree of righteous energy in this score seems to make it more suitable for concert performance than for performance in church. Certainly it is one of Haydn's truly great works.

The works that put the final touches to his fame were two choral works written in the last decade of his life: the great oratorios the *Creation* and the *Seasons*.

Haydn received the impetus to write the *Creation* in London. A text that was supposedly originally intended for Handel was put before him. When he got back to Vienna he decided to write the work after the Baron von Swieten, a staunch friend of Haydn's in word and deed, had translated the original English text into German. Haydn worked at the project from 1795 to 1798, an enormous expenditure of time and energy when you consider the speed with which he usually worked. But the work received its just reward: even the first performances were a terrific success. In a short space of time, the *Creation* was being enthusiastically acclaimed throughout musical Europe and the highest honours were conferred on its creator.

The material for the *Creation* was particularly close to Haydn's heart and it set fire to his imagination. The tripartite layout of the text and the subdivision into recitatives, arias and choruses are the same as in Handel, Haydn's great forerunner. But apart from these formal externals, Haydn's work is imbued from the first note to the last with a consummate originality, illuminated by the highest creative power. The story of the creation forms the content of the oratorio, and this is told by the three Archangels, Gabriel (soprano), Uriel (tenor) and Raphael (bass), in recitatives and arias, interspersed with choral commentaries. The chorus is also used to underline the dramatic climaxes. The orchestra is large, and the way Haydn exploits its possibilities as well as those of each individual instrument, the nuances, and the way he mixes his colours is all quite flabbergasting. The score of the *Creation* is a model for all conceivable refinements of instrumentation.

The instrumental introduction to the first part is headed 'The representation of chaos'. It would be mistaken to expect Haydn to attempt a representation of chaos with all the machinery of modern tone-painting; nothing could have been further from his mind than a realistic representation. By purely musical means he attempts to awaken in the mind of the listener the idea of how harmonic formations slowly evolve out of a formless nothingness of inert, slithering sequences of notes, with unprepared dissonances and so forth, of how life slowly starts, and how movement and, finally, order emerge from the chaos. The archangel Raphael announces the opening words of the creation story; the chorus enters in extreme *pianissimo*, only to break out in a radiant *fortissimo* with the words, 'And there was light', supported by the full orchestra. The next aria of Uriel tells how 'The gloomy, dismal shades of darkness vanish', how 'The throngs of hellish spirits flee to endless night', and how 'A new created world springs up at God's command'. The chorus takes up this last idea with a cheerful childlike note. Chaos is no more. The big recitatives, as opposed to the arias which are almost all in a lyrical vein, are executed dramatically and supported by marvellous tone-paintings. Every new idea is interpreted in terms of music. Of the arias in the first part, the charming soprano aria, 'With verdure clad the fields appear', is worthy of special mention; melodically, it is one of Haydn's most beautiful inspirations. The mighty chorus, 'The heavens are telling the glory of God', concludes the first part.

The second part describes the creation of all living beings. The soprano aria tells how 'Birds may fly above the earth', and Haydn imitates the songs of birds with delicate coloraturas and trills. The bass tells of lions and tigers, of deer and horses, of insects and worms, while the orchestra plays evocative interludes. The tenor aria, 'In native worth and honour clad', praises the creation of

mankind. Finally, the chorus breaks out with the rejoicing hymn
'Achieved is the glorious work'.

The third part depicts the idyllic harmony of paradise where the
first of mankind enjoy life in peace and happiness. The music
evinces a rare depth of emotion and warmth of feeling; everywhere there is harmony and joy. The mood is set in the slow introduction by an idyllic trio of flutes. With the chorus, Adam and Eve
praise and glorify their Creator, and then turn their attention to
their common happiness. Haydn finds the most fervent notes to
depict the mutual love of the first human beings in a magnificent
duet. This wonderful piece is the last musical climax of the work,
which now proceeds to its mighty close with the chorus, 'Sing the
Lord ye voices all'.

The overwhelming success of the *Creation* induced von Swieten
to propose a new oratorio text to Haydn. This also had to be translated from the English (an adaptation of James Thomson's poem),
and was called the *Seasons*; Haydn started work on it straight away.
The subject matter and text of the *Seasons* proved a happy bride to
Haydn's individuality. The *Seasons* may lack the grandeur of concept that is the unique property of the *Creation*, but to make up for
this, it touches on a different, but equally endearing side of Haydn's
genius, namely the humorous side.

The general plan of the *Seasons* is, of course, in four parts, with
one section for each season. An uninterrupted performance of the
whole work tends to be slightly tiring. Broadcasting corporations
in Germany (such corporations not being faced with the necessity
of providing a full evening's entertainment of the same sort) have
initiated the praiseworthy custom of performing the appropriate
section of the work at the beginning of each season of the year,
and, despite their brevity, the individual sections are each capable
of creating a powerful effect.

The *Seasons* takes the usual form: choruses alternate with recitatives and arias. Gay, secular songs are sometimes inserted in place
of the arias, and this accords very well with the general character
of the work. The soloists are the farmer, Simon (bass), his daughter,
Jane (soprano), and the young farmer, Lucas (tenor). The introduction to the first part (devoted to spring) represents the transition
from winter to spring: storms and blizzards give free rein to their
fury, the wind whistles. The greyness lightens only when the solo
voices enter and announce the withdrawal of winter. The oboe
strikes up a delicate song, forming the bridge to the chorus. The

peculiar magic of the work blooms for the first time in the chorus, 'Come gentle spring'; here for the first time one remarks the sweet grace that contributes so much to the atmosphere of the *Seasons*. The listener is immediately captivated by the swaying melody, which revels in its own euphony. The first aria is one of the most famous pieces in the score: Simon sings 'With eagerness the husbandman his tilling work begins', as he walks, whistling, after the plough. The song that he 'whistles' is the charming melody of the andante from the *Surprise Symphony*, well-known by this time to all Viennese music-lovers. The farmer sings 'With measured step and liberal hand he then throws out the seed' while the orchestra walks with him every step of the way. The duet between Jane and Lucas, accompanied by a small chorus, is particularly striking among the following songs of gratitude. The sincerity of feeling in this song keeps it young despite the ineffectual text, and its freshness never fades. A powerful chorus of thanksgiving closes the first part.

The section devoted to summer is subdivided into five scenes that follow the course of a summer's day: sunrise, the heat of midday, a rest in the shade of a wood, an evening storm, and a thankful chorus at the close of the day. The musical highlights occur chiefly towards the end of this sequence. What wonderful depth of feeling there is in Jane's great scene in the wood! The general mood of this and some of the detail seem to anticipate the big Agatha aria in Weber's *Der Freischütz*. In both cases, besides the magical details in the representation of nature, there is a rare emotion in the expression. After anxious *pizzicato* and gloomy rolling of the kettledrums, an angular flute phrase introduces the storm, which breaks out in a passionate chorus. The climax is reached with the wild cry 'O Heaven', and then comes the uncanny effect of the sudden *pianissimo*, shuddering occasionally with the flute's lightning. The evening chorus that closes this sequence expresses wonderful calmness. The country people's hearts are filled with thankfulness; they strike up a happy song and gay dance figures are introduced, while the chorus in unison evokes the bells of evensong.

Besides the pretty but somewhat extended love duet between Jane and Lucas, it is the two marvellous choral scenes, the hunting chorus and the harvest chorus, that form the musical nucleus of the autumn section. Though Haydn uses well-worn methods of characterization—the festive horn sounds for the hunt, and the doodling clarinets and bagpipe bassoons in the dance scenes—it is the way he uses these methods that gives these bewitching musical scenes their enormous charm. The choruses with Halali and Juchuh, which are apt to be coarse, are attractive in the same way as an old Dutch painting. One finds the same atmosphere in Breughel's Kermis pictures: an atmosphere of *joie de vivre*, fullness of life, heartiness and pristine health.

At the centre of the winter section stands the enchanting spinning scene with the chorus of spinning women and Jane's amusing song, 'An honest country girl there was', which are model examples of Haydn's brand of refined humour, expressed better by a chuckle than a laugh. But the reflective side of his genius is not entirely absent: Simon's aria about the transience of life towards the end of the work has a profound effect despite the musty, sentimental text. Haydn feels each phrase honestly and experiences each thought, so that one really can, must, believe the final emphatic words, 'Only virtue remains'. The work ends magnificently with a large double chorus calling on God and praising Him.

The première of the *Seasons* took place in Vienna in 1801 and it provoked as much enthusiasm as the *Creation* three years earlier. Haydn's popularity rose to unprecedented heights; medals were minted in his honour, poems were written in praise of his art, the town of Vienna made him an honorary citizen, homage was conveyed to him from all over the world, and he was honoured and celebrated to an extent that can hardly have been equalled in the case of any earlier musician. The genius who had conferred such bounty on the world was recognized and accepted with gratitude by his contemporaries—a just reward!

WOLFGANG AMADEUS MOZART

born Salzburg 27 January 1756
died Vienna 5 December 1791

The boy Mozart received his musical education from his father Leopold, himself an excellent musician. At the age of six, little Wolfgang already had some reputation as a pianist and composer; concert tours took the prodigy to Vienna, Munich, Mannheim, Paris and London. In 1769 he took the position of leader of the orchestra in Salzburg. In the same year he travelled to Italy, admired and celebrated wherever he went; the youthful artist's fame spread further and further afield; the whole of the musical world loved and spoiled him. In 1781 he gave up his job in Salzburg and tried to build himself a new life in Vienna, supporting himself by his compositions and by giving music lessons.

In 1782 he married Constanze Weber. He wrote his greatest masterpieces in the following years: operas, symphonies, Masses, sonatas, quartets streamed from his pen and were performed everywhere with the greatest success. But Mozart was constantly battling against financial crises. His continual worries and excess of work when his health was extremely delicate led to his untimely death at the age of nearly thirty-six. He did not even leave sufficient funds for a decent burial; Mozart had a pauper's grave, which it is now impossible to identify with any certainty. Thus ended the life of the child prodigy who had once been the darling of the whole world.

Mozart is perhaps the most versatile musical genius of all time. There is no field in which he did not produce masterpieces of the highest order. It is the liberation and happiness of his music that we love, the artless self-evidence of his musical ideas. The magic of eternal youth inspires the music of an early awakened and early perfected genius. And here the perfection of classical symmetry is achieved in the coupling of gaiety with profound feeling.

Compared with Haydn, who initiated a new world of music and who was able to create a new style, Mozart had not nearly such a revolutionary effect on symphonic music. But he transformed everything he laid his hand to, and his last symphonies constitute a decisive enrichment of symphonic form. What seemed so new about Mozart's music, and yet so happily self-evident despite its novelty, was the vocal element in his melodic style, the 'cantabile', as his contemporaries called it, that he introduced into instrumental music. Even in Haydn, freely extended melodies only appear in the slow movements; his allegros are all based on rhythmically accented themes. Mozart had a natural gift for the vocal line; even in his earliest compositions there are allegro movements in which the theme is not a scamper of quavers and semiquavers but a broadly flowing melody in minims or even semibreves. This trait was gratefully taken up by other composers, and Mozart's influence can be distinctly traced in the later symphonies of Haydn himself. We may arbitrarily pick out this vocal element in his melodic style, the nobility of his *cantilène*, as one important characteristic of Mozart, but it goes without saying that everything that this unique genius touched was transformed into some precious substance previously unknown to the world.

The extent of Mozart's achievement in the field of orchestral music alone is hardly credible in view of the brevity of his life. The thematic index of Mozart's works edited by Ludwig Köchel lists fifty-two symphonies, more than thirty serenades, divertimenti, some forty instrumental concertos, among them twenty-five piano concertos. Mozart's works are numbered according to this list, called the Köchel Index, instead of by opus numbers as is usually the case. The great majority of his symphonies are juvenile works; despite interesting details they seem pale in comparison with the last three, the *E-flat major*, *G minor* and the *Jupiter Symphony*, written in 1788. The *Prague Symphony*, written in 1786, is also important, and there are a few others that have secured a place in the concert repertoire.

The most remarkable among Mozart's early symphonies is the *Symphony No. 25 in G minor*, K. 183. The first allegro is dark in colour, though the second subject is set in the major key in the exposition. A new theme is introduced in the short development section, and in the reprise the lighter second theme appears in the minor key. The brief major key (E-flat major) andante also turns towards the minor at the end. In the minuet movement, the trio is in the tonic major key and scored for winds alone. Mozart's early maturity is well displayed throughout this symphony, in particular in his free handling of the tonality. The finale presents the urgent and exciting side of G minor again with a second subject in the relative major.

The symphonies K. 200 and K. 201 are also worthy of mention. The first of these is in C major and the great Mozart authority Alfred Einstein places it just before the *G minor Symphony*, K. 183— both were written towards the end of 1773. The presto finale is the most remarkable movement, and the whole shows a growth of seriousness in symphonic writing, which makes it a landmark on the way to Mozart's final symphonic perfection.

The *Symphony in A major*, K. 201, dates from the following year. Though it is scored for only oboes and horns, besides strings, it achieves considerable intensity and scale. Already in this symphony we find Mozart using the contrapuntal methods that later became for him such an essential means to emotional intensification.

The *Symphony in D major*, K. 297, was written in 1778 for the
Concerts Spirituels in Paris, and is sometimes referred to as the
'Paris Symphony'. It is scored for two each of flutes, oboes, clarinets, bassoons, horns, and trumpets, with timpani and strings. It is
in three movements: allegro assai, andante, allegro. The work was
commissioned by the director of the Concerts Spirituels, Le Gros,
who was very satisfied with it, referring to it as the 'best symphony
ever written for the Concerts Spirituels' (Einstein). However, he
considered the middle movement too long and complicated and
Mozart had to write a shorter one. The symphony made several
concessions to current Parisian taste—this also accounts for the
omission of a minuet—but it is brilliant and genuine Mozart. The
second subject of the last movement, which is in sonata form, is
developed fugally.

The *Symphony in B-flat major*, K. 319, dates from 1779; or rather
three of its movements do, the minuet being added three years
later for performance in Vienna. The final allegro demonstrates the
melodic profusion that we associate with Mozart. Dance rhythms
hold the whole together. In the development Mozart introduces
the four-note motif that is so familiar from its appearance in the
Jupiter Symphony.

The andante moderato presents three melodies, the first two of
which are recapitulated in reverse order. The later minuet is a
stately one with considerable modulation and development; the
trio has the characteristics of a *ländler*. The finale again presents a
profusion of melodies, and the movement is again predominantly
dance-like, with triplets in ²/₄ giving it the flavour of a tarantella.

After this, Mozart wrote the *Symphony in C major*, K. 338, in Salzburg in 1780. This symphony, the preceding K. 319, and K. 385
which followed in 1782, are three transitional works ranking high
above the early symphonies on account of their genuine personal
Mozartian flavour, but they offer nothing approaching the ripeness
and perfection of the later works. The three Salzburg symphonies

occur at the stage when Mozart was also concerned with plans for his operas *King Thamos* and *Zaide*, both written in the Italian style, which means that they precede his decisive break-through with *Il Seraglio*. But at this time, Mozart the symphonist was much freer than Mozart the dramatist; they have in common their wonderful youth and freshness of invention and sensitivity.

The little *C major Symphony*, K. 338, exudes a happy feeling of life. The minuet is missing, so there are only three movements. The first movement has a festive, mobile character, somewhat in the manner of the Italian overtures of the period; Mozart employs happy march rhythms, and only occasionally does the music take a reflective turn. The festive first theme also dominates the end of the movement with its shining trumpets. The second, romanza-like movement is for strings alone; stepping gracefully, it is a dance of untarnished youthfulness. The last movement is in a gay mood, and by its brilliant and elegant playfulness again gives expression to the feeling of life that above all distinguishes the world of the delightful young Mozart.

The Symphony in D major, K. 385, called the *Haffner Symphony*, was originally written as a serenade. Mozart wrote the serenade in Vienna in response to an urgent request from his father to write a small party piece for the burgomaster Haffner's family in Salzburg, with whom his father was on friendly terms. He sketched and completed this in a few weeks in the summer of 1782, despite the interruption caused by his marriage to Constanze at this time. Then, when he was re-reading the piece in the following spring, he was so impressed with the charm of the music that he decided to develop it into a symphony, by omitting the opening march and one of the minuets and filling out the instrumentation. This symphony is not to be confused with the *Haffner Serenade*, which Mozart wrote in 1776, and which also happens to be in D major. We will return to that work when we come to assess the serenades. In accordance with its original function the *Haffner Symphony* is extremely festive and animated in mood. It opens with a splendid, fiery theme which includes powerful leaps over two octaves, and the pregnant dotted rhythms in the third bar that characterize it so strongly. This theme is admirably suited to contrapuntal working and Mozart dispenses

with any obvious second theme. Small subsidiary ideas surface
briefly, only to disappear again immediately. The charming andante
is expressive of joyful anticipation; the violins sound as if their
hearts were beating in expectation of the bright jubilation that
breaks out at the end. The minuet steps along with a gay swiftness,
with the seductive melody of the trio in effective contrast. And now
the relaxed finale, a presto that sprays along in exuberant, unrelent-

ing mobility, joyously fulfils all our expectations; graceful little
subsidiary ideas pop up, but are immediately run to ground by the
cheeky rondo theme.

The little Symphony in C major, K. 425, called the *Linz Symphony*, also belongs to this group of transitional symphonies, in
which Haydn's influence is still strongly in evidence. Mozart wrote
this one in 1783 for the Linz Music Society. The middle movements are quite enchanting: the fervent feeling of the adagio and
the pristine freshness of the minuet with its *ländler*-like trio. The
outer movements are not so convincing. Though they are strongly
felt, the themes are not very fertile, and there is a certain conven-
tionality about them. But the fiery swing of the whole makes up
for these defects.

With the Symphony in D major, K. 504, Mozart achieved complete mastery of the symphonic idiom. He wrote this symphony,
generally known as the *Prague Symphony*, in 1786, at which time
he already had the *Marriage of Figaro* behind him. If we compare
the work with whatever operatic masterpiece was written at about
the same time, it is to *Don Giovanni* we must look, for in the *Prague
Symphony* there is a presentiment of the demonic grandeur so
characteristic of that opera. There is very little trace of that 'sunny
gaiety of the darling of the gods' which sentimental devotees of
Mozart often regard as the sole significant characteristic of his
genius. Mozart's later works show only too clearly how wrong
such a one-sided view is. What would Mozart be if the enchantment of his melodies were not filled with profound sensibility and
passionate feeling, and if the demonic strength of his genius did
not also pursue the most secret impulses and sufferings of the heart.

In this symphony there is more trace of depth of suffering sensibility than of the abundance of divine gaiety that animated his

earlier symphonies. The introductory adagio shudders with gloomy presentiments, and after an unavailing lunge towards a lighter mood, it ends in tired resignation. The main theme of the allegro presses forward nervously; nothing can disperse the general anxiety. Even the consoling subsidiary idea is transposed into the gloomy minor key. Heavy pressure is brought to bear in the subsequent development, but there is no liberation. Nor does the extended andante permit of any friendlier preoccupations. The graceful second theme lightens the mood for an occasional moment, but it is superseded by threatening passages in the bass which lead back to the weariness of the opening. There are dramatic accents in the development section, but they, too, are unable to elucidate the situation and the depressed mood persists right to the end. The minuet is missing, and it is probable that Mozart decided to dispense with a dance movement so as to preserve the unity of his long-faced symphony. Even the finale is far removed from the usual gaiety of a last movement; there is uneasy agitation in the

main theme with its faltering syncopations. The second theme, of a precious bourgeois cosiness, is impotent in the face of this agita-

tion and remains merely a contrasted episode within a joyless world.

Mozart's three last and greatest symphonies appeared in quick succession in the summer of 1788, a time of severe business worries and artistic rebuffs. The summery quiet and isolation that he enjoyed in his suburban house outside Vienna must have made it possible for him to achieve, despite all his worries, this triptych of his most beautiful symphonies.

A solemn adagio opens the *Symphony in E-flat major*, K. 543. Its entrance is proud and magnificent, but it sinks down into mysterious quiet before the allegro begins. The delicate cantilena of the

allegro theme grows out of this stillness, and then acquires a powerful accented character in its second phrase. Brilliant scales in the
violins underline this element of liveliness and the first group ends
with some energetic accents. The second theme, suggested timidly
by the violins, has a melancholy character, particularly when the
wind take the lead. The development section is exceptionally short,
and is mostly dominated by the energetic final accent from the first
thematic group. A general pause snatches us away from this development and three reserved bars of wind music lead us back to the
reprise of the first theme. The recapitulation ends with fanfares.

The second movement, a slightly martial 'andante con moto', is
kept simple and perspicuous as regards its outward form. Three
clearly contrasted thematic groups are played in succession and then
repeated in the same order; the first idea reappears once more to
close the movement. The first group, which is played first by the
strings alone, is a delicate, almost transparent image in a clear
A-flat major, whereas the second theme reaches us in a powerful
minor tonality. The little third theme takes the form of a duet between bassoon and clarinet with a lovely simple line. And Mozart's
spirit inevitably combines these themes, diverse as they are, into a
higher unity.

The minuet of the *Symphony in E-flat major* is probably the most
famous movement Mozart ever wrote: every music-lover knows

and loves it, for it is often played on its own. The trio holds a
peculiar enchantment: the clarinet takes the lead with an inspired
melody.

The final movement is Mozart in one of his gayest moods. All
the parts are engaged in spinning out the lines of joyful relaxation
with a busy mobility, and when the bassoon takes part in this game,
the effect is entrancing.

Apart from the serious, dignified introduction, and the occasional melancholy note in the slow movement, Mozart's *E-flat
Symphony* is full of confidence and *joie de vivre*. Mozart's creative

imagination was above the petty worries that threatened him; he seemed able to transplant himself out of the world around him and give expression to the world within him.

The *Symphony in G minor*, K. 550, is filled with painful, melancholy emotions, unlike the *Jupiter*, and the *E-flat Symphony* we have just discussed. But the emotional world of the *G minor Symphony* is so rich, the melodic writing of such surpassing beauty, and the composition of such immaculacy, that one has to give it the crown as the most wonderful of the three (I am succumbing to the ready temptation to compare them).

There is a consistency of mood in all four movements of the *G minor Symphony* that is seldom to be found in Mozart. The note of suffering, struck in the first bars, is sustained throughout. Many people describe this work as a document of tragic pessimism, but this interpretation is foreign to me, for there is a transfiguring grace in all the melancholy ideas, that gives even the most painful of them a lovely flavour of consolation.

The first allegro begins without palaver with a spun-out theme

in the violins that sounds like subdued sighing. A brusque twist into a sudden *forte* leads to the second theme with its long-suffering, downward chromaticism. But the first theme soon takes the lead again and retains it throughout the development section. Mutinous outbursts are followed by humble, mournful complaints. The movement ends in a burst of painful energy.

The fundamental character of the andante is one of delicate melancholy. There are sighs here too in the hesitant motion of the theme. The little motif at the end of this thematic group is particularly expressive; it is a pleading cry raised alternately by the strings and the woodwind, with great delicacy of feeling. The opening of the minuet is powerfully combative, as dissonances underline the defiant, energetic character of the movement. The delicate trio in G major introduces a note of consolation.

The finale has a demonic disquietude: it expresses passionate

feelings intensified to the point of wildness. Nor does the painful chromaticism of the quieter second theme lead to any mitigation of the general atmosphere, and bitter energy dominates the symphony right through to the final bars. But this whole dark world is illuminated by the purity of Mozart's spirit and the grace of his expression.

Mozart's last symphony, the Symphony in C major, K. 551, composed in 1788, is, to outward appearance at least, his greatest creation in the field of symphonic music. It acquired the nickname *Jupiter* probably to characterize the truly Olympian greatness of its themes and structure. There is a classic perfection in the equilibrium of the work that has some affinity with the spirit of the ancients who, with their elevated sense of the beautiful, were able to transmute every feeling into art. The masterful headline of the symphony

is distinctly reminiscent of the main theme in Gluck's *Iphigenia* overture, representing the imperious demands of the gods. In this case, however, the masterful theme is answered in a sensuous singing vein, and indeed it is the dualism and conflict of masculine and feminine that gives the movement its dramatic character. The emotional second theme is followed by a flirtatious third theme which plays an important part in the development section. The first theme reasserts itself only very gradually, but when the reprise does come, it is powerful and festive.

The andante cantabile is a single drawn-out song, amazingly expressive and profound. A soulful subsidiary idea is contrasted with the tender main theme, but the latter is only temporarily ousted. A little motif of triplet semiquavers appears towards the end of this second idea, like an imploring request, wafting a slight air of melancholy into the movement. Even the big climax in the development section is helpless against this tenacious strain of melancholy. The minuet, too, with its descending steps of a semitone, is far removed from the gaiety of the dance.

The finale is the most important movement of the *Jupiter*. It represents the peak of Mozart's contrapuntal achievement in the field of symphonic music. The main theme, a procession of semibreves, is extremely characteristic and after being played once in

Allegro molto

full regalia with an extended concluding phrase it is developed into a simple fugue—which is, however, abandoned after five entries! But though it never turns into a properly executed fugue, fugal technique plays a decisive rôle in the further course of the movement. Secondary themes, such as the large-scale triple fugue at the beginning of the development section, are derived from the main theme and these also take part in the fugato, but they are soon submerged in the stream of Mozart's imagination, despite the fact that he employs every imaginable contrapuntal device. The fact is that Mozart could not conceive of a fugue as an end in itself: even in this Jupiter of a symphony it is only an auxiliary means to achieving the most marvellous climaxes. The extraordinary transparency of the thematic work is a miracle in its own right; thanks to the significance of the themes it is not difficult to follow even the most complicated contrapuntal ramifications. The impression created by this finale is one of true liberality: it is the triumphant finale *par excellence*—worthy, in fact, of a Jupiter.

Mozart never scorned to write pure entertainment music besides his great concert works. Various pieces by his father were charming models for him in this genre; Leopold Mozart's divertimento *The Farmer's Wedding* can still be heard occasionally. Not all Mozart's serenades are really orchestral music; many of them were originally written for single strings and can be played purely as chamber music. Their form is related to that of the old suite, but a march usually takes the place of the overture as the first of the movements. Mozart did not restrict himself to sequences of different dance forms; the influence of the symphony makes itself felt and some of the individual movements are executed on a large scale. He probably intended these works to be played orchestrally, and an orchestra is really preferable for their performance. This is certainly the case with the *Haffner Serenade*, K. 250 (1776), which Mozart scored for two each of oboes, bassoons, horns and trumpets. There would have to be several strings against such a corps of wind instruments. The *Haffner Serenade* is unusually long for Mozart, and of its eight movements, the allegro and the two andantes achieve symphonic proportions. The introduction opens with a fanfare of horns, and is followed by an exuberant allegro. The second of the three minuets, in G minor, is especially remarkable: strange sounds creep in under cover of the general animation. But all dreary cobwebs are swept away by the theme of the next andante, a lovely melody which reappears as a rondo theme in a variety of disguises. These charming variations are the cream of this very rich crop of movements. Preceding the finale is a reflective adagio like a melancholy retrospective glance. But it merely toys with serious thoughts before the work closes in a flurry of exuberance and gaiety.

The three serenades for wind instruments form a trio of real treasures. The one that is played most often is the *Serenade in B-flat major*, K. 361, for thirteen wind instruments, that Mozart wrote in 1781, his last year in Salzburg. The thirteen parts are taken by two each of oboes, clarinets, bassett horns and bassoons, with four horns and a double bassoon as bass. The bassett horn is a version of the clarinet, a form of alto clarinet, that has now fallen into disuse. Each instrument is handled as if it were a soloist, and its sound and technical possibilities are exploited with great virtuosity.

The serenade begins with a big, slow introduction of great tension, in which the melodic lead is taken by the clarinet. The clarinet also leads in the short, pregnant main theme of the allegro. This gay and playful movement is dominated throughout by a little four-bar motif, which strays through all the parts.

The following adagio is strange. The characteristic colour of the movement is given by an accompanying figure in quavers, a motion which is retained throughout the movement, and which produces a mood of mystery and disquiet. Delicate melodic lines are spun over the quavers, by the oboe chiefly, but later taken up and extended by the clarinet or the bassett horn.

A gaily animated minuet with a *ländler*-like trio forms the transition to the fourth movement, a romanza. This romanza is another treasure: the enthusing melody of the opening is in clear contrast to the ghostly scherzo in the minor key that constitutes the middle section. The busy mobility of the bassoons provokes the atmosphere of unrest. At the close, oboe and clarinet take up once more their enthusiastic song.

The fifth movement is a theme with variations. The theme is very simple, in a binary form that is easy to grasp. Individual instruments are given the chance to display their virtuosity in the pleasing figurations of the first three variations: the first exploits the

oboe, the second the bassett horn, and the third the bassoon and
clarinet. A small fugato leads to a variation in the minor key, and
this is followed by an adagio variation. This adagio is the climax
of the variations: the little piece exudes a magical mood of mystery
with its cobweb of accompaniment figures. The final variation, a
minuet, forms the bridge to the rondo finale, a lively coruscating
movement that cannot fail to charm the listener with its youthful
joy of music-making, whether in the happy shower of its main
motif or in the *alla turca* of the subsidiary themes.

The *Serenade for wind instruments in E-flat major*, K. 375, was
written in 1781. It is scored for two each of oboes, clarinets, horns
and bassoons. The first movement is almost symphonic in its layout
and proportions, but for the rest, Mozart departs from the symphony. The second movement is a minuet and trio, and the third
an adagio. This shows an admirable mastery of the thick, sweet
accompanying textures peculiar to combinations of wind instruments, and some lovely contrapuntal work for oboes and clarinets.
A second minuet and trio follows, and lastly a spirited rondo movement. The last wind serenade is subtitled *Nachtmusik*, K. 388,
which presumably means that it was to be played in the open air
(for instance outside someone's window). The work is scored as
for K. 375, and it is a genuine symphony for wind instruments in
C minor, a surprising key for a serenade, with four movements—
allegro, andante (with a lovely 3/8 dotted rhythm, and numerous
cross-accents), minuet (a serious canon at the distance of one bar in
treble and bass) and trio (a canon by inversion, *mezza voce*) and
allegro finale. The last movement is extended by frequent repetitions of short, sharply characterized variations. It ends with a brief
fanfare.

Mozart's best-known serenade is *Eine kleine Nachtmusik*, K. 525;
of all his orchestral works this is played most often. The orchestra
consists of strings alone. Written in 1787, *Eine kleine Nachtmusik*
bears all the marks of Mozart's great mastery, though it was intended purely as occasional music. The four movements correspond
to the movements of the symphony as regards both form and expression, but on a considerably smaller scale, with the result that
understanding of the form is greatly facilitated. In the first movement the gracious coquettish reserve of the second, feminine theme
is contrasted with the masculine wooing of the first fanfares. This
wooing is presented in a more fervent form in the andante romanza.
In the minuet and trio, the male-female conflict reappears quite

clearly, and then, in the animated finale, the two are reconciled in

delicate pillowtalk. This enchanting music is the most fragrant rococo, and delicious to the ear.

Mozart was greatly interested in concerto form and was never at a loss for new ideas with which to revivify it. After all, he had an exceptional affinity with the temper of the concerto, its virtuosity and element of social elegance. In the violin concertos, Mozart must have taken Vivaldi for his model, whereas it was Johann Christian Bach, the 'London' Bach, who provided the stimulus for his piano concertos. The concertos are all in three movements, and the forms are always delineated with great clarity, especially the first movements, with their opposition of solo and *tutti*. The solo parts are written in a very effective style, with elegant passage work, but Mozart never loses himself in the purely external elements of effectiveness: the circus tricks of virtuosi are completely foreign to him.

In 1775, when he was nineteen years old and leading the orchestra in Salzburg, Mozart wrote five violin concertos in quick succession, and at least the last three of these, the *Concertos in G major, D major* and *A major*, are among the most popular of all violin concertos.

The *Concerto in G major*, K. 216, has a wonderfully melodious adagio, which comes after a rather superficial, but very brilliant allegro. This adagio flows along in a broad stream of song, ending very delicately and dreamily. The richly varied rondo is also very gratifying. The gay main theme frames some charming secondary ideas: first a lovely tune ornamented with trills, accompanied by *pizzicato* strings, and later a happy, rusticated folk melody with open-string drones.

The allegro movement of the *Concerto in D major*, K. 218, is magnificent, with its march-like main theme; everything about this movement is brilliant. The andante cantabile has a memorable song theme and a lovely contrasting secondary idea. The song of the

solo instrument flows throughout in a broad stream, uninterrupted
by orchestral interludes. The final rondo is highly *capriccioso*: the
gravity of the strutting main theme *à la gavotte* lapses each time
quite unexpectedly into a happy tune. In the middle of this charming movement, as it were a musette, there stands a tiny folk song
movement complete with bagpipe effect of the open-string drone
just as in the G *major Concerto*.

The *Concerto in A major*, K. 219, deserves the crown amongst
these concertos. After the introductory adagio, the big allegro
movement unfurls its elegance, awakening a happy, festive mood
in the responsive listener. The broad lines of the adagio are shaken
by pangs of profound agitation. But the rondo, particularly the
busking 'allegro alla turca' with the wild interruptions from the
orchestra, is magical in its effect.

A second *Concerto in D major*, K. 271a, Mozart's last violin concerto, written in 1777, was rediscovered at the beginning of this
century. (Its authenticity has been questioned.) The andante is
valuable, with the solo instrument's delicate embroidery of the
folk song melody played by the orchestra. In sighing suspensions
and trills the simple melody is extended and amplified with great
virtuosity and poetry.

The *Sinfonia Concertante* or *Double Concerto for violin and viola in
E-flat major*, K. 364 (1779), also enjoys great popularity. In Mozart's
day, concertos for several soloists with orchestra were called concertante symphonies, in memory of the fact that this juxtaposition
of a group of soloists with the orchestra originally sprang from the
concertino in the concerto grosso. In contrast to the somewhat
rigid monumentality of the orchestra in Mozart's concertante symphony, the solo themes are very expressive. The themes, most of
them in a tone of delicate pleading or friendly conciliation, are
played by the two instruments alternately. Sometimes the two
soloists play together, but mostly in thirds, and the virtuoso passage
work is divided between them: the instruments bandy their elegant
figures about from one to the other, bar by bar. The sublimity of
the andante springs from a profoundly felt melody in the minor
key. The structure of the movement is large and significant, and in
a weighty *serioso* tone it rises up to a suggestive, fateful climax. In
the closing cadenza the soloists timidly repeat the expressive main
theme, and abandon it with resignation. The third movement dissolves the tension of the two dramatic movements in unencum-
bered good humour.

Mozart's *Sinfonia Concertante in E-flat major*, K. App. 9, for oboe, clarinet, horn and bassoon with orchestra (oboes, horns and strings) was for a long time believed lost, for Mozart sold the work to the promoter of the Concerts Spirituels and did not keep a copy for himself. For some reason the performance was cancelled, and Mozart did not retrieve his score. He expressed the intention to rewrite the work from memory later, and may have done so. The text used now was not discovered until the 1860's and there is no way of telling whether it was Mozart's original score or his revision of it. These are the problems of musicologists, and need not worry the general listener; it is sufficiently established that the work we hear stems from Mozart. It was written in 1778, which places it in the neighbourhood of the 'Paris Symphony' (K. 297). The work is in three movements. The first allegro starts with an orchestral exposition leading to an exposition in which the concertino takes part. A cadenza for the concertino is written out just before the end.

The adagio opens with heroic dotted rhythms and *sforzati*, but the main body of the movement is flowing and expressive. The finale is an andantino with variations. The concertino takes most of the responsibility of stating the theme; only the last phrase is handed to the orchestra. The first variations expose the clarinet, the second the bassoon, the third contains a dialogue for clarinet and bassoon. In each case the orchestra takes the tail phrase of the theme. The horn soloist can show off his tone at the lovely beginning of the seventh variation, and his dexterity at the beginning of the ninth. After the tenth variation Mozart inserts an adagio that ends as a pause in the sixth bar. A 6/8 allegro with a *piu mosso* to come rounds off the animated piece.

The piano concerto held a special place in Mozart's affections. He produced his first efforts in the field at the tender age of eleven, but these were really arrangements of other people's compositions for piano. More than twenty concertos appeared in the following decades, and Mozart wrote his last piano concerto—*Concerto in B-flat major*—in the year of his death. His love of the piano concerto is perfectly understandable; Mozart was generally considered the best pianist of his day, and what could have been more natural than for him to extend the repertoire—still relatively small in those days—of the instrument of his choice, thus creating a wider range of choice for himself in his own concerts. The form of Mozart's most mature creations in this genre was already established in the first of his piano concertos. Here Mozart follows in the footsteps of

Bach and his sons, Carl Philipp Emmanuel and Johann Christian (the 'London' Bach referred to earlier, who had such a significant influence on Mozart). The duologue between the soloist and the orchestra, the actual 'concertizing' is carefully constructed in Mozart. The orchestra has a significant part to play, and Mozart was very particular about instrumental shading. The ideas and expression of the individual movements are tightened up with the intention of achieving greater unity in the whole.

Mozart wrote his *Piano Concerto in E-flat major*, K. 271, at the age of twenty-one. It is not his first piano concerto, but it is the first to achieve true Mozartian proportions. The first movement opens with an attacking unison of one bar and the soloist repeats his answer. Only then does the allegro motion get under way with a melody for violins. The work is characterized by its extraordinary neatness of execution and nicely judged sonorities. The soloist seems to ride the orchestral sound, to be borne along on it and then take off and fly on his own when the orchestra stops. After the cadenza in the first movement the orchestra enters with the contrary motion figure of repeated notes that we remember from the exposition. Then a soft variant of this starts up in the violins; after two bars the soloist starts a high trill which covers the entrance of oboes and horns. Two more bars of the motif, and then four cadential chords send the soloist skittering down a broken chord. This procedure is twice varied and the movement is over.

The middle movement is a lovely andantino in C minor. The violins state a melody canonically. The soloist enters with a lovely narrative line after sixteen bars of instrumental exposition. Again

there is a cadenza passage just before the end. The final presto is a brilliant imaginative journey. The piano starts the chase, the orchestra gets off to a start only after thirty-four bars. A fantasia-like cadenza with frequent tempo changes precedes a repeat of the opening stages of the chase. However, this is soon interrupted by a further cadenza cascade, and then the soloist strikes up a minuet (in

A-flat major). Note the lovely *pizzicato* counter-subjects in the varied portions of the theme. After four variations this stately dance is interrupted in its turn, also by cadenza passages that gradually bring us back to the opening chase. This now pushes on to the end. What a remarkable episode!—one can hardly believe that it actually happened. It is as though a child was out chasing butterflies, and suddenly falls under some spell. She wakes up what seems like years later and finds herself still in the middle of chasing the same butterfly. The memory of the spell fades quickly and soon she can only remember that it was an enchanting butterfly chase.

In Vienna in 1782–83 Mozart wrote three piano concertos in quick succession. They are the concertos K. 413, 414 and 415. Mozart writes about them in a letter: 'These concertos are neither too hard nor too easy. Extremely brilliant and pleasant to listen to, they never deteriorate into the vapid, of course. There are some places that will only be fully satisfying to the connoisseur, but even they are so written that the less learned cannot fail to enjoy them, without knowing why.' K. 415 is scored for a larger orchestra than the other two, and Mozart is known to have played it himself, at least twice. But the *Concerto in A major*, K. 414, is valued more highly by contemporary musicians. Mozart's alternative cadenzas are available for all three movements.

The layout of this concerto is simpler and more conventional than the one discussed above. The first movement starts with a full-scale instrumental exposition ending with a full close in the tonic. The soloist then enters with the theme and in the sequel the orches-

tra accompanies. The constructional simplicity of the work frees the listener's mind to concentrate on the beauties of the melodies and figurations.

The andante opens *sotto voce* with the string quartet in beautiful four-part harmony. Later the pianist elaborates the same theme. The whole movement is extremely beautiful, in the best sense, or in the sense in which we think of natural phenomena as being beautiful. The allegretto finale opens with a jumpy tune over a *staccato* accompaniment. Then in unison we hear a smooth creeping melody. The piano enters with a third melody, very simple.

The movement develops from the interplay of these; but chiefly from the combinations of the smooth, creeping theme with itself. The cadenza is a pseudo-contrapuntal development of this second theme.

In 1784 Mozart embarked on an unparalleled spate of activity in the field of the piano concerto. He wrote twelve concertos in the space of two years, during which time he did not neglect other fields, of course. K. 449 in E-flat major is a small-scale work written for Mozart's pupil Barbara Ployer. The two following concertos— K. 450 in B-flat major and K. 451 in D major—belong together like a pair of gloves. They are large and conventional in form and yet bursting with vitality in every bar. In K. 451, which uses flute, bassoon, trumpet and timpani besides the usual oboes and horns, the andante is the most remarkable with its crawling theme, subtle contrasts of registration, and unexpected counterpoint. However, the energy of the second element of the exposition of the first movement—a considered leap of an octave down, followed by an impetuous tumble of dotted rhythms over the scale encompassed by the leap—is not to be forgotten. This is developed contrapuntally from the outset.

K. 452 is a piano quintet and does not concern us here, but K. 453 is again a piano concerto. This is the *Piano Concerto in G major*, dedicated to Barbara Ployer. This work is unique among Mozart's concertos on account of its extreme grace and subtlety of orchestration and movement. The opening is symptomatic; the first violins alone enunciate a motif that falls from dominant to mediant and trills its way back to the dominant, very quiet. A tonic pedal point from the horns gives a wonderful calm to the texture. Winds play an ornamented tailpiece to each of the phrases of the theme. After the orchestral exposition, the soloist executes a delicate run up to the dominant note that begins the theme. This repeated dominant seems to give the melody a certain poise, as though it were holding its breath, and quite happy to continue doing so. However, the thick dominant seventh of the second half of the theme provides something in the nature of an exhalation. The thematic material of this movement is more limited than is usually the case in Mozart's concertos.

The andante opens with an accompanied melody for violins that is closely related to the second thematic group of the first movement. There is a pause, and some expressive work for the woodwind follows. The instrumental introduction closes on a tonic pedal (this movement is in C) with dramatically descending sixths in imitation above it. Of a wound one can say that it is more tender than actually painful; the same is true of the grieving character of this andante. The pianist's statement of the theme is of the utmost simplicity; two separate pauses lead us into the dominant minor and the mood changes. The work ends with an enchanting allegretto with well defined themes; in fact the first theme is so well characterized that a pet starling of Mozart's succeeded in learning it!

The *Piano Concerto in B-flat major*, K. 456, was written for the blind pianist Maria Theresa Paradis, a gifted pupil of Mozart's rival in Vienna, Leopold Kozeluch. The simple theme of the first movement is stated first by the strings, and then by the wind chorus with ligatures in the strings. The juxtaposition of wind and strings is a characteristic feature of this concerto; a striking example occurs in the second movement, a theme with variations. The second variation begins with the theme in flutes and oboes with a jumping accompaniment from the bassoons, and strings filling in harmonically. The repeat is given to strings with demisemiquaver figurations for the piano. The second half of the melody is treated similarly.

The pianist starts the ball rolling in the finale; the theme is in $^6/_8$ with light repetitions of the dominant, hence the light 'toy character' of the melody. The answering phrase is lightly accompanied by violins and violas. The winds emphasize the repeated chords in the orchestral statement. There is a remarkable passage in B minor soon after the return of the main theme; the piano plays a flowing melody in $^2/_4$ against a $^6/_8$ accompaniment.

All Mozart concertos possess the same rococo magic, but there is a unique profundity of expression in the *Concerto in D minor*, K. 466, which raises it above the others. Written in 1785, the concerto presents a strange combination of gloomy reserve and luxuriant, emotional warmth, which gives it quite a romantic character. This explains the great popularity enjoyed by this concerto in the nineteenth century. The first movement is dominated by the passionate agitation of the orchestral theme which opens the concerto, with its flickering syncopations in the strings against the threatening

triplet figure in the bass. The piano solo is always trying to mitigate this threatening, fateful character with its friendly gestures; the piano's themes plead with it and seek to purify it. But the mood lightens only temporarily, and the dark, fateful theme succeeds in retaining its ascendancy. The romanza takes you by the hand and

leads you into a light world of peace, though hints of the agitation of the first movement are in evidence in the middle section. The rondo takes up the passionate tone once more; over against the uncanny agitation of the main theme, played by the piano, Mozart

sets two friendly secondary ideas, the second of which—partly in the major and partly in the minor—introduces the final twist into the light major key, in which the work ends. The consistency of line that Mozart sustains in this concerto is quite extraordinary, and the effect created by this concerto far surpasses any experience of virtuoso playfulness.

The *Piano Concerto in C major*, K. 467, is a triumphant and affirmative work. The first movement opens with a quiet march of separated quavers, and it is this element that dominates the movement, reaching a triumphant statement at the end.

The andante is in F major and begins with a bar of harmony before the aspiring melody for muted violin appears. The bass line of separated *pizzicato* quavers appears as a direct sequel to the march element in the first movement and persists almost uninterrupted throughout the movement.

The finale is based on a delicate rising and falling theme in tenths, with quiet chordal interjections from the wind chorus. A second melody in the tonic is introduced by the soloist: plain unisons ascending the triad with lower octave grace-notes; that is, a variant of the theme of the andante! The iambic rhythm of the dominant-key melody provides Mozart with opportunities for delicate exploitations of the chordal wind interjections.

Einstein believes that Mozart was being deliberately engaging or winning in his *Concerto in E-flat major*, K. 482. At that time, the standing that a composer enjoyed with a specific public was a matter of paramount importance, a matter of bread and butter in fact. In Vienna, Mozart had constantly to spar with the public's taste, and he was healthily preoccupied with problems of keeping within the range of his audiences' understanding. The standard juxtaposition of *tutti* and solo passages—for example, the quiet suspensions that answer the first heroic *tutti* statement—should not make us insensitive to such beauties as the exquisite contour of the second theme with its sweet octave leap.

However, there is no question in the andante variations of any mere pandering to popular taste; here Mozart is totally immersed

in his own world, and one has an overpowering impression of how alone he was in this world. Mozart was surprised when the audience demanded an encore of this movement. Many times here one is struck by a certain reluctance to move on into the next bar, and this is partly responsible for the undertones of shrinking poignancy that characterize the music. The repeated bar just before the strings complete their initial exposition of the theme is beautifully filled out in the pianist's variation. The accompanying string *sforzati* trail a leaping octave in the piano's right hand, and the resulting sonority is as heavy as lead and yet ringing like glass.

The final movement is all smiles; it is based on a hunting theme. However, a surprise andantino cantabile insertion in 3/4 before the reprise reminds us that life is not simply a gay dash from birth to death. It also reminds us of the *E-flat Concerto*, K. 271, with the inserted minuet in the finale.

The *Concerto in A major*, K. 488, was written in 1786. It opens up a world of grace and light. But behind the shine and gaiety some reflective and even melancholy ideas are hidden. Thus you hear all too soon the bitter accents that creep into the sweet, rocking melody of the andante. However, these are soon dispersed. The finale is lively and relaxed, with no trace of melancholy marring its happy mood.

The first movement of the *Concerto in C minor*, K. 491, is extremely serious, almost tragic. There are traces of Beethoven in this work; it is like a presentiment of that master's *C minor Concerto*. The main idea of the first allegro is gloomy and taciturn; this theme evokes a strange mood with its leaps of a seventh and downward crawling chromaticism. Right through to its dreamy ending the movement is filled with an air of mystery. There are fervent heartbeats behind the song-like melody of the larghetto. The finale takes the form of a set of variations: a simple, expressive allegretto theme, filled with a soft melancholy, goes through marvellous transformations, and the whole embodies such richness of imagination and strength of expression that one cannot but think of Beethoven again. There is also humour in this movement, but it is humour brushed up the wrong way as it were, a defiant, bitter amusement.

The piano *Concerto in C major*, K. 503, is scored for a large orchestra including trumpets and timpani. The first movement is headed *allegro maestoso* and the opening bars lead us to expect a large, masterful movement. This it is, but there are contrary elements, for instance the emphatic C minor of the soft march theme in the exposition.

The andante is a very serious movement; its theme falls slowly over the triad of F major and sinks heavily into a prolonged dominant seventh. The movement contains some beautiful ornamental writing with exciting *ostinato* leaps over against it.

The final movement is almost Haydnesque in its opening. The strings enunciate the melody *allegretto* and *piano*. Clearly, the winds answer with an echo of the march theme from the first movement. This rondo derives considerable excitement from the exploitation of triplet semiquavers in the solo part.

The *Concerto in D major*, K. 537, the 'Coronation Concerto', of which Mozart himself gave the first performance in Frankfurt in 1790, for the coronation of Kaiser Leopold II, is characterized by its magnificence. In both of the extended allegros the piano part is extremely brilliant; the character of the work is determined by the rich passage work and elegant runs. But there is a fervent note in the lovely romanza theme of the middle movement; technically speaking, the movement is simple and artless, everything is subordinated to genuinely Mozartian, song-like expressiveness.

Mozart's last piano concerto, the *Concerto in B-flat major*, K. 595, was written in 1791. It is relatively seldom that one gets a chance to hear this marvellous work in the concert hall, which is strange, because the piece presents a rare combination of all Mozart's excellences. The character of the concerto is established straight away in the first few bars; the dreamy, lyrical melody for strings is answered by a powerful call from the wind, and this romantic antithesis dominates the movement. However, the element of conflict is pushed further and further into the background to make room for strong, lyrical feeling. The larghetto is in the familiar style of the romanza, and the piano part is very striking. The finale hurries by, fresh and happy, in a springing $^6/_8$ rhythm: an exuberant flight, extremely lively and brilliant, with cadenzas inserted at three different points. These cadenzas are carefully written out by Mozart himself.

Mozart also wrote a concerto for two pianos and orchestra. Written in 1779, this *Concerto in E-flat major*, K. 365, was obviously intended for Mozart and his sister to play together. The concerto goes with a swing; both pianists are given ample opportunity to display their pianistic talent, and the dialogue between them is charming. Most of the time the two soloists converse harmoniously about the same theme, which they repeat one after the other. Occasionally they conflict, however: they have contradictory ideas, or interrupt each other. But they very quickly come to an understanding again.

The *Concerto for flute and harp*, K. 299, dates from 1778. Mozart wrote it for two aristocratic amateurs, and consequently made light of the technical capacities of the instruments. The three movements are charming and unproblematic. The slow movement is andantino and the finale is a rondo in gavotte tempo.

Seen as a group, the concertos for wind instruments are extremely straightforward. The two *Concertos for flute*, K. 313 and 314, are in G major and D major respectively. K. 314 is a transposition of an earlier oboe concerto, and is very light and nimble. The later concerto, K. 313, is remarkable for the imaginative treatment of the slow movement.

Mozart wrote four horn concertos, three of them for a hornplayer named Ignaz Leitgeb, who was active in Salzburg. Mozart's relations with this man were good-natured and joking; he wrote in various coloured inks to confuse him, and bespattered the scores with jocular words of encouragement. The first is *Concerto in D*

major, K. 412, and consists of two unrelated movements, allegro
and rondo. The remainder are all in E-flat major; K. 417 and
K. 495 were also written for Leitgeb, a player whose technique was
apparently limited, for the concerto K. 447, which was written
for someone else, makes considerably greater demands on the
soloist.

The *Concerto in A major for clarinet*, K. 662, was written for Mozart's clarinettist friend, Stadler, who had already inspired the great
clarinet quintet. This is a work of Mozart's final period, and in
craftsmanship and invention it is superb. Mozart and Stadler between them deserve almost all the credit for the subsequent acceptance of the clarinet as a 'beautiful' instrument, rather than merely
as a penetrating one.

The overtures to Mozart's operatic masterpieces have always had
a place in the concert repertoire. Mozart fulfils Gluck's require-
ment (that the overture should anticipate the content of the opera
and take the place of a table of contents) in so far as he expresses all
the most important ideas of the opera in the overture, throwing
light on all their various aspects so as to get the audience in the right
mood to appreciate the spirit of the work. The overture to *Il
Seraglio*, written in 1781, captures the mood of mystery in the first
few bars. We hear a whispering and a murmuring, and then the
orchestral entry in all its glory transports us right into the magical
world of the orient. The large percussion section, cymbals, triangle
and bass drum, gives the music its Turkish flavour. The agitated
music continues, constantly alternating between *piano* and *forte*,
between expectant murmurs and the shrill music of the janissaries.
Suddenly it stops; you hear a romanza melody, full of longing. It
is Belmonte's aria, with which the opera begins. Belmonte is
searching desperately for his beloved, whom he believes lost, or
hidden in the seraglio. But the scene of sadness and longing has
already melted into thin air, and we are once more under the spell
of the mysterious glitter and rowdy uprush of the whole fantastic
situation.

The overture to the *Marriage of Figaro*, written in 1786, is surely
the most wonderful of all Mozart's overtures. The piece is an unparalleled fountain of joy and life. Its sparkle makes it the prototype
of the comic overture. This music has a whirlwind quality: like it
or not, one is caught up and whirled around in it. It steals up softly—
the strings in unison with the cheeky, chuckling bassoon against

them; reserved brass sounds take it up, and then out jumps the full orchestra in a jubilant *fortissimo*. There is no holding the music now, as it constantly jumps up and down, and springs out at one from all sides. New themes appear with provocative *sforzati* or happy dance rhythms; everything is carried along irresistibly on this Bacchic maelstrom of the life-force in flood.

The overture to *Così fan tutte*, written in 1790, is filled with the same spirit of comedy. It is an uninhibited presto, a crazy whirl-wind that makes one think all the spirits of earth and heaven are let loose in it. But the three somewhat shortwinded themes seem to lack the polished elegance of the *Figaro* themes; despite all the gaiety, this overture never quite achieves the unique sense of release and animation that you find in the *Figaro* overture. A short, slow introduction precedes the overture like a motto: the oboe plays a love-sick motif, and this is followed by the basses with the title quotation from the opera: *Così fan tutte*, 'that's the way they all carry on'—meaning women.

In accord with the larger dramatic concept, the overture to *Don Giovanni*, written in 1787, is laid out on a much larger scale, both as regards structure and development, than Mozart's other over-tures. The slow, gloomy introduction conjures up the higher pow-ers, the supernatural forces of a threatening fate, personified in the action of the opera by the stone statue. Rigid syncopations and strident *sforzati* emerge, and above the *tremolo* of the violas you hear menacing scale passages played by the violins. The basses rise up imperiously, and all the supernatural powers unite in a disturb-ing *forte*, which re-echos and dies away as if in a great void. Out of the sudden *piano* emerges the constant surge of the main theme of the allegro, with its knightly echo in the winds. Tremors of demonic strength and sensuality shake this music. The second theme opens with masterful unison steps and is answered by a lightheaded, trifling gesture—one more aspect of the shining, frivolous cavalier. In the large-scale development section, these themes are alternately played off one against the other and com-bined, and the genial exchange rounds out the picture into an ex-pression of unbridled lust for life. The ending is remarkable: after twisting into the subdominant minor key, the overture ends, totally unexpectedly, in a pale C major.

The three solemn, ascending wind chords that open the overture to the *Magic Flute*, 1791, immediately transplant the listener into a world of total unreality. It is a fairy tale world: the benevolent despotism of the supernatural powers surrounds us like a magic circle. The finely worked equilibrium of the allegro theme (which

first appears as a fugato, and is subjected to all sorts of contrapuntal treatment in the sequel) becomes a symbol of divine symmetry, perfect equilibrium and eternal harmony. A feeling of festivity animates the music, though it is suffused with sublime seriousness. The work possesses a rare luminosity, and conveys a really salutary feeling of liberation.

The key of C exerted a persistent attraction for Mozart in his church music. As early as 1768 he wrote a *Mass in C minor* (K. 139) for the consecration of the Waisenhaus church; this was scored for soloists, chorus, strings, oboes, three trombones, four trumpets and timpani, and is a solemn work to have been written by a twelve-year-old. A year or so later he wrote another large Mass—the *Dominicus Mass* in C major, K. 66. (The higher Köchel number of the earlier *C minor Mass* is due to a one-time misconception about its origin; internal evidence seemed to indicate a later date.) The *Dominicus Mass* contains some secular moments, particularly the notorious Kyrie waltz.

This monumental beginning of a career in church music was followed up by a number of very brief Masses, partly, no doubt, because the worthies who commissioned them wished them to be brief. Mozart brought the Missa Brevis form to a high level with his *Credo Mass* of 1776, again in C major (K. 257). Here, he discards all accepted canons of church composition and creates a type of church music that Einstein describes as 'song-like'—simple and childlike. This work is followed immediately by two further Masses in C, the *Spaur Mass*, K. 258, and the *Organ solo Mass*, K. 259. These were followed a year later by a further Missa Brevis, this time in B-flat major (K. 275) which again disintegrates the distinction between secular and sacred. The simplicity and 'popularity' of style in this Mass has borne fruit; it came into widespread and frequent ecclesiastic use in South Germany, as is testified by the fact that manuscript copies of it existed in many church music libraries in that area.

Mozart wanted to write another large Mass. In 1778 he began one in E-flat (K. 322) but did not get further than the Kyrie; the Mass he completed in the following year is in C major and is called the *Coronation Mass* (K. 317). This work is by no means a Missa Brevis, but it is concisely planned, and is again characterized by song-like simplicity and generally homophonic choral writing.

The Kyrie is in ternary form: the first part is choral, with regular *fp* dotted rhythm statements of the word 'kyrie'; the second part is a beautiful melodic statement by soprano and tenor soloists; the third part returns to the maestoso of the opening, but the chorus plays a more important part, and a soft coda is added. The Gloria is marked 'allegro con spirito' and again we find a blocked, dotted rhythm choral enunciation of the word 'gloria'. There is a great deal of interplay between soloists and chorus in this movement. The opening material returns with the word 'quoniam' and an abbreviated recapitulation and coda follow.

The Credo (allegro molto) opens with an orchestral introduction that sets up a stream of running semiquavers in the violins that does not let up until the sudden quiet adagio for the quartet of soloists, 'et incarnatus est', where the violins are united and play delicate descending passages. The rushing semiquavers return with 'et resurrexit'. New material is given to the soloists at the words 'et in spiritum sanctum'. This motif had already been used for the Agnus Dei of Mozart's *Litanae Lauretanae*, K. 195 (in the key of D), and was to be used later in the slow movement of the *Hunt Quartet*, K. 458 (in the key of E-flat). In this Credo it is *alla breve* and in the key of F, as a secondary theme in the subdominant.

The Sanctus is homophonic throughout, and Mozart specifies that the voice parts should be doubled by trombones. The movement is in two sections; an andante maestoso for the Sanctus, and an allegro assai for the Osanna. The Benedictus is likewise in two parts: first a lovely song for the quartet of soloists, and then a reprise of the Osanna from the Sanctus.

The Agnus Dei opens with an extended solo for soprano, which leads straight into a restatement of the central section of the Kyrie, in which the full quartet of soloists join at the end. The chorus proper now enters deliriously with a speeded-up version of the lovely andante melody we have just heard so beautifully sung by the soloists. The end is simple and festive, with the trombones joining in for the *tuttis*.

Incomparably larger in scale is the incomplete *Mass in C minor*, K. 427. There is no Agnus Dei for this Mass, and only two sections of the Credo. Attempts have been made to complete this work by substituting movements from other Mozart sources. Alois Schmitt is the most notable proponent of this procedure, and we have to be grateful for his efforts towards performing and editing the work in the early years of this century. However, the size and content of the existing movements make it almost impossible to conceive of completing it successfully, since there is nothing else even in Mozart's church music that can approach this level. Only minor editorial additions are necessary to perform the existing movements as they stand, and this is the procedure that is generally followed. There was no Süssmayer available to do for this masterpiece what he did for the great *Requiem*.

The 'Christe' section of the Kyrie Eleison was written with his wife Constanze in mind; note the sharp contrasts of register in the passage with pauses in the central section. Soft choral passages are interspersed in the long soprano solo. The richly developed counterpoint of the Kyrie is recapitulated.

The Gloria is subdivided into seven movements. The first movement is in C major and opens with a fanfare of repeated chords; immediately a fugue develops, and the feeling of this movement is contrapuntal right through to its quiet close. 'Laudamus te' is a solo for soprano (Constanze again) in a light allegro. The vocal line is highly elaborated and very difficult, with much exploitation of the different registers of the voice. This movement is in F major. The 'Gratias agimus tibi' is a highly chromatic adagio for five-part chorus and orchestra; the key is A minor. For the Domine Deus, a duet for two soprano soloists with strings and organ accompaniment, we move to D minor. The full orchestra returns for the fifth movement, 'qui tollis'. The key is G minor and the repeated chromatic descent in the bass recalls the crucifixion passacaglia of Bach's *B minor Mass*. However, the double-dotted rhythm of Mozart's movement gives it a feeling of agitation that is peculiar to this work; the music seems to progress compulsively. The wind chorus doubles the eight-part double chorus of voices, except for brief exposed 'misereres' and 'suscipes'. Trumpets and woodwind share the choral antiphony of the 'miserere' passage at the end of this overwhelming movement.

The E-minor 'Quoniam' is an animated trio for two sopranos and tenor with oboes, bassoons and strings. The last movement is preceded by a short adagio 'Jesu Christe' (at last we are back in C major) as a prelude to the enormous fugue *alla breve*, 'cum sancto spiritu'. In this fugue every kind of contrapuntal device is used, the theme is inverted, and appears in a number of different *stretti*. Bach's *Art of Fugue* was bearing fruit at last.

Just how much Mozart had absorbed of the colossal influence of Bach at this stage is well shown by the opening of the first Credo fragment. Drum-beat figures for strings and organ are used antiphonally against passages in thirds for oboes with bassoons and horns. The same music returns when the chorus enters, but the five-part choral writing is strictly homophonic, as though Mozart intended to symbolize perfect solidarity. The strongly articulated rhythm implements this view. At the words 'et invisibilium' the texture dissolves into imitative counterpoint, but the drum rhythm is maintained in the orchestra. The music continues through this movement in one unbroken line, but fresh material is often introduced and treated in the most graphic manner: a musical illustration of a literary *point* is afforded by the close antiphony of 'deum de deo, lumen de lumine'; verbal imagery in the Bachian sense is obvious at 'descendit in coelis'. Always at the return of the word 'credo', Mozart reverts to the compelling solidarity of the opening. The *allegro maestoso* semiquavers of this movement are also reminiscent of Bach. The only other extant fragment of the Credo is the beautiful 6/8 soprano aria, 'et incarnatus'.

The Sanctus and Benedictus form a close-knit whole. The long Osanna fugue of the Sanctus is briefly recalled after the Benedictus, and the Benedictus itself stands like a contrasted lyrical central passage (in the relative minor) with the semiquaver subject of the Osanna fugue making an appearance several times like a ritornello. The Sanctus itself is a noble largo, standing like a monumental prelude to the Osanna fugue.

Mozart left his last work, the *Requiem in D minor*, K. 626, unfinished. However, work on it has gone so far that there were sketches at least, even of the final movements. Süssmayer, a pupil of Mozart's with whom he had spent some time while he was working on the *Requiem* and to whom he had probably revealed a lot about the work, then undertook to complete the score. Musicologically speaking, the matter of the extent to which Süssmayer's completion is based on Mozart's indications has never been cleared up, and probably never will be. But we can assume that Mozart's influence was very extensive, for these completions seem perfectly genuine, and unmistakably in Mozart's spirit.

There has always been a romantic legend built up around the story of the composition of the *Requiem*, which is doubtless one of the reasons why it has become so extraordinarily popular. And, as it turned out, this legend was firmly founded in fact. The stranger who commissioned Mozart to write a Mass for the Dead, and paid him on the spot, was actually representing a certain Count Walsegg, who was very devoted to music and had already commissioned several works from well-known composers with the intention of passing them off as his own work. These are the sober facts about the origin of this strange commission. But the mysterious stranger may have appeared to Mozart to be a messenger from beyond the grave, instructing him to write his own Requiem. In any case, his imagination was deeply stirred by the commission, and it must have given him a feeling of heavy responsibility. In this state of mind he produced the child of his final artistic maturity; nowhere else in Mozart do the mysteries of life and death find such expression.

The first section of the *Requiem*, the plea for eternal rest for the dead, is filled with deep mourning. The bassoons and bassett horns plaintively enunciate the serious theme of the *Requiem* in the short introduction, which is closed by four bitter chords in the trombones. The chorus enters with a gloomy *forte*, singing the theme with close overlaps, accompanied by pleading syncopations in the violins. After a short interlude, the mood of mourning is greatly intensified. Glowingly, the soprano sings 'Et lux perpetua luceat eis', only to be re-extinguished in the *piano* of the chorus. The following entry of the double fugue is extremely powerful: themes that are strangely baroque articulate the words 'Kyrie eleison' and 'Christe eleison' and are combined in the broad stream of the mighty double fugue. This network of voices gives rise to a peculiar feeling of unrest, an anxious excitement, as if in anticipation of an imminent horror.

In the Dies Irae the Last Judgement descends on us in all its power and glory, and the choral parts are introduced with a harsh plasticity of expression. Peace emerges from this agitated mood when the tenor trombone enters with its majestic triads. The following section, up to and including the 'Lacrymosa', all belong to the Dies Irae, and all together they make up the second large section of the *Requiem*. The solo voices sing the Tuba Mirum: the bass soloist takes up the majestic trombone motif, the tenor sings the theme in diminution transplanted into the minor key; the mood of darkness is slowly dispersed when the contralto enters, and thereafter, the effect of the soprano's entry is bright and luminous, expressive of pious confidence. The mighty chorus, 'Rex tremendae majestatis', is again overpowering and awe-inspiring. This ends with the fervent plea, 'Salva me'. The 'Recordare'. which follows this, sung by the quartet of soloists, forms a wonderful climax to the work: uncertainty is charged with anxious hope. Then all the sufferings of fearful mankind break out again in the 'Confutatis maledictus', resolved in an urgent plea for grace in the 'Lacrymosa dies illa'.

The climax of the Offertorium is reached in the fugue, 'Quam olim Abrahae promisisti', which is repeated after the solemn 'Hostias'. The Sanctus is formally brief, but highly expressive, with its little Hosianna fugue, and the Benedictus, sung by the quartet of soloists, emerges from this with a delicate reserve. The last movement, the Agnus Dei, is full of profound piety: the faithful humbly bow themselves before God's compassion. At the close, the big double fugue from the Kyrie is reintroduced with the words 'Cum sanctis tuis in aeternum'. Whether Mozart intended this repetition, or whether it was simply a fortunate solution *in extremis* of Süssmayer's will probably never be known.

The *Requiem* had its première in Vienna in 1792 under van Swieten. The extraordinary qualities of the work were immediately recognized; Haydn remarked that Mozart deserved immortality for this work alone. Within a short space of time the work was supreme throughout the musical world, and had ousted all works of a similar nature from the concert repertoire, however illustrious their composers.

Any survey of Mozart's music would be incomplete without a postscript mentioning some of his concert arias.

In the course of his career Mozart returned fairly regularly to this genre. He was of the opinion that an aria should 'fit the singer as perfectly as a well-made suit of clothes' and it is consequently of some interest to know for whom he wrote his arias. For general background and information concerning the singers of the time and Mozart's dealings with them the reader should refer to Alfred Einstein's excellent survey. Here, we must restrict ourselves to a few of Mozart's most mature creations in this field.

In 1873 Mozart wrote a scena and an aria for his sister-in-law. These were to be inserted into an opera by a composer named Pasquale Anfossi, but Mozart did not trouble to adjust his style of composition to the music that already existed. Paradoxically, the scena, 'Vorrei spiegarvi', K. 418 is rather lyrical, but the aria, K. 419, is highly dramatic and brilliant. The aria is in two parts; the words of the first part are 'No, che non sei capace', and the music is a vigorous allegro with plenty of display work for the soprano. She reaches for a top E, and then a repeated semiquaver run leads through a pause into the second section, allegro assai, with the words 'Vanne! t'aborro, in grato'.

For inclusion in the same opera Mozart wrote a rondo for one Valentin Adamberger: 'Per pietà, non rivercate', K. 420. Of this piece—which Mozart never heard—Einstein writes: 'It represents an intensification of emotion from concealed agitation to the most open and passionate excitement. There is hardly another piece in which Mozart used so many *tremoli*, *crescendi* and *sforzati* in the strings. If this aria were in *Figaro* or *Don Giovanni* it would be world famous' (*Mozart*, p. 369).

Though they were both written within the space of a few days (in 1787), the two bass arias, K. 512 and 513, were not written for the same singer. 'Alcandro lo confesso ... Non so d'onde viene' (K. 512) is a scena from Metastasio's *Olimpiad* that Mozart had set many years earlier as a soprano aria for his sister-in-law. This version he wrote for the excellent bass Carl Ludwig Fischer. It begins with a dramatic recitative, and the aria is an andante with syncopated throbbing accompaniment. There is an allegretto middle section in 6/8 to the words 'Nel seno a destarmi si fieri contrasti' (In my bosom are aroused such violent conflicts).

The second aria 'Mentre ti lascio' ('As I leave you my love'), K. 513, was written for a young friend of Mozart's, Gottfried von Jaquin. It begins with a larghetto with a beautifully elaborated orchestral part. This builds up to 'I depart. You weep? O God!' and then moves into an allegro 'I ask of you one moment only'. The pain of parting generates considerable agitation—one can think of the piece as a crescendo of indecision: 'I leave, Goodbye. You weep? O what a bitter parting. O God! What a cruel torment! My love, I am going, I leave you. Goodbye! ...'

Mozart wrote his last aria for his sister-in-law in 1788; the words are again from Metastasio: 'Ah se in ciel, benique stella', K. 538. The writing makes the utmost demands on the singer's agility and

endurance, and it has been called a 'concerto for voice' not without
good reason. Mozart executes such *tours de force* with exquisite
precision, but this is not what makes him the composer he is. The
last aria I shall discuss was written shortly after 'Ah se in ciel',
but the two are worlds apart. This is the aria for bass, 'Un bacio di
mano', K. 541, written for Francesca Albertarelli, who had played
the title rôle in *Don Giovanni*. This aria was also for insertion into
a comic opera by Anfossi; and the text consists of a Frenchman's
advice to an uninformed lover. He seems to recommend that the
poor man should allow his wife to do as she pleases, and swallow
his pride, 'close his eyes, his ears, his mouth'. This lovely allegretto,
though short, contains many beautiful comic devices: the up-beat
*fp*s that accompany 'andante a studiar'; the way the orchestra
pushes in through the wife's door, which must of course be left
yawningly 'aper........te'.

LUDWIG VAN BEETHOVEN

born Bonn 16 December 1770
died Vienna 26 March 1827

Like Mozart, Beethoven came from a musical family; he received
his first music lessons from his father, and later ones from Christian
Gottlob Neefe, the respected song-writer. Already in 1783, Beethoven was a member of the electoral orchestra in Bonn, and in
1785 he became Second Concert Organist. A short period of study
with Mozart in Vienna led to a second trip for study in 1792.
Thanks to his excellent connections in Vienna, through the Elector
and the recommendation of Count Waldstein he was soon able
to find his feet, and these advantages must also have given him the
idea of residing there permanently. In 1795 Beethoven introduced
himself to the Viennese public as a composer and pianist, and
shortly afterwards his trios, opus 1, appeared in print. He was soon
highly appreciated; the higher strata of Viennese society supported
and adored him and his success increased steadily year in, year out.
At quite an early stage, around 1800, he began to suffer from
a severe malady of the ear which was to lead, in twenty years,
to total deafness. A letter written to his brothers in 1802—the
'Heiligenstädter Testament'—tells in the most moving terms about

the enormous internal conflicts caused by the recognition of his
disease, a particularly fatal one for a musician.

Beethoven's nine symphonies form the central block of his creative activity; besides these there are numerous other instrumental
works of great significance, including thirty-two piano sonatas and
sixteen string quartets. The opera *Fidelio* was Beethoven's difficult
child; it was first performed in 1805, and reworked in 1806 and
1814. Beethoven never accepted a permanent post, though he
received several honourable offers. And he never married. An enormous web of legends has been spun about his relations with women;
to whom, for example, did he write his wonderful letter 'to the
immortal beloved'? Such questions are in all probability unanswerable. The chief works of his final years are the *Ninth Symphony*,
written in 1823, and the *Missa Solemnis*, written in 1824, both of
which had a terrific impact when they were first performed. His
string quartets on the other hand (the ones dating from 1825–26)
were very coolly received. He made countless plans in his final years,
for a tenth symphony, for instance, and for a 'Faust', but did not
live to execute them.

When Beethoven left for Vienna, Count Waldstein wrote that
he would receive 'Mozart's spirit from the hands of Haydn', and
this prophecy was marvellously fulfilled. His trios, opus 1, and his
first piano sonatas and string quartets, still more his first symphonies and piano concertos, follow quite clearly the lines laid down
by his great predecessors. However, it is equally apparent, even in
his earliest works, that his is a unique personality, the mouthpiece
of a completely new spirit in a completely new era. Beethoven
never composed commissioned works; he was not tied down by
any job. When he wrote, he followed only his own inner impulses,
and was answerable only to his own artistic conscience. 'Music
should strike fire from a man's spirit'; this saying of Beethoven's
indicates the high critical standards he applied to his work. He
lacked the facility with which his great precursors were so for-
tunately gifted. Beethoven would file away at his work with the
strictest self-criticism; his sketch books are evidence of this serious,
constructive detail-work. Each of Beethoven's works is at the same
time an experience and a credo. The form arises out of the passionate sentiments of the content, and so does the manner of expression
of his personality. Beethoven was perfectly aware that he was great
and that he was unique. He did not fight shy of writing to his great
admirer, Prince Lichnowski, in a very proud vein, when the latter

wanted him to play for his guests (officers of the French army) in 1806. He writes: 'Prince, you are what you are by chance and by birth; I am what I am by my own hand alone. There have been and will be many thousands of Princes but there is only one Beethoven.' There is another, even prouder, saying of Beethoven's that characterizes very strongly his mighty battling nature: 'Strength is the morality of men who are distinguished from the rest, and it is also mine.'

Beethoven's *Symphony No. 1 in C major*, opus 21, written in 1800, follows, as we have already mentioned, in the symphonic footsteps of Mozart and Haydn; but it would be very wide of the mark to suppose, as many people do, that it is in imitation of his two predecessors. There are ideas in each of the four movements that show a strength and boldness of thought that could only be Beethoven's. The basic character of the symphony is joyous and animated; strength, gaiety and grace are the elements that motivate this music. Preceded by a short, dramatically tense introduction, the allegro of the first movement has a powerful main theme and

lyrical subsidiary ideas, and conveys a feeling of confidence. The andante develops fugally from a gracefully stepping theme; it is an

enchanting sound-picture of dreamy musings. Beethoven calls the
third movement a minuet but it is nothing like the minuets of his
predecessors; the bold, storming scherzo so characteristic of Beethoven's later symphonies is already here, complete with all its

Allegro molto e vivace

characteristic capriciousness, sudden *sforzati* and soft sounds and
surprising twists. The reflective simplicity of the trio forms a perfect
contrast to the stormy scherzo. The last movement sparkles along
with a gay absence of inhibition. Critics have tried to make out that
this enchanting movement is less significant than the others, but
the little introduction alone shows the injustice of this: the violins
climb up timidly, and repeatedly fall back for a fresh run up, before
they finally manage to articulate the animated theme. A good per-

Allegro molto e vivace

formance will make the listener hold his breath in suspense, before
succumbing to the freedom and charm of the finale itself.

The *First Symphony* was widely applauded when it was first
played in Vienna and Beethoven's name spread like wildfire all
over Germany. But the next, *Symphony No. 2 in D major*, opus 36,
which was played for the first time three years later, in 1803, did
not receive anything like the same warm reception. Without
doubt, Beethoven's *Second Symphony* is far removed from the
classical symphony, and to the public it seemed strangely bold
and even repellent in its novelty. At that time no-one had any
idea of the enormous step forward Beethoven was to take with his
third symphony, the *Eroica*, in which his symphonic peculiarities
find their first powerful expression. That the *Second Symphony*
could estrange anybody seems incomprehensible to us today, when
the language and structure of the music has become so familiar.
The four movements of the symphony are very close-knit, and
the fundamental line of the work is healthy and vigorous. Beethoven's later demonism, with its combative, self-willed obstinacy,
appears only fleetingly here. A slow introduction precedes the first
allegro. The pleasurable melody which flows quietly at the begin-

ning of the adagio molto is supplanted by threatening powers: an anticipation of the main theme of the *Ninth Symphony* emerges in a hard unison. The gloom of this scene lightens soon enough as the homely promise of the allegro theme raises itself from the basses.

The secondary theme is a fresh, march-like melody, first intoned strongly by the winds and then triumphantly taken up by the full orchestra.

The second movement of the symphony is of a very special nature. This larghetto, built on one of Beethoven's most fervent melodies, has always enjoyed great popularity. It is often to be

heard on its own in programmes of popular music, which is doubtless the reason for its being one of Beethoven's best-known pieces. The wonderful melody exudes peace and happiness, and in the course of the movement it is juxtaposed with ideas that are sometimes dreamy and idyllic, sometimes gay and playful. The scherzo has a hearty, robust humour, while the finale raises the mood of gay animation to one of powerful grandeur.

Beethoven completed his Symphony No. 3 in E-flat, opus 55—the *Eroica*—in 1804. As is well known, Beethoven originally wanted to dedicate his heroic symphony to Napoleon, but tore up the dedication in a rage when he heard the news that Napoleon had declared himself emperor. The work then appeared in 1806 under the title 'Heroic Symphony, dedicated to the memory of a great man'. The ideas, content and programme of the *Eroica* are generally outlined by that dedication. It would be misguided to look for individual scenes in the life of a hero in the four movements. The man of battle, the great man in general, is the hero of the heroic symphony; the man marked off by his aspirations and strength, and yet no stranger to the world of love and pain.

The first movement is the picture of a hero in general outline. After two short introductory strokes in the orchestra the 'cellos

play the main theme. The horns pick it up with a little more weight and then, after some hard, driving syncopations, you hear it briefly in all the finery of the full orchestra. Doubt begins to infiltrate: over against the proud, active potential of the main theme sound querulous, complaining woodwind, but they are ruthlessly sup-

planted by imperious unison steps. These contrasts constitute the characteristics of the first movement of the *Eroica*, and they also indicate Beethoven's particular view of heroism. The strength, the aspirations and the deeds are always served up with a sauce of suffering. The elegiac undertones reappear in new guises, the most significant being the melancholy song of the oboes that forms such

an impressive sequel to the *fortissimo* outbreak of the orchestra at a later stage in this giant allegro. But as the movement continues these painful threatening cries and complaints are progressively overshadowed by powerful heroic ideas. Marching basses, the heroic call of the horns, the brilliance of the string passages, subdue all resistance. The movement is brought to a victorious close.

Difficult though the first movement of the *Eroica* may be to understand, the second movement is very direct in its appeal. It is headed

'Funeral March', and Beethoven has erected an indestructible
monument to the dead hero. The main theme is a gloomy march
melody, played first by the strings, *pianissimo*, and then by the
woodwind. After the appearance of a conciliatory counter-melody,

the plaintive main theme recurs. Then there is a new, luminous
idea in a light C major that seems like a vision, an apotheosis of the
hero. Rising out of the most delicate colours, this vision is elevated

to the heights of victory. But the torn and painful rhythms of
mourning are muttering again, and the development continues
with an energetic fugato. This, too, is interrupted by the lament
of the main theme. A wonderfully delicate melody in the violins
seems temporarily to mitigate the general gloom, but it fails to
penetrate. The straining rhythms of the opening reappear, and the
movement ends as they die away, melancholy and lamenting.

The shaking experience of the funeral march is followed by a
scherzo filled with mysterious voices. The natural horn sounds that
shine in the trio are immediately superseded by the stealthy dealings
of fantastically interwoven series of notes. The whole movement
is enshrouded with a stealthy, mysterious urgency, a drive of untiring activity that reaches its climax in the wildly animated coda.

The finale, which opens with a passionate outbreak in the strings,
is a set of variations. A simple theme is gracefully decorated by the
strings for the first two variations. In the third variation a counter-

theme of a heartrending, sunny clarity appears in the form of a folk-song melody. The variation theme provides the bass for this. The variants mount up in a rich profusion expressive of the fullness and joy of life. It is in the transfiguring andante of the folk-song-like second theme that the climax is reached. The end is heralded by a veritable storm of enthusiasm.

Beethoven's *Eroica* is a mighty work, not only as regards its size, but in the endless wealth of its ideas. The heroic grandeur of the rushing first allegro, the melancholy transfiguration of the funeral march, the mysterious scherzo, and the finale that pulsates with *joie de vivre* and spiritual grandeur, each movement is a world in itself.

The fundamental mood of the *Symphony No. 4 in B-flat major,* opus 60, written in 1807, is one of happiness. After a dreamy, reflective introduction, the main theme of the first allegro enters with a

robust freshness; a merry secondary idea joins in as a complement

rather than in contrast to the first theme. In the development section the issue is slightly confused: an emotional lament of a melody appears and, under its spell, the gay mood becomes overcast. Only very temporarily, however, for soon the voices unite, first timidly and then with increasing confidence, and lead back energetically to the recapitulation. The movement ends with a jubilant *fortissimo.*

The adagio, one of the most marvellous movements Beethoven ever wrote, is brimming with contentment. No shadows mar its clear beauty. Happy confidence is expressed in the fervent melody of the main theme, and this confidence is further underlined by the marked rhythmic accompaniment, which always reappears as the faithful consort of the main idea. I would like to draw particular

attention to the dreamy, intense clarinet melody that forms the

second theme of the movement. This soulful song emerges from the twilight of a sudden *pianissimo* and perfumes the air with the magic of high romance.

The scherzo of the *B-flat major Symphony* is very gay, but—genuine Beethoven—fantastical-demoniacal elements are injected into the exuberance. These are, however, unable to divert the music from its fundamental gaiety. A simple song-melody in the trio contrasts perfectly with the scherzo. Emerging from a delicate *piano* in the woodwind, it raises itself in a stream of emotional, luminous song. The finale makes a jovial end to this happy symphony. Brilliant and fiery or light-hearted and graceful, as the occasion demands, this finale dance sparkles along in the gayest of moods. There are few works by Beethoven that are so consistently sunny of disposition as this *Fourth Symphony*. But it would be presumptuous to maintain on this account that it lacks depth or significance.

The *Symphony No. 5 in C minor*, opus 67, was first performed in 1808, and it was immediately apparent that here was a unique experience, a titanic spirit at work, but one speaking such a clear language that people spontaneously understood and appreciated it. The extraordinary unity and natural clarity of the work have resulted in the fact that the *Fifth Symphony* has become the most popular of all symphonies, despite the sublime and profound quality of the material.

The *C minor Symphony* has often been called the 'Symphony of Fate'. This refers to the remark that Beethoven is supposed to have made about the theme of the first movement: 'thus fate knocks at the door'. This interpretation is certainly very convincing. The threatening strokes of fate at the beginning of the symphony intimate a passionate struggle that is to draw all the energies of life

into its fateful wake. The whole long movement evolves out of this one theme which stands like a cipher at the opening of the work: life storms along, hard and inexorable; softer ideas attempt to make their mark, but none succeed: fate proceeds ruthlessly along her chosen path.

The second movement, 'andante con moto', takes place in a totally different world. The lower strings open with a wonderful

melody, and this is complemented by a march-like theme in the woodwind. The latter takes a victorious, radiant turn; both themes,

artfully altered, recur several times in the course of the movement. Emotionally, the movement has its ups and downs—the weather is changeable—but there is no lapse of confidence; the movement is full of faith in happiness and beauty.

The third movement returns to the world of ideas manifested in the first allegro. A theme that seems to wish to escape from the low

region where it started leads to a derivative of the fate motif. As it feels its way ahead with gliding limbs, the strokes of fate recur, now hard and threatening, and then later, softly reverberating in the distance. An animated dance is introduced by the basses; a

game that is an attempt at gaiety. This pales and flies off into nothingness. The dark lines start their climb as at the beginning, and the fate theme returns again, but with less life than before. An uncanny, heavy mood starts to spread, a mood of scary suspense, and it is from this that the victorious last movement breaks out, in all its

elemental strength. 'Through darkness into light' seems to be one of the archetypal themes of symphonic music, and here it finds the most marvellous expression imaginable. The movement is a song of triumph for the subjugation of the powers of fate, an uninhibited, victorious procession.

Beethoven's Symphony No. 6 in F major, opus 68, is exceptional in so far as it is the only symphony for which Beethoven provided a programmatic sketch. Written in 1808, he named it the *Pastoral Symphony*. Its content is a profound musical expression of life in the country, the life of nature. Beethoven has given an explanatory title to each movement, though he wrote somewhere that anyone who had any idea at all about life in the country could not fail to understand the work, even without the titles.

The first allegro is headed 'the awakening of pleasant sensations on arrival in the country', and Beethoven's indication that 'it is a matter rather of the expression of feeling than tone-painting' applies to this movement in the highest sense. It intimates a most pleasant experience of nature. A delicate, early morning atmosphere holds sway at the outset; natural life wakes up only gradually. Here and there you hear the theme played by individual instruments; short subsidiary ideas appear and disappear only to be

taken up again; everything is awake and moving. A marvellous poem of nature coming to life, the effect of which is so perfectly open and direct that one cannot help but listen, enchanted.

The atmosphere of peace and sunlight at noon is created by the second scene, which Beethoven entitles 'scene by a stream'. One hears the melodic murmuring of the stream, and out of it arises a song-like tune. The small, secret creatures of nature go about their business in the grass and leaves, the birds start to sing and at the end of the movement, clearly distinguishable, is a gay trio consisting of a nightingale, a quail and a cuckoo.

The third movement is devoted to a lusty gathering of country people. It must be getting on for evening now; dance music beckons from a distance and the lads and lasses choose their partners. A distant growl of thunder puts a hasty end to all the gay activity; everyone is scared away by the sudden outbreak of the storm. The bad weather breaks with a grandiose clamour: lightning flashes, the rain rattles down and the thunder rolls. The storm passes over, and peace is gradually restored; the transition to the final movement is formed by a pastoral dance in the clarinets and horns.

'Shepherd's song', writes Beethoven over the last movement,

and it expresses the shepherd's thankful feelings after the storm. The first movement's mood of pleasant communion with nature is taken up again. The thematic work, unified to a high degree, is simple and fervent, and the movement forms a wonderful close to this divine symphony of Pan.

Beethoven's *Symphony No. 7 in A major*, opus 92, written in 1813, is often referred to as a 'Dance Symphony'; it is usual to describe it as a grand apotheosis of the dance. I agree with this interpretation only with large reservations, for besides the dance elements that give the symphony its particularly sparkling, affirmative character, it contains serious, reflective episodes that are constantly pointing out that, despite the gay animation apparently holding sway, there is no excluding the idyllic and reflective side, the serious ideas that keep on cropping up, sometimes even in quite a threatening tone.

Even the first movement begins with a slow introduction, a large-scale tone-painting that conveys feelings of idyllic peace. If you wish to conjure up the sublime atmosphere of the regions of the blessed in heaven as Orpheus experienced it, it is all there in this introduction. The main section of the first movement is dominated by a sprung, dancing rhythm. The lively, compelling 6/8

rhythm takes the driver's seat for most of the time, racing along with joyful animation. However, it is often threateningly interrupted by inhibitory *piano* episodes. Perhaps the most impressive instance comes just before the end of the movement, where the bright jubilation of the overwhelming final climax builds up slowly out of a mysterious *pianissimo* in the basses.

The second movement, allegretto, is one of Beethoven's most popular movements. Even at the first performance, conducted by Beethoven himself, the audience understood it straight away and clamoured for an encore. At the beginning there is a wind chord of an indefinable quality and this transports us into the world of dreams. A quietly stepping theme emerges from the basses and a longing, lamenting melody consorts with it; both themes are com-

bined, and rise steadily in pitch. The stepping theme is intensified
with all the radiance of the full orchestra to a pitch of sublime
grandeur, and then slides back into the mood of the opening. Like
a vision, a wonderfully delicate, happy melody in the major key

emerges. But this luminous idyll is severely interrupted, and the
first theme, in a bitter, combative guise, dominates the rest of the
movement. The melody in the major key crops up again, but only
for a short time, and the movement ends, as it began, with the
mysterious wind chord.

The third movement turns on a contrast similar to that in the
allegretto. After the lively sparkle of the whirlwind scherzo comes

a note of reflective calm in the trio. The melody of this trio con-

firms once more the spiritual counterpoise to dancing animation
in this symphony. This melody is extremely simple, but words are
impotent to describe the wonderful sound-picture that Beethoven
manages to conjure up in these few simple notes.

The final movement is devoted entirely to the unfettered joy of
life. Besides the animated opening melody, there is a triumphal

secondary theme, and the whole movement is borne along on a

frothing, vigorous wave. The music rises to a rapturous frenzy in
the final climax.

The *Symphony No. 8 in F major*, opus 93, written in 1814, is filled with robust gaiety. The whole work exudes a bright joy that, nevertheless, by no means excludes more profound and powerful undertones. But the character of sunny joy is never entirely banished, and in accord with this general idea, Beethoven decided against a slow movement proper. The first allegro opens with a gay, festive theme that sets the tone for the jovial current of the

movement. There is real exuberance in the development section where a happy octave motif in the basses pushes the music along, and the end of the movement is exuberant too, in its way: the main theme is played for the last time by the strings *pianissimo* like a slight, gracious bow of farewell.

The second movement, allegretto scherzando, a charming game of nimbly hurrying notes, is particularly graceful. The minuet is blunter: a fresh, countrified dance, very robust. The idyll of the trio deserves special mention; the horns and clarinets carry on a conversation which is presently joined by the violins, who introduce a delicate, succulent flavour. The *tour de force* of the symphony

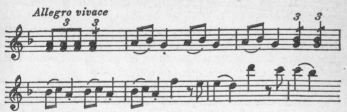

is the finale. The main idea has a humorous side; the secondary theme is warm and fervent. This movement—the brilliant crown

of a symphony of joy—is an irresistibly vigorous stream of feeling, and inexhaustible in its freshness of invention.

Beethoven's *Symphony No. 9 in D minor*, opus 125, written in 1824, is not only the final step in his symphonic development, it is also an apotheosis that sums up all that went before. All the fundamental ideas of his dramatic symphonies are united in the *Ninth*: the heroics of the *Eroica*, the fateful quality of the *Fifth*, and the affirmation of the *Seventh*. Beethoven's intensive preoccupation with the *Symphony No. 9* is unparalleled in any of his earlier works; there are sketches for it that date back as far as 1815! For decades he had been toying with the idea of setting Schiller's *Hymn of Joy*. But he only decided to include part of it in the final movement when the other three movements were almost finished. Richard Wagner believed that this innovation was in effect 'a declaration of the bankruptcy of instrumental music', but when one thinks of the enormous intensity and expressive strength of the last quartets one can hardly agree with him. In his *Choral Fantasy* (opus 80, 1808) Beethoven had already attempted to introduce the chorus into a purely instrumental work—a piano concerto. His decision to make the same exception for the *Ninth Symphony* must have sprung from his desire to intensify still further, by the inclusion of the human voice, the expression of joy and the most elevated affirmation of life—to which he had already given such overwhelming expression in his *Seventh Symphony*.

Something twitches and bubbles its way up out of darkness, over mysterious open fifths. Slowly the mood lightens in the course of an exciting *crescendo* and then, with elemental power, the mighty main theme breaks over us. It grows and flourishes with demonic intrepid-

ity, only to sink back into the murky twilight of the opening. It picks up again and rises to still more powerful strokes. The content of the grandiose first allegro of the *Ninth Symphony* is the battle against the threatening powers of fate, the fight of some proud, heroic personage, for whom retreat is quite inconceivable. Peaceful scenes and moments of blessed calm disappear as quickly as they came in the flares of renewed fighting. The musical drama is shaken by the feeling that something is being sought and striven for, but there is no glimpse of fulfilment in the clashes of one force against the other. None the less, the hero's courage and intrepidity are unimpaired.

The same demonically excited mood dominates the second movement, molto vivace. At the start there is the mysterious quietness of the fugato, which then boils up wildly in a passionate tumult;

temporarily things take a soothing turn, but the wild demonism flares up afresh. There is a pastoral note in the middle section,

similar to that in the scherzo of the *Seventh Symphony*, and here too the idyllic mood is taken up briefly once more just before the end. With a few harsh strokes the movement breaks off abruptly.

The adagio leads into a totally different world. The B-flat major melody is expressive of calm, and its long lines lead to a lovely

subsidiary idea, in which there is an element of childlike faith. This

statement of the themes is followed by variations, first using both themes, later only the first theme. The whole is a dream of harmony and happiness, a hymn of faith in the loftiest and most beautiful of human ideals.

We are snatched away from this dream-world by the *fortissimo* outbreak with which the last movement opens; all the storms of the first movement seem ready to break over us again. The 'cellos and basses raise their voices warningly in a powerful recitative, and memories of the foregoing movements that try to intervene are thrown out again by the basses. At last the oboe plays a new tune;

it is an anticipation of the melody of joy. Once more you hear the
recitative of the basses, but played this time with a note of assent:

they take up the theme themselves and play it first as a single line
in the most delicate *pianissimo*. This is the wonderfully simple
melody that is later taken up by the chorus with the words 'Praise
to joy, the God-descended daughter of Elysium'. This first appearance of the melody is sublimely effective, though it is virtually a
popular song nowadays. The main theme is now handed over to
each instrumental group in turn in the course of a long build-up,
but at the climax Beethoven falls back once more on the chaotic
scene from the beginning of the movement. This is the point where
the human voice enters: the baritone soloist leads with the words,
'O friends, no more these sounds continue. Let us raise a song of
sympathy, of gladness'. Then the soloist takes up the song of joy,
and the chorus joins in enthusiastically, followed by the quartet of
soloists. The hymn comes to a temporary close with the sublime
words, 'and the Seraph dwells with God'. A march-like variation,
beginning *pianissimo*, leads to the tenor solo, 'Glad, glad as his suns',
and this opens out with a violent build-up, supported by the male
chorus, into a wild, battling fugato. The full chorus takes up the
song of joy with hymnic enthusiasm. The section that follows with
the words 'O ye millions, I embrace ye' is the gripping climax of

O———   ye mil - lions, I——   em - brace ye

the choral finale. There is an overwhelming grandeur in the unison
entry of the men's voices, exultantly followed by the women. This
transcendental effect is perhaps even surpassed by the mystical
transfiguration of 'World, dost feel thy maker near? Seek him o'er
yon starry sphere'. Jubilantly the great double fugue now opens
and the melody of joy is combined with the grandiose theme of
'O ye millions, I embrace ye'. Once more we are transported into
that celestial mood, and it is given to the solo voices to bring us

back with their delicate, foreboding entry. Then all the jubilation rushes up again with constantly increasing enthusiasm into a veritable tumult of joy; the movement ends at the highest pitch of ecstasy.

Beethoven's overtures can be divided into two groups. *The Consecration of the House, Fidelio* and *Prometheus* constitute one group. These overtures have an introductory character, and do not penetrate the content of the coming drama in any detail. *The Consecration of the House* is, in fact, not associated with any drama, and stands on its own. The overtures of the second group do concern themselves with the drama that supposedly follows; in this second group belong the *Leonora Overtures*, and the *Egmont* and *Coriolan Overtures*. These last can almost be regarded as symphonic poems, similar to the great Weber overtures and the preludes to Wagner's music dramas.

The *Coriolan Overture*, written in 1807, comes from the same period as the *Fifth Symphony*, the *Waldstein Sonata*, the *Appassionata*, the violin concerto, to mention only a few of the important works dating from these happy years of his most fruitful creative period. Like the *Fifth Symphony*, the *Coriolan Overture* is in C minor, Beethoven's tragic key, and, in fact, there are many traits in the overture that seem to point to the *Fifth Symphony*. A tragedy by the poet Collin provided the literary plan for Beethoven's marvellous overture, not, as has often been supposed, Shakespeare's Roman drama of the same name. Beethoven was very impressed with Collin's tragedy: he was sympathetic and enthusiastic about Coriolanus' whole personality, his character and fate. With passionate pride, Coriolanus rises against his people and the laws of his society, and this brings about his downfall. The overture is devoted to the portrayal of this tragic personality. Gloomy, clenching harmonies, lightning syncopations, a defiant rising theme, astringent *sforzati*—this is how the overture opens; everything is

steeped in the dark minor key, but with an air of bitter, powerful

decision. As a contrast to this intractable toughness, Beethoven
introduces a secondary theme with lighter harmonies in the major

key. This turn for the better is very brief, and the astringent, combative sounds reassert themselves and retain their ascendancy despite the renewed gentle warning of the major key harmonies.
Finally, the heroic theme is taken up once more in all its tragic
significance, and—collapses! The hero has destroyed himself, and
the overture ends in a gloomy *pianissimo*.

The *Egmont Overture*, written in 1810, based on Goethe's tragedy,
is also a piece of programme music, in the ideal sense of that expression. The content of the tragedy is the great battle for freedom
fought by the Dutch against their Spanish oppressors. Egmont is
the hero who is to liberate his people, but he falls victim to a Spanish
plot, is taken prisoner and condemned to die by the executioner's
axe. In his overture, Beethoven does not depict Egmont's fate as
an individual, but with broad strokes pictures the suffering of the
people (the slow, heavy introduction) and their struggle with their
oppressors (the passionately animated allegro). This section of the
overture closes on a hard, warlike note; and then, from the delicate
sounds of the woodwind, victorious jubilation emerges in the
strings, symbolizing the death and transfiguration of the hero, and
indicating simultaneously the people's liberation from their oppressors' yoke at a later stage.

As is well-known, Beethoven wrote four different overtures for
his only opera, *Fidelio*: three in C major called the *Three Leonora
Overtures* (after the original title of the opera), written in 1805, and
a fourth in E major, which he wrote in 1814 after reworking and
renaming the opera, and which is called, accordingly, the *Fidelio
Overture*. This last is the one that is always played with the opera
nowadays. It has also become a common practice to insert the
Leonora Overture No. 3 before the final scene of the opera. Whether
or not this is justifiable is a moot point, but the fact that it is done
is evidence at least that the *Leonora No. 3* is an extraordinary piece
of work musically. It is far beyond the sort of overture that is
merely an introduction to an opera. The spiritual essence of the
Leonora-Fidelio drama is magnificently depicted in this tone-poem:
the suffering of the innocently incarcerated Florestan (Leonora's

husband), his wife's heroic decision to liberate him, her struggle
and her success, and then, as a marvellous apotheosis, the stormy
jubilation and thanksgiving for his release and the reunion of the
couple. After a slow introduction depicting the suffering of the
innocently condemned man with the fervent theme of Florestan's
aria, the main idea, glowing with blessed confidence, is introduced

in the fast main section of the work, progressing with a passionate
swing from a timid *piano* entry to a brilliant, powerful *fortissimo*.

The long-suffering Florestan's delicate theme is sounded again, but
this time borne aloft by fighting impulses. The courage of battle
and confidence of victory dominate the further evolution of the
tone-poem; the pressing main theme constantly comes out and
leads powerfully to the first dramatic climax. A trumpet-call sounds
in the distance, announcing—in the opera—the arrival of the min-
ister, and also freedom, since the trumpet is the symbol of Florestan's imminent liberation. A reserved interlude leads to a second
trumpet-call, this time not so far away, and there is a surge of confidence. With a delicate swing, the main theme is played by the
flute and this surges forward to the entry of the battling idea, completely confident of victory. Florestan's subsidiary theme appears
once more, and leads to a shower of victorious rejoicing. Then,
with a great uprush in the strings, we hear the greatest hymn of
victory that Beethoven ever wrote.

The *Leonora Overtures Nos. 1 and 2* can be regarded as prelimi-
nary studies for the great *Leonora Overture No. 3*. In this context,
the first can really only arouse historical interest, but the *Leonora
No. 2* is very stirring and direct in its effect, even though one has
to do without some of the details that were finally perfected in the
Leonora No. 3, such as the trumpet-call and the wonderfully reserved interludes.

Seen beside its C major sisters, the E major overture, or *Fidelio
Overture*, seems quite modest. It is plain that Beethoven simply

wanted to write some festive, introductory music for his opera, without going into any of the details of the drama. The first few bars in unison immediately set the tone of happy excitement, and these bars constitute the main theme and also the germinating cell

of the overture. After a tense introduction the allegro takes up this main idea and develops it, storming onward with joyful animation. Before the coda, the luscious horn sounds from the introduction appear once more, and the rushing *stretto* of fanfares enters for the final, stormy triumph.

The layout and thematic work of the little overture for the ballet *The Men of Prometheus*, written in 1800, is reminiscent of the first movement of the *First Symphony*. An animated theme follows the slow introduction. From its mysterious beginnings, the allegro hurries past like an irresistible river; slowly, life stirs, new ideas are added in the secondary themes and the whole builds up to a happy, jubilant close.

Beethoven wrote his last overture for the opening of the Josef-stadt Theatre in Vienna in 1822, and *The Consecration of the House* is purely representative in character. It is an opulent, festive over-ture, somewhat in the style of Handel. The slow introduction opens on a solemn note; fanfares appear and disappear. The strings take the lead and, timidly at first but with increasing purpose, attempt to form a theme that can serve as a thread to guide them. In the allegro this theme takes on its final shape and, like Handel, Beet-hoven builds up a fugal fantasy in a free style, rich in changes of mood, powerful in its climaxes. The final effect is overwhelming.

Beethoven wrote only one violin concerto, *Concerto in D major*, in 1806, but it is one of the most beautiful and significant works in the repertoire. It has been a favourite with every great violinist both in this century and the last, and is a standard work that every violinist must come to terms with. The large first movement breathes an air of peace and fortunate humanity, and the thematic groups contain hardly a single contrast. The unique quality of Beethoven as a man flows out of this cornucopia of wonderful melodic ideas; in this work he sings his song of songs for the soul's peace with harmonious perfection. This mood is at its most pronounced in the hymn-like song of the second theme, in the simplicity of its ascending line. It is this wonderful melody that dominates

the end of the movement: in a reserved *piano* it is introduced once more after the virtuoso solo cadenza like a peaceful transfiguration. The lyrical mood is still more pronounced in the second movement. The theme of the larghetto has a delicately romantic air; its melody is played first by the strings and later by the horns and clarinets, gracefully ornamented by the solo violin. A cadenza forms the bridge to the final movement. Twice, the violinist plays a dancing, animated theme that is then jubilantly taken up by the

full orchestra. This rondo forms the brilliant endpiece of the concerto. The mood is uninhibited and happy and the handling of the orchestra and particularly the solo instrument is brilliant. The latter's glittering, playful runs lead the movement—and the concerto—to its lively close. The orchestral part of the concerto is laid out on a symphonic scale, and it is with reason that the work is sometimes referred to as Beethoven's 'tenth symphony'.

The juxtaposition of piano and orchestra has always been one of the most stimulating forms of instrumental music, and almost all the great symphonists have contributed something to the repertoire. Though it was Bach and Mozart who gave birth to this form, it required Beethoven's mighty genius to take the decisive step in the field of the piano concerto, as indeed in almost all fields of instrumental music, and create the type of the modern piano concerto in its symphonic sense. Beethoven wrote five piano concertos, if we leave out the juvenile *D major Concerto* and the *Fantasy for piano, chorus and orchestra*. The first two—*Concertos in C major* and *B-flat major*—are still dependent to a large extent on the form of the Mozartian concerto; the layout and thematic work are very much in the style of the times. However, both works are so rich in excellent points that it will always be a pleasure to hear them in the concert hall. The first of Beethoven's piano concertos is the *Concerto in B-flat major*, opus 19, which was, however, written in 1795 and is referred to as his second on account of its higher opus number. The first movement is a playful allegro, very effective with its runs and passage work. But the still, dreamy adagio is incomparably more significant. There is no doubt about it, however, that the delightful rondo deserves the crown, with its impudent main theme exuberantly accenting the weak parts of the bar. The cheeky twist into the minor key is especially piquant! And then, how charming is the close of the concerto, with gradually fading trills in thirds in the piano part.

Reckoning by the date of composition, the *Concerto in C major*, opus 15, is the second of his piano concertos. Written in 1798, it still belongs clearly to Beethoven's first period. In the lively *C major Concerto* there is no sign of the astringent accents, the grandeur and profundity of, say, the *C minor Concerto*, written only two years later. The first allegro is extremely virtuoso and is laid out on a grand scale. The beautiful song-like main theme of the adagio exudes a reflective quietness and a beautiful richness of sound. But the sunny finale is undoubtedly the most beautiful movement of the concerto. It is characterized by great exuberance; the piano enters almost rudely with the main idea, and this is then joined by secondary themes that are graceful and charming, or again folky and dance-like. The whole finale sparkles and the listener is put in mind of an animated local festival.

The third piano concerto, the *C minor Concerto*, opus 37, is the first that bears the genuine Beethoven seal. Hitherto, the solo concerto had been purely for the benefit of the soloist and his virtuosity, with the orchestra in the subordinate rôle of mere accompanist. In his *C minor Concerto* Beethoven broke with this tradition, and the orchestra is on an equal footing with the soloist; they create a sort of dualogue in which both parties are of equal importance and equally expressive. The salient virtuosity of the piano part is checked for the sake of the symphonic character of the whole.

Beethoven wrote the *Concerto in C minor* in 1800, approximately at the same time as he was writing the *Pathétique* and *Moonlight Sonatas*, which appeared shortly before and after the concerto. The passion and magic of these masterly sonatas is also present in the *C minor Concerto*. The accent is on strength and grandeur in the first movement. The themes are presented in an orchestral introduction of considerable length: the delicate melody of the subsidiary idea is contrasted with the powerful steps of the main theme.

Allegro con brio

The energetic character of this theme reasserts itself towards the end of the orchestral introduction and forms the bridge to the piano's entry. After some powerful, preparatory runs, the pianist takes up the main idea and from then on he dominates the subsequent course of the allegro. The soloist is always the driving force in the interplay between the piano and the orchestra, and the extensive passage work, free from mere virtuosity, is filled with terrific expressive power. The second movement, largo, is a tender dream. The marvellous melodic writing contains all the scent and magic of romantic rapture. A hard orchestral chord leads to the rondo, which overflows with wanton wilfulness. The main theme, with its almost obstinate character, dominates the movement in a multitude of small variants. The whole movement is full of restless, sparkling life.

The *Concerto in G major*, opus 58, the fourth of Beethoven's piano concertos, had its première together with the *Fourth Symphony* in 1807. It was performed again, this time with Beethoven himself playing the piano part, in 1808, in the big Beethoven concert in the Theater an der Wien, in which the premières of the *Fifth* and *Sixth Symphonies* took place, and also the *Choral Fantasy*. Remarkably enough, these were the only two performances of this concerto in Beethoven's lifetime, which is almost incomprehensible since it is not only one of the most beautiful piano concertos in the repertoire, but also one of the most rewarding to play. It is a tone-poem of rare delicacy and feeling, but also with a great deal of fiery impetus. A lyrical, delicate line dominates the first movement, and it is only occasionally that it girds up its loins for a more powerful display; reflective reticence remains the basic mood. We are told that Beethoven modelled the second movement on Orpheus' plea in the underworld. The orchestra enters with the strings in octaves, hard and inexorable. Against this, one hears the quiet, pleading melody of the piano solo. The result is a profoundly moving conversation between the soloist and the orchestra: on the one side Orpheus' pleas, and on the other the adamant attitude of the spirits of the underworld. Gradually the hard rhythms in the orchestra reverberate into softness as the strong feeling of Orpheus' fervent prayer emerges victorious. The final movement takes up this idea with great joy: it is dominated by a very lively, animated theme with an almost march-like character. Needless to say, the vivacity and joy of the ideas is always elegantly harnessed.

The Concerto No. 5 in E-flat major, the *Emperor Concerto*, opus 73, completed in 1809, is still larger in concept and execution. Notice the opulence of the introduction! The soloist preludes the work with extended cadential figurations, as if taking stock of his instrument before the orchestra enters. Contrasted with the main theme, there is a strange subsidiary idea, first in the minor key, like

a distant funeral march, and then immediately afterwards in a quiet, affirmative major-key variant. The subsequent entry of the soloist is extremely effective: the main theme is reached by a chromatic run against the fading orchestra. The second theme is prepared with rare felicity: it appears first in a delicate *pianissimo* variant, and is then taken up by the orchestra in a very warlike tone. The character of the movement is determined by the element of animation, plunging ahead with great power, and this gives the soloist the opportunity to celebrate real triumphs of powerful virtuosity. The second movement has a dedicated flavour. The strings strike up a solemn song and the delicate piano theme descends as if from some luminous pinnacle, finding its way towards the other parts only by gradual degrees. Finally, the piano unites with the others and takes up the noble, song-like theme with free figurations. A step of a semitone in the orchestra introduces the last movement; the piano anticipates the theme of the finale, dawdles on a pause . . . and then the rondo theme bursts forth in all its frothy lustiness, with a remarkable, angular rhythm. The movement flows along in the most exuberant mood, brilliant and festive.

The *Triple Concerto for piano, violin and 'cello and orchestra*, opus 56, completed in 1806, is the least effective of Beethoven's concertos, and not very gratifying for the players. The first movement conveys the strongest impression, and the largo also strikes home, with its soulful song for the solo 'cello. But the closing rondo sounds really conventional: a not very interesting polonaise, despite a couple of charming details.

The last of Beethoven's piano concertos, the *Fantasy for piano, chorus and orchestra*, opus 80, already mentioned, has a special position among his works. Here he burst the formal bonds of the traditional piano concerto by introducing a chorus and dissolving to a large extent the usual three-movement allegro–adagio–allegro scheme. The fact that the chorus is utilized in the concerto makes the *Choral Fantasy* seem like a presentiment of the *Ninth Symphony*.

The strange work begins with a big prelude for the soloist. Beethoven improvised this at the première, working it out on paper only later when the work was to be published. The introduction to the *Choral Fantasy* is a rhapsodic dream for the piano, in which sombre colours predominate. Now gentle, now excited, this tone-painting achieves no particular shape; Beethoven leaves it open, with constant changes of mood.

The march rhythms emerge from the orchestral basses, at first as if from a distance. Gradually, other orchestral parts join in, until the horns and oboes break out with their bright cry. At this point the piano introduces the main theme of the work, a simple folk melody. The orchestra extends this melody and variations on it emerge from the variegated interplay of soloist and orchestra. The most important sections to be distinguished in these variations are a wildly excited C minor allegro, a tender, sensitive adagio, and finally a triumphal march. Then the march rhythms of the opening make themselves felt again, and this time they are answered by the chorus, who take up the main folk tune theme of the work with the words 'The harmony of our life sounds pleasing and lovely'. The chorus unfolds with great simplicity, ornamented with lively passage work from the piano. The graceful work ends with a brilliant *fortissimo*.

The *Missa Solemnis* rises like a gigantic peak among Beethoven's vocal works. Alongside this mighty work his other choral works seem of little importance, and they are hardly ever heard in the concert hall. The oratorio *Christ on the Mount of Olives*, written around 1801 but not performed until 1803, is one of the few pieces by Beethoven that were a great success in his lifetime, only to be forgotten by future generations. Apparently Beethoven himself did not have a very high opinion of this work, and there are certainly serious lapses concerning the text and form. The poet's feeling for the layout and structure of the text was quite operatic and he worked it out accordingly, thus determining the external shape of the work. Jesus becomes an operatic tenor singing beautiful arias, and Peter a blustering bass *buffo*; the Seraph passes the time in graceful ornamental song. This sort of version of the events in the garden of Gethsemane is hardly palatable to us nowadays. Of course, it would not be Beethoven if there were not some very impressive passages strewn along the way; one of these is the characteristic chorus of angels, and another is the atmospheric orchestral introduction right at the beginning of the oratorio, saturated with melancholy. These beautiful details, however, hardly tip the scales against the misconception of the total layout.

The *C major Mass* was written in 1807, and thus cannot be regarded as a piece of juvenilia, as can the *Christus Oratorio*. However, the monumental *Mass in D major*, written in 1823, put this work so much in the shade that it has slowly been forgotten just like the *Christus Oratorio*. The *C major Mass* is genuine Beethoven from the first note to the last. Although the traditional form is strictly adhered to, Beethoven's personal sensitivity and experience enlivens every detail. The motivic relationships between the individual main themes of the various sections are very remarkable, and the almost instrumental treatment of the voices is unique, anticipating the later *Missa Solemnis* and the *Ninth Symphony*. Taken as a whole the work is not difficult to understand, but it must have seemed very new and daring to his contemporaries, if a man like Prince Esterhazy—who had requested Beethoven to write the work, and who was musically a highly cultivated man—could say to Beethoven after the performance in his castle, 'But, my dear Beethoven, what have you been up to, writing this?'.

Beethoven's mightiest vocal work, the *Missa Solemnis in D major*, opus 123, is occasionally referred to, like the violin concerto, as the 'tenth symphony'. It is again not completely ridiculous, for the work is instrumentally conceived and the structure purely symphonic. Here is a brief outline of how the work came to be written. In 1818 Beethoven planned a new Mass to be ready in time for the enthronement of his pupil, the Archduke Rudolf, as Archbishop of Olmütz. But the work acquired such gigantic proportions that it was only finished in 1822, when the external motive for writing the work was long out of date. The forces he employs are four solo voices, chorus, orchestra and organ. For the most part the solo voices function as a closed ensemble, a sort of chorus of soloists juxtaposed to the full chorus. Independent *arioso* sections do not occur at all, and even instrumental introductions or interludes occur only where the textual scheme of ideas can properly accommodate them. Everything is subordinated to the formal symphonic structure in five giant movements: Kyrie, Gloria, Credo, Sanctus and Agnus Dei.

The Kyrie and the Gloria belong together in somewhat the same relation as the slow introduction and long allegro in the first movement of a symphony. Both parts are in D major, the main key of the work. The sublimity inherent in the concept of God's majesty is represented by the solemn grandeur of the opening theme. This is first played by the orchestra and then taken up by the chorus in three mighty outbreaks, interrupted each time by a call from a solo voice, comparable to a priest's intonation. The chorus then retains the lead with an unusual interchange of *forte* and *piano*, symbolizing the light-dark atmosphere of a church interior. The solo voices do not reassert themselves until their entry with the animated, melodic figuration of the delicate Christe Eleison. This plea is softer and milder; God's sublime grandeur gives way to the mild benevolence of the Redeemer. The chorus repeats the soloists' plea and the section fades away to *pianissimo*. And now God's majesty is asserted anew, as the solemn calls of the Kyrie rise and build up to a mighty climax, and disappear.

The Gloria is a mighty, soaring flight, a powerful, extended allegro movement. It starts with a great and joyful enunciation: 'Glory be to God on high'! This is followed by a *piano* chorus in the lower register to the words 'and peace on earth', a quiet, sublime subsidiary idea that is immediately followed by a repetition of the main theme, 'We praise Thee'. The 'Gratias Agimus Tibi' is another delicate interlude, and this becomes the starting point for the steep crescendo that culminates in the chorus' ecstatic cry of 'Pater Omnipotens'. For the first time in the score, with the full orchestra and the roar of the organ, Beethoven writes a *fortissimo* trombone chord. Everything is marked *fff* to give expression to the very highest ecstasy. The middle section, with its trembling 'Qui tollis peccata mundi, miserere nobis', forms a strict contrast to the first main section, immersed in happier emotions. This interlude flows like a still, quiet prayer. The majestic ideas of the opening are taken up again at the words 'Quoniam tu solus sanctus', laid out in the form of a grandiose fugue which builds up with ever-increasing breadth and power to a pitch of happy enthusiasm. The movement closes with great noise and jubilation after the re-entry of the Gloria theme.

In the huge building that is the Credo Beethoven retains the same clarity and concision of form. The formal subdivisions are not demarcated by exact recapitulations of the individual themes in these gigantically extended movements; the character of a sec-tion is determined rather by tonality and time-signature, or by cer-tain motifs, and the formal divisions are created by the recurrence of areas of similar mood. The orchestra's opening of the Credo is large and powerful, as are the following choral entries, 'I believe'. This is a confession of absolute faith in the power of God; it is belief in God in the most heroic sense. The middle section sub-divides into two smaller sections: first comes a turbulent adagio representing the sufferings of Christ, and then the radiant allegro for the Resurrection. 'Et incarnatus est' emerges in a psalmodic *pianissimo* from an almost mystical darkness. The solo voices give expression to the impassioned pain of the 'Crucifixus'. The section ends with the perplexed 'Passus sub Pontio Pilato' and the pro-foundly moving 'Sepultus est', where all the voices lose themselves in their lowest registers.

Hardly have the sounds of burial reverberated away into noth-ingness, than the tenor rises up with his luminous 'et resurrexit', which is taken over by the chorus in a radiant *a cappella* section. 'Ascendit in coelum' is expressed, as directly as in Bach, in sailing, ascending scales; triumphantly the song of jubilation unfolds in honour of the grandeur of the kingdom of heaven. And that brings us to the reprise of the main section: the Credo from the opening is sung by the individual choral parts in turn, with profound con-viction, and alongside it, in a psalmodic tone, runs the text of the confession of faith. The music builds up slowly, reaching its peak with the words, 'et expecto resurrectionem mortuorum'. This is followed by the mighty coda of this giant movement: the fugue on the final words of the creed, 'et vitam venturi saeculi, amen'. As if wishing to present the highest form that the promise of ever-lasting life could take, Beethoven constructs a form that makes the greatest imaginable demands both on the performers and the audience. It is only with the entry of the solo quartet in the trans-figured Amen at the end of the choral fugue that oil is poured on the mighty motions of the choral masses. This breathtaking tone-painting ends on a note of total unreality, like a dim pinnacle in an azure haze.

Beethoven's Sanctus constitutes a decisive departure from the usual mode of presentation. Everything in the Sanctus is merely a preparation, or frame, for the Benedictus, which Beethoven sees as the kernel of the Sanctus. The introductory Sanctus is devotional and followed by two short fugues, 'Pleni sunt coeli et terra gloria tua' and 'Osanna in excelsis'. At this point Beethoven inserts an orchestral prelude to prepare the way for the miracle that is to come. A mysterious devotional melody appears in the remarkably matt instrumental mixture of low flutes and violas; in holy trepidation it collapses into the depths and disappears. There is not a sound. From ethereal heights descends the delicate sound of the solo violin, supported by two high flutes. Against this, the choral basses intone the opening words of the Benedictus, 'Blessed be he that cometh in the name of the Lord', in a restrained psalmodic tone. The solo violin floats up to the heights again with a melody of unimaginable, weightless grace, prophesying the blessed message, and retains the lead right through the progressive entries of the vocal parts—soloists first—in a timid *piano*. Now another 'Osanna in excelsis' is folded in, full of joyful certainty: the prophecy has been fulfilled. The delicate song of the solo violin floats up once more into the heights from whence it came.

The Agnus Dei represents an even more radical departure from tradition than the Sanctus. The few words of text, 'Agnus Dei, qui tollis peccata mundi, miserere nobis. Dona nobis pacem', inspired Beethoven to develop a tone-painting of enormous proportions to form the gigantic ending to a giant work. An ardent prayer forms the introduction; the bass soloist raises his voice, the male chorus repeats his words, and then the other solo and choral voices join in. Dully the chorus pleads 'Miserere nobis', and the following 'dona nobis pacem' sounds like a message from heaven. The parts intermingle in a fugal texture and then unite for a short, harmonious *a cappella* section, that is to recur later on, sung by the quartet of soloists. Rumbling timpani strokes, anxious string figures and trumpet-calls constitute a warning as to the interim nature of this peace, and once again are heard the perplexed cries for help: 'miserere nobis'. The threatening forces disappear as suddenly as they came when they hear the solo soprano's troubled call; the joyful message of the 'dona pacem' is repeated by the solo voices

and powerfully taken up by the chorus. But peace is not yet assured:
a wild orchestral fugato starts up, with various orchestral groups
battling together. Once more the danger is averted by the passionate cry to the Agnus Dei (Lamb of God) for help, and peace now
settles finally over the land. The fervent harmonies of the *a cappella*
section, first timidly suggested in *piano*, glow now with an inner
radiance; the orchestra lends its support and the *Missa Solemnis*
ends on a note of solemn grandeur.

CARL MARIA VON WEBER

born Eutin 18 November 1786
died London 5 June 1826

The son of a theatrical impresario, Weber became acquainted with
the life of the stage at quite an early age. In 1804 he was already
leader of the theatre orchestra in Breslau, but by 1806 he had sunk
to the post of music teacher at the court of the Prince of Württem-
berg in Stuttgart. His unstable life took him from place to place,
but at last in 1813 he got the job of leader at the Landestheater in
Prague, and by 1817 he was in a position to take over the direction
of the German Opera in Dresden. He received his musical education
at the hands of Michael Haydn in Salzburg, and later he studied
with the famous Abbé Vogler in Vienna and Darmstadt. Weber's
early works—several operas, two symphonies, some songs and
piano pieces—did not attract very much attention. But the première of *Der Freischütz* in Berlin in 1821 turned out an unprecedented success, and thereafter the composer's name was on everybody's lips. It was chiefly on account of its unfavourable text that
Euryanthe was not very widely acclaimed in Vienna in 1823.
Oberon, which Weber wrote for London, turned out to be his
swansong. He lived to direct the première there in April 1826, but
shortly afterwards he succumbed to an infection of the lung. In
1844 Richard Wagner had Weber's body brought back to Dresden.

Weber's name goes down in history as the creator of romantic
opera. In his best works, a new musical world raises its head; the
forces of nature, the elements, come to life in this music. Demonic
ghosts and supernatural forces are unleashed and the vitality and
sensuousness of the romantic perception of nature takes musical

shape. It was the work of great genius to find such a telling expression of nature, and in doing so Weber found it necessary to make drastic revisions in the field of orchestral sound, of instrumentation. The conscious exploitation of the characteristic sound of the individual instruments of the orchestra and the individual use of the various registers of the instruments, the low notes of the flute or the clarinet, for example, every effect to be found in romantic orchestral music—and the romantic orchestra hardly exceeded Beethoven's in size—can be traced back to Weber. He opened up a new world to music, an enchanted world in the truest sense of the word.

Weber was a dramatist through and through, and consequently his most significant work was in the field of opera; his symphonies have been almost entirely forgotten. His operatic overtures, on the other hand, have come to occupy a prominent and honourable position in all our concert programmes. Weber's great overtures are not only introductory music for the operas, whose moods they intimate so ideally; they are symphonic poems, perfectly complete in themselves.

The *Freischütz Overture* must be one of the best-known works in the whole literature of music, especially in Germany. Hearts are opened at the first sounds of the adagio introduction; souls are flooded with blessed mystery at the entry of the horn melody. 'Never was there a more German musician,' says Wagner of Weber, and in another place, 'O my wonderful German homeland, how I love you, how you fill me with enthusiasm, even if only for the fact that *Der Freischütz* was written on German soil.' Hans Pfitzner writes, 'The heart of *Der Freischütz* is that indescribably fervent and acute ear for nature; the main character of *Der Freischütz* is the German woods'.

The slow introduction to the *Freischütz Overture* is a masterful portrayal of nature: the sounds of the horns, rising out of a delicate

pianissimo, go straight to the heart, evoking the woods at dusk. A gloomy *tremolo*, a dull thumping of the kettledrums, and the peaceful mood is banished. The 'cellos sigh; there is an uncanny burst of orchestral sound which dwindles into *pianissimo*.

The passionate allegro opens with a feeling of the closeness of dark, stormy weather. Steeply, the wild excitement reaches its climax and then comes a radiant horn chord, in the dwindling reverbèrations of which, above a *tremolo* in the strings, the clarinet fades in with its happy melody, full of the promise of bright trans-

figuration. Disturbing and anxious elements attempt once more to

come to the fore but the mood of gloom and fear is successfully suppressed, and the second theme is free to pour out the sweetness of its lovely melody. In the development section the forces of dark-

ness again take the upper hand; the delicate second theme, which shyly pokes its head out on two occasions, is brusquely shown the door by the threatening trombones.

The reprise opens in a mood of passionate animation, but after a restless build-up, the first theme breaks off abruptly. A *tremolo* shudders gloomily and the violins sigh. An expressive repetition in the 'cellos leads to complete calm. Then, with overwhelming effect, comes the final hymn, the rejoicing song of the second theme.

The *Euryanthe Overture* is the perfect expression of the romanticism of noble knights. In the first few bars we are straight away transported into the world of medieval romance by the bold and passionate swing of the introductory string passages and by the noble gravity of the march-like theme in the winds. The first thematic group is developed with gripping momentum, after which a delicate bridge by the 'cellos leads into that wonderful melody, the love-song of a Minnesänger, a melody filled with the most

profound feeling and yet with a really courtly flavour. The animated rhythms of the main theme reassert themselves. The middle section of the overture is clothed in supernatural darkness: the mysterious string sounds emerge from a delicate, reserved *pianissimo* and brush by us like a breath from the beyond. Then, by way of a lead-back, we hear a march theme in the bass, which builds up

rapidly into a fugato and culminates in the radiant rejoicing of the reprise of the main theme. Afterwards we hear the wonderful love-song once more, but this time in all the glory of the full orchestra, and this forms the climax of this unforgettable overture.

The *Oberon Overture* (1826) is also quite unique in its perfection. The big allegro section is preceded by a slow introduction in which we stray through the fairy world of the elves; the sound of Oberon's

horn forms the key to this magic realm. The forest rustles and the elves whisper amongst themselves, a little march is played, goblins hobble by, and the rustling of the woods swells up again in the sound of the lower strings. But our romantic dreams are abruptly shattered as we find ourselves in the allegro, which begins by depicting Huon, the hero of the opera, battling with the various

dangers that beset him; his love for Rezia guides him in all things.
We hear a fervent melody played by the clarinet, which is to be-

come his guiding star, and from the strings—first timidly, but with

increasing strength—we hear Rezia's love-call: 'My Huon, my
husband'. But there are still a few adventures in store, and the
various themes line up antagonistically. The fervent feeling of the
motif of Huon's longing overcomes all obstacles and the animated
ending is reached with unquenchable confidence of victory, the
whole jubilantly crowned by Rezia's love-song.

The *Jubel Overture* is an extremely effective piece written by
Weber on the occasion of a celebration in the royal palace. After a
solemn introduction symbolizing honour and respect for the king
comes a driving presto of jubilant celebration. Formally, the presto
is marvellously clear; two contrasting themes are introduced in the
exposition, to be juxtaposed and combined in the development
section. After the reprise, which ends with a brilliant *fortissimo*, the
full orchestra intones 'God save the King' with a solemn grandeur
that is quite breathtaking.

The *Preziosa Overture* stands out from among Weber's smaller
overtures—which are all possessed of great atmosphere and charm—
as a real museum piece. The scene is set in the introduction: an
extended bolero, whose characteristic rhythm is forcefully underlined by the strings, leaves no room for doubt about the locality of

the drama. We are in Spain. Now in the distance we hear a little gypsy march in the woodwind accompanied by triangle, drum and tambourine. This gypsy melody becomes the main theme of the

allegro that follows. A delicate song appears as a contrast, but in such a stormy development section it is unable to hold its own against the returning gypsy rhythms that lead back for the reprise and on to the jubilant close of this sparkling little piece.

Weber's overtures constitute the transition to romantic *instrumental* music as distinct from music for the stage. The tone-painterly aspect, the programmatic side of his overtures, was the most important contribution to the break-through to programme music, to the symphonic poems of Liszt and Berlioz. There is virtually no trace of this new spirit of romanticism in Weber's symphonies, which are definitely to be regarded as juvenilia. Understandably, these conventionally classical symphonies have lapsed into obscurity, and his piano concertos have gone the same way, though their brilliant piano writing and occasional melodic beauties make them quite effective and graceful to play. The smaller *Concert piece in F minor*, on the other hand, a piece of pure programme music, has always been very popular. It consists of three relatively short movements, played without a break: there is a first movement, allegro, preceded by an introductory larghetto of some length; then comes a march as the middle section, played by the orchestra alone, and finally an extremely lively and virtuoso finale. Weber provided a complete programme for this: the lady of the castle is sitting on the balcony looking out into the distance, her heart filled with melancholy foreboding. Her knight has been away in the Holy Land for years; will she ever see him again? (Introduction). In a vision she sees him being slaughtered and lying dead on the field of battle (allegro passionato). But what is that sound in the distance? Nearer and nearer come the horsemen and pages, all bearing the sign of the cross (orchestral march), and the lovers fall into each other's arms amid general rejoicing (finale). The work is laid out like a big operatic scene, with the piano taking over the function of the voice part. The expressive thematic work and the brilliance of the piano writing guarantee the work its success.

Weber's concertos for clarinet and orchestra have also survived, though their admirers are chiefly to be found in academic conservatoire circles. The reason for this is perhaps to be sought in the relatively conventional layout of the concertos; the operatic charm of the concert piece just described is lacking, and with it the most substantial aspect of Weber's genius.

FRANZ SCHUBERT

born Lichtenthal 31 January 1797
died Vienna 19 November 1828

Schubert's short life was marred by constant, and understandable, anxiety about his syphilitic condition and also by recurrent periods of poverty, but his friends and the music that was in him made it rich and well worth living. For a time he applied himself to helping his father as teacher in the Volkschule, but soon he gave up all thoughts of a steady job and devoted himself entirely to composition. This one decade in which he cultivated his talent produced a miraculous harvest. He left over six hundred songs, the most wonderful music for piano and a lot of chamber music, not to mention eight symphonies, seventeen overtures, Masses, operas and choral works.

The flood of Schubert's work and his tremendous industry are only to be compared with Mozart's ease and naturalness in composition. In Schubert's mind everything becomes music; everything he touches seems to sing; every poem he likes is already half-way to being a song. His refinement in the art of writing *lieder* is mirrored in his instrumental music, where each feeling conjures up a thousand possibilities of expression. The vocality of his instrumental melodies, his irridescent feeling for harmony, the rhythmic declamation of his themes, everything he does betrays his mastery of the *lied*. Thus Schubert's instrumental music also develops its own free individuality; the Austrian vocal tradition is carried along and developed concurrently, and even Hungarian folk elements are to be found in his works. There is a wonderful bloom on Schubert's sound, every note pulsates with a warm current of feeling, and—as did Weber—Schubert shows us the magic of the romantic world of sound.

Schubert wrote eight symphonies, of which the last two are so immeasurably greater than the rest that the others are usually considered insignificant. In some cases this is a very mistaken judgement. The first two, the *Symphony in D major*, written in 1813 when Schubert was sixteen years old, and the *Symphony in B-flat major*, written in 1816, are dependent to a large extent on Schubert's great classical predecessors, but they are not to be dismissed as juvenilia. Sir Thomas Beecham's recordings have revealed more individuality in the works than had hitherto been suspected.

The *D major Symphony*, to be sure, is fairly conventional; the inventive schoolboy nags at his material for something interesting, but does not have sufficient poise to sustain it when he chances on it. However, the finale is a lively, sparkling movement. Is it possible that Schubert, having written a movement, was occasionally left unsatisfied in some way, perhaps by a lack of musical solidity, and that this spurred him on to write the most important music in the codas?

The *Symphony No. 2 in B-flat major* represents a substantial gain in assurance and control. The introductory largo leads us from heavy chords into *pianissimo* for the light-footed violin figure of

the vivace. Here Schubert's imagination drives him and leads him at the same time and the movement is successful. The andante is again reactionary, though beautiful, but the last two movements pick up the momentum of the first, and the final presto vivace builds up a compelling rhythm which encourages the young composer to depart from the accepted canons of his musical forebears.

His *Symphony No. 3 in D major* again betrays the influence of classicism, but in its freshness of invention it is superior to the two earlier symphonies. Schubert wrote this symphony in one go: all four movements were written within a fortnight, and this free-flowing work is very noticeable in the piece. Over the whole is an atmosphere of leisured gaiety, never letting a sombre tone come to the surface, except for a few serious and warning passages in the slow introduction. The development of the first allegro contains hints of dramatic development, but they remain only modest hints.

The central movements are especially charming: an allegretto full
of delicate grace and a boisterous scherzo (which Schubert still calls
a minuet), for which the trio is a simple and lovable *ländler*. The
final presto dances away, led by an exuberant theme in the rhythm
of the tarantella.

The *Symphony No. 5 in B-flat major* possesses the same *joie de
vivre*, and Schubert wrote this one, too, in only a few weeks, in the
autumn of 1816. The size of the orchestra—besides strings, there is
only one flute, and two each of oboes, bassoons and horns—derives
from the fact that Schubert wrote the piece for an amateur orchestra that used to play in his father's house occasionally. But consequently Schubert was able to hear this symphony, whereas the
others, with the possible exception of the *First*, were never played.
It is a scandal and an undying cause for shame that Schubert's great
symphonies, even the *Unfinished*, had to wait decades after their
composer's death before they were performed.

In its fresh thematic work and the unworried stream of its development, the *B-flat major Symphony* is reminiscent of Haydn's spirit.
But the pregnant forms and the layout of its development sections
lean more towards Beethoven. The atmosphere of charm is set
right at the start with the *pianissimo* wind chords and the delicate
theme enunciated by the violins after a short run up, then echoed
bar for bar by the basses. The vocal second theme emerges significantly from the animated main idea. Everything, even the clearly
demarcated development section, is kept very brief; indeed the
whole movement is over all too soon. The 'andante con moto' is
laid out on a somewhat larger scale, the simple grace of its theme
being modelled on similar movements in Haydn. The subsidiary
theme, on the other hand, strikes a very romantic note: the accompaniment rustles intimately, and the violins and oboe play a delicate
duet in which the flute, sweetly languishing, also engages. The
minuet is very austere in the minor key, with its *ländler*-like trio in
the light and friendly major. The theme of the final presto could
also have been written by Haydn; the movement, which is short
and charged like the first allegro, is dominated by a feeling of
uninhibited gaiety.

Schubert later called his Symphony No. 4 the *Tragic Symphony*;
this is the one in C minor, written in 1816, between the two happier
symphonies in D major and B-flat major respectively. The symphony is not really tragic in a Beethovenian sense, however, much
Schubert may have striven for Beethovenian greatness, particularly

in the outside movements. The adagio introduction to the first movement is perhaps the most moving part of the work, with its melancholy, resigned suspensions and syncopations. The following allegro is then, unfortunately, rather conventional. The andante has a noble theme, but Schubert spends too much time on it; the scherzo is striking and original, but its trio is rather colourless. The last movement is very similar to the first, both in feeling and structure. Here again we find the break-through from the darkness of C minor into a bright C major, but the darkness is far removed from that demonic darkness that we find in similar movements in Beethoven.

The *Symphony No. 6 in C major*, sometimes called the 'Small C major Symphony', is incomparably greater. It was completed in 1818 and can be regarded as a transitional work. Schubert's individuality is noticeable in many details: in the treatment of the wind (they become an independent body), and in the polyphonic layout of the development sections, and particularly in the remarkable growth of harmonic richness. What is astonishing is the fact that the thematic work is still very dependent on his great predecessors. It is only in the middle movements that we encounter the real Schubert: in the song-like andante, handled almost like a piece of chamber music, and in the very characteristic and interesting scherzo. The big allegros, though powerful and brilliantly effective, are still rooted in the classical spirit. Only very occasionally do we hear traces of romanticism in, for instance, the delicately spun subsidiary idea of the first allegro.

There is no other work in the literature of great symphonic music that has achieved such unprecedented popularity as Schubert's Symphony No. 8 in B minor, universally referred to as the *Unfinished Symphony*. 'Unfinished', because it consists of only two movements; there exist sketches for a scherzo, but Schubert never took it up again. He laid the fair copy of the score of the first two movements on one side, thinking he could not continue the symphony, despite the fact that he was at the peak of his creative strength at this time and great works ran uninterruptedly from his pen. Today these two movements seem wonderfully complete in themselves, a perfect miracle, and Schubert himself may have considered this juxtaposition of the two movements and the perfect balance between the contrasted moods to be complete, even though it represented such a radical deviation from the normal four-movement scheme of symphonic form.

The first movement is headed 'allegro moderato'. Out of mysterious depths of gloom there emerges a burning question from the

basses, and in a tone of sensuous longing the oboe and clarinet in unison intone the answer over the delicate whirring of the violins.

A sudden twist introduces the wonderful 'cello melody that is so familiar to us all. But the mood of transfigured melancholy that

flows from this melody is not long sustained and the fateful question of the opening raises its head again. This leads to a grand, dramatic build-up of the emotion of suffering, after which the reentrance of the two main ideas recreates the melancholy mood. This wonderful movement expresses a great mournful plaint that moves us to the inmost depths of our being. The radiant clarity of the 'andante con moto' forms a beautiful contrast to the first movement. There are melodies of unearthly beauty that take us into walks of the soul that are of an eternal purity and a divine equilibrium. It is the radiant balance achieved by Schubert in setting this movement against the melancholy elegy of the first movement that gives the work its wonderful, self-contained quality, the finished perfection that is peculiar to this unique *Unfinished Symphony*.

It was in 1822, six years before his death, that the twenty-five-year-old Schubert performed the miracle of composition that is this B minor symphony. The manuscript lay unremarked for four decades before someone dug it up and arranged a performance of it. It took some time after that for the work to be recognized as a true masterpiece of Austrian symphonic music.

The *Unfinished* is generally thought of as Schubert's eighth symphony, and the great *C major Symphony*, which was composed much later, is always referred to as his seventh. This muddle has been taken over by all the important editions of Schubert's works. The *C major Symphony* is not only Schubert's last symphony, it is the crowning glory of his symphonic works. He completed this masterpiece in 1828, only a few months before his death. Schubert's contemporaries did not recognize the greatness and significance of the work and the Viennese Society of Friends of Music declined to perform it on the grounds that it was bombastic and difficult to understand. So Schubert never heard this either, his symphonic masterpiece. It took no less a man than Robert Schumann to discover the work, ten years later, and ten years after the composer's death, amongst Schubert's papers. Schumann immediately recognized the value of the work and wrote an enthusiastic and impressive article in the Leipzig musical journal, whereupon the symphony was played in the Leipzig Gewandhaus in 1839. Then, once and for all, the *C major Symphony* assumed its rightful place beside the symphonic masterpieces of the classical period. Schumann's remark about the 'heavenly length' of Schubert's instrumental movements has often been quoted in connection with the *C major Symphony*, and certainly the four movements of the symphony are laid out on an extraordinarily grand scale. Sometimes it has been the custom to perform a shortened version.

The symphony is preceded by a big introduction: the horns enunciate a marvellous, genuinely romantic theme—hesitating be-

tween the major and minor key—that is like a questioning of fate. The woodwinds repeat the melody, the 'cellos prolong it until it achieves a mighty extension in the strings and trombones. The winds intone the theme once again, *piano*, decorated with triplets in the violins, and then, with a radiant crescendo, pass on to the allegro. The strings strike up with a proud, knightly motif, which

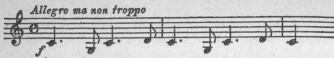

is taken up each time by the woodwinds with bright triplet figures. This rushes on with youthful vigour until the oboes and bassoons in thirds introduce the second theme, somewhat reserved to start with. But this becomes more and more dance-like until it bubbles

with uninhibited gaiety. The development is romantically myste- rious; the themes are woven into one another and together they swing up to luminous peaks of sound. Then the trombones raise their voices warningly; it is a motif from the big theme of the introduction that they are intoning. This passage is overwhelming in its effect, but it is perhaps even surpassed at the end of the move- ment, when the wonderful theme of the introduction is heard in all its magnificence; this time its powerful grandeur represents the answer to the reserved question that the same theme seemed to pose when played by the horns at the opening.

The second movement, 'andante con moto', offers a colourful cascade of charmingly contrasted melodies, each more expressive than the last. The grace of the main theme makes way for the fire

of the subsidiary melody, and the central group is delicate and sen- sitive. Schubert achieves an effect that is simply magical when, at the end of this second thematic group, the horn answers the strings, calling as if from the far distance and creating the dreamiest mood imaginable. The melodies of the first thematic group present themselves again, and this time the fiery subsidiary idea is able to come more into the foreground, and the whole rises to great heights of impassioned grandeur. By a delicate, unmistakably Schubertian stroke, the 'cellos find the transition, in a variant of

the main theme, to the lovely dreamy world of the second thematic
group. The graceful main idea appears once more at the end of this
very extended movement; Schubert finds it almost impossible to
abandon this melody and the ending is postponed time and time
again. But he succeeds finally, and first in the brass, then in the
woodwind, *pianissimo* chords close the movement on a note of
gentle melancholy.

The scherzo opens in the strings, rough and rusticated. Loosely

and decoratively, the woodwinds vary the idea and throw a bridge
over to a happy, swinging *ländler* melody that is taken up ecstati-
cally by the violins. An enchanting game evolves out of the contrast,

and one priceless idea supplants another. The trio is especially effective: the overflowing fervour of its song-like theme is comparable
with the best of Schubert's songs. The finale opens with a stormy
Reveille, and the storm shows no sign of abating; the movement

rushes along in rollicking triplets and excited dotted rhythms, impatient, irresistible and full of joyful anticipation. The broad, flowing second theme, bringing fulfilment, offers warmth, comfort and
security after the tumult of the first thematic group. The lovely
melody is entrusted to the woodwind, and the strings soon provide

an accompaniment of mysterious rustlings which rushes by and fades like the beating of enormous fairy wings. This finale rises to festive brilliance in the long development section and again in the coda. Despite its gargantuan proportions, this movement is beautifully balanced, and its unquenchable zest forms a fitting close to this great symphony.

Of Schubert's numerous overtures, some written for stage works, some purely for concert overtures, it is really only the *Rosamunde Overture* that has survived the test of time. Schubert wrote it in 1820 for the melodrama *The Magic Harp*, but he later used it as music for the drama *Rosamunde*. It is obvious from this fact alone that Schubert was not following any particular programmatic idea such as you find in Beethoven or Weber; it is simply a beautiful piece of music of a gay kind, expressing the happy tension of joyful anticipation. After a short andante introduction, in which the soulful melody is taken first by the oboes and later by the violins, we pass straight on to a very swift allegro. Three typical comedy themes are strung together and, without getting involved in a development, these are repeated after a short lead-back, and the unproblematic piece ends with a brilliant coda. The work owes its deservedly great popularity to its enchanting melodic ideas.

It is an amazing fact, considering the decisive activity of Beethoven and Mozart in this form, that Schubert showed no interest at all in the concerto. The only concert piece he left is a little *Rondo for violin and string orchestra*, written for some specific occasion. However, it is a very charming and successful piece. After a slow, pretty introduction the *Rondo* enters with lively freshness. The constant exchange between the two gay and gracious themes and a lyrical subsidiary melody creates a very animated movement. All Schubert's lovable peculiarities find expression in the little work: the grace and fervour of his melodies and the dance-like animation of his rhythms. The *Rondo* exudes the magic of unspoiled youth: it is light and unproblematic, and expresses an unmistakable feeling of happiness.

Another occasional work of Schubert's, the *Sonata for arpeggione and piano*, has been arranged by the Spanish 'cellist Gaspar Cassadó as a *Concerto for 'cello and orchestra*. In 1823 the Viennese instrument maker Georg Stauffer had built a stringed instrument with a sound not unlike the gamba, which he called the arpeggione. Schubert wrote his sonata in 1824, probably to please Stauffer, though it may have been a commission. We do not know if the piece was ever played at that time.

The concerto has the usual three movements, the first of which, however, is lyrical in character. The main theme, which is extremely noble and beautiful, is played first by the orchestra and then by the soloist, with great richness of figuration. A rhythmic subsidiary idea forms the bridge to the second theme, also very song-like. The development section sees a more animated type of movement, in which the solo instrument plays a large part, though its activity never deteriorates into mere virtuosity. A long cadenza for the soloist then leads back to the reprise. The final bars of this first allegro are particularly charming: first the wind and then the solo 'cello take their leave with one last earnest little melody.

The second movement is kept very simple: the 'cello sings a Schubertian *lied*, whose cantilena fades finally into *pianissimo*. A sharply rising figure then takes us straight into the last movement. This rondo is possessed of really magical charm. The graceful rocking motion of the main idea, which always appears in a reserved *piano*, is contrasted with two secondary themes. Of these, the striking staccato theme in the minor key with its charming echo effects is especially impressive. It is obvious that Cassadó had to change some things and reshape others when he arranged the arpeggione sonata for 'cello and orchestra. But with the sureness of touch of the tasteful and refined musician, everything he has done is quite successful and perfectly in accord with Schubert's spirit.

Schubert wrote six Masses. The first four are really juvenilia, happily melodic, but without deeper significance. The *Mass in A-flat major*, completed in 1822, is much stronger. But Schubert's last, the *Mass in E-flat major*, is still more personal in feeling and structure. He wrote it shortly before his death, at about the same time as he was working on the great *C major Symphony*. Fundamentally, the *Mass* is very lyrical in feeling; the world of the great master of the *lied* is recognizable in countless features in the work.

The beginning of the Kyrie is plunged in mystical darkness; the basses thump restlessly against the solemn chords of the trombones, and the voices enter *pianissimo*. The Christe Eleison is bright and stirring with its luminous triplet accompaniment. Coming after the powerful middle section, the return of the mystical Kyrie is particularly effective. This time the Kyrie is spun out to a greater length until, after a glowing climax, it dies away to nothing. The unaccompanied chorus opens the Gloria powerfully; all is joy and rejoicing. Only at the words 'adoramus te' does the enthusiasm die down and give way to depression. The 'gratias agimus tibi' forms an earnest and devout interlude, with an expressive melody. The second part of the Gloria is characterized by solemn grandeur: there is a formidable *forte* entry for the trombones, with the strings' passionate *tremolo* as a backcloth; the male voices of the chorus enunciate the words 'domine deus, agnus dei' in fibrous octaves. The form is completed when the 'quoniam tu solus sanctus' takes up the main theme of the Gloria once more. For the words 'cum sancto spiritu' Schubert writes a large choral fugue as a coda to the Gloria, and the overwhelming swell of the Amen constitutes the climax of the movement.

The beginning of the Credo casts us back into the mysterious depths of the Kyrie: dull rolls from the kettledrum and the *pizzicato* notes of the basses underline the mystery of the confession of faith; as before, the chorus is strictly homophonic. The Incarnatus episode, sung by the quartet of soloists, is of a truly moving loveliness. The Crucifixus is filled with gloomy passion, the Resurrexit powerful and radiant with its lively succession of joyful entries. This forms the bridge to the final fugue, sung, in accord with tradition, to the words 'et vitam venturi saeculi'.

The adagio of the Sanctus is overwhelming in its explosive dynamism. The cry to God takes place at a *fortissimo* level and is followed immediately by a sudden *pianissimo*. The melodic writing in the Benedictus, again sung by the solo quartet alone, is of an unearthly delicacy. This lovely episode is framed by the powerful swing of the Osanna fugato. But it is the final movement of the Mass, the Agnus Dei, that conveys the strongest impression. The bass begins it, plaintively, supported by the trombones, with restless syncopations in the background. The theme is reminiscent of a motif in the wonderful Doppelgänger song, and the mood is similar. From the depths of depression Schubert struggles for grace. But the 'Dona Nobis Pacem' is full of promise, and the discouragement of the preceding plaint is successfully vanquished; the plea for peace gains steadily in confidence. The desperate mood of the Doppelgänger makes another attempt, but it soon has to give way to this irresistibly peaceful mood. At the end, where it rises to a radiant *fortissimo*, this longing for peace is filled with a strength that is positively passionate.

ROBERT SCHUMANN

born Zwickau 8 June 1810
died Endenich, near Bonn 29 July 1856

Originally educated for the law, it was only in 1830 that Robert Schumann was able to devote all his time to the study of music. The renowned piano pedagogue Friedrich Wieck became his teacher. But he had to abandon his career as a pianist when he lamed the fingers of his right hand by his unnatural habits of practice. In 1834 he started a *New Journal of Music* which developed under his guidance into the leading musical paper of the time. He wrote assiduously in the support of musical romanticism; his articles were very spirited and not a little sharp in criticism. In 1837 he became engaged to Clara Wieck, the daughter of his teacher, and they were married in 1840, against the will of her father. Clara Schumann developed into the most important pianist of her day, and proved to be the ideal interpreter of her husband's compositions. Schumann, despite his unchallengeable reputation as a composer, was unable to find his feet professionally; at the end he tried unsuccessfully for a conducting job in Düsseldorf, but already at this stage he was suffering from a disease of the brain. In 1854, in a fit of depression, he tried to drown himself in the Rhine, but he was saved and had to spend the last two years of his life in total darkness in a lunatic asylum.

In the critical writings of the last few decades, musical romanticism has been very out of favour. Goethe's remark 'feeling is everything', which was to become a slogan of romanticism, is almost irritating to our too sober sensibilities. We are misled into referring to exuberance of feeling as stupor or giddiness, we confuse sensibility with weakness, and sometimes we go so far as to deny that Schumann, the chief figure of musical romanticism, possessed any strength of passion at all. Schumann can afford to be temporarily misunderstood; his very real genius will easily survive such periods of obscurity. His music is certainly filled with a superabundance of feeling, and with a sensibility not previously encountered. But besides this, Schumann had a truly battling nature, which finds constant expression in his work. What power there is in his rhythmic writing, what passion in his climaxes and outbreaks, and what colossal and enthralling grandeur is represented by the structure of his thought. How much the poorer our musical heritage would be without Schumann's life-work and his influence, which has been active right up to the present day.

Schumann's greatness as a man, particularly the battling side of his character, is admirably documented in his passionate articles in favour of Chopin, and later in favour of Brahms, whose career was considerably smoothed by Schumann's mediation. His compositions for the piano are, of course, his most individual and unmistakable works; he made this field peculiarly his own and it is not for nothing that all the works written in the first decade of his creative activity were for this instrument. It is quite extraordinary the way he is constantly stimulated afresh by the instrument, and is always discovering fresh aspects of it for exploitation. His most beautiful works are for the piano; only his later songs can compare with them. What is amazing is how little his imagination was fired by the orchestra as a medium; his compositions in this field fall far short of his piano works. In his piano compositions his mode of expression can be refined down to the lightest difference of shading in the sound, whereas his orchestral style is remarkably dry, the works themselves somewhat uniform and the instrumentation very unromantic. Seen in this context it is only to be expected that Schumann's best orchestral work is not purely orchestral, but in the form of the piano concerto, and such a concerto as takes its place, amongst Beethoven's last concertos and the two by Brahms, at the summit of all piano concertos.

The *Concerto for piano in A minor*, opus 54, is one of the great climaxes of Schumann's career. Everything that appeals to us in Schumann is brought together here with the highest degree of perfection: the wonderful melodic style, the bold, virile rhythmic structure of his ideas, the richness, imagination and clarity of the layout of the movements and, not least, the marvellous piano writing. The most beautiful aspect of all is undoubtedly his never-failing melodic strength. The melodies are so remarkably unified as to style that one hardly realizes what a cornucopia of great ideas the work contains. The first movement is the largest; it is a typical Schumann movement in that the two poles of his world of ideas are combined in complete harmony. The contrasting elements confront each other straight away within the first few bars of the first theme, as the fiery strength manifested in the first outburst from the solo instrument is answered by the emotional and luxuriant cantilena in the woodwind. The luxuriant tone occasionally gets the upper hand, but the powerful, knightly motif prevails more

and more as the movement progresses and at the end, after the
piano's wonderful cadenza, it embraces everything in its spell,
even—by a bold rhythmic transformation—the emotional main
theme.

The second movement is gentle and gracious, in the form of a
short intermezzo. The wonderful song of the 'cellos in the middle

section, dreamily ornamented by the piano, is particularly beautiful. A note of melancholy nostalgia creeps in at the end of this
movement where the orchestra refers gently to the main theme of
the first movement. Immediately, the piano breaks through into
the powerful world of the last movement. As in the first movement, Schumann draws on an apparently inexhaustible reservoir
of ideas. Just when you think the movement is about to end, a new
idea is taken up leading to a new climax; the solo instrument shines
with even greater brilliance, and leads the work on to its breathtaking close. There is one place in the last movement, where the
second theme appears, which is quite electrifying: a memorable
march-like theme in the orchestra is superposed on the original
metre which is continued in the piano part. This rhythmic-metric
game has an almost enervating charm.

Schumann's other concert works cannot scale the heights conquered in the piano concerto. The *Violin Concerto*, published eighty
years after the composer's death, has had no more success than the
Fantasy for violin and orchestra, and even the *Concert pieces for piano
and orchestra* have been completely forgotten, although the first of
these, in G minor, includes some lovely details. The *Concerto in A
major for 'cello and orchestra* (1850), on the other hand, is a brilliant
work, though not so perfect as the piano concerto. It is certainly

the most significant 'cello concerto of the classical-romantic period,
and, after Dvořák's, the most frequently performed and popular
work in this genre.

Firmly rooted in the usual three-movement form, allegro–
adagio–allegro, Schumann's *'Cello Concerto* nevertheless departs
from it in that the movements are played without a break, thus
forming a single long movement. The soloist is in the foreground
throughout the work, right from the first bars where he introduces
the beautifully vocal theme. The work makes great demands on
the soloist's technique and intonation, especially in the high register,
and the writing is highly virtuoso, in the best sense. The possibilities of the instrument are valued and exploited, but empty passage work and merely effective cadential writing is strictly shunned.
The musical climax of the work is the slow middle section; the
melody is the purest Schumann, infused with romantic warmth.
The last movement is lively and brilliant; the excitable main idea
is contrasted with a vocal subsidiary idea that is rich in interplay
between the soloist and the woodwind. A large-scale cadenza forms
the effective close of the work.

Schumann's *Symphony No. 1 in B-flat major*, opus 38, was also
his first work for orchestra. In 1840, after the ten years in which he
composed exclusively for the piano, Schumann produced his most
beautiful songs, and only in 1841 did he turn his attention to the
orchestra. He was at the peak of his strength and filled with a superabundance of the joy of creation he sketched the *B-flat major Symphony* in a mere four days. He often referred to this work as his
'Spring Symphony', and also said of it that it was 'born in one
fiery hour'. It opens with a call in the high register. This call in the
trumpets and horns is the main theme of the first movement. The
slow introduction is solemn and grand to start with, but with the
entry of the solo flute it takes on an aspect of idyllic calm. Soft
motions in the strings gather themselves for an impulsive rush into
the fresh pulsating life of the 'allegro molto vivace'. This fast movement is like an irresistible river of ideas. Its unmistakable character
is set up in the dotted rhythm of the theme's first bar, and the other
themes cluster around this first motif, which constantly crops up in

new guises. One wonderful climax is the reprise of the main theme, played by the full orchestra with triumphal breadth. Almost at the end of the movement, after some *pianissimo* wind chords, there appears a truly lovely Schumann melody in the strings that is particularly moving after the irresistible pressure of the preceding music. This moving fervency is also the language of the second movement, larghetto. A broad theme is played three times, first by the violins, then, blossoming, by the 'cellos, and finally by the oboe and horn. The movement ends on an uncertain note, and the scherzo follows immediately. The main section of the scherzo is energetic, almost brusque. As a contrast to this comes a marvellously original sound-picture, with light harmonies and a gentle up-and-down motion. After the reprise of the energetic main section comes a second trio, of a lively, fiery character. A brief reappearance of the first magical interlude heralds the *pianissimo* ending of the scherzo. The finale recaptures the mood of the first move-

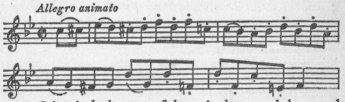

Allegro animato

ment. Gaiety is the keynote of the main theme, and the second theme's controlled confidence forms a contrast. The symphony ends with a happy swing.

The first symphony was a success, and shortly afterwards Schumann wrote his *Symphony in D minor*. So this is really his second symphony, though it is generally known as the *Symphony No. 4*, opus 120, because it was published only much later. It was written in Schumann's greatest period and displays all the hallmarks of the composer at his best. The symphony is of a marvellous unity: themes from the first movement recur in the later movements and do much to determine the general mood of the work. The four movements are played without a break, but, of course, the divisions between them remain quite clear and recognizable.

A slow introduction precedes the first movement; a soft, tentative theme feels its way along and gradually reaches a sphere of powerful decision. The tempo increases by degrees and the violins press forward energetically with a figure that gradually solidifies into the lively, powerful main theme of the work. This animated

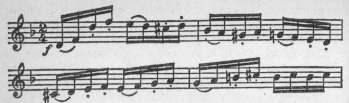

figure dominates the subsequent evolution of the movement, it is
the driving force in almost every bar. Several significant subsidiary
ideas are juxtaposed with this agitated texture, in particular the
romantic warning of the trombones, a motif of mystery, repeated

four times and with greater intensity each time. There is also a
march-like thematic group, joyful and animated, which attaches
itself to a blooming, superbly Schumannesque melody. A picture
of victory emerges from the fiery swing of this movement; an
affirmative, virile and accented piece.

A minor chord in the wind that is almost demonic in its effect
leads to the second movement, a romanza. A melody like a folk
song is played by the oboe, and the tentative theme from the slow

introduction to the first movement is used as the secondary theme.
With charming ornamentation in the solo violin this melody is
transposed into the major key, and so initiates a sunny, peaceful
mood. The scherzo is brusque and powerful, and in the trio the
dreamy mood of the middle section of the romanza reappears.
After repeating the energetic scherzo, Schumann takes up this
dreamy idea yet again and prolongs it to form a delicate ending.
The music has now ceased entirely, everything is quiet, almost
disquietingly so, and out of this darkness, groping its way, comes
the tentative figure from the first movement. Kettledrums roll
dully, the trombones and horns poke out, and the antenna-like
figuration in the violins reaches forward until the march-like theme
from the first movement breaks out in all its glory as the opening
of the finale. The movement progresses with fiery rhythms; a host

of gallant melodies join in and the movement rushes to its jubilant close with great boldness and strength. Only very occasionally is this movement disturbed by calmer elements.

The *Symphony in C major*, opus 61, was published before the *D minor Symphony* and is consequently referred to as the second symphony, although actually the third. The spread of this symphony indicates clearly that Schumann wanted to say something very special in it. Unfortunately, not all parts of the work are equally successful, and next door to wonderful details come sections that are disappointing; it is the sad fact that Schumann could no longer achieve the wonderful consistency and balance of the *D minor* and *B-flat major Symphonies*. However, the introduction to the first allegro is really great and significant. A fanfare motif is entrusted to the brass while the strings and woodwind weave a mysterious web of counterpoint around it. The dotted rhythms that are to dominate the fast section are already twitching prophetically. This great *sostenuto* section is a truly Faustian struggle, a search for clarity, a battle for truth. The allegro does not really live up to this preparation; only occasionally does it rise to any pitch of intensity, and these climaxes have to last us for long stretches of freewheeling. The scherzo, on the other hand, is real Schumann, an enchanting movement which conjures up all the poetry of nature. The scurrying main section frames two trios, the first of which has a particularly delicate grace.

The wonderful adagio is the climax of the symphony, one of the most beautiful movements that Schumann ever wrote. It is built on a single theme, one that conveys a most wonderful feeling of

peace and encouragement. Schumann draws out this beautiful melody with marvellous skill, and when it is played yet again by the woodwind with the violins descending from the heights in delicate trills, the listener finds perfect fulfilment in a dream of better worlds. Recollections of this theme also appear in the finale, in the guise of the second theme. The violas and 'cellos sing this song of romantic longing in contrast to the almost march-like main theme, and their melancholy emotion pushes the main theme more and more into the background; the place where it slowly disappears in three general pauses is particularly moving. Schumann twice attempts a fresh start after this, but is unable to get away from the melancholy mood of farewell, until finally, with the recurrence of the fanfares of the opening, a radiant climax is reached to end the symphony.

The *Symphony No. 3 in E-flat major*, opus 97, was written in 1850, and is generally known as the 'Rhenish Symphony'. It is not clear how far Schumann was responsible for this title; he is supposed to have mentioned the fact that it was a view of Cologne cathedral that originally gave him the idea of writing the symphony. The gay mood of the work can certainly be understood as a reflection of life in the Rhine country, or indeed of the famous Rhineland jocular bumptiousness. The first allegro opens with a

broad swinging theme, which makes the melodious second theme seem somewhat complacent. This second theme spreads itself and dominates the beginning of the development section almost entirely; this increases the effect of the re-entry of the fiery first theme, which then proceeds to grow to an enormous size and displays itself in all its glory, *fff*, in the reprise. The scherzo is a broad, rustic *ländler*, and might have served to depict a local festival were it not for its extraordinary middle section, where the woodwinds sing their melancholy song *pianissimo* over the pedal-point *tremolo* of the basses. The small A-flat major andante has a delicate air, and the gloomy E-flat major adagio that follows it is incomparably

stronger in its effect. Schumann originally headed this 'in the character of an accompaniment to a solemn ceremony'. At any rate, the movement represents a church scene in the grand style. As if it were an organ, Schumann pulls all the stops of the orchestra, from the dull trombone sounds to the radiance of the high winds. Fearful voices are to be heard mingled with the general elevated mood: are these doubts that assail the faithful? The finale is again festive and happy, and it rushes to its end without posing any problems.

In 1841, the year of the *D minor Symphony* and the *B-flat major Symphony*, Schumann also wrote some music which he reworked and published in 1845 as his *Overture, scherzo and finale*. This piece is a small symphony without a slow movement. The fast movements are brief but rich in ideas. Gallant romanticism is the keynote of the overture with its impulsive main theme and singing subsidiary ideas. A powerful motif that was introduced in the slow introduction plays the decisive rôle in the development section. The swift scherzo is similar in character: adventure beckons and the two trios hold a promise of tender rewards back home. The main theme of the first movement is reintroduced at the end of the scherzo, which underlines the close relation of the two movements. The finale sets off with a swing; there is something infectious in the pull of this movement, even though the themes themselves are none too significant. The fiery music storms forward carrying everything along with it, and the climax is reached with the restatement of the main theme augmented.

Of Schumann's many overtures, only two have retained their popularity, namely the *Genoveva* and *Manfred Overtures*. The opera *Genoveva* has fallen into disuse despite the marvellous music; all attempts at reviving it have fallen down over the hopelessly undramatic text. But the overture, perhaps the greatest piece in the opera, persists in reminding us of this unfortunate child of Schumann's genius. Every bar exudes the atmosphere of romantic knighthood, but dark powers and demonic shades are conspiring to destroy all noble feeling. The gloomy introduction intimates the complications of the plot that is hatched in the passionate allegro. A weird, slinking motif takes the lead, and all delicate feelings are pushed aside. The horns blow a promising fanfare, but this ray of light is quickly dimmed. The development spends itself in wild passion, reaching a gloomy climax with the recapitulation of the main theme. Only in the coda do nobler feelings force their way through and jubilantly announce the triumph of truth.

In 1848, at the peak of his career, Schumann wrote some music for Byron's dramatic poem *Manfred*. The character of Manfred had long fascinated Schumann, almost as much as Goethe's Faust. The passionate, stirring side of Manfred's character, the restless struggle for supreme knowledge no matter how riven and undecided his feelings, had a profound attraction for Schumann's passionately sensitive nature. Thus there appeared a portrait in the most inspired musical language, a grandiose painting of his hero's soul. After the broad strokes of the brooding introduction, the allegro breaks over us like a cloudburst of passionate feeling, sometimes interrupted by stretches of a softer sensibility. The main idea of the work attempts with fierce energy to break through, but collapses in the melancholy ending. The torn, dejected quality of this music, unable to choose between supreme effort and doubtful resignation, makes a most wonderful unity of the whole, despite the raw contrasts inherent in the idea.

FELIX MENDELSSOHN-BARTHOLDY

born Hamburg 3 February 1809
died Leipzig 4 November 1847

Mendelssohn had an excellent education, and his main teacher in music was Zelter, a close friend of Goethe's. He appeared in public as a pianist when he was only nine years old and at the age of seventeen composed the overture for the *Midsummer Night's Dream*. At twenty he gave a performance of the *St Matthew Passion* in Berlin, a work that had fallen into complete obscurity. Mendelssohn was, indeed, largely responsible for the revival of Bach's music. After 1835 he was active as conductor of the Gewandhauskonzerte in Leipzig, and in 1843 he founded the Leipzig conservatory. Mendelssohn's life was an unbroken chain of brilliant successes. His outstanding gifts as a composer, conductor and pianist, the charm of his personality, and financial independence through the riches of his father, all these circumstances contributed to his extraordinarily successful career.

The recognition he enjoyed in his lifetime soon faded after his death. Yet Mendelssohn will always remain the most important representative of musical romanticism after Schumann. Schumann, who was an adherent of the *Sturm und Drang* movement, revealed himself anew in every work, whereas Mendelssohn is more reasoned, and more at home in the classical forms, which he had mastered even in his earliest works. Consequently, he has been accused of a certain lack of depth, much more so than Schumann, but when his music was revived after the time of national socialism (during which it was idiotically banned), its scope was recognized and the injustice rectified. Mendelssohn's melodic writing is truly inspired; his tunes are enchanting, but only seldom are they really moving. The expressive strength of Mendelssohn's musical language is clearest in his small-scale works, such as the *Songs Without Words*, for piano, but his violin concerto is generally recognized as his most important work.

Mendelssohn wrote his *Concerto for violin in E minor*, opus 64, in the summer of 1844 in Soden near Frankfurt, where he had retired with his family to a quiet country residence. The harmonious beauty of these summer weeks is expressed in the concerto. In the spring of 1845 it was performed by the violinist Ferdinand David, a friend of Mendelssohn, who had also given him much useful advice about the elaboration of the violin part. The main charm of the concerto lies in its abundance of melodic ideas. The solo instrument, after a brief orchestral introduction, directly introduces the expressive main theme over delicate quaver figures in the strings.

Allegro molto appassionato

This builds up in whirling triplets and is repeated by the orchestra *fortissimo*. A subsidiary melodic phrase which is to be much in evidence in the course of the movement leads to a vivid virtuoso section with brilliant runs, passages and double-stops. When peace has been restored, the violin climbs down from the high regions in a tender *pianissimo* and, on reaching the low G, holds it for eight whole bars. The clarinets and flutes play a wonderful melody over this pedal-point, and the soloist reproduces it with the utmost tenderness. The orchestra reintroduces the first theme over the fading arpeggios of the cadenza, first *piano*, but with ever-increasing strength, supported throughout by the soloist's broad arpeggios, and culminating in a passionate outburst in *fortissimo*.

The andante follows without a break, and the violin unfolds a truly beautiful melody with infinite sweetness. The main theme is

Andante

repeated with great effect after a slightly agitated middle section. A short bridge leads to the brilliant finale, which is full of fairy magic, reminiscent of his *Midsummer Night's Dream*. The rhythmic main theme dominates the whole movement; all subsidiary phrases

are developed from it, and the effect achieved is one of extraordinary unity. The languishing violin melody can be regarded as a second theme, appearing first, however, as a counterpoint to an altered version of the main theme. Later, the rôles are reversed and the orchestra takes this tune while the solo instrument plays the main theme. A brilliant coda ends the work.

The first *Piano Concerto in G minor*, opus 26, is the only work of Mendelssohn's in this genre that is still performed. The *Concerto in D minor* and various other of his concert pieces are only used as examination pieces now. They are all brilliant technically, but otherwise conventional. But the *Concerto in G minor* is certainly a masterpiece in its own way. It was written in 1831, and first performed in Munich, where Mendelssohn himself played the solo part with great success. After a brief but effective exchange between the orchestra and the piano, the solo instrument introduces the main theme, soon followed, after a brilliant development, by a song-like melody. Everything is short and clear, and the soloist has ample opportunity to display his talent. The recapitulation restricts itself to the first theme, and the subsequent fanfares serve as a bridge to the andante. The melody of the andante is tender and folk-song-like. It is played first by the orchestra and then by the pianist, who gradually dissolves it in colourful variations. The same fanfares that introduced the andante now introduce the last movement. The soloist executes brilliant passages and runs before embarking on the effective rondo theme. This finale is typical of Mendelssohn's brilliance and charm, and forms an effective end to the concerto. Just before the coda, we hear once more the melodious second theme of the first allegro and this underlines the unity of the three movements played without a break.

Of Mendelssohn's five symphonies the two last ones, in A major and A minor, are still great favourites in the concert world. They are really his third and fourth symphonies, for the so-called *Reformation Symphony* was later remodelled and came to be known as his fifth symphony. The Symphony in A major, opus 90, generally known as the *Italian Symphony*, was finished in 1833 and published as his fourth symphony. Mendelssohn found inspiration for his work in the course of his travels through Italy in 1830. The first part is fresh and youthful: the violins start the first theme straight off, without special introduction, in a vivid 6/8 rhythm, accompa-

nied by quick quavers in the woodwind. The characteristic 6/8 rhythm animates the whole movement and even affects the calm subsidiary theme in the woodwind. The joyfulness of the first

allegro may be regarded as an expression of the bright southern landscape and the eternal blue of the sky in Italy. However, it is impossible to make similar interpretations for the short expressive andante and the graceful 'con moto moderato'; only the last movement, a wild saltarello, takes us back to Italy.

In 1829 Mendelssohn visited Scotland, and there found great inspiration not only in the landscape but also in the reminders of the life of Mary Stuart. 'I believe I have found the beginning of my Scottish symphony today,' he writes after his visit to the gloomy royal castle of Holyrood. But it took almost thirteen years for him to finish his symphonic masterpiece. The *Scottish Symphony*, opus 56, is in A minor. The first movement is rather melancholic;

the theme of the introduction is serious, as is the main theme of the allegro. One secondary idea is slightly livelier, but it is quickly supplanted by the plaintive second theme. The mood throughout is reserved, and expressive of gentle resignation. The merry theme

of the scherzo is an imitation of Scottish folk melodies, without recourse, however, to the favourite effect of the bagpipes. The adagio is very effective with its contrast of a tender song theme and a gloomy, solemn funeral march. The last movement falls into two sections: the *allegro guerriero* (warlike allegro) builds up to a dramatic climax in the *allegro maestoso assai*. The work ends on a note of hymnic grandeur.

Mendelssohn's journey to Scotland found more direct expression in the famous *Hebrides Overture*, opus 26. He sketched the main theme of this original work on the spot, so great was the effect of that miracle of nature, Fingal's cave. Richard Wagner called it 'one of the most beautiful works of music', but it had to wait a year before it was performed. The *Hebrides Overture* is, of its kind, a perfect symphonic poem and creates a very real impression of its subject. 'Cellos, violas and bassoons introduce the mysterious little figure that dominates the whole work and symbolizes the stalactite

formations in the cave. The song-like second theme is also introduced by 'cellos and bassoons and then taken over by the violins.

An energetic call is added to the two previous themes in the development section, and within the reverberating cave we hear the wind instruments calling to each other, accompanied by *tremolos* in the violins.

In 1828 Mendelssohn wrote the overture *A calm sea and a peaceful voyage*, a piece of programme music based on Goethe's well-known poems. The slow introduction depicts the calm of the sea and a crawling up-and-down motif symbolizes the peace of nature. At last the motion ceases completely. A short piccolo solo forms the transition to the joyful allegro: the mists disperse and the voyage can begin. A flourishing song theme develops out of the short motif which dominated the introduction. The coda announces the happy return of the ship with rising scales and resounding trumpets.

The overture *The Fair Melusine*, opus 32, composed in 1833, is
also a little symphonic poem. The graceful motif depicting the

motion of the waves was later used by Wagner for the Rhine-
maidens' scene in *Rheingold*. In the main part, which tends towards
the minor key, the beautiful nymph Melusine emerges from the
murmur of the waves. She desires to experience the joys and the
sorrows of human love and this turns out to be her downfall. The
tragic first theme is followed by a beautiful love melody, the whole
accompanied by the waves, now threatening, now restrained.
When the love theme dies away in a desperate sobbing, the reconciling waves still accompany it, soothing all pain.

Mendelssohn's most beautiful overture, however, is the *Midsummer Night's Dream*, opus 21, composed in 1826. This is the work
of genius that made the young composer famous. In the overture
each theme is remarkably characteristic and beautiful, and ideally
suited to the colourful world of Shakespeare's comedy. In spite of
all its contrasts the music is of a rare consistency. The romantic
chords of the wind instruments introduce us to Oberon's magic
realm; the violins play the dance of the fairies in the moonlight.

The two themes unite in a festive climax: Oberon, the king of the
fairies, arrives and the dance of the fairies recommences. The clari-

net then introduces a tender love theme which is continued by the
violins as the lovers walk in the moonlight. Suddenly horns, trom-

bones, flutes and clarinets strike up the dance of the goblins, interrupted by the cry of the donkey, and at last we hear the festive
flourish of the trumpets of the royal hunt. The whole company is
assembled in the woods. The music subsides again into the whispering dance of the fairies. Oberon's theme bids us farewell in a most
tender *pianissimo*, and the mysterious wind chords from the opening die away to nothing.

When Mendelssohn composed the overture for Shakespeare's
comedy he was not thinking of composing incidental music for the
play; he regarded his overture as a concert piece like a symphonic
poem. It was only seventeen years later that he decided to write the
complete music for the play, and he then used the themes of his
overture for the incidental music in the various scenes. Besides this,
he composed quite a number of little pieces of delightful musicality,
which, collected into a suite, can frequently be heard in concerts.
The most delightful of these is the scherzo in G minor, fairy music
of infinite grace. The rhythm of the main theme is quite captivating
and holds your attention through all the variations. The intermezzo
is languid in expression, and at times strongly passionate. This is
followed by a burlesque allegretto for the entry of the workmen.
The nocturne with the dreamy horn solo is a typical expression of
Mendelssohn's musical character. The best-known piece in the
suite is, of course, the Wedding March, chock-full of original ideas.

In connection with the music of the *Midsummer Night's Dream*
we have to mention OTTO NICOLAI (1810–49) and the overture for his opera *The Merry Wives of Windsor*. Like Weber's
Oberon and Mendelssohn's *Midsummer Night's Dream* this overture
is pervaded by the romantic spirit. Of Nicolai's works only *The
Merry Wives* has survived—deservedly, for it is a masterpiece. The
overture, which re-opens fairyland to our delighted eyes, is naturally unthinkable without Weber and Mendelssohn, but it is so perfect in its form that this seems unimportant. The work curtains an
abundance of the most wonderful melodies. The introduction is

Andantino moderato

captivating: a tender, dreamy melody rises from the basses and the
united violins shiver in long sustained notes above it, as the moon
rises over the nocturnal wood. Fairies and goblins giggle and plan
to play a trick on fat Sir John. The confused activity of the masked
dance breaks out, and is followed by a blissful love song as a second
theme. The development section opens with the burlesque rhythms
of stamping feet for, unlike those of the *Midsummer Night's Dream*,

the fairies are actually only merry, masked humans playing in the
moonlit wood of a summer's night.

Of Mendelssohn's numerous choral works the *St Paul* and *Elijah
Oratorios* are the most outstanding. Many people consider them the
most important choral works of the nineteenth century and worthy
of a place beside the great choral works of Bach and Handel.
Mendelssohn combined his own style admirably with the inspiration he found in the works of those two masters of the baroque
period. His stylistic dependence is particularly noticeable in *St Paul*,
written in 1836, where he remains firmly rooted in the traditional
forms as laid down in Handel's great biblical stories and in Bach's
Passions. The text of *St Paul* is taken mainly from the Acts of the
Apostles. Usually, the words of the narrator are sung by the solo
soprano, and only occasionally by the alto or tenor soloists. Some
of the arias are in the nature of lyrical commentaries, but in general
it is left to the chorus to comment on the action and these choruses
do much to determine the general mood of the work. The chorus
also takes most of the dramatic work though sometimes, as in
Handel, the arias lend a helping hand.

St Paul consists of two parts. The first part depicts the stoning
of Stephen and St Paul's conversion; the second part shows the
Apostle in action after his conversion. Thus, the dramatic climax is
in the first part, and the true subject of the whole work is the conversion to the new faith and the idea of enlightenment. The chorale,
'Sleepers, wake, a voice is calling', the symbol of this main idea,
appears for the first time in the overture and again at the conversion
of St Paul. The overture begins with a very simple chorale in the
low register of the orchestra. This builds up only gradually and,

after reaching a mighty level of sound, again sinks back into twilight. The following excited fugato expresses the doubts and qualms
of conscience that assail the soul searching for salvation. The chorale
theme joins in, at first like a serious exhortation, then as a promise
of salvation, and leads the overture on to its powerful close.

The first choruses and recitatives depict everyday life in an early
Christian community, and tell of the wonderful doings of Stephen,
against whom the scribes are trying to incite the general populace.
The passionate chorus of the people is contrasted with the calm
nobility of Stephen's recitative (tenor). The musical climax of this
section is the wonderful soprano aria, 'Jerusalem, Jerusalem, thou
that killest the Prophets'; its brevity and conviction lend it a truly
classic grandeur of expression. A wild chorus accompanies the
stoning. The narrator's announcement that Stephen is dead is followed by the chorale, 'To Thee, O Lord, I yield my spirit', which
is very moving in its Bach-like simplicity. Paul, full of hatred and
destruction, is introduced in a grand aria in the style of Handel.
Before the great moment of his conversion, Mendelssohn inserts
a very expressive alto arioso, 'But the Lord is mindful of His own'.
A four-part female chorus, supported by high wind chords, enun-
ciates the words of Christ that move Paul so deeply. A wonderful
excited crescendo in the orchestra leads to the powerful chorus
'Rise! up! arise! rise, and shine!' depicting Paul's conversion and
vocation. The chorale, 'Sleepers, wake, a voice is calling', forms
the radiant conclusion of the chorus, musically and ideologically a
significant climax of the work. Our Lord strikes Paul blind, and he
accepts his punishment with deep contrition. His aria, 'O God,
have mercy upon me, and blot out my transgressions according to
thy loving kindness', is one of Mendelssohn's most wonderful
inspirations. It is the prayer of a man that is ready to repent, but a
man of great heroism, who recognizes his guilt only before God.
A radiant soprano solo then announces that Paul has regained his
sight. The chorus concludes the first part with convincing melodic
clarity with the words 'O great is the depth of the riches of wisdom
and knowledge of the Father!'.

The second part depicts the Apostle's activity amongst the
heathen, his miraculous healing of a lame man, his struggle against
idolatry, and how the people constantly turn against him and his
religion. After the expressive double fugue of the introductory
chorus, 'The nations are now the Lord's, they are His Christ's, For
all the Gentiles come before Thee', the great five-part chorus, 'But

our God abideth high in heaven', is the climax of the second part.
In the preceding aria Paul tries to convert the people to the true
religion. This aria reaches its climax in its conclusion, 'For the
temple of God is holy, which temple ye are', a theme which is
taken up by the chorus. The chorale 'In one true God we all believe' is interwoven as a *cantus firmus* by the second soprano. The
populace want to stone Paul, but Our Lord supports him and gives
him strength; the tenor cavatina 'Be thou faithful unto death'
brings him consolation from above. The action ends with the
Apostle's departure from his community. Originally, Mendelssohn
planned to include Paul's martyrdom, but he abandoned this plan.
The last soprano recitative gives only a brief indication of the trials
in store for Paul and also mentions the just reward Our Lord will
bestow on him. The final chorus is an elaborate double fugue in
praise of God.

The first performance of *St Paul* took place in 1836 in Düsseldorf, with the composer conducting. It was an enormous success,
but Mendelssohn still corrected it a great deal before he had it
printed.

Mendelssohn's second great oratorio, *Elijah*, opus 70, is much
freer as regards its text than *St Paul*, which kept fairly strictly to
the words of the Bible. In *Elijah*, the narrator (equivalent to Bach's
Evangelist) is almost entirely absent; the action is carried forward
in arias and dialogues, and often by the chorus. Lyrical commentaries in the form of arias and solo ensembles take up a lot of space,
and Mendelssohn hardly uses chorales at all. On the whole, *Elijah*
is very close to Handel's oratorios, and this is particularly plain in
his treatment of the big choral scenes. The oratorio divides into
two parts, and Mendelssohn disposes his musical and dramatic
climaxes so cleverly that both parts are equally rich. The work was
first performed in Birmingham in 1846. Mendelssohn again conducted, and it was a triumphant success.

Elijah himself opens the work with a short recitative. What he
says is hard to accept: 'As God the Lord of Israel liveth, before
whom I stand, there shall not be dew nor rain these years, but
according to my word.' The overture which follows is a large fugue
on a dull theme rising from the bass, intended to represent the per-
plexity of the people when they realize what they will suffer under
this curse. From an anxious *pianissimo* to a *fortissimo* of alarm this
movement is a single steep crescendo, culminating in the ecstatic
outburst from the strings that leads to the first chorus, 'Help,

Lord!'. A fugato, 'The harvest now is over', gives telling expression
to the inconsolable mood of the populace by means of uniform
chromaticism. The following duet for soprano and alto, 'Zion
spreadeth her hands for aid', is extremely exciting and has a strangely
penetrating odour, underlined by the chorus, which recurrently
murmurs 'Lord! bow Thine ear to our prayer!' in a psalmodic
tone. Of the following scenes, the double quartet, 'For He shall
give His angels charge over thee', is noteworthy, and also the big
duet between Elijah and the widow whose son is brought back to
life by the prophet. This scene is very dramatic and forms an effective contrast to the lyrical choruses that frame the duet. The climax
of the first part is Elijah's argument with the priests of Baal. The
idea is that first the priests and then Elijah shall conjure up their
respective gods 'and the God who by fire shall answer, let him be
God'. Powerfully, the priests of Baal call for their god in the eight-
part 'Baal, we cry to thee', and when nothing happens their pleas
become more and more urgent. Elijah laughs at their expectations
with scornful words. 'Hear our cry, O Baal' becomes ever more
passionate and ends with fanatical cries of 'Hear and answer!'. The
quiet humility of Elijah's prayer has a great effect; his 'Lord God
of Abraham' ends with a delicate chorale for the quartet of soloists,
and everyone holds their breath in expectation of the miracle. The
orchestra enters *fortissimo* and the chorus shouts the news: 'The fire
descends from heaven'. The scene where Elijah, in front of the
assembled populace, pleads with God to send rain to their thirsty
land is similar in its dramatic effect, though musically not nearly
so interesting. The final chorus of the first part, a song of thanksgiving for rain, is musically immensely significant; the full orchestra lends majesty to this rejoicing hymn.

The second part opens with the wonderful soprano aria, 'Hear
ye Israel'. The specific threat of the adagio is followed, after a brief
recitative, by a radiant allegro movement, 'Be not afraid! thy help
is near'. The people rise up against Elijah, and following God's
advice, he flees into the wilderness. His F-sharp minor aria is another
musical climax: 'It is enough'; the prophet is tired and brought low
by the ceaseless struggle to save his people's soul. Exhausted and
dejected, he falls asleep, and in a dream a trio of angels, *a cappella*,
encourages him with one of Mendelssohn's loveliest melodies,
'Lift thine eyes to the mountains'. The best chorus of the second
part is the one describing how God appears to Elijah. An angel has
instructed Elijah to step out on the mountain and cover his face,

for the Lord is near at hand. The chorus opens with a mysterious unison, 'Behold! God the Lord passed by!' a wind blows, 'But yet the Lord was not in the tempest' whispers the chorus. Earthquakes mutter, flames flicker up, and the chorus builds up passionately, 'But yet the Lord was not in the fire'. The following *pianissimo* is very effective after this ecstatic outburst: 'And after the fire there came a still small voice; and in that still voice, onward came the Lord.' Quiet motion in the strings forms a delicate backcloth to the mysterious, lulling whispers of the chorus. Choruses of angels, 'Holy, holy, holy is God the Lord', sound out with increasing grandeur, and an eight-part chorus bears the good tidings to the ends of the earth. The final chorus to the words 'Lord, our Creator, how excellent Thy Name is in all the nations' is laid out on a still larger scale, and crowns the work with true magnificence.

FREDERIC CHOPIN

born near Warsaw 22 February 1810
died Paris 17 October 1849

Chopin was only nine years old when he first performed in public as a pianist. In 1830 he settled in Paris where he was celebrated both as a pianist and as a composer. There he met Liszt and Berlioz and became friendly with Heine and Balzac; he fell in love with George Sand, the poetess. His premature death was brought about by a serious disease of the lungs.

Chopin was an extraordinary and unique character. The son of a Polish woman and a Frenchman he united within himself the good qualities of both races—Polish elegance and French *esprit*. A child of his time, he is a representative of romanticism; the sensitivity of his musical expression represents the very climax of the romantic period. Chopin's main instrument is the piano and his style of writing for this instrument has an unusual and extraordinary quality. His melodies are decorative and sometimes lose themselves in vague variations. The chromatic scale finds strong emphasis in his music, and for this reason alone he can be considered one of the great forerunners of musical impressionism, which reached its peak in Debussy. Chopin concentrates exclusively on the piano, the orchestra means less to him than it did even to Schumann. He only used it for the accompaniment of his piano concertos. Of Chopin's numerous works for piano and orchestra, fantasias, variations and suchlike, only two concertos, in E minor and F minor, are still performed. The piano writing, needless to say, offers the pianist great opportunity to display his ability.

The *Piano Concerto No. 1 in E minor*, opus 11, composed in 1830, is a youthful work, of course. But it shows the eminent characteristics of the composer's maturity with its elegant thematic work and brilliantly differentiated technical mastery of the piano. The disadvantage of this concerto lies in the fact that all the opportunities arising out of the orchestral accompaniment are scarcely elaborated at all. For instance, the grand orchestral introduction to the first allegro introduces the three main themes of the work, strangely enough all in the same key, but after that the orchestra immediately withdraws completely, as if its task has been fulfilled; all further development of the themes is left to the soloist. The soloist repeats the themes, the first very energetic motif followed by the plaintive

second idea. An enchanting, playful episode concludes this first section. The subsidiary theme is extraordinarily melodious; sensitive and simple at the outset, and then dissolving in brilliant variations. The development section and reprise also produce fresh, technically interesting figurations in great profusion. The second movement, romanza, is a truly inspired nocturne full of those dissolving sounds and colouristic effects that are so characteristic of Chopin's world. The most beautiful part is the conclusion of the romanza where the piano plays tender arabesques and variations round the theme in the orchestra. The last movement, a rondo, is

typically French: graceful and charming. The subsidiary theme is highly original; it is given to the pianist, who executes it in simple octaves. The further development of this capricious idea is correspondingly simple and the effect is positively electrifying. Needless to say, the last movement gives the pianist endless opportunities for brilliant display and *bravura*.

The *Concerto No. 2 in F minor*, opus 21, was actually written before the *E minor Concerto*, although the opus number of the work indicates a later period. It was composed in 1829, and also belongs to Chopin's early youth. In a way it may be considered more brilliant still than the *E minor Concerto*, though the thematic work is not quite so precise. The themes of the first movement especially are rather blurred, and even the brilliant runs and passage work cannot disguise the fact. The larghetto is the most important movement. Like the romanza of the *E minor Concerto*, it is actually a nocturne. A luxuriant melody with enchanting decorations and variations evokes the unique mood of Chopin's nocturnes. The piano breaks out with great intensity in the middle section; the longing, desirous writing climbs to the peak of passion over the orchestra's *tremolo* and then, with a delicate figuration, the soloist leads back to the quiet mood of the opening. The allegro vivace is a virtuoso waltz rondo, similar to a *perpetuum mobile* in its restless motion. This

last movement can be fascinating to listen to, if played with grace and brilliance by a real virtuoso.

LOUIS-HECTOR BERLIOZ

born Côte-St-André 11 December 1803
died Paris 8 March 1869

Berlioz dedicated his life entirely to music against the wishes of his father, and, consequently, had to fend for himself without any parental support. He won the Prix de Rome at the Paris Conservatoire and this made his life a little easier for a while. In his lifetime Berlioz had no success with his music; a small number of people were interested in him, but they did not succeed in making him known. Even a professorship was denied him and he had to be content with the post of curator and, later on, librarian at the Conservatoire, which was a recognition of his capabilities as an author rather than as a composer. A great Berlioz cult came into being in France after his death, but even this soon subsided.

Berlioz is a tragic phenomenon. His ideas were mocked at and his music disregarded. He struggled passionately for his ideals, but his rewards were constant bitterness and disappointment. He believed himself the successor of Beethoven, and suffered a great deal from the latter's greatness. His burning ambition drove him to attempt speculative and revolutionary feats, but his musical genius proved insufficient to express the superabundance of ideas presented to him by his highly developed imagination. However, for all our scepticism, we are nowadays filled with genuine admiration for Berlioz the innovator, and his works are frequently performed.

Berlioz is the first composer of programme music as such, music, that is, inspired by external objects, poetry, art, or nature. Naturally, numerous works of absolute, or abstract, music have been inspired by these things, but only when a definite programme or title is given to a work can it be considered real programme music. Music, however, always remains subject to its internal architectonic laws, so only such pieces of programme music that are composed according to the conceptions of absolute music can have any meaning. This entails that really good programme music must be perfectly understandable musically, even without the explanation of the programme. Whether it produces in the listener the same pictures that inspired the composer, however, is dubious.

Programme music had already existed for quite a long time. The most famous examples from the beginnings of musical history are, of course, the *a cappella* tone-paintings of Jannequin, written in the sixteenth century; amongst other things he attempted to depict a battle. The most important example of the classical period is naturally Beethoven's *Pastoral Symphony*. But Berlioz is the first conscious champion of programme music, which he believed to be a totally new step in the development of music. He was the first to make a hard and fast distinction between absolute music and programme music, and between the expression of inner feelings and depiction of outer events. Such a statement loses its meaning when one realizes that music is *always* an expression of inner feelings and that these cannot be distinctly differentiated from outer events in the process of musical composition. But his theory led Berlioz to a new, subtler and more intense exploitation of the orchestra. Instrumentation became a highly specialized art in its own right. Berlioz is the father of the modern orchestra, and with his true feeling for orchestral sound laid the foundation on which Wagner and Strauss were later to build.

Berlioz' first great work, the *Fantastic Symphony*, opus 14, is also his most important, and the most significant in the evolution of programme music. This symphony was written in 1829, only two years after Beethoven's death, and its daring conception seems literally overwhelming. The subtitle of the symphony, 'Episode in the life of an artist', tells us that Berlioz wanted to depict one of his own personal experiences. Schumann believed that Berlioz' passion for the English actress Henriette Smithson was his inspiration. The symphony consists of five movements. The first movement bears the title 'Rêveries. Passions'. Berlioz' programme tells us about a young musician who for the first time meets a woman who corresponds perfectly to his ideal. The beloved image always appears in connection with a musical thought. This motif, a kind of *idée fixe*, pervades

all the movements of the symphony. The slow introduction depicts the man in love, longing for his beloved, in a largo of a languid restlessness, clothed in vague twilight. The allegro section introduces the clear, radiant melody that is the image of the beloved, played by flute and violins, at first unaccompanied. The whole orchestra takes up this motif after a fiery development. There is no second theme; even the development is based entirely on fragmentary themes taken from the main melody. This movement is full of passionate impulses expressing a vast variety of moods, from tormenting anxiety to the height of exhilaration.

The second part is entitled 'A Ball'. After a light introduction comes a tender waltz from which the *leitmotif* of the beloved

gradually detaches itself, at first in the flute and oboe and later *pianissimo* in the clarinets. 'In the country' is the title of the third

movement. Two shepherds are playing their pipes: the cor anglais begins and is answered by the oboe; both are accompanied by the strings. Gradually, the whole orchestra is affected by the pastoral mood. An excited figure in the bass instruments rudely interrupts the idyll, the leitmotif is heard in flute and oboe, and the orchestra answers passionately. According to Berlioz' programme these are the artist's doubts as to his beloved's fidelity. The clarinet introduces a quiet theme and the pastoral mood is reinstated. The idyllic main theme is heard again in the violins and is harmóniously united with it. 'One of the shepherds again strikes up the simple melody, but the other does not answer... sunset... distant rumbling of thunder—loneliness—silence.'

The fourth part is called 'March to the Scaffold'. The programme gives the following explanation: 'When the lover is certain that his love despises him, he drinks poison and sinks into a deep, death-like sleep. He dreams he has murdered his beloved; he was condemned to death and is being led to the gallows. The walk to the gallows is accompanied by a march that is sometimes gloomy and wild, sometimes resplendent. The noisiest eruptions are followed directly by gloomy, measured steps. Finally, the leitmotif appears briefly like a last thought of love in the midst of death.' The gloomy mood of this movement corresponds perfectly with the feeling of French romanticism prevalent at that time. Berlioz understands this scene perfectly and finds the perfect means to translate these gloomy thoughts into musical terms. After a short introduction dominated by the rhythm of kettledrums, the basses play an impressive theme which probably represents the death sentence. Then follow march rhythms which build up and consolidate themselves to broad, solemn steps. An excited crowd has gathered; the noise and shouting of the people is distinctly audible. The climax is reached when the tragic main theme is played in unison, *fortissimo*. The execution is near, the music builds up wildly, then suddenly stops. The shrill tone of the clarinet reminds us of the leitmotif, and hence of the beloved and then the axe falls, expressed by a *fortissimo* stroke from the orchestra, *pizzicato* of the lower strings and a wild roll of drums and kettledrums...

The *Fantastic* was the first symphony to exceed the prescribed four movements. The fifth movement depicts a dream of a witches' sabbath in an extraordinary orgy of sound. 'Strange sounds, groaning, shrill laughter, distant shouts' lend a mysterious mood to the introduction. The crow of a cockerel in the flutes, then in horns *cuivré*, leads to the leitmotif played by the clarinet in a distorted manner, and accompanied by drums and kettledrums. This distortion of the *idée fixe* develops into a coarse dance melody: the former loved one turns up at the witches' sabbath and is cordially welcomed by the witches! This scene suddenly stops, and the basses play a solemn recitative, thematically related to the death sentence of the previous movement. Now comes a gloomy sound of bells, the bells of death, playing a parody of the Dies Irae (the Last Judge-

ment). The tubas and bassoons play a gloomy chorale, trombones and horns repeat the theme in abbreviated form, the violins repeat it doubly abbreviated, intended obviously as a parody. The ringing of the bells obliviously accompanies the whole frightful scene. Then the wild witches' dance starts: a fugue begins, breaks off and begins again; there is a threatening hint of the Dies Irae, but this is overwhelmed by the theme of the fugue in chromatic distortion, before the two themes unite. In a wild build-up all the possibilities of orchestral sound are used and lead up to a *fortissimo* conclusion. The first performance of the *Fantastic Symphony* raised a great deal of discussion. Paganini, Liszt and especially Schumann supported Berlioz' ideas wholeheartedly, but Mendelssohn condemned the symphony outright.

Paganini was the indirect originator of the *Harold in Italy Symphony*, performed in 1834. Paganini had asked Berlioz to compose a viola concerto for him, but when he saw the first sketches he was disappointed. So Berlioz decided to use these sketches for a symphony with a long viola solo in the middle. As a programme for the symphony he chose episodes from Byron's *Childe Harold*. This work, too, has a *leitmotif*; in this case it is Harold's theme that pervades all four movements of the symphony. It is played mainly by the solo viola, who thus comes to represent the hero of the symphony. The first movement, subtitled 'Scenes of sadness, of happiness and of joy', depicts Harold in the mountains. The big, slow introduction shows the character of the hero. A pensive fugato passage is followed by the main theme played by wind instruments, at first in the minor key. Suddenly the mood changes for the better:

the solo viola plays the theme in the major key, gently accompanied by the harp. The melancholic hero turns his face towards life. Now follows an emotional dialogue between the orchestra and the solo viola, in which the main theme is treated canonically with the viola following the orchestra. The mood of darkness and mist is completely dispelled, even in nature, and a joyful, pastoral theme introduces the allegro. The viola resists at first, but the swinging melody soon overcomes it. The measured second theme, played first by bassoon, then by the solo viola, spreads general calm, but only for a short while, for the joyful rhythms of the first theme dominate the movement. Towards the end of the development, Harold's theme is restated in a short fugato starting softly in the bass, and this leads quickly to the reprise to conclude the first movement with an effective dithyrambic swing.

The second movement is headed 'March of the Pilgrims singing their Evening Prayer'. In the distance the song of the pilgrims is heard, gradually approaching, their pious chant constantly inter-

rupted by monotonous psalms. Harold meets the pilgrims and decides to join them. His theme accompanies the pilgrims' song. Towards the middle of the movement the simple song reaches its climax in a hymn, and the solo viola joins in the solemn tune. Gentle *pizzicati* in the basses mark the march rhythm of the pilgrimage. The song gradually fades away in the distance, until only a few notes of the song are audible. Bells are heard, as at the beginning, and the poetic movement fades into the twilight of evening. The third movement is 'Serenade of a mountaineer of the Abbruzzi to his Mistress'. Piccolo and oboe play a merry folk

melody, and the clarinets and bassoons imitate the bagpipes accompaniment. After this short merry introduction an enamoured peasant starts his song; the English horn plays a languid melody, accompanied by *pizzicati* in the violins and basses. Harold appears. At
first he plays his own theme, but this becomes absorbed by the
melody of the serenade. In fact he continues playing it dreamily on
his own after the village musicians have ceased. The finale, 'Orgy
of the Brigands', is most strange. The movement begins with
reminiscences of the previous movements, interrupted by the noisy
shouting of the robbers. Harold dreams of better days and plays
nostalgic melodies on the viola—the adagio of the introduction,
the song of the pilgrims, the serenade—but the coarse dance tunes
of the robbers' wild orgy contaminate all the pictures of memory.
At the end. the pilgrims' song is heard once more from a distance.
Harold reaches for his viola, tries to play his theme, but is unable
to find the right intervals. His playing fades, and he is dead. The
robbers continue their wild tumult.

Berlioz gives the subtitle 'Dramatic Symphony' to his third
great symphony, *Romeo and Juliet*, opus 17. It is like a concert
opera. He wanted to leave the possibility open of having it performed as a dramatic symphony either in the concert hall or on the
operatic stage, but the work does not really feel at home in either
rôle. Berlioz' *Romeo and Juliet* consists of eight parts which are
partly instrumental and partly choral and the chorus has a significant part to play. Three instrumental sections have won constant
places for themselves in the concert hall, and these are, indeed, the
most beautiful pieces Berlioz ever wrote. The first of the three
pieces is entitled 'Grand feast at the Capulets'. It begins with a slow
introduction, depicting Romeo's gloomy mood. He is overcome
by great excitement (*tremolos* in the strings and kettledrum rolls);
he sees Juliet's image (tender melody by the oboe, accompanied
by 'cello arpeggios). The following allegro is a brilliant dance
movement, of which the main theme is a powerful march. The
climax of the allegro is reached where Juliet's theme is played by
the horns over the dance rhythms. The coda is threatening and
combative and banishes the festive dance music. The 'Love Scene'
is a long adagio of absolutely enchanting orchestral sound. The
introduction depicts nature: the low strings represent a mild summer night and the woodwinds imitate the sound of birds. A tender,
languid melody in the horn and 'cello expresses Juliet's longing and
love, and the wind instruments announce Romeo's approach. The

following dialogue is serene and untroubled, interrupted only occasionally by passionate impulses.

The most famous movement of the *Romeo Symphony* is the scherzo 'Queen Mab, fairy of dreams'. Queen Mab has very little to do with *Romeo and Juliet*: there is only a casual mention in the drama of the tiny fairy queen who rides in a nutshell and gives beautiful dreams to sleeping people. Berlioz uses this story as an excuse to write a piece of fairy music which is well worthy of comparison with those of Weber, Mendelssohn and Nicolai. Technically, Berlioz' orchestration even surpasses that of the German romantics. The main section is a wild *prestissimo* and the quiet middle section forms a contrast, as, with great sensitivity, Berlioz uses violin and harp harmonies to create the magical beauty of the fairy world. A simple dance melody played by the flute and cor anglais moves gracefully through the strange fairy landscape. The piece is full of unusual sound effects and charming surprises.

It would be natural to suppose that Berlioz, as the composer of programme music *par excellence*, would also see new possibilities in the form of the overture and that he would build up his overtures into small symphonic poems. But surprisingly this is not the case. His overtures retain the form of those of Weber and Beethoven, namely the opposition of two main themes. Berlioz' most famous work of this kind is the overture for the opera *Benvenuto Cellini*, 1837. The main theme expresses a festive carnival. This mood is broken off abruptly by a threatening theme introduced by the basses, *pizzicato*, and joined by clarinet and flute in a plaintive melody. Finally, the trombones and lower woodwind raise their threatening voices. The festive mood reappears interwoven with a tender love-theme. After a sudden break the first threatening theme returns, but this once more gives way to the animated final hymn.

The *Carnaval Romain* overture was written in 1843. It is based on the motifs of Berlioz' opera *Benvenuto Cellini*, and was later used as an *entr'acte* in the opera. *Carnaval Romain* is very similar in character and form to the *Benvenuto* overture, but perhaps still more brilliant. After a short festive run up Berlioz uses a languid love melody (the love duet in the opera) as a slow introduction to the allegro. The allegro itself is written in a fiery 6/8.

The greatest tragedy of Berlioz' life was the fact that after the unsuccessful performance of *Benvenuto Cellini* in the Paris Opera House this Institution completely disregarded him, despite all his successes elsewhere. The injustice compelled him to limit himself to concert pieces and this gave rise to such strange mixed forms as the 'Dramatic Symphony', *Romeo and Juliet*, and later the dramatic legend, the *Damnation of Faust*. *Romeo and Juliet* was not an opera, and the *Damnation of Faust* was not an oratorio. Three dazzling orchestral pieces from the latter have maintained their position in the concert repertoire and these persist in reminding us of Berlioz' contribution to the Faust legend.

Berlioz handled Goethe's work with exceeding freedom; his version is centred round the Gretchen scenes. Incidentally, one of Berlioz' chief concerns was to find effective material for his larger choral and orchestral pieces. Thus, he transplants the first part of the Faust story to Hungary, simply because he wished to use the Rákóczi march in the music! Berlioz had already planned a gripping march based on the well-known Hungarian melody and this met with considerable success at its first performance in Vienna. It is still a favourite piece. It begins softly, as if in the distance, and approaches gradually, its gloomy, warlike atmosphere momentarily lightened by a friendly section in the major key. The symphonic development concentrates on the main theme which becomes ever more compelling and ends with mighty *fortissimo* passages for the tubas and trombones. The reprise, which is a shortened version of the main section, triumphantly concludes the march. The dance of the sylphs is extremely delicate. The violins play a soft waltz melody in *pianissimo*. A very gentle accompaniment of flutes, harp harmonics and muted figurations in the violas completes the dreamlike mood, over the constant pedal point of the basses. The dance of the Will o' the Wisps is less convincing. It is a minuet with a czardas-like rhythm and is interesting more for its brilliant instrumentation than for any musical or melodic content.

The *Grande Messe des Morts*, or *Requiem* (1837), is a work that was obviously conceived on the grandest scale; Berlioz' intentions were transcendental. However, the work does not now seem as modern as it must have when it appeared, and it requires an exceptional performance to hold the listener's attention throughout. But performances of any sort are rare on account of the enormous forces required by the score, which includes fifty brass instruments.

The *Te Deum*, opus 22, is scored for three choruses (of which the third consists of sopranos and altos only), with orchestra and organ. Again, this work is characterized by its extreme opulence and grandiosity, and it must have been an overwhelming experience to hear the first performance, which Berlioz himself described as

'Babylonian, Ninivite', that is, super-colossal. There are seven movements in the *Te Deum* proper, and a final orchestral march for the presentation of the colours on military occasions. An interesting feature of both this work and the *Requiem* is the spatial distribution of the choral and orchestral forces. In the *Te Deum* the three choruses are separated, and the orchestra and organ are at opposite ends of the church; and in the *Requiem* the brass are divided into four sections, one at each corner of the orchestra. Here is irrefutable evidence that Berlioz was coming to regard the various points in space from which the sounds were to issue as an element in the music itself. This was in the 1840's!

L'Enfance du Christ is one of Berlioz' most readily accessible and enjoyable works. It is an oratorio in three parts: the dream of Herod, the flight into Egypt, and the arrival at Sais. A brief epilogue follows in which the narrator calls attention to the fact that Jesus lived for many years among the gentiles and was supported by them. The following devotional chorus 'O my soul' forms a quiet climax.

Berlioz wrote his own libretto for the work, and used several solo singing characters: Mary, Joseph, Herod, a centurion, for instance, besides the chorus. The most illuminating survey of the work as a whole is provided in a single sentence by the German poet and friend of Berlioz, Heine, who had not even heard it himself: 'I hear on all sides that your oratorio is a perfect bouquet of sweet flowers of melody, and a masterpiece of simplicity.'

FRANZ LISZT

born Raiding, Burgundy 22 October 1811
died Bayreuth 31 July 1886

Liszt's father was trustee of Count Esterhazy. He and several of his Hungarian friends made it possible for the prodigy to study with Czerny in Vienna. Liszt appeared in public as a pianist when he was nine years old. Later on he settled in Paris, and was celebrated as a great pianist, and his concert tours throughout Europe substantiated his reputation as the greatest virtuoso of his time. From 1848 till 1861 he worked as court conductor in Weimar, and was able to give real support to the views of Wagner and Berlioz. Meanwhile he had given up work as a pianist entirely, and dedicated his time to composing. In 1861 Liszt moved to Rome, and went into the church. His pedagogic activity was influential during the last decades of his life; his great talent seemed to live on after his death in the prowess of his numerous pupils.

The influence exerted by Liszt on the musical life of his time was quite extraordinary; he was an inspiration to his contemporaries in all fields of musical activity. One of the main qualities of this great character was his capacity for supporting other people's artistic efforts and creations entirely selflessly and with great enthusiasm. He was admired more as a pianist, a great teacher and an extraordinary man than as a composer. His significance in this field was recognized only very late.

Together with Berlioz, Liszt is rightly regarded as the co-originator of programme music. When Berlioz' attempts proved a failure, Liszt came to his support and championed his 'music of the future'. In his work he even surpassed the intentions of his friend Berlioz. He did not share the opinion that the poetic idea had to be fitted into the shape of a symphony in four movements. For Liszt the programme was such a strong factor in the composition that it even determined the form, and his symphonic poems, for instance, are mostly in one movement. His creative spirit injected new life into all the different musical forms. Liszt even dared to part company with the canon of classical harmony, that a piece should be in one key; in particular his systematic use of the augmented triad provided him with new harmonic combinations. He was the most significant forerunner of musical impressionism. In the motivic elaboration of his themes he also trod new ground—the hand of the innovator is traceable in everything he wrote. Unfortunately, Liszt did not have the same strength of imagination. His themes are often weak, not very original, and his repetitions seem tiresome. This may be the reason why only a small number of Liszt's orchestral works are still played today. Of his twelve symphonic poems only a very few are still heard in our concert halls.

The most beautiful of these is certainly *Les Préludes*. A programme is not necessary for an adequate understanding of this work: Liszt himself added the words of Lamartine only later. According to this programme the work depicts life and its struggles—the happiness and grief of love, the consolation of nature and the perpetual renewal of struggle. There are only two themes, and these are constantly opposed or united in different ways. This economy of means gives the work great unity and simplicity. The main theme is introduced by the strings in a soft unison and taken up after a short development by the trumpets and trombones. This

brilliant fanfare section reappears at the end of the piece. A further theme develops out of the main motif, and this is followed by the second theme, a languid love melody. The end of this beautiful section is indicated by a general pause. Storms threaten when the basses reintroduce the main motif, and then soon burst violently. An energetic fanfare motif, derived from the triplets of the main theme, takes over the lead. The middle section is an allegretto pas-

torale: after his struggle, man seeks consolation in the silence of nature. A tender theme is taken up alternately by different wind instruments and gradually settles down into an even stream of melody. The love melody is introduced and artfully interwoven with the pastoral tune. In a slow, constant build-up the idyllic melodies disappear and a powerful march motif, again derived from the main theme, spreads itself triumphantly. The love theme, too, develops to heroic proportions, and the whole majestic stream of melodies ends with the brilliant fanfares in the trumpets and trombones.

Besides *Les Préludes* the symphonic poems *Tasso, Orpheus* and *Mazeppa* are still performed occasionally. *Tasso* was originally intended as an overture to Goethe's *Tasso*, and after reworking it in 1854, Liszt called it 'Tasso, Lament and Triumph'. This title gives a clear indication of the programme. The strings introduce the main theme which dominates the whole work with its triplets.

The allegro evolves from grief to passionate rebellion, and the mood of gloomy excitement is underlined by a chromatic falling motif. Then Tasso's theme moulds itself into a funeral march, the chromatic motif joins in with the mournful sounds, and from this Tasso's theme emerges with solemn grandeur played this time by the trumpets in the major key. A melancholy bridge passage leads to the middle section: the Tasso theme becomes a minuet; the poet is in the court of Ferrara. The minuet develops into a wooing, passionate crescendo, the language of the poet becomes more powerful, and he dares to lift up his eyes to the princess; demandingly the horns sound Tasso's theme. Then the hard sounds of the first allegro again enwrap the unhappy poet and his life is extinguished. However, his powerful, defiant motif forms the bridge to the second part, announcing the poet's triumph. His theme is repeated in the major key as a triumphal march; this gets louder

and more festive and the work concludes on a note of overwhelming enthusiasm.

The symphonic poem *Orpheus* is simply a song in praise of music. Distant sounds emerge from mysterious darkness and consolidate into a melody; more and more instruments join in and participate in the slow *crescendo*. This ends in an overwhelming climax and the original theme is played at a brilliant *fortissimo* level. Suddenly, this is broken off and the music recedes into outer space, dissolving in tender harmonies. This poem is pure Liszt, the mythical singer Orpheus is taken purely as a symbol, and transformed into a musical experience of the highest order.

Liszt was fascinated by the figure of the Cossack, Hetman Mazeppa. He had already published the great concert-study *Mazeppa*, the sketches for which date back to when he was fifteen, and in 1851 he finished the symphonic poem *Mazeppa*, which was based on the earlier piano work. Liszt had a poem by Victor Hugo in mind, and the music follows the descriptions in the poem. Mazeppa, under sentence of death, is tied on a horse by his enemies, and the horse rushes towards the steppe. It races along for days, persecuted by wild horses, accompanied by swarms of vultures waiting for their prey. At last the horse collapses, the vultures circle round their prey, but Mazeppa has not given up. He still dreams of being saved and, indeed, he is saved. The orchestra starts with a *fortissimo* of wind instruments to a clash of cymbals: a lash of the whip drives the horse out into the steppe. Wild triplets in the strings depict its aimless galloping, and *ostinato* figures in the bass indicate the desolation of the landscape. The rhythm of the hoofs is distinctly heard, accompanied by the shrill piccolo. Trombones now introduce the powerful theme of Mazeppa, a great heroic melody. The horse races on; it is tired, but still runs on. Birds are represented in chromatic scales running up and down: ravens clack their beaks (*tremolo, pizzicato*, and *col legno* effects). The woodwind play a painful distortion of the main theme, which is then scattered into a multitude of tiny motifs. The whole orchestra goes into a crescendo as the horse collapses. One last rumble from the kettle-drums, and horn and 'cello give vent to the animal's last sighs. Then trumpets announce Mazeppa's theme; he is saved, and a brilliant triumphal march, using rhythms that are as typically Hungarian as they are Ukrainian, leads the hero to his apotheosis.

Liszt's most significant symphonic creation is the *Faust Symphony*, written in 1854, a great work of genius. The idea of giving symphonic expression to Goethe's work was very inspiring to Liszt. He does not depict the action of the Faust drama, he is content to paint musical portraits of the three main characters of the Goethe tragedy: Faust, Gretchen and Mephistopheles. Thus, the first movement, devoted to Faust, gives us a picture of titanic struggle; the second movement gives poetic expression to the character of Gretchen; and the third movement deals with the destructive spirit, Mephistopheles. Then the *chorus mysticus* concludes the symphony with the final words of Part Two of Goethe's drama. The formal structure of the separate movements is very unconventional; the form is totally subjected to the poetic idea, and often the listener gets the impression of a free fantasia. The main themes are used somewhat as *leitmotifs* and reappear in the separate movements, either in their original form or in some new guise. It is not easy to follow the musical development of the three movements, and the surest guide is the programme. If one imagines the poetic idea of each movement with some intensity, one can obtain a very strong impression of this atmospheric music.

The first movement of the symphony, devoted to the central figure Faust, depicts the various aspects of the Faustian nature in a number of themes. The slow introduction has a gloomy motif; the tension of the augmented triads played by the unison of strings

expresses the doubts and sadness of the philosophical mind. A brusque twist opens the main section, *allegro agitato*, and an excited theme characterizes the affirmative Faust with his face turned towards life. A tender andante contrasts with the allegro, depicting a Faust that can love and hope, and give himself up to tender anguish. A heroic theme, powerfully executed by trumpets, symbolizes his energy and power. The opposition of these four main

themes constitutes the first movement. After a highly impassioned section the gloomy mood of the beginning reappears; the love theme and the heroic theme also return, but cannot sustain themselves, and the movement dissolves in anguish and longing.

The second movement is devoted to Gretchen. A very tender melody played by the oboe paints simply and beautifully the in-

nocence of Gretchen. The second theme is also very tender. In the

development section we hear some of Faust's motifs from the first movement, and also a beautiful love scene now tender, now exuberant. A reprise of the main section of the movement brings us again to the Gretchen theme, played this time by four solo violins in a delicate transfiguration of the image of Gretchen.

The Mephisto movement presents no new themes; Mephisto is characterized by the way in which he distorts all Faust's themes and tries to destroy them. A fantastical scherzo culminates in a crazy

fugue. Faust's themes are dismembered and interwoven with sa-
tanic laughter. Only when the Gretchen theme appears is Mephisto
powerless; we hear this in all its original beauty, and eventually it
reconciles the opposing themes. The moving climax of the symphony is reached with the organ's mysterious entry. A male chorus
sings Goethe's immortal words, 'All things corruptible are but a
parable'. A solo tenor is heard above these with motifs from the
Gretchen movement to the words 'Eternal Womanhood leads us
above'. The repetition of the *chorus mysticus* presses forward to a
mighty climax, and vanishes in quiet transfiguration.

The poetic idea for Liszt's symphonic poem *Dance in the Village
Inn* is an episode from Lenau's *Faust*, not Goethe's. Faust and
Mephisto come to a village inn, where a marriage is being celebrated with music and dancing. Mephisto seizes the violin and plays
himself. The dancers are enchanted by the demonic melodies and
the dance develops into a Bacchic tumult. Faust finds himself a girl
and disappears with her out of the circle of dancers. The *Dance in
the Village Inn* is subtitled 'Mephisto-Waltz'. It is a wild, demonic
dance. The elemental rhythms of the main section are followed by
a languid, restlessly rocking middle section, but this melodic theme
is distorted and drawn into the general tumult. The dance concludes
with a tender theme by the solo 'cello answered by the violins; the
flutes imitate nightingales, and in accord with the words of the
poem, the orchestra rushes up once more to the pitch of ecstasy.

Liszt's *Dante Symphony*, 1856, does not consist of three parts, as
one might imagine from the layout of the *Divine Comedy*, it has
only two parts: Inferno and Purgatory. Richard Wagner expressed
his doubts about representing Paradise in music, and Liszt gave up
his plan, deciding instead to conclude the second movement with
a Magnificat for female chorus, which, in its hymnic transfiguration really seems to reveal Heaven to the eyes of man.

The terrifying inscription on Dante's gate to Hell, 'Per me si va
nella città dolente' with the depressing concluding words 'Lasciate
ogni speranza voi ch'entrate!' (Abandon hope all ye who enter

here) is also the title of Liszt's Inferno. The hellish inscription is

indicated by trombones with a majestic *fortissimo* reverberating in
the kettledrums and gong. This theme is repeated twice, each time
with greater intensity, then the horns and trombones repeat it yet
again in merciless monotony: Abandon hope! The following section depicts the horrors of Hell. The whole orchestra is wild with
excitement and out of this Liszt develops two chromatic themes

that raise their brash heads repeatedly and then disappear. The movement ends with the old monotonous cry: Abandon hope! Harps,
flutes and violins now set a new scene with Paolo and Francesca,
Dante's classic lovers. The cor anglais plays a fervent melody with

arpeggio figures and glissandi, which leads into a soulful love song

played first by the 'cello, and then passionately by the whole
orchestra. This dream is snatched from us, however, by the 'Lasciate'
theme, and Hell rears its dreary head for the last time.

After the horrors of Hell, Liszt shows in his second movement
the blue of the sky as seen from the heights of the Mountain of
Purification. Here there is calm, peace and light, and hope of salvation. The woodwind create a mood of idyllic peace, and a pious
melody takes shape, like a prayer. Then the violas begin a distorted,

tormented theme which develops into a strange fugato, repre-

senting purification. Resigned once more, the pious theme reappears and forms the bridge to the Magnificat, the conclusion of the symphony. The female chorus, accompanied delicately by the orchestra, sings the song of praise and thanksgiving addressed by the Virgin Mary to her Creator. The Magnificat dissolves in a mystical transfiguration.

Liszt's piano concertos rank among his most important and best-known works. The *E-flat major Concerto* was composed in 1848. It is a work of extraordinary unity, for the energetic main theme,

introduced at the outset by the orchestra, dominates the first as well as the last movement. All the other important themes also recur several times in the course of the work. The concerto has four movements, all relatively short and played without a break. After four bars of the main theme, the piano enters with octave triplets and proceeds with a powerful cadenza, in which the main theme is skilfully elaborated. The piano's subsidiary theme is very melodious, but is impotent against the main idea. The movement ends with delicate arpeggios and runs in the piano part, while the orchestra asserts the main theme. The following adagio is a dreamlike melody executed by the piano, accompanied by wide arpeggios. In an excited recitative passage the beautiful melody is taken to pieces, and a passionate climax follows. Then the flute enters with a lovely melody, while the pianist's trills die away to nothing. The scherzo's character is largely determined by the glistening sound of the triangle and the brilliant cascades of the piano. The movement ends as the powerful, gloomy main motif is stated *pianissimo*, and a development similar to that at the beginning of the concerto leads up to the triumphant final movement. This brilliant finale unites all the themes of the work: first the adagio melody is converted into a march, and the graceful flute melody is given virtuoso treatment by the pianist, then the brilliant theme of the scherzo leads into a vivid *stretto*, in the course of which the main theme of the work triumphs, and forces the conclusion. Dazzling thematic work and interesting form are not the only features of this concerto. The elaboration of the piano part and the consummate instrumentation are perhaps responsible to a greater extent for the work's lasting success.

The *A-flat major Concerto*, composed in 1848, and remodelled in 1856, is also based entirely on its main theme, and this determines the character of the work. As opposed to the rather energetic main theme of the *E-flat major Concerto*, the main theme here is of a lyrical nature. There the rhythmic element was the decisive factor, here it is the transfigured harmony. The theme appears first very dreamily in the woodwind, then in the strings decorated by the piano. Finally, it is taken up properly by the solo instrument and developed in magnificent variations. A very gloomy march forms

a strange contrast to the sensitivity of this introduction. An excited orchestral theme, accompanied by blistering fanfares concludes the exposition. The middle section is the most beautiful episode of the concerto; an earnest dialogue between piano and solo 'cello, in which the main tune is taken by the 'cello. The brilliant climax of the work is the reprise, where the main theme, now transformed into a march, is played by piano and orchestra. Thus, the lyrical idea triumphs in the end over all the dramatic counter themes.

RICHARD WAGNER

born Leipzig 22 May 1813
died Venice 13 February 1883

Wagner only began to study music seriously when he was at university. In 1834 he took the part of conductor in Magdeburg where he wrote his opera *Das Liebesverbot*. In 1836 he worked in Königsberg, and in 1837 in Riga. Wagner went to Paris in 1839 in order to settle there as a self-employed musician; but in this he was unsuccessful. During the hunger years in Paris he completed *Rienzi*, which was performed with great success in Dresden in 1842. On the strength of this Wagner obtained the position of court conductor in Dresden. He was involved in the 1848 revolution and had to take refuge in Switzerland. He was able to return to Germany only in 1861, and in 1863 Ludwig II of Bavaria summoned him to Munich, where *Tristan* and the *Mastersingers* had their premières in 1865 and 1868 respectively. Intrigues forced Wagner to flee once more to Switzerland, and there he married Cosima von Bülow, Liszt's daughter. In 1871 he moved to Bayreuth, and laid the foundation stone of the opera house in 1872. In 1876 the first complete performance of the *Ring of the Nibelungs* was staged in it, and in 1882 the first performance of *Parsifal*.

Richard Wagner is the chief representative of high romanticism. His revolutionary musical style led him to break almost entirely with the existing musical tradition. Wagner's music is the forerunner of twentieth-century musical development. Although his music is limited exclusively to music drama, the novelty of his style is so significant that it has had an important influence on all fields of music. His melodic line, his 'endless melody', his dramatic harmony which almost breaks with the traditional concept of tonality, his characteristic instrumentation, his extraordinary refinement of the *leitmotif* technique—with all these characteristics of his art, Wagner became the chief influence on subsequent musical developments for a long time to come.

Purely instrumental works play a very small part in Wagner's work. His *C major Symphony*, a work of his early youth composed in 1832, is only interesting from a historic-biographical point of view. During his years in Paris, in 1839, Wagner intended to write a Faust Symphony, but after completing the first movement he abandoned the work. In 1855 Wagner remodelled this movement and published it as his *Faust Overture*. The motto for the overture is the following words by Goethe: 'The god who dwells enthroned within my breast can stir my inner vision's deepest springs, but he who binds my strength to his behest brings no command to sway external things. Thus life has taught me, with its weary weight, to long for death, and the dear light to hate.'

This longing for death expresses Wagner's state of mind during his years in Paris. The mood of the *Faust Overture* is similar to that of the *Flying Dutchman*, but the idea of salvation which finds expression in the latter overture is missing here. Tubas and basses presage the Faust motif in a gloomy measured rhythm over a timpani roll. The strings answer with a complete enunciation of the Faust theme with its striking octave steps. After a steep swing up, the slow introduction ends. The following allegro is dominated by the excited figure in the strings. The forward pressure and resigned downfall of this figure, which constantly undermines the powerful octave motif, form a striking expression of the mood of impotent despair. The delicate melody of the second theme appears first in the oboe. It seems to bring light into the darkness, but only for a short episode. The reprise is wild and unbridled, and even pulls the conciliatory second theme into its wake. The tone-painting ends on a gloomy note of self-destruction.

In the preludes to his music dramas Wagner continues the tradition of Beethoven and Weber, whose overtures can really be regarded as symphonic poems in the romantic sense. Wagner's preludes bring this line of development to perfection. They are complete musical poems in themselves, and as such have become very popular with concert audiences.

The *Rienzi Overture* of 1842, however, cannot be regarded as a symphonic poem in this sense. It is a great piece of introductory music in which the three themes of the opera are elaborated in the usual way. This music is characterized by its gripping swing, and the climaxes are breathtaking. The master dramatist is evident in every bar. The slow introduction states the noble melody of

Very sustained

Rienzi's prayer, at first delicately in the violins and 'cellos. A mighty build-up leads to the *fortissimo* orchestral repetition of the theme.

A note on the trumpet played three times, each time starting softly
and rising in a crescendo to *forte*, leads into the allegro. A wild
battle begins; a *fortissimo* war-cry in the trombone incites the warriors. Rienzi's prayer has a warlike sound played at double speed,

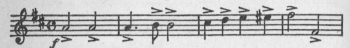

and this culminates in the war-cry, now executed by all the brass
instruments and leading to a war march. This starts *piano*, as if from

a distance and builds up slowly to a powerful *fortissimo*. The development section represents the battle in full swing; it presses forward powerfully to the triumphant reprise of the march theme.
A brilliant *stretto* ends the work.

In his overture to the *Flying Dutchman*, written in 1843, Wagner
provides a brilliant description of his romantic opera. This overture
is a symphonic poem of such clarity as is hardly to be found before
or after Wagner. The Dutchman is condemned to live at sea under
the terms of a curse; his only chance of release lies in the fidelity of
a woman. The two main motifs of the poem, his curse and the
possibility of release from it determine the ideas and structure of
the overture. The basic mood of the music is given by the representation of the sea: the key is a bald D minor, the woodwind play
high and shrill, and hard *tremolos* are heard in the strings. Horns
and bassoon add the Dutchman's call of open fifths; the basses

storm upwards with wild chromaticism and tumble down *fortissimo*; the Dutchman's call is heard again and a howling storm in
the full orchestra spends itself and runs down. Now comes a delicate

statement of the release motif in the cor anglais; the oboe repeats
the theme like a ray of hope. However, the Dutchman's call returns,
and the short idyll is drowned in the excited waves of the strings.
The storm breaks with wild passion; the release motif tries several
times to break through, but is immediately drowned in the howling
of the storm. The merry song of the sailors is like a vision of a
passing ship, but this friendly image is also swallowed up in the
violence of the storm. The release theme makes another attempt,
becoming more and more powerful, until at last it gains the upper
hand over the menacing elements, with a passionate crescendo in
the strings. The curse motif tries to break through, once more, but
is submerged in the waves; the release theme remains victorious
and ends the work on a note of promise.

The *Tannhäuser Overture* can also be regarded as a complete
symphonic poem on its own. The work presents the whole content
of the opera with such unity that this symphonic interpretation of
the material seems just as exhaustive as the opera itself. Wagner
himself recognized this and declared repeatedly that the *Tannhäuser
Overture* should be included in concert programmes. The content
of the opera, and thus of the overture, is the division in Tannhäuser's personality. The sensual side of his nature, symbolized in
his yearning for the world of Venus, stands in opposition to his
morality, which leads him back to life as a Christian knight. These
two worlds are represented by the beguiling charm of the Venusberg music on the one hand, and the ascetic grandeur of the melody
of the pilgrims' chorus on the other. The overture is based on the
contrast inherent in these two themes. The music of the pilgrims'
chorus is heard at the beginning and at the end of the work. The
big middle section consists of the Venusberg music and its extinction. This section is also very clear in the succession and repetition
of the various themes and thematic groups. After the collapse of
the magic world of Venus the music of the pilgrims' chorus closes
the work with great sensitivity and grandeur of expression.

The Venusberg music, composed later, is also frequently performed in the concert hall. The revival of *Tannhäuser* in Paris in
1861 was the incentive for the composition of the *Venusberg-
Bacchanale*. The Grand Opera House in Paris was at that time
Europe's leading opera house and it was absolutely essential to have
a ballet interlude in the second act. This would have meant composing ballet music for the Wartburg act, and Wagner refused for
artistic reasons which are understandable; he was willing, however,

to write pantomime music as an introduction to the Venusberg scenes. Actually, this was purely a formal reason; he really wanted to write some new music for Venus. The Paris version of *Tann-häuser* is changed only in the Venus scenes, which, after twenty years, seemed to Wagner not passionate and ecstatic enough. The music of Elizabeth and the knights he left untouched. The incomparable charm of the new Venusberg music is reminiscent of *Tristan*, but his renunciation of the world is replaced by a new-found sensuality. The concert performance of the *Bacchanale* generally consists of a shortened version of the *Tannhäuser Overture*, leaving out the reprise of the pilgrims' chorus and inserting in its place the first scene of the opera in the Paris version, the *Bacchanale*. After the introduction of the pilgrims' song we hear the themes of the Venus music. Tannhäuser's knightly love song is played twice and then the veil is torn from our eyes and we are carried away by the wild sensuality of the new Venusberg music. The well-known themes of the old version of *Tannhäuser* appear in a completely new form. The motifs are shorter, often only brief intimations of themes; the harmonies, the orchestration, everything is new, more colourful, wilder, delirious. A longing call, reminiscent in its chromaticism of the *Tristan* music, gets progressively more demanding and passionate and develops into a wild dance underlined by the rhythm of castanets and other percussion instruments. The climax is a shrill *fortissimo* of the full orchestra, in which familiar string figurations from the overture reappear in a dancing rhythm. Gradually repletion sets in, the call of the sirens sounds from a distance, the wild rhythms fade away, and Wagner's brilliant improvisation ends in a lovely melodic style.

The prelude to *Lohengrin*, written in 1850, signalizes a new type of operatic introduction. It is another symphonic poem, but in its form and content it diverges widely both from the overtures of Beethoven and Weber and from Wagner's own *Flying Dutchman* and *Tannhäuser Overtures*. In the prelude to *Lohengrin* Wagner does not rely on a dramatic contrast. A single theme, one idea, is sufficient to express the musical action, the descent of the Holy Grail. The strings evolve light harmonies out of the delicate harmonies of the violins, and a celestial melody sways above them. Gradually, the range of the music is extended downwards and the woodwind take the lead melodically, and later the horns. With the entry of trumpets and trombones the climax is reached; the full orchestra states the Grail theme in all its glory, which gradually ebbs away again and disappears into the weightless harmonies from whence it came.

The same unity is characteristic of the prelude to *Tristan and Isolde*, written in 1859. This prelude, too, is based on only one theme, the theme of longing and love. In concert performances of

the *Tristan* prelude Wagner used to follow it with the concluding scene of the opera, the 'Liebestod' scene. Thus the beginning and end of the music drama, the two opposing poles of the work, are brought together to form a unity in themselves. This mysterious piece has a unique position not only among Wagner's works, but in the whole literature of music. Wagner said himself that he chose longing, constant disruptive desire as the theme of the prelude of his drama of love—unfulfilled longing with all its hopes and fears, joys and tortures, eternally newborn desire for ecstasy. This music of longing and desire builds up constantly, but collapses at its climax and returns to the first shy phrase of the wooing motif in the beginning. After the theme has disappeared the melody of the first song is introduced, at first delicately, and then ever broader and higher. This is not Isolde's 'Liebestod', as this wonderful song is generally but erroneously called, but Isolde's transfiguration, the transfiguration and eternal union of the lovers in infinite space, 'without bonds, without partings', to quote Wagner's own words.

The prelude to the *Mastersingers* is characterized by its clear C major tonality, as opposed to the *Tristan* prelude. With each new work Wagner creates a new world of sounds, and this is immediately plain in the prelude. The special atmosphere of the *Mastersingers* music is created by the plastic clarity of the themes within the artful polyphonic web of parts. The music is expressive of festivity, *joie de vivre* and powerful feeling. The full orchestra introduces the main theme. After a short transition a mighty fanfare motif is struck up by the brass, and then brilliantly adopted by

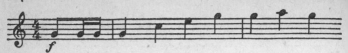

the strings and powerfully developed. A lively syncopated motif leads to the second theme, a love melody which is a version of Walther's *Prize Song*. The wooing becomes more demanding and

the strings more and more brilliant. Abruptly the music breaks up; the woodwind play the theme of the *Mastersingers* at double-speed like a caricature while the strings prolong the love melody. A theme from the mocking chorus in the third act is added, and a wild build-up leads to the reprise in a radiant C major, which unites all three main themes in a brilliant climax. The basses play the powerful theme of the *Mastersingers*, violins, 'cellos and horns sing the love song, while second violins, violas and woodwind play a *scherzando* version of the fanfare motif. The fanfare motif takes the leading rôle in the big build-up that follows and then gives place to the main theme which ends the work on a festive, joyful note.

The prelude to *Parsifal* belongs in the group of Wagner's preludes that have no dramatic structure and only one main idea to express the action of the opera. It gives musical expression to the mystery of faith. Strings and woodwind introduce the motif of the Lord's

Supper, and the oboes and trumpets repeat the melody, accompanied by string arpeggios and silvery woodwind chords. This strange tone-painting is repeated in the minor key and then dissolves in light chord sequences in the flutes and clarinets. With a deep breath the trumpets and trombones intone the theme of the

Grail, which reverberates to nothing in the woodwind. Horns and trumpets take up the motif of faith in unison, and this is extended by the woodwind and strings. The pious melody builds up in long phrases, higher and higher, like a great dome of faith. The motif of the Lord's Supper re-emerges from this melody, with a tragic and expressive air. Finally, in the distance, the magical chords of the Grail motif are heard once more.

Two passages from the final opera of the *Ring* (*Götterdämmerung*) are often played as concert pieces. The first is *Siegfried's Rhine Journey*, which links the prelude of the opera and the first act. Siegfried, protected by spells of invincibility woven by Brünhilde, sets out on fresh adventures. On the stage we see Brünhilde looking fondly after him as he leaves, and we hear the music that expresses her love for Siegfried. Then the music of the Rhine appears and various other motifs connected with the drama.

The other passage is the *Funeral March* after the death of Siegfried. This superb piece of rhythmic cumulation opens with timpani alone, playing the rhythm:

on a low C-sharp. This rhythm, deployed chordally, in combination with expressive mourning material, builds up to shattering climaxes that leave us in no doubt as to the stature of the departed hero. The piece ends quietly with moonlight reflected in the Rhine, and the rhythmic figure subdued and subterranean, again in the timpani (C-natural).

Apart from some juvenile works and his Wesendonck songs, there is only one work by Wagner which can stand beside his great music dramas, namely the *Siegfried Idyll*, which he composed in 1870, as a birthday surprise for Cosima. It expresses his devotion and gratitude to his wife, who had just given birth to their son, Siegfried. The *Siegfried Idyll* is scored for small orchestra, and its themes are taken from the third act of *Siegfried*, on which Wagner was working at that time. The first main idea is played by the strings. In *Siegfried* this is the theme of Brünhilde's words, 'Deathless was I, deathless am I'. The clarinet plays the contrasting theme,

'O Siegfried, Herrlicher! Hört der Welt!', which is fervent in ex-

pression and of a profound sensitivity. Both themes are developed,
varied and combined, and other motifs from the *Ring*, for example,
Brünhilde's slumber motif, are added. In the dense, but transparent
polyphonic texture the joyful sound of Siegfried's horn is heard as
a climax. As a reserved conclusion, the strings gently recapitulate
the two main ideas of the work.

Wagner's songs with orchestra to words by Mathilde Wesendonck show his mastery of the small, closed form of the *lied*. The
first song 'The Angel' is a gentle melody that rises quietly from the
low register over a rocking accompaniment. The second song
'Stand thou still' begins as a *perpetuum mobile* of semiquavers in $^6/_8$—
'endlessly galloping steeds of time'—but by the end, the tempo has
evaporated to 'langsam' (slow), and over quiet chords, the singer
sings emphatically: 'For man has touched the summit of life.' The
third song 'Im Treibhaus' (In the Conservatory) is particularly
interesting because it is obviously a preparatory study for the music
of *Tristan and Isolde*. The poem describes pathetically the 'yearning
and imploring' of the exotic plants for their far-off homes. The
crawling, chromatic music describes the cloying, sweet perfume of
the imprisoned plants. The fourth song 'Schmerzen' (Tears) is the
strongest of the group. The tempo is slow, the feeling broad and
heroic. The strong harmonies and rhythms reach a climax at the
words 'O wie dank' ich, dass gegeben solche Schmerzen mir Natur'
(Then may we give thanks to Nature for the boon of pain and
tears). The key is A minor, but the song begins with a first inversion
and ends with a second inversion. The final song 'Dream' begins
softly in F major so that E, the dominant of A minor and the bass-
note of the last chord of the preceding, appears as the leading note
to the new key.

JOHANNES BRAHMS

born Hamburg 7 May 1833
died Vienna 3 April 1897

Brahms was the son of a double bass player, and was brought up in poverty. However, he received excellent musical tuition from the Hamburg composer Marxsen, who recognized the extraordinary talent of his pupil and tried to further it. Brahms appeared in public as pianist and accompanist at quite an early age, and the great violinist Joseph Joachim discovered him and recommended him to Schumann and Liszt. In 1853 Schumann wrote his famous article in the *New Journal of Music* which proclaimed the name of Brahms far beyond purely musical circles. After working for a few years as a director of music in Detmold, and then attempting to settle in Hamburg, in 1863 Brahms finally resolved to move to Vienna. There he wrote his greatest works, the *Requiem* and the symphonies. Against his wishes, the almighty critic Hanslick drew him into a quarrel with Wagner and Bruckner which was entirely alien to his nature.

The phrases 'Wagner versus Brahms' and 'Bruckner versus Brahms' which were heard for decades in the musical world have now vanished entirely. However, this conflict shows clearly that even at that time Wagner and Brahms were recognized as the most significant musical spirits of the second half of the nineteenth century, who between them brought about a vast enrichment of musical literature. Bruckner is Wagner's complement in the field of absolute music, whereas Brahms and Wagner are complementary in every sense; they are at opposite poles. With the universality of his ideas and the classical feeling of his forms, Brahms is the immediate successor to Beethoven. He is also a complete romantic; his musical language is a romantic language, but of his own specific variety, quite distinct from that of Wagner or Schumann. For Brahms it is never the sound alone that is decisive, nor the expression, but the line of his music, the draughtmanship of his phrasing.

Like Schumann, Brahms turned his attention to the symphony only quite late in his career. His first symphony was published in 1876, when he was forty-three years old. The sketches for this powerful symphony date back as far as 1854, which is an indication of the cautiousness of Brahms' approach to symphonic form. His previous orchestral works, the first piano concerto and the two

serenades, can be regarded as studies in the symphonic field, but his
most important step on the way to the symphony was his *Variations
on a theme by Joseph Haydn in B-flat major*, opus 56, written in the
summer of 1873 in Tutzing. Haydn's theme, the *St Anthony Chorale*, starts with two five-bar phrases, instead of the usual four-bar

phrases. The dotted rhythm of the first bar dominates the development of the simple theme, whose end is marked by a B-flat repeated
five times. The first variation harps on this ending; basses and high
woodwind alternate with the five repetitions of the tonic and the
strings build a network of delicate figurations around it in quavers
and triplets. This is constantly interrupted by the bell-like B-flat.
The second variation takes up the characteristic dotted rhythm of
the theme and prolongs it in passages in sixths for clarinets and
bassoons. In the third variation first the oboes and then the violins
play a flowing melody derived from the theme. The horn leads in
the fourth variation, and the melody is shifted into the minor key.
The fifth and sixth variations are *scherzando* in character. The
seventh variation is especially effective: its graceful melody appears
in a rocking $6/8$ rhythm. The last variation forms a strange contrast
to this idyll; it is *pianissimo* throughout, and runs in the muted
strings, with bassoon, clarinet and piccolo performing a ghostly
dance. The finale is a kind of passacaglia; a bass line of five bars
modelled on the theme is repeated seventeen times, with seventeen short variations over it. This leads into the triumphal repetition of the Haydn theme.

Brahms had been working on plans for his first symphony for
nearly two decades, before he published it at the age of forty-three.
After its long period of incubation, however, Brahms' symphony
proved a worthy successor to Beethoven. This *Symphony No. 1 in
C minor*, opus 68, is related in character to Beethoven's *C minor
Symphony*. Through darkness into light, through struggle to victory, is Brahms' motto for his symphony.

The first movement starts with overwhelming power and grandeur: the theme climbs up in semitones over a gloomy pedal point.
The chromatic ascending motion of the first three notes forms the
basis of the movement. It recurs again and again in different voices,
and even becomes the germinating cell of the whole symphony.

Un poco sostenuto

After the grand introduction, the various parts are, as it were, auditioned; the strings start the main theme tentatively but soon revert to the powerful organ point, and after a short interlude we pass on to the excited allegro. Chromatic ascent is also the characteristic of the first allegro theme, though it is largely triadic. This first

Allegro

part expresses painful longing increased to a pitch of tormenting excitement. Calm descends only gradually. The second theme starts

p espress.

imploringly with the oboe and is continued by the clarinet and horn. This friendly episode is interrupted by a harsh motif in the

p pizz.   *arco*

strings. Titanic struggles are followed by a melody like a chorale which offers consolation, but this is thrown back by the opposing powers. The struggle goes on, but gradually it has to weaken. The grand theme of the slow introduction reappears and the main theme looks towards the major key. The movement ends in a soft melancholy mood.

The second movement, andante sostenuto, is dominated by the

desire for peace and quiet. Peace, however, does not appear immediately. Chromatic figurations still disturb the harmony. Only at
the end of this melodious movement does Brahms succeed in iron-
ing out the disturbing elements, and the solo violin and horn play
a delicate melody together. The third movement has little to do
with the usual scherzo. The first theme is expressive of quiet satisfaction, and the trio, with its beautiful dialogue between woodwind and strings, is also calm. The themes join up, separate again,
and the dance ends with a feeling of indecision. The last bars sound
like a fugue, waiting for an answer, and the answer is given by the
powerful finale, one of the most wonderful movements in symphonic literature. The gloomy mood of the first movement is
present again: there are bars of excited *pizzicati*, a passionate recitative in the woodwind, a *fortissimo* timpani roll drowns everything
as it storms forward and then fades away; the orchestra holds its
breath. The horn plays a wonderful simple melody—an unforgettable experience for any receptive audience. Joyfully, the flute

takes up this melody, and a short chorale interlude in the trombones
emphasizes the solemn mood. The repetition of the wonderful
horn melody then leads to the main part of the finale, the allegro.
The allegro starts straight away with the main theme, which in

character and melody is a conscious reference to the melody of joy
in Beethoven's *Ninth Symphony*. A triumphant hymn of joy develops out of this grand melody together with several other joyful
motifs. It represents the final liberation from all the forces of darkness that were active in the first movement; all doubts are overcome. The grand horn theme forms a brilliant climax, and the joyful *stretto* is crowned by the chorale theme from the introduction,
played now by the full orchestra. Brahms' *First Symphony* makes
large demands on the listener; the spiritual world of this monumental work cannot be entered without considerable mental concentration.

Brahms finished his *Symphony No. 2 in D major*, opus 73, in 1877, one year after the *First Symphony*. The composition of the *First Symphony* took Brahms more than ten years; the *Second Symphony* was completed within a few months. A happy summer holiday at Lake Wörther in Kärnten inspired the composition, and in the autumn the great work was completed. Happy, affirmative feelings are expressed in this symphony, though, as is natural in Brahms' great works, serious ideas also have an essential part to play.

The first movement can be thought of as a summer idyll. After an introductory bar with a figure in the bass that is to be significantly exploited in the development section, the horn starts the main theme, which is then continued by the woodwind. This

theme, based on the tonic triad, is followed by a lovely subsidiary theme in the violins which really establishes the allegro character

of the movement. A delightful subsidiary idea in the oboes leads to the languid second theme, in the high register of the 'cellos. This

melody is followed by animated rhythmic themes, which drive the movement on. Powerfully accented steps in the high violins lead back again to the second theme. The development section starts with the idyllic main theme, played solo by the first horn in F major, which produces the effect of an echo coming from a distance. The horn plays an important part in the whole of this movement. Especially beautiful is the horn part at the end of the movement: after the reprise is finished, the horn states a beautiful

p dolce

longing melody, and this little episode seems a microcosmic expression of the basic character of the whole movement.

The second movement, 'adagio non troppo', is of a serious nature. A characteristic theme played first by the 'cellos dominates

poco f

the movement. During the development the atmosphere of gloom becomes almost depressing, and the return of the main theme has a calming and consoling effect. The third movement, allegretto

Allegretto grazioso

grazioso, is a very genial piece. The way the charming oboe theme is transformed rhythmically in the two trios is quite enchanting.

Presto

The final movement starts softly and mysteriously, but the basic character of the movement is powerful and brilliant. The second theme, executed mainly in sixths and thirds, is especially impulsive and affirmative. This theme is almost march-like in character and is

very prominent throughout the movement. The conclusion is loud and triumphant.

Brahms completed his *Symphony No. 3 in F major*, opus 90, in 1883, when he was fifty years old and at the peak of his creative power. Brahms never spoke much about his own works and his biographers are correspondingly voluble. Some regarded Brahms' *Third Symphony* as his heroic symphony, others compared it with Beethoven's *Fifth* and called it a symphony of fate, others again called it a symphony of nature. Whatever the fashionable opinion may be, it is generally agreed that this symphony is the perfect expression of Brahms' maturity in every aspect, be it form, idea, or spiritual greatness.

A particular characteristic of this symphony is its major–minor ambience, the continuous shifting between the two modes. The first bars give immediate expression to this dualism, and it is evident

in the passionate main theme. The leading motif is heroic in character, and recurs in many variants, now triumphant, now calm and

transfigured. The second theme is idyllic. The effective melody is played first by the clarinet like a folk tune, and then taken up by

other instruments, but it soon fades like the memory of a dream. Powerful ideas assert themselves and lead back to the heroic basic character of the movement. The development section is dominated by a mood of virile decision, transformed and carried along by the powerful currents. Slowly the excitement ebbs and gives way to one of the most effective sections of the symphony: the little motto motif is extended into a drawn-out melody played by the horn. The music takes on an aspect of transfigured calm; even the resolute main theme is reduced to a mysterious *pianissimo*. However, the

calm is only apparent. A timpani roll leads to a *forte* restatement of
the motto, and the recapitulation opens with the main theme in all
its original strength. The idyll of the second, folk-like theme is also
recapitulated, but is soon absorbed in the dominant character of
the movement. The wonderful movement ends calmly, but this
should not be interpreted as resignation; on the contrary, it is the
calm that comes after a successful struggle. This idea also forms the
basis of the great last movement, thus bringing the two outer
movements together and closing the symphonic circle. The middle
movements are an andante and an allegretto. Both movements are
characterized by their clarity of form and melodic expression.

A folk tune forms the basic idea of the andante. It stirs up beautiful memories and creates a host of new images in its many guises.

These are all of a happy nature, and the occasional heavier variants
cannot mar the general ease of the movement. In the allegretto the
'cellos play a languid nocturnal melody whose long phrases are

later taken up by the violins, and then by the horn. A charming,
sweetly harmonic subsidiary theme contains intimations of dance
rhythms. This episode is supplanted by the horn playing the melody
from the opening. The finale is mysterious and excited in mood,

and this is intensified when the trombones enter *piano*; then a passionate struggle breaks out. A confident horn call is juxtaposed
with this excited texture; gradually the tumultuous music fades
and peace returns. The concluding section is broad, and crowned
by the heroic theme of the first movement. The great man finds
peace and equilibrium after a long struggle.

Brahms' last symphony, of 1885, is the *Symphony No. 4 in E minor*, opus 98. The drear and bitter character of the minor key pervades all the music, even the middle movements, written in E major and C major respectively. The basic character of this symphony is its sincerity; it is like a final reflection on the seriousness of life and fate, and how, despite transitory strength and enthusiasm, bitter resignation is the lot of mankind.

The first movement is narrative in character: it is like a nordic ballad about heroes and heroic deeds, and also about their bitter experiences. The climax of the movement is the recapitulation of the main theme after a relatively short development section. The

second movement, andante moderato, is a romanza. The main

motif is strangely old-fashioned, and though the middle section is a little livelier, the mood of the whole is one of quiet melancholy.

The third movement, too, despite its tempo indication *allegro giocoso*, is not gay, but excitable, almost wild, obstinate and brusque, although lighter, graceful subsidiary themes are introduced as effective contrasts.

The powerful crown of the work is the fourth movement, a brilliant set of variations on a simple eight-bar theme introduced by the brass. This theme is a short climbing melody, of which each

note has a bar to itself. This theme is repeated thirty-one times, sometimes in the bass, sometimes as the melody or in one of the inner parts. It runs right through the whole movement, like a *cantus firmus*, thus giving it the character of a passacaglia. First, the theme is repeated in *pizzicato* by the strings, then woodwind join in with a figure that takes the rôle of the main theme. The mood gets more excited and more passionate and then this suddenly ebbs away, leaving absolute quiet. The middle section of the movement is introduced in an expressive variation for the flute, followed by a dialogue between the oboe and the clarinet. The tempo has become broader, E minor changes tc E major, the rhythm becomes calm and a solemn melody is played by the trombones. The seventeenth variation begins the recapitulation with passionate grandeur. Besides despair, the end of the work expresses resignation and acceptance of the inescapability of fate.

Besides his four symphonies Brahms wrote another gigantic cycle of works, namely the four concertos: two piano concertos, one violin concerto, and a double concerto for violin and 'cello. All four are works of unity, clarity and perfection, each one a world unto itself.

Brahms' *Concerto No. 1 for piano in D minor*, opus 15, is not a concerto in the usual sense, in which the solo instrument takes the leading part. This concerto is more like a symphony in which the piano has a decisive part to play, but *with* the orchestra rather than against it. In fact, Brahms had originally, in 1853, designed the *D minor Concerto* as a symphony. Later he remodelled it and wrote it as a sonata for two pianos, and only in 1861 did he give the work its final form. Of the three movements of the concerto the first, maestoso, is the most powerful and effective. The main theme is

introduced *fortissimo* by the orchestra at the outset. The powerful thematic idea is extraordinarily gripping and hard, but it is mitigated by gentler subsidiary themes. The piano introduces one such theme after the elemental outburst in the orchestra has faded to *pianissimo*. In its structure this melody is reminiscent of pre-classical themes, and it, too, is filled with an inner tension. The second theme played by the piano alone is lyrical and reconciling. In this movement the piano is often the harbinger of friendly, conciliatory ideas. The development section opens with wild octave passages for the pianist; the dark powers are in the ascendent. The climax of the movement is reached with the return of the main theme, this time played by the piano, *fortissimo*, and accompanied by thunderous timpani rolls. The consoling subsidiary theme is again played by the pianist with beautiful simplicity, but the movement ends as gloomily as it started.

The second movement forms an enormous contrast; it is a peaceful adagio. A pious hymn rises to sublime heights and dies away in a reserved *pianissimo*. The final movement starts with its main theme, introduced by the piano soloist. The theme is robust and almost brusque, and sets the tone for the whole finale. Despite some playful subsidiary themes, the dominant character of the movement is very virile. Struggles and conflicts that are reminiscent of the dramatic first movement are here brought to a powerful and happy conclusion.

However gentle the second movement and however lively and interesting the finale, the most significant impression of Brahms' *D minor Concerto* is undoubtedly the first maestoso. The passionate grandeur of this movement is unique in the history of music. Its main theme is said to have been inspired by the news that Robert Schumann, Brahms' dearly beloved friend and master, had attempted suicide.

Brahms' piano concertos are so large in form and technique, that they are referred to as 'symphonies with obligato piano'. This description fits the *B-flat major Concerto*, opus 83, Brahms' second piano concerto, particularly well, for the solo instrument is organically interwoven with the symphonic structure. The first movement is romantic in character. The concerto begins with a fervent horn theme and this is taken up and delicately extended by the

woodwind. The piano part struggles against this theme. The whole allegro is built on this contrast of moods; the main theme passes through a series of transformations, and at the end takes on quite an assertive character.

This complicated movement is followed by a tough scherzo, with only occasional soft undertones. The third movement, andante, is full of languid melodic work of which the solo 'cello takes a large share. One beautiful 'cello theme is a variant of Brahms'

song, 'Sleep, ever lighter through my grieving'. In the middle
section this is juxtaposed with a further quotation from Brahms'
song, 'Todessehnen' (Longing for Death), played by the clarinet.
The piano ornaments these melodies with great delicacy. The conclusion of the andante is particularly poetic. The final movement is a happy rondo with a merry, dance-like main theme. The
second thematic group in the style of Hungarian dances is very
effective, especially the episode with the clarinets *pianissimo*. The
movement ends gaily and affirmatively with a *stretto* of the main
theme.

Brahms' *Concerto for violin in D major*, opus 77, was written in the
summer of 1878 in Pörtschach in Kärnten. This places it between
the *Second* and *Third Symphonies*, and traces of both are united in
the violin concerto. Thus we find the idyllic side of the *Second
Symphony* giving way to the serious and heroic aspect of the *Third*.

Characteristic of the first movement is the *joie de vivre* that prevails throughout and asserts itself in defiance of all vague dreams.
This contrast is clearly recognizable in the thematic structure of the
work. Even before the entry of the solo violin, the disposition of
themes is clearly indicated in the introductory orchestra *tutti*. The
first theme, based on the tonic triad, is simple and of a joyful, festive

character. This theme is energetically developed, but soon loses
itself in a lyrical, reflective atmosphere. The rhythmic second
theme, in the minor key, tears us away from this mood and forms
a brilliant contrast to the main thematic group. The solo violin
then takes up the second theme, and both thematic groups are repeated. During the development section a number of new ideas are
introduced, and the music progresses stormily to the recapitulation
of both themes. In the middle of a *fortissimo* climax the orchestra
breaks off, and the cadenza follows, without accompaniment. The
most beautiful part of the concerto begins with the re-entry of the
orchestra: the solo violin floats above the orchestra and repeats the
main theme like a vision of happiness, and a steep uprush concludes
the movement. The noble idyll of the adagio forms a contrast to
the powerful first movement. The main idea is played first by the
oboe, and then prolonged and freely developed by the solo violin.

This adagio expresses a lofty, earnest and yet delicate feeling for nature. The final movement is again healthy and vigorous. The

second theme, especially, with its ascending octaves, is virile and affirmative. The solo part is very virtuoso, especially the lively triplet variant of the main theme, which brings the work to its powerful close.

The first performance of the concerto was given by Joseph Joachim, who had doubtless been a great help to his friend in advising him on the layout of the solo part. The concerto proved technically insurmountable at that time, which is probably the reason why it did not get better known. Today it is part of the repertoire of every concert violinist and is recognized as the most significant and beautiful work in this genre since Beethoven's violin concerto.

At this point we must mention another violin concerto that has become a standard work, namely MAX BRUCH's *Violin Concerto in G minor*, which is a perfect jewel in the literature for the violin. The second movement is perhaps the most rewarding piece of music that has ever been written for the violin. This middle movement is in every sense the kernel of the concerto. Max Bruch (1838–1920) wrote his concerto from the violinist's point of view: every bar sings, the cantilena writing is wonderful in all registers, and every passage is perfectly violinistic. The allegro movements that frame the adagio are brief but full of virtuosity. The first movement serves as an introduction: a rather melancholy phrase in the orchestra is answered twice by the solo violin in freely developed cadenzas. Then, an orchestral *fortissimo* forms the bridge to the rhythmic main theme which, played first by the violin, dominates the short movement. At the end of the movement, the melancholy phrase from the opening returns, again answered by violin cadenzas, and the movement ends *pianissimo*. The slow movement which follows immediately is full of expressive melodic material. The fervent main theme is played by the violin, and the subsidiary theme by the orchestra with virtuoso embellishment by the soloist.

The main theme glows again in a big build-up and then sinks back
into *pianissimo*. The last movement offers a light dance-like main
theme and a dramatic subsidiary theme in contrast. However, the
dance theme prevails, and with a fiery swing, brings the concerto
to a brilliant close.

To return to Brahms. His *Double Concerto in A minor for violin,
'cello and orchestra*, opus 102, composed in 1887, is much less frequently played than his other concertos. Brahms wished to continue the tradition of the concerto grosso, just as Beethoven had
with his triple concerto. The lack of enthusiasm for this work is
accountable chiefly to the difficulties inherent in its execution; it
is not often that one can secure two eminent soloists who are entirely attuned to one another. However, it is worth the effort, for
this work is just as beautiful and rich in ideas as Brahms' more
popular concertos. The first allegro is laid out on a grand scale,
perhaps a little too grand in relation to the other two movements.
After an introductory cadenza for the two solo instruments, the
orchestra states the themes of the movement. The melodious second
theme is especially memorable. The solo instruments play a decisive
part in the development of the movement, sometimes in harmony
and sometimes contrasted. Sometimes they play simply in octaves,
for instance in the flowing melody of the andante, the wonderful
climax of the work. The final rondo is highly virtuoso. The main
scherzando theme is contrasted with several subsidiary themes,
among them a rhythmic dance theme played by the soloists in
thirds, and a tender melody introduced by the clarinet, with embellishments in the solo instruments. Brahms develops a brilliant
finale out of this superabundance of thematic material; it is a very
rewarding piece for both soloists.

Brahms wrote both his overtures, so disparate in feeling, in 1880,
which puts them between the second and third symphonies. Their
titles are the *Academic Festival Overture* and the *Tragic Overture*.

The *Academic Festival Overture*, opus 80, is Brahms' musical
thanksgiving for the reception of an honorary doctorate from the
University of Breslau. Brahms used well-known student songs for
the themes of his overture and this was severely frowned on by the
music critics. The general public, on the other hand, accepted this
humour with great enthusiasm. Despite its merriment the overture
bears traces of melancholy; it is the reflection of the mature man
on his bygone youth. Everyone is still asleep as the strings open the

work. Delicately, the trumpets then play the beautiful melody 'Wir hatten gebauet ein stattliches Haus', which is continued by oboes and clarinets and leads up to the introductory motif, now bright and powerful in the major key. Further on we hear 'Hört, ich sing das Lied der Lieder', and finally the bassoon introduces the fox song, 'Was kommt dort von der Höh?'. The various themes are beautifully handled stylistically in the development section. The reprise brings back the main melodies, and the work ends with a majestic orchestral statement of the 'Gaudeamus igitur'.

The *Tragic Overture*, opus 81, is not one of Brahms' happiest creations and it is played relatively seldom. The main theme starts straight off after two strokes from the orchestra and a kettledrum

roll. This builds up rapidly with a strange alternation between the major and minor modes. A mysterious motif in the trombones reminds us of the eternal enigma of fate. The second theme is friendlier, but cannot assert itself, and the section ends as it began with two strokes from the orchestra. Over the kettledrum roll the main theme strides by and dissolves to nothingness, accompanied by pale wind chords: a very effective moment! Dotted rhythms step in to fill this vacuum and form up into a funeral march, only to dissolve again to nothing. Once more the struggle starts, but the main theme asserts itself in all its power and grandeur. There is nothing that can resist fate.

Brahms' *Requiem* is his greatest choral work, and also the most popular. Its success has never waned since its first performance in 1868. The *Requiem* made Brahms' name famous throughout the musical world. The work is written in a very personal style; the ascetic quality of Brahms' expressiveness is intensified by the text. However, the wonderful clarity of its formal layout has a profound impact, and it is always greeted with fierce enthusiasm.

The *Requiem* consists of seven movements. The first three tell of the sadness in the transitoriness of life. The movements of the second half bring consolation and promise of eternal life. Brahms composed the text for the *Requiem* himself, out of words from the Bible. Since he knew the Bible very well, it was easy for him to compile a text that would accord with his conception.

The first part is solemn: 'Blest are they that mourn.' In character it is calm and devotional, its colours muted, and only occasionally lit by delicate harp sounds. The second movement is full of a rigid grandeur. The orchestra sets up a march-like rhythm and the chorus sing a chorale tune in unison to the words 'All flesh doth perish as the grass'. A consoling middle section commends patience, but the chorus resumes its chorale. The movement concludes with the joyful prophecy: 'And the ransomed of the Lord shall return.' The third movement is chiefly given to the baritone soloist: 'Lord, make me know what the measure of my days may be, let me know all my frailty, ere Death o'ertake me.' The chorus reiterates the desperate cries of the soloist. The solo outbursts are urgent and fearful, but the choral reiterations are at first resigned. However, during the course of the movement the chorus becomes progressively infected with the soloist's anguish, even with the words 'Lo! how surely every man living doth at his best live vainly'. Consolation comes with the climax, 'My hope is in Thee', which leads into the concluding fugue, 'But the souls of the redeemed are in the hands of God'. The fugue builds up like a grandiose cathedral of polyphony and forms an overwhelming ending to the first part.

The second part starts with an extremely graceful chorus, 'How lovely are thy dwellings fair', the first indication of the beauty of eternal life. The fifth movement, a soprano solo, offers consolation from above: 'Ye now are sorrowful', to which the orchestral accompaniment is very delicate. The chorus softly repeats the consoling words, and above, the high soprano voice sounds like a heavenly promise. The sixth movement is the dramatic climax of the work, the Dies Irae of the *Requiem*. The baritone solo leads. After an introductory choral funeral march, 'On this earth we have no continuing home', the soloist hints at the eternal mystery: 'We shall all be immortalized.' The chorus bursts out *fortissimo*, 'Then shall sound the trumpet, and the dead shall all be raised incorruptible', and develops a choral passage of great passion depicting all the horror, but also all the sublimity of the Last Judgement. The movement ends with a grand choral fugue: 'Lord, thou art worthy of praise and glory, honour and power.' The final movement reverts to the mood of the first movement: 'Blessed are they that die in the Lord', and the *Requiem* ends on a note of quiet devotion and transfiguration.

The *Schicksalslied* (Song of Destiny) for mixed chorus and orchestra, opus 54, written in 1868, is one of Brahms' largest choral works.

In concept it is very close to the *Requiem*. It is based on a poem by Hölderlin which contrasts the peace of the gods with the insecurity of humanity, doomed to perish. The chorus sings of the eternal peace of the gods in a broad melody with clear rhythms. Then the orchestra bursts out wildly, expressing the anguish of tortured humanity. Distracted and breathless, the humans call to one another and unite in a cry of disgust. The kettledrum beats out its disembodied rhythm: Fate is merciless! The chorus ends at this point. For Brahms there is no escape from this antique conception of Fate; he repeats the orchestral introduction depicting the eternal peace of the gods. This vision of a better world is conciliatory—but slightly bitter.

Brahms' *Rhapsody for alto, male chorus and orchestra*, opus 53, is quite frequently performed. For this work he chose Goethe's strange poem, 'Journey through the Harz in Winter'. They are wonderful verses, but not easy to understand. When Goethe wrote this poem he was trying to forget his love for Frau von Stein by taking a walking tour in the Harz country. The poem is full of suffering; the poet is in disagreement with the world, his tortured soul seeks peace and consolation in nature. The poem ends with a wonderful prayer to the Almighty.

Brahms' composition for the poem consists of three parts. In the first part the orchestra takes the leading rôle: in gloomy colours Brahms depicts the tortured man. Heavy melodies are heard in the bass, the strings play hard accents and excited *tremoli*. Later the solo voice joins in with a rather declamatory style. The second part begins with the words: 'Who can comfort his anguish, who, if Balsam be deadly?' The orchestra retreats into the background and the solo voice mourns above it in extended melodic phrases. The climax of the work is reached with the entry of the male chorus in the third part. Over the accompanying men's voices the alto soloist's moving melody sways like the song of angels. The words of this song are, 'But if from Thy Psalter, all-loving Father, one strain can but come to his hearing, O enlighten his heart'. This melody is truly moving in its simplicity, and forms the crown and climax of the composition. The final movement of the *Rhapsody* is naturally the most intense, for Brahms was here expressing his own most personal thoughts and his absolute faith in the deity.

ANTON BRUCKNER

born Ansfelden, Austria 4 September 1824
died Vienna 11 October 1896

Bruckner received his first musical tuition from his father who was village schoolmaster in Ansfelden. When he died, the thirteen-year-old choirboy entered the monastery of St Florian near Linz. During his later career as assistant teacher Bruckner continued to improve his knowledge of counterpoint and organ playing with the help of various teachers. He pursued his studies with great industry right up until 1863; meanwhile he had obtained the position as organist in St Florian and had developed into an outstanding player. His acquaintance with the work of Wagner was of decisive significance for Bruckner as a composer. In 1868 he settled in Vienna as professor of organ and counterpoint at the Conservatoire and it was in Vienna that he wrote all his symphonies except the first, which was written in his time at Linz.

In relation to the extraordinary significance ascribed to Bruckner in our time, his symphonies were originally very coolly received. The Viennese press persecuted Bruckner as an adherent of Wagner. His works were even ridiculed, and Bruckner suffered a lot from all this hostility. In spite of all this, his genius did not go totally unremarked and unrewarded; his organ playing was much admired in Paris and London, and during the last decades of his life he was reasonably secure financially. The University of Vienna appointed him an honorary doctor, and the Kaiser was always interested in his work. The first performance of his *Seventh Symphony* in Leipzig in 1884, by Arthur Nikisch, spread his fame further afield, and a further performance of this symphony in Munich was a triumphant success for the composer (Bruckner was present at the performance). Various symphonies were performed in important cities, and his *Third* and *Seventh Symphonies* were even performed in America. However, this interest in his work soon faded; only a small circle of people really understood it, and Bruckner's life was overburdened with disappointments.

Appreciation of Bruckner's music was difficult not so much because of the scale of his symphonies but because of their formal novelty, which made the enormous extent of the movements necessary. The classical forms, which were still present in the symphonies of his great contemporary and rival, Brahms, were disregarded by

Bruckner, and the conservative Viennese public could not forgive
him this. The classical principle requires that each theme has to
appear at first as a whole; only then can it be elaborated and dis-
sected into separate motifs during the development section. Bruckner, on the other hand, starts with the short motifs, which gradually
develop into the theme. Thus instead of a theme we find a large
coherent group of themes, which contains within itself the development of the theme as well as its statement. Bruckner creates the
first idea, the main theme of the symphony, out of nothingness, or
chaos, and we watch its growth into a theme, just as we do in Beethoven's *Ninth Symphony*. In Bruckner's symphonies the first
thematic group is very dramatic; the second, lyrical thematic group
introduces the song theme. But now Bruckner appends a further
thematic group of considerable dimensions. Bruckner's famous
biographer August Halm refers to this third group as the epic
group, because here the thematic work is quieter and more coherent than the dramatic first group. In contrast to the lyrical group,
however, this third group is larger and more grandly rhapsodic, and resumes the ideas of the first group. To state these
three thematic groups requires a certain length of time; they also
require a very long development section; the recapitulation is,
of course, long and is followed by a long coda. So the movements spread themselves to a length that was unheard of in
those days. The final movements are similar in construction, but
often, in addition to the three thematic groups, he adds themes
from the previous movements which makes the construction
appear even more complicated. A Bruckner finale is a powerful summing-up of all the previous ideas. They usually start with
great impetus and end with hymnic grandeur. The classic grace
of the middle movements, the adagio and the scherzo, makes
quite a contrast to the gigantic outside movements. They are
relatively easy to comprehend, though they, too, are of unusual
length.

The form of Bruckner's symphonies is superdimensional, but
their content is infinite. Bruckner dedicated his last symphony to
'Dem lieben Gott'. All his work is dedicated to God; it is divine
service in the most elevated sense. Much has been written about
Bruckner's strict religiosity, his childlike piety. This religious sensibility lay at the very roots of his character; his youthful imagination had been indelibly affected by the years in St Florian, and
his music was the natural expression of his devotion to God.

Bruckner—alone in the nineteenth century—temporarily concludes the line of the great mystics of previous centuries.

Before Bruckner finally turned to the form of the symphony, he devoted decades of his life to strict theoretical studies and the composition of church music. He wrote psalms, motets, a Requiem and his early Masses, all considerable choral works beside which his few instrumental pieces pale into insignificance. Of these numerous choral compositions the two last Masses in E minor and F minor are the best known.

The *E minor Mass*, written in 1860, is firmly rooted in the tradition of old church music. The thematic material, which is based on the Gregorian Chant and the frequent use of the old church modes, clearly indicates a strong connection with liturgical forms as employed by the masters of the *a cappella* period. The orchestra uses no strings; a few wind instruments are used for accompaniment, if anything. The Kyrie is almost entirely *a cappella*. In the *fortissimo* passages, horns and trombones are brought in for sonorous support. The Kyrie, Sanctus and Agnus Dei are written for eight-part chorus; there are no soloists in the *E minor Mass*. The Kyrie Eleison starts, mysterious and disembodied, with the women's voices. It builds up step by step like an organ to *forte* and *fortissimo*, and the horns lend their assistance for the first time. The men repeat the Kyrie and lead to the 'Christe Eleison' which again is delicately introduced by the women. Then it is taken up by all the voices and builds up to a powerful climax. The concluding Kyrie fades into the distance *a cappella*. The two main dramatic movements, Gloria and Credo, are very powerful and declamatory. Quietly, in unison, the women begin the Gloria, 'et in terra pax', only to burst out *fortissimo* in the 'Laudamus te'. The middle section is dominated by the tender 'Qui tollis peccata mundi'. The 'Quoniam tu solus sanctus' resumes the theme from the beginning and thus represents the reprise. The Amen fugue forms the grand conclusion of the movement. It starts with two themes, of which the second is abandoned in the course of development, and the chromatic main theme gains in significance through *stretti* and inversions up to the hymnic-homophonic climax.

In the Credo the woodwind repeat the one-bar theme each time in unison, effectively emphasizing the obstinate character of this movement. The ostinato, which starts with the first bar of the Credo, dominates the whole of the exposition and also the recapi-

tulation, which resumes the mood of the opening with the words
'et in Spiritum sanctum'. The middle section starts with the 'et
incarnatus est de Spiritu sancto', a mysterious *a cappella* adagio.
The 'sepultus est' is hardly breathed, and follows the brilliant allegro
of 'et resurrexit'. The climax of the middle section is reached in the
passionate unison of the 'iudicare' with its hammering rhythms.
The brilliance of the Sanctus is contrasted to the quiet faith of the
Benedictus. The unison choral entries of the Agnus Dei are very
moving, each one accompanied by a rising theme in the woodwind
like an imploring gesture. After the desperate 'miserere nobis'
the Mass ends with a prayer for peace: 'dona nobis pacem',
which reverts to the mood as well as the thematic ideas of the
Kyrie.

In length as well as in instrumentation, Bruckner's *F minor Mass*
is much larger than his *E minor Mass*. It was written in 1867 and
1868, while the composer was working on his *Second Symphony*.
In the meantime, Bruckner had become acquainted with the music
of Richard Wagner, an experience that was to have so decisive an
influence on his life. Many details of the *F minor Mass* show
Wagner's influence. The orchestra is of symphonic proportions,
with a full complement of strings; four solo voices are added to
the chorus. A short introduction repeats the simple main theme
several times and then the women enter with the Kyrie Eleison.
The muted mood is enlivened when the solo soprano sings the
'Christe Eleison', which builds up only to melt away again to
pianissimo at the end of the movement. The allegro of the Gloria
starts with great impetus. After a tender 'Gratias agimus tibi' with
the soprano and alto soloists, the first great climax is reached with
the 'Pater omnipotens'. The adagio middle section is centred on
the 'Miserere', and the 'Quoniam tu solus sanctus' starts the recapitulation, which ends in a grand fugue. The striking theme of the
fugue is used significantly later on, in the final movement.

Chorus and orchestra open the Credo in unison, with a great
motif that climbs up to the major third. This theme spans the
whole gigantic movement. It returns in the middle section in 'et in
spiritum sanctum' and again as the subject of the grand final fugue.
The familiar phrases of the confession of faith are effectively elaborated, especially the 'Crucifixus' with a mysterious climbing syncopated figure in the violins, which strays into the bass at 'passus'.
The last words are breathed *a cappella* by the chorus and bass soloist
pianissimo. The trombones then conclude the movement.

In contrast to the usual brilliant setting of these words, the beginning of the Sanctus is soft and gentle. Only with the 'pleni sunt coeli et terra' and the solo soprano entry with 'Hosanna in excelsis' does Bruckner give free rein to his enthusiasm. The Benedictus has a long and expressive orchestral introduction; a delicate movement for strings with a dialogue of violins and 'cellos. The strings also accompany the chorus with delicate figurations, and the light ascent of the soprano soloist forms a wonderful climax. The Agnus Dei starts in quiet humility and builds up slowly with the 'miserere nobis' where the soloists are accompanied by passionate outbursts from the chorus. The Mass ends with a conciliatory 'dona nobis pacem'. The woodwind play the theme of the Kyrie, now in the major key; the chorus takes it up, and goes on to sing the great plea for peace in unison to the theme of the Gloria fugue. After this climax the movement ends on a note of quiet devotion.

Bruckner completed his *Te Deum*, his grand hymn of praise to God, in 1883. He had been planning the work for years. It is probable that the news of Richard Wagner's death gave him the impetus he needed to complete it. In the shadow of this great shock Bruckner also wrote the wonderful adagio of his *Seventh Symphony*. The first bars of the great *Te Deum, fortissimo*, are direct and decisive in their effect: over three octaves, the strings play this energetic motif of a falling octave divided into two component intervals of the fourth and fifth. This motif symbolizes the majesty of God and

gives a feeling of monumentality to the *Te Deum*. Although only an accompanying motif it is the most characteristic and memorable feature of the work; its power and rhythm dominate it entirely. It ceases and gives way to softer tones only twice, and it is thanks to this that the form of the *Te Deum* gains enormously in clarity.

The chorus, supported by trumpets and trombones, bursts out in a triumphant unison: 'Te Deum laudamus', the solo voices entering straight afterwards with 'Tibi omnes angeli proclamant'. The trio (soprano, alto and tenor) floats calmly above the delicate orchestral accompaniment, which soon ceases completely. The reintroduction of the string motif *pianissimo* in the basses is very mysterious; over it the chorus breathes the soft Sanctus which, with a rapid build-up, emerges in the *fortissimo* of the 'pleni sunt coeli et terra maiestatis gloriae tuae'. Great effects are achieved by the direct juxtaposition of *pianissimo* and *fortissimo*, as when the joyful outburst suddenly stops and dies away in soft sighs to the words: 'Tu de victo mortis'—with such sharp, dissonant writing! However, the mood of hymnic ecstasy returns consistently.

Two calm middle movements express doubt and imploring: 'Te ergo quaesumus' and 'Salvum fac populum tuum'. The first is performed by the solo quartet, and the second, following the powerful, solemn chorus 'Aeterna fac', is in anxious, psalmodic vein. The reprise opens with the powerful choral outburst of the 'Per singulus dies benedicimus te'. As in the beginning the full brass supports the chorus and the string motif falls powerfully. The final fugue, 'In te, Domine, speravi', is relatively short. After two short developments the theme disperses in anxious outcries from the separate voices. Slowly the trombones build up a chorale theme, and the chorus joins in. The orchestra builds up powerfully and the chorus strides majestically into the key of C major, the triumphal final chords of the hymn.

The *Te Deum* is frequently performed straight after Bruckner's *Ninth Symphony*, with a view to creating a parallel to Beethoven's *Ninth*. It is supposed to complete the three movements of Bruckner's unfinished symphony, but it does not achieve this in any true sense, for the two works have no inner connection with one another.

Like Brahms, Bruckner embarked on the composition of his symphonies late in life. He wrote his first symphony in 1865, when he was forty-one years old. He had already written two symphonies, in E minor and D minor, but did not regard them as fully valid and did not publish them. Since then, the *D minor Symphony* has appeared in print and has even been performed occasionally under the title 'Symphony No. Nought', but it has not made much impression.

Bruckner's *Symphony No. 1 in C minor* bears all the hallmarks of style that we discussed at the beginning of this chapter. The work has a wonderful unity. The defiant first movement is complemented by the battling grandeur of the finale, and in between are the sorrow and joy of the adagio and scherzo. The great outside movements each have three themes. The first allegro opens directly with the main idea. The violins build up a taut, dotted rhythmic melody over calm march rhythms. Soothing sextuplets try to subdue this defiant theme, but the dotted rhythm prevails. The second theme, played first by the violins, and then by horns and 'cellos,

seems marvellously soft and peaceful by contrast with the main theme. But this idyllic melody is soon ousted by the powerful third theme; the trumpet comes through and leads up to the climax of the trombone entry. All three themes take part in the short, dramatic development section, which expires in a general pause. The recapitulation runs parallel with the exposition, but before the climax of the third theme is reached the impetuous music breaks off and the coda presents a further development in the course of which the powerful dotted rhythm of the main theme successfully asserts its mastery.

The second movement starts like a plaintive adagio; the strings breathe mournful sighs and build up to a painful outburst. Flutes start a reconciling tune, the strings rush up gently and lead over to a peaceful andante. In the reprise of the first section the theme is played by the woodwind, accompanied by the strings; there are the same sighs, but milder and softer than in the beginning. The scherzo is of a bright rusticity and presents no problems; the trio strikes a gentler note. The finale reasserts the battling mood of the first movement. The allegro starts with a grand fanfare and once again the dotted rhythms are in the ascendent. The second theme is no contrast this time; although it starts softly, it is soon absorbed by the powerful brass of the third theme. During the dramatic development the second theme plays the decisive part. The energetic trill that characterizes the theme comes out resolutely. The recapitulation moves over into C major and triumphantly concludes the movement.

Bruckner's *Symphony No. 2 in C minor*, written in 1871 and 1872, is in the same key as his *First Symphony*. But despite this and the fact that the two symphonies were written at almost the same time, they differ widely in character. The allegro of the *Second*

Symphony is much clearer and more controlled. However, it has a genuine, longwinded, broad Bruckner theme, full of longing. The 'cellos announce the vocal second theme. A peaceful idyllic mood spreads, accompanied by the singing of the violins—a mood of evening drawing to a close. This movement is like a happy experience of nature; Bruckner's usual dramatic conflicts are hardly in evidence at all. The andante, touchingly delicate and simple, is like a prayer of thanksgiving, full of fervid piety.

The scherzo is robust and happy and incorporates a graceful trio. The ending is especially charming, when the lovely song of the violas ceases, and the wind parts are softly prolonged before everything merges into silence. The repetition of the scherzo ends with a coda summing up the charming, typically Austrian love of dancing. The finale starts with a mysterious, long crescendo. The tension snaps in an energetic theme which leads to powerful climaxes in the course of its development. Two subsidiary themes are introduced to balance this elemental main idea: a graceful, pastoral one and later a chorale theme for strings. The finale is built out of these three very different sound-pictures. The battling main theme leads fairly constantly and, according to classical tradition, ends the work with a brilliant C major *stretto*.

Bruckner's *Second Symphony* embraces all the elements of his music that we honour and love: the powerful main themes, the tenderness of the subsidiary themes, love of nature, and religious piety. It is, however, only seldom performed, perhaps because it is not quite so grand and significant as his later works. It presents hardly any problems; despite their expansiveness, the separate movements are never exaggerated in expression.

Bruckner completed his *Symphony No. 3 in D minor* in 1873, and with this work he proves his complete mastery of symphonic form. He dedicated the symphony 'To Richard Wagner with the most profound respect'; Wagner intended a performance of the work, but unfortunately the plan came to nought. It was first performed in December, 1877, in Vienna, with Bruckner conducting. However, a concert-scandal ensued and the audience fled the concert hall. Today Bruckner's *Third Symphony* is a great favourite. It is the first of his symphonies to show clearly his feelings about life and God. Formally, it is more readily understandable than his later works, and it seems utterly incomprehensible that it could have been rejected at its first performance.

The main theme emerges in the trumpet from the disembodied

twilight of a D minor chord. It falls down via the fifth to the lower octave, then climbs up again freely to the initial tone. The horn

develops the melody, the woodwind repeat the last tones like an echo, and the theme builds up slowly, gathering tension; the orchestra bursting out in a powerful unison with the final phrase. After a short interlude the theme is repeated. The second theme introduces some calmer feelings: the horn sounds a languid melody, accompanied by strings and woodwind who develop a triplet figure that gradually gains in importance and finally takes the lead. A chorale-like melody in the trumpets leads to the climax, the powerful return of the main theme in the trombones, followed immediately by the horns in canon. The exposition ends quietly. The development begins equally quietly, but builds up into a mighty argument. God and Nature stand now in opposition, now in harmony with man. Feelings of bitter struggle and real resignation dominate the magnificent movement, which is nevertheless constructed with great clarity.

The slow movement of this symphony is also full of dramatic conflicts. The peaceful rhythms of the strings are superseded by

plaintive calls from the woodwind, culminating in desperate outcries. The second theme is a tender melody of the violas which stands in contrast to a mysterious march of the strings. Bruckner wrings great tension from this contrast, and the movement rises to intoxicating heights to end in a delicate mood of transfiguration.

The following scherzo is a magnificent piece of work, rustic and rather coarse like most of Bruckner's scherzos. The main theme, indeed the whole movement, is centred on the key-note. A waltz

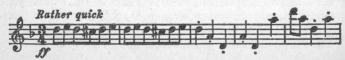

appears as a subsidiary theme, but is soon absorbed by the main idea. The trio depicts a pastoral idyll: sounds of nature, the cries of the birds and the rustling of the leaves, and then the scherzo is resumed.

The excited string figure of the scherzo still lives on in the finale, but demonically transformed. The mighty main theme is played *fortissimo* by the brass, rhythmically reminiscent of the main theme of the first movement. After a stormy climax the excitement suddenly ceases and is directly superseded by a dancing theme, which makes a very strange impression. To this melody in the strings the wind add a chorale theme which is developed very expressively, but always accompanied by the graceful dance melody. This strange

combination of dance and chorale is one of the most controversial points in Bruckner's symphonies. It has been explained in a variety of ways, as a juxtaposition of happiness and grief, gaiety and seriousness; dance-hall and church often stand side by side in human life. However, such explanations cannot shift our discomfort at the strange disparity of the passage. During the development the voice of the fateful main idea becomes menacing, and the theme grows to gigantic size in the reprise. The childlike piety of the chorale theme (still accompanied by the dance melody, but somehow much more balanced that at the beginning of the finale) forms a contrast. The movement ends with a vivid crescendo, and the main theme of the first movement reappears in a brilliant D major.

Bruckner's *Symphony No. 4 in E-flat major* was composed in 1874. It is subtitled 'A Romantic Symphony'. Bruckner gave no further explanation of this title, and it is frequently referred to as a symphony of the woods. The forest is certainly noticeable in the music, but such a title is much too narrow to explain everything comprised by this work. It would be better to describe it more generally as a Nature Symphony, and interpret the word 'Romantic' as expressing a longing for perfect union with nature. Bruckner's 'Romantic Symphony' is a symphony of nature in the sense that all powers of the universe unite in sublime harmony. Comprehensible symbols for this expressive world are musical moods that can be understood as depicting nature.

The first movement particularly is full of such moods. The calm *tremolo* of the strings gives birth to the horn motif which is the main idea of the first allegro, and is later significantly referred to in

the finale. This horn motif rings up the curtain on a romantic representation of nature: the calm *tremolo* becomes more vivid and the orchestra, *fortissimo*, plays a powerful striding theme. A held note on the horn leads to the second group of themes, when above the lovely vocal viola motif the violins play something like the cry of a bird. This episode in nature is succeeded again by powerful steps: man, the thinking, striving animal, is also part of nature. This thought may be of help in understanding this first great allegro movement. Be it the mysterious life of the wood, be it light, be it the cries of the birds, or the mood of a fresh morning, man is always present in nature. He feels himself in harmony with the power of nature: the theme of nature is sounded by the horns, full of colour, light and life. Despite the gloom of the somewhat funereal main theme, the andante of the symphony is of a tender nature. 'Cellos begin a mourning melody which finds a consoling answer in the violins. After the funeral march, a chorale melody is introduced and soon followed by a fervent melody in the violas. The soft *pizzicato* notes that accompany the viola melody are a characteristic feature of this second main theme. In the middle section the funeral march theme builds up and is transformed; this time the consoling answer is given by the violas. At the conclusion, the funeral theme reaches a solemn heroic climax and then dissolves in *pianissimo* timpani strokes.

The scherzo of Bruckner's *Fourth Symphony* is generally known as the 'Hunting Scene'. It definitely represents the romantic mood of the woods, interrupted by the joyful sound of hunting horns, and fanfares of trumpets softly accompanied by the strings. The trio is a country idyll, a dance in the sunlit meadow, typically Austrian in character. The great main theme of the finale struggles

up out of a depressing twilight; it stands before us, *fortissimo*, displaying all the fury of fate. Played in unison by full orchestra, it has a mysterious, tragic character. Gradually, the menacing mood fades away, and the horn theme of the first movement reappears in all its triumphant beauty. The grandeur of this first section is contrasted with the joyful melodies of the second group of themes. The initial gloomy mood gradually acquires serenity. The contrast of these two groups of themes is extraordinarily effective. During the development section the gay, childlike mood of the second theme is hardly touched, and the tender melody is transformed into a moving wind chorale of great effect. The basic feeling of this movement is one of piety.

Bruckner wrote his *Symphony No. 5 in B-flat major* in 1875, immediately after the *Fourth*. In the following years he made serious alterations, and the work was completed only in 1878. He never heard this symphony, which had its première in 1894 in Graz with Franz Schalk conducting, when Bruckner was ill and could not attend the performance. Schalk's extensive cuts, especially in the finale, were approved by Bruckner, and the symphony was printed in its shortened form. The earlier version was discovered only recently, and after some discussion, it came to be accepted as more authoritative, despite Bruckner's sanction of the later version. The cuts were introduced in order to make the symphony more easily comprehensible.

The adagio is introduced by mysterious *pizzicati* with a timid melody from the oboe. A mood of heavy depression is inherent in the main idea of the adagio. The main theme appears three times during the movement, each time richer and more beautiful, a solemn procession, twice interrupted by a wonderful melody for strings.

The scherzo of the *Fifth Symphony* is thematically very closely related to the adagio, a very rare occurrence. The mysterious *pizzicato* accompaniment of the adagio is here considerably intensified and pushes the music along. A *ländler* is introduced, and the scherzo runs on in a playful mood. The trio is a pastoral idyll that begins with a plaintive horn note, and then develops into a friendly dance tune. The adagio and scherzo are framed by the two great dramatic outside movements. In expression and even in thematic work these two movements are closely related. A slow introduction precedes the first allegro. The tentative melody of the strings is contrasted with a powerful *fortissimo* for the full orchestra, which is in turn answered by a radiant and confident chorale in the wind. This wind chorale introduced at such an early stage does much for the magnificence of both dramatic movements. The confidence expressed in the chorale is the basic idea of the whole work. Before the confidence is resolved, however, great struggles have to take place. The main theme is powerful, but changeable and ambiguous

in its major-minor ambience. Its majestic power gradually subdues the shy song theme and the final thematic group. In the course of the development section the main theme takes the lead, and also dominates the end of the movement.

The finale is similar in structure, but more grand. As in Beethoven's *Ninth*, it begins with a backward glance at previous movements. In the introductory adagio we hear the powerful main theme of the first movement and the timid oboe melody from the second movement, each time interrupted by the masterful octaves of the final theme, which then unfolds in a powerful fugato. A rich group of vocal melodies is presented as a contrast, before the main idea of the movement is unfolded—the great wind chorale. Bruck-

ner constructs this grand movement out of all these elements, the masterful octave theme, the melodious subsidiary theme and the confident chorale, and, in the development section, the great theme of the first movement. The brilliance of this piece of work can only by recognized after a very close study of the score. Fugues and double fugues are interwoven with the separate themes and masterfully executed. The direct impression conveys only a small part of this grandeur, but this impression alone is unforgettable. The brilliant wind chorale triumphantly crowns the work and creates an almost super-sensitive vision in sound.

Bruckner's *Symphony No. 6 in A major*, written in 1881, is only seldom performed. The reason for this is, perhaps, that it has neither the grandeur of the *Fifth* nor the sublimity of the *Seventh Symphony*. However, anyone who knows and loves Bruckner would not be without his *Sixth Symphony*, for the language and character of its music are a pure expression of his personality. The strongest impression is conveyed by the first theme, proudly emerging from the basses. This powerful main theme is mainly given to the brass, whereas the melodious subsidiary theme borrows its tenderness from the strings. The mood of this section is dreamy and reserved, but the movement as a whole is dominated by the powerful gesture of the main theme.

The adagio is the most expressive movement of the symphony. The first theme is sad; the oboe raises its plaintive sighing voice

over the melody of the strings. The sad mood gradually develops into a delicate, serene melody, mainly executed by the strings, and this melody is in its turn followed by solemn march-like music, expressive of an almost dejected devotion. These three ideas are then repeated: the element of sadness gains strength, the sighs this time entrusted to horn and trumpet, whereas the second, happy theme is repeated almost without alteration. The movement ends peacefully. The scherzo is strange; the fantastical mood of the main section is contrasted to the pastoral idyll of the trio. The grand finale continues the ideas of the first movement. Subsidiary themes introduce naïve folk-tunes, but the energetic themes predominate. The work ends with the return of the brilliant main theme of the first movement.

Bruckner's *Symphony No. 7 in E major*, written in 1883, was first performed in 1884 in Leipzig, under Arthur Nikisch. It was very successful and was subsequently performed in all the most important German towns. From this time onwards Bruckner's music began to be more generally appreciated. The main characteristics of his *Seventh Symphony* are triumph and victory, though naturally a work of such quality sounds the whole scale of human emotions, from deep suffering to triumphant joy.

The first movement can be understood as a hymn to the greatness and loveliness of nature. The main theme is introduced in the first bars and becomes the emblem of the symphony. First it is sounded by horn and 'cellos, then taken up by the violas and 'cellos and reaches fulfilment in the brilliance of the full orchestra. A

melodious subsidiary theme is added, and is caught up in the brilliant *fortissimo* which suddenly ceases. A new theme appears, and so
on. Emotional images follow one another, without any great conflict. The ceaseless pulse of nature enlivens this music, and it builds
up to climax after climax. The movement ends with a broad
hymn in the full orchestra, and the listener simply basks, as if in the
never-failing brilliance of the sun.

The following adagio creates as strong an impression as the first
movement. Bruckner wrote this wonderful 'Mourning for the
Dead' in premonition of Richard Wagner's imminent death. He
completed the movement after he had heard the news of his death,
an event which moved him to the depth of his being. The conclusion of the adagio thus became a heroic song of greatness unimaginable at the beginning of the movement. The solemn main
theme is played by the quartet of tubas. During the course of the

movement it appears three times, each time with greater intensity
before reaching that indescribably beautiful C major passage,
where the gates of Eternity burst open with a triumphant cymbal
clash and the hero is welcomed into Walhalla.

The scherzo is compelling in its masterful development and
clarity of form. A powerful motif of nature, introduced by the
trumpet like a brilliant signal, dominates the movement. In contrast, the trio is a fervent melody for strings.

The finale takes up the ideas of the first movement. The ecstatic
main theme dominates the course of the movement with recurrent
outbursts of resolution and strength. A chorale-like melody that
builds up like a grandiose hymn constitutes the subsidiary theme.
We are again in the presence of nature, as in the first movement,

but here the form is still more dramatic. The *E major Symphony* ends with a hymn to the majesty and grandeur of almighty Nature.

Bruckner worked on his *Symphony No. 8 in C minor* from 1884 till 1887, a happy creative period initiated by the success of his *Seventh Symphony*, which had brought him hard-won recognition. So much the greater, then, was his disappointment when his closest friends appeared absolutely baffled by the finished score and advised enormous alterations. The *Eighth Symphony* was published in 1891, after Bruckner had carried out the alterations suggested by his friends. Since then the original version of the work has been re-discovered and published, and the symphony is usually performed in this version. A performance takes about eighty minutes, and for this reason it is generally played on its own. For it really makes enormous demands on the audience, if they are to understand it.

Bruckner's *Eighth Symphony* can be regarded as man's mighty argument with fate; the man who accepts and affirms his fate can proceed victorious. The motif of fate, with its sharp, dotted rhythms, extremely striking and memorable, emerges threateningly in the basses and mercilessly subdues the imploring sighs that

Allegro moderato

appear in the woodwind. The melodious second theme develops out of a transitional triplet figure. Violins, woodwind and horns, all join in and get the happy mood well under way and the song streams through the whole orchestra, with flourishes of the trumpets. However, the trumpets cease; it is early yet for triumph. The motif of fate grows gloomily, dominating the development section as well. Separate motifs from the fateful theme appear and disappear. The reprise is a *fortissimo* of the theme of fate; the return of this main theme makes futile the attempts of the subsidiary melody. The horns and trumpets content themselves with repeating the incisive rhythm of the theme, against long-held chords in the orchestra. Fate descends heavily; any resistance is crushed. Small, partial motifs make a painful effort in the strings and in the clarinets, the timpani rumble gloomily, and the movement ends with deadened *pizzicato* notes. Bruckner referred to the end of this allegro movement as the clock of death. The second movement, as in the later *Ninth Symphony*, is a scherzo. It is dominated by a one-bar ostinato with a rhythm that is wilful and almost perverse. The

scherzo breathes so much strength and joy of life, that the listener cannot fail to be captivated. In the trio we are absorbed in dreams; it is full of delicate images that transport us into the colourful world of fantasy.

The first two movements of the *Eighth Symphony* are relatively easy to understand, but difficulties arise with the adagio. However, if the listener is conscious of the fact that this whole vast movement is based solely on the contrast and opposition of the two main themes, and is able to recognize the main characteristics of these, then this wonderful adagio is not really more difficult to understand than many other, more compact movements. The main theme is closely related to the fate theme of the first movement,

and is played mournfully over gloomy syncopations. However, the theme frees itself, becomes more confident and ends brilliantly. A consoling melody is contrasted with the solemnity of this theme. It appears first in the 'cellos, is answered by the flutes and continued

by the tubas. Both thematic groups appear twice, broadly transformed. The orchestra rises to greater and greater heights; the current of the main theme is overwhelming. It reaches its climax when it appears for the third time, in augmentation, majestically carrying the quintuplet figure before it. Once more, the violins play the tender second theme and the clarinet brings consolation in the shape of a gently gliding figure which, at the end of the movement, gives a lovely warm feeling to the final statement of the main theme.

The finale of the *Eighth Symphony* is one of the most gigantic movements Bruckner ever wrote. Three, even four, complexes of themes are built up during the exposition. The basic idea of this movement is the struggle with fate, the aim is the triumph of struggling mankind. The main theme, sounded by the brass, is grand and solemn and its main characteristic is the solemn festive rhythm of the grace-notes in the strings, which always accompany the brass. The second theme is calm and at its most impressive when the high 'cellos take the lead. This represents a peaceful moment in which to gather strength for fresh struggles which appear with the third theme, powerful and march-like in unison in the strings. This energetic and resolute idea is contrasted with a calm figure in the woodwind. The final group is dominated by a strict rhythmic motif, closely related to the main theme of the first movement. Bruckner builds the development freely out of this abundance of material. All the struggles of life are fought in the mighty ebb and flow of the music, until the main theme is regained with its iron grace-notes. The reprise is shorter than the exposition; the themes pass calmly. The coda rises majestically out of a gloomy *pianissimo* to a brilliant *fortissimo*. All the main themes of the symphony appear once more; the rhythm of fate from the first movement, the rigid ostinato from the scherzo, and the main theme of the adagio, all join forces with the triumphant main theme of the finale. Man has conquered himself at last, and thus retains his victory over fate.

Bruckner's *Symphony No. 9 in D minor* remained unfinished; the finale is only sketched. However, the three existing movements are so gigantic that the finale is hardly missed. The third movement, the adagio, is the crown of Bruckner's symphonic achievement. Bruckner referred to the wonderfully impressive horn part in the first interlude of the adagio as a 'Parting from Life', and this adagio was indeed for Bruckner a parting from life: he did not live to hear the symphony performed. Seven years after Bruckner's death, in 1903, the symphony had its first performance in Vienna under Ferdinand Löwe, and left a deep and permanent impression. This work reflects to perfection the abundant creativity of Bruckner's life.

The first movement consists of three grand thematic groups. Bruckner divided his thematic groups from one another by means of clear caesuras, even general pauses, and this does much to facilitate their comprehension by the listener. It is impossible to intimate the abundance of ideas that fill this first movement with a mere few words. It has frequently been called a 'Dialogue with God'; Bruckner headed the movement 'Mysterioso'. The first cycle of themes appears timidly, as if from some mystic primeval beginning, sounded by horns and ending in a wonderful melodic build-up. Slowly the first group struggles towards its climax, with grandiose octaves for the full orchestra. Two very tender and melodious groups stand in contrast to the gigantic main theme, which remains in the ascendent right through the development section as well as in the recapitulation and the final section. Even the most beautiful melodies, be they humble or seductive, must give way to the hard greatness of the main idea. The movement ends, rigid and merciless, with an open fifth. The second movement is called a scherzo, but it has little in common with the conventional scherzo. It is mysterious and demonic and absorbs all the more delicate emotions of the subsidiary themes. The scherzo starts with wild *pizzicato* runs; the sudden *fortissimo* outburst, dominated by the kettledrum, is breathtaking. The shy oboe melody is mercilessly suppressed and even the trio is only a brief episode within the demonic whirlpool of this scherzo.

The adagio of this symphony was to be Bruckner's swan song. Indeed, the movement seems like one long song, an almost infinite chain of the most wonderful and deeply moving melodies. It is as though Bruckner had surrendered himself, with faultless faith, to the strength of inspiration, and the result forms a wonderful close to his pious life.

Bruckner brought Wagner's spirit to the height of perfection in his symphonies; HUGO WOLF (1860–1903) developed it in the field of the *lied*. Wagner's symphonic style was decisive also for Wolf, but for Wolf as for Bruckner, there was no danger of his becoming an epigone. Wolf dedicated his creativity almost exclusively to the composition of *lieder* and hardly touched the field of purely instrumental music.

Wolf's only great orchestral work is his symphonic poem *Penthesilea*, written in 1883. This broad symphony was based on Kleist's tragedy. Wolf called the first movement 'Departure of the Amazons for Troy'. The introduction is powerful and noisy, expressing the excitement in the Amazon camp. From all sides sound flourishes of trumpets as the Amazons arm themselves for their journey.

The main theme, starting *pianissimo*, depicts the ride of the Amazons with its dotted triplets. A powerful and melodic subsidiary theme expresses the excess of their energy. The reprise follows immediately, and the movement ends as if the Amazons were riding off into the distance. The slow movement is called 'Penthesilea's Dream of the Feast of Roses'. The melody is broad and calm, accompanied by harp and violas *divisi*. This beautiful melody also appears in the third movement, entitled: 'Fights, Passions, Madness, Extinction', which builds up to the height of passion with a love theme that recurs constantly throughout all struggles. The reprise opens with wild passion and the theme of the introduction to the first movement returns. Penthesilea dies and, mournfully, the love theme dies with her.

The *Italian Serenade* for small orchestra is a very charming work. A posthumously discovered piece, it was probably intended as the first movement of a larger cyclic work. But just because of its brevity and unity, the serenade is extraordinarily convincing. After a short orchestral introduction the viola plays a tender wooing theme accompanied by the strings *pizzicato*. The melody becomes more and more passionate, new melodies are added, now languishing, now demanding, until the main theme returns. Then recitative phrases appear; they sound like question and answer. But everything is carried along by the graceful dance, which hurries by like a whisper and finally fades away with infinite tenderness.

ITALIAN ORCHESTRAL MUSIC

VIVALDI — SCARLATTI — LUIGI CHERUBINI — GIOACCHINO ROSSINI
NICCOLÒ PAGANINI — GIUSEPPE VERDI — OTTORINO RESPIGHI

In Italy the most important forms of instrumental music were richly developed during the seventeenth century. Names like Gabrieli, Corelli, Vivaldi, Geminiani and Alessandro Scarlatti exerted a powerful influence on Italian instrumental music even far into the eighteenth century.

ALESSANDRO SCARLATTI (1660–1725) was the leader of the Neapolitan musical world, while CORELLI (1653–1713) was active in Rome. Corelli established the modern style of violin playing, and his pupil GEMINIANI (1687–1762) brought his skill to

England, where Corelli's music was considered practically un-playable. All these musicians were expert composers who wrote a great deal of music, but not all of it is equally interesting.

Corelli's *Twelve Concerti Grossi*, opus 6, deserve to be mentioned, as they are perfect manifestations of this form. At their London première in 1724 it is said the musicians played them all through without a break, by popular demand. They are scored conven-tionally for a concertino of two violins and 'cello, with ripieno strings and continuo.

The finest flower of this period in Italy is the Venetian composer and violinist VIVALDI (1675–1741). A testimonial to his liveliness and originality is provided by the fact that Bach arranged several of his concertos (for violin), as piano concertos. Many of these are extremely popular to this day. More recently, however, Vivaldi has become popular in his own right, largely through the efforts of enterprising gramophone record companies, who discover and record the works in their authentic style. The cycle of four violin concertos representing the seasons, opus 8, is generally known simply as *The Seasons* (Le quattro stagioni), and performed as a single work. Each concerto is prefaced by a sonnet on the season in question, and Vivaldi follows these sonnets fairly closely and programmatically. However, even without these poetic references the music is supremely satisfying. Vivaldi seems never at a loss to invent a new texture for the string orchestra, and a fresh way of combining *soli* and *tutti*. Yet his skill is not merely technical: the melody of the slow movement of the last concerto (Winter) is a masterpiece of expressive writing quite apart from the subtle *pizzi-cato* accompaniment. It is easy to understand why Bach was in-spired to enlarge and adapt this composer's music into large-scale concertos for the harpsichord.

In the second half of the eighteenth and in the nineteenth cen-tury—that is for almost the whole of the classical and romantic eras in Germany—opera was prominent in Italy, and symphonic music, as well as chamber and piano music, was totally neglected. So the Italian contribution to our orchestral concerts is small in compar-ison to the number of operatic overtures written in the nineteenth century.

LUIGI CHERUBINI (1760–1842), following in the footsteps of Gluck, helped to found the grand tradition of French opera. His most important work, *The Watercarrier*, was rated high even by Beethoven. Cherubini's operas have now disappeared from the

repertoire, but their overtures will always remain standard pieces
of classical instrumental music. They are introductory pieces of a
festive character, which prepare us for the opera without touching
on the content. Cherubini does not emphasize the Spanish character in his famous overture for the opera *Les Abencérages*, written
in 1813, which depicts the fate of a Moorish generation of heroes,
as Weber did so masterfully a little later in his *Preziosa Overture*.
A powerful heroic motif introduces the largo of the *Abencérages
Overture* with a delicate love melody in the flutes, as a contrast;
a gloomy, dotted figure in the strings leads to the excited main
section. A hard, fateful motif in the strings played in unison directly

following the rather conventional main theme is very impressive.
The second theme is simply charming, executed *pianissimo* by

strings and woodwinds canonically. The main theme returns briefly,
and after an interrupted cadence, the reprise commences directly
without development, and work ends with a festive coda and enlivening fanfares.

The *Anacreon Overture* is Cherubini's most popular work. It was
written in 1802, and the thematic writing is much more concise
and subtle than in the *Abencérages Overture*, the layout more symphonic. Here, too, the main section is preceded by a brief, solemn
introduction. The allegro opens mysteriously, and the vocal main
theme evolves out of an accompaniment figure. This Mozartian

idyll is rudely interrupted by the excitement of the second theme.
The bridge passage is a wonderful piece of work: the excitement
dissolves to nothing, and the development picks out related fragments from both themes, which makes it plain that really the whole
movement is based on a single theme, but one with two faces. The

excited aspect dominates the development section, and the reprise opens accordingly with the passionate second version. Peace returns only with the re-entry of the idyllic main theme. Strings take up a gracious new figure which becomes significant as a counterpoint to the main theme. The final section is extended; theme, accompaniment and counterpoint are combined afresh in refined permutation and in a slow, constant build-up the idyll aspires to the heights of classical grandeur.

GIOACCHINO ROSSINI (1792–1868) represents the first great climax of Italian opera in the nineteenth century. Rossini's melodies created storms of enthusiasm throughout Europe, and his masterpiece, *The Barber of Seville*, is the most firmly established component in the repertoires of all operatic companies throughout the world. Its enchanting overture is a great favourite in the concert hall. The allegro possesses incomparable charm; like Mozart's *Figaro Overture*, it seems inspired by a real spirit of comedy. The listener is always captivated by the grace and swing of all the melodies: the breathless main theme, the somewhat arrogant wind melody, and the wonderful plunging final theme.

Rossini's greatest success with serious opera was *William Tell*, a real masterpiece. Apparently, after the unprecedented triumph of this opera, Rossini forswore opera for evermore, although he was only thirty-six and had thirty-eight more years to live! The overture, laid out in four brief movements, is pure landscape painting. First comes the expressive melody of the solo 'cello accompanied by basses and four further 'cellos; then a storm that rises in the distance, breaks all about us, and finally dies away; then a lovely pastoral duet for cor anglais and flute which breathes the air of mountain heights; and, at last, horn sounds lead to the final allegro of the overture, which begins with sprightly rhythms *pianissimo* and then breaks out in the magnificent jubilation of the full orchestra.

The *Semiramis Overture*, 1824, is perhaps still more effective, and has become a show piece for every orchestra in Italy. The opening is magical: over a drum roll we hear the delicate beginnings of an enormous orchestral crescendo. The horns introduce a naïve pastoral melody that is repeated later by the oboes. The spell of this graceful idyll is always shattered by powerful orchestral outbursts. The following allegro unites three typical comedy themes in a charming dance. Rossini dispenses with a development section and contents himself with a few bars of lead-back before cheekily announcing the reprise. This runs strictly according to schedule, and leads the piece to its infallibly effective close.

Rossini wrote his *Petite Messe Solennelle* in 1863, thirty-four years after his last opera, *William Tell*. This remarkable personality held out for that long against the urge, which finally—in his seventy-first year—became irresistible, to write a large-scale religious choral work. The 'petite' in the title is misleading; the work lasts at least an hour. Perhaps he was thinking of the scale of performance, for he premièred it with twelve singers, two pianos and harmonium! At a later date he orchestrated the work. On the last page he wrote this letter: 'Dear God, well, this poor little Mass is now completed. Have I for once written real "musique sacrée", or merely "sacrée musique." (cheap music)? As thou knowest, I was born for comic opera. Little skill, but some heart, that about sums it up. So blessed be thou, and grant me Paradise. G. Rossini.'

The music, however unpretentious, displays a marvellous clarity of articulation, which must be attributed, despite his protestations to the contrary, to Rossini's great technical mastery. The 'feeling' of the music is free and uninhibited, expressive of an unconscious heartfeltness that reminds one of Mozart's smaller works in this genre.

NICCOLO PAGANINI (1782–1840) was the most colossal virtuoso of the violin that the world had ever known. Quite consciously, he pushed the technical limits of his instrument to the furthest extremes, and in the process discovered a domain of possibilities hitherto undreamed of. The novel, virtuoso character lends a specific shine to his compositions for the violin. He wrote two violin concertos, and the first of these, *Concerto in D major*, is still played quite often. The concerto was originally in E-flat major; the solo part was notated in D and the soloist had to tune his instrument a semitone higher (Paganini believed he could achieve still greater brilliance by this means). The concerto makes quite exceptional demands on the soloist, and the real music has to take a back seat while all the technical possibilities of the violin are exploited. Melodically, the work is in the style of Rossini. The festive main theme is contrasted with a vocal second theme which acquires greater and greater prominence in the course of the movement. In the extended, fantasia-like development section Paganini introduces a graceful third theme in the minor key. The passionate adagio is a very expressive piece, but the final rondo reverts to the technical virtuosity of the first movement. However, the main theme is full of ideas, and recurs in constantly fresh variations. Technically, this movement is even more demanding than the first, full of doublestop harmonies and so on.

The *Concerto No. 2 in B minor*, called 'La Clochette' after the bell melody of the rondo, is hardly ever played, though Liszt used the Clochette melody in his brilliant 'Campanella' concert-study.

As Rossini's reputation began to fade, GIUSEPPE VERDI (1813 –1901) became the leading light of Italy's musical life, and reasserted Italy's priority in the field of opera. However, Verdi did not have an easy time to begin with. The examiners of the Milan Conservatoire rejected him as a student lacking in talent, and his early operas brought him no success. *Nabucco*, 1842, set him on the road to fame, and thereafter he was known as Italy's leading composer of opera. The operas *Rigoletto*, 1857, *Il Trovatore*, 1853, and *La Traviata*, 1853, are his most popular works, and their success was exceeded only by *Aida*, 1871. After *Aida*, that is to say, at the peak of his career, Verdi wrote his only concert piece, the *Requiem*, which was first performed in Milan in 1874. He wrote the work as a memorial to the great Italian poet, Alessandro Manzoni, who died in 1873.

The first movement is full of delicate melancholy and childlike faith. The introductory steps in the bass are quiet and serious, and the chorus whispers the 'Requiem aeternam'. Consolation radiates from the delicate orchestral 'et lux perpetua luceat eis'. The Kyrie Eleison is firm and confident. From timid beginnings this strange and beautiful movement builds up to a wonderful climax in the solo soprano's entry with the words 'Christe eleison'.

The Dies Irae rushes out like a mighty operatic finale. The thought of the horror of the Last Judgement unleashes a storm of despair; chorus and orchestra howl their chromatic passages, and excitedly recite their plaints before the movement ends, resignedly, with the words 'Quantus tremor'. Trumpets in the distance introduce the second section of the Dies Irae, 'Tuba mirum', which builds up to a sublime *fortissimo*. The bass solo, 'Mors stupebit', is shattering in its effect, with the expressive motif of the basses underlined by the dull sound of the drum. There is uncanny grandeur in the alto solo 'liber scriptus proferetur', and the chorus' fearful interjections of 'Dies irae' intensify the general gloom. The plea 'Quid sum miser', sung by solo soprano, alto and tenor, forms a consoling interlude. As a contrast to the frightening 'Rex tremendae maiestatis' comes the pious melody of 'Salva me, fons pietatis'. The following sections, which are particularly beautiful musically, are handled quite operatically, first the expressive duet for soprano and alto 'recordare', then the tenor solo 'ingemisco', with its strangely oriental flavour in the orchestral accompaniment, and then the powerful bass aria 'confutatis maledictus', after which the chorus reintroduces the cruel images of the Dies Irae. This long series of movements ends with the great prayer 'Lacrymosa dies illa'.

The offertorio is given to the quartet of soloists. The lovely delicate melodies seem to be trying to obliterate the memory of the Last Judgement. The Sanctus is a big double fugue for double chorus, and in the following Agnus Dei, the soprano and alto soloists introduce a simple melody in octaves, unaccompanied, which is repeated by the chorus *pianissimo*. In the subsequent music, this simple melody gains in brilliance and expressive strength from a twist into the minor key, the chorus dividing into several parts and the increasing richness of the orchestral accompaniment. The melody itself remains simple. The 'Lux aeterna luceat eis' is steeped in the most delicate colours: the trio of soloists fades into a shimmering twilight.

The soprano solo takes the lead in the last movement 'Libera

me, Domine'. The way the psalmodic whispers of the opening lead
into the anxious solo is very impressive. After a pause, the chorus
howls in an attempt to recreate the horrors of the Dies Irae, but
after a mighty climax the movement ends on a note of deadened
anxiety. The peace of salvation appears in a magical *a cappella*
movement, with the solo soprano soaring over the rich harmonies
of the chorus. A reintroduction of the psalmodic idea forms the
bridge to a powerful fugue. Finally, we hear the soprano solo singing a radiant, confident 'Libera me', and suddenly the hopeful
atmosphere dissolves to *pianissimo*, and only a depressed whispering
and pleading remains, which dies away to nothing.

The introductions to Verdi's operas are mostly brief preludes,
little more than short introductions to the mood of the first scene
of the opera. In the concert hall we encounter only two Verdi
overtures, but both of these are magnificent pieces, with their
glowing melodic style.

The overture to *La Forza del Destino* (The Power of Fate), 1862,
opens with threatening strokes from the woodwind, and the bassoon and clarinet excitedly state the gloomy theme of fate, which
plays such a decisive rôle in the opera as a sort of *leitmotif*. The
overture, too, is completely dominated by this motif; it recurs
constantly, in juxtaposition with the various themes, all of which
are precedents of the most beautiful melodies in the opera. Against
the melancholy woodwind andantino the violins play the motif of
fate, and in the wonderful cantilena for strings, we hear it in the
'cellos and bassoons, and later in the trombones. The first part ends
with a brief reappearance of the delicate andantino. Two new
melodies from the opera are introduced in the second part of the
work, which is set in the radiant major key. These, too, are interrupted by the fate motif. This motif, which is constantly flaring
up in new variants, serves to mitigate somewhat the *potpourri* character of the work. However, rather than criticize this overture
from the point of view of symphonic craftsmanship, I prefer to
remark the overflow of lovely melodies, and the *brio* with which
the whole, but especially the second part, is executed.

The overture *Sicilian Vespers* is much more symphonic in structure. The slow introduction is veiled in dark colours; a delicate
melody emerges only to return whence it came. The allegro opens
with a battling theme, which grows to passionate heights. The
second theme is a love melody, whose long and lovely phrases give
way to a dallying, typically Italian march melody. The develop-

ment concerns itself with the first theme, and a dramatic build-up leads to the reprise of the love melody. The march theme forms the transition to the *stretto* that ends the piece.

In 1898, three years before his death, Verdi wrote two choral pieces, both of a religious character: the *Stabat Mater* and the *Te Deum*. These, together with two slighter works of the previous decade, a Dante setting 'Laudi alla Vergine Maria', and an Ave Maria, make up the four *Pezzi Sacri* that we hear in present-day concert programmes. These 'Sacred Pieces', Verdi's last works, are an excellent example of his later style. In them, his religious feeling, which had been obscured by other interests or even rejected in the past, moulds the music again, and he expressed the wish that the final prayer of the Te Deum should be buried with him.

The Italian composers of the twentieth century turned their attention back to symphonic music. Pizzetti, Respighi, Casella and Malipiero all wrote chamber music and symphonic works besides their operatic undertakings. Of these composers, it seems that only OTTORINO RESPIGHI (1879–1936) is enjoying any sort of permanent success. His symphonic poems, particularly the *Fontane di Roma* (Fountains of Rome) and *Pini di Roma* (Pines of Rome), are very well-known. These tone-poems are written in the style of the impressionists, a school which came into being in France at the turn of the century and whose chief exponents were Debussy and Ravel. Respighi preserves his unexceptionable Italian sense of melody against the impressionistic tendency to dissolve the melody entirely, and the result is a very happy combination of melodic and thematic content with the resplendent and colourful orchestral technique characteristic of impressionism.

His symphonic poem *Fontane di Roma*, 1916, is preceded by the following programme note: 'In this symphonic poem the composer wished to express the feelings awakened in him by four Roman fountains, at the particular times of day when their peculiarities made the greatest impression on him, or struck him as particularly integrated with their environment.'

The first part expresses the composer's attitude to the fountain at the Villa Giulia, and the music paints a landscape with shepherds. The shepherds' pipes are heard in the dewy early morning mist. Clarinets and oboes exchange their melancholy, long melodies with a delicate feeling of reserve. The morning breeze rushes in the violins, and harp and celesta gleam silver in the morning sun.

The second part is introduced by a powerful horn call, and depicts the Triton fountain in the fresh sunlight of the forenoon. The horn call is the signal for the naiads, nymphs and tritons to come to life and begin their lively dance under the spray of the fountain. At first there are only a few participants, but new groups join in and the dance gets livelier and freer, without, however, marring its general graceful spirit. At the end of the lively piece we hear echoes of the dance in the flutes, and light, grotesque reminders in the muted trumpets.

The third section, the Trevi fountain in the heat of midday, opens with a solemn theme. In the course of the piece the brass make a big build-up with this triumphal theme; fanfares sound, and Neptune's chariot rolls by with its train of sirens and tritons over the golden surface of the water. The procession moves off and muted trumpets are heard in the distance.

Dark has fallen, and the final section opens with a plaintive theme for cor anglais. This section depicts the fountain of the Villa Medici. The cor anglais theme is succeeded by a melody for solo violin; the air is filled with the sound of bells, the twittering of birds and the rustling of leaves—it is the hour of sunset. Finally, everything melts and dies in the great silence of nature.

In these four scenes, Respighi offers us his view of nature from morning till sunset. The sections follow on without a break, but his characterization of the moods is so clear that one can follow the development of the poem without any trouble.

The symphonic poem *Pini di Roma* is very similar in form to the *Fontane di Roma*. This work, too, is in four sections played without a break, and again the brusque changes of mood and the consistent thematic work differentiate the four scenes quite clearly from one another. Respighi entitles the first scene 'The pines of the Villa Borghese' and adds the following explanatory text: 'Children are playing among the pine trees of the Villa Borghese. They dance in a ring, make military marches and battles, and are intoxicated by their own cries like swallows in the evening. Then they run off.' This first movement is characterized by its extremely lively tempo. Childish songs and ringing laughter are interspersed in the gay cries of the orchestra. The bright activity breaks off *fortissimo*.

A low string chord emerges from the fog like an organ; the curtain goes up on the second scene. We are standing in the shadow of the pines at the entrance to the catacombs, and a melancholy song reaches us from the depths. This builds up into a solemn hymn and fades away again. The lovely melody played by a trumpet in the

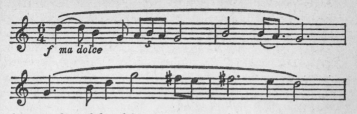

distance, framed by delicate string sounds, is one of the most memorable episodes in this movement.

A light, scintillating piano cadenza forms the bridge to the third scene, 'The pines on the Janiculum', which starts with a dreamy clarinet melody. This movement uses only the most delicate orchestral colours, with threads of melody now in the oboe, now in the violin, and finally again in the clarinet with a nightingale's song as a timid competitor. The movement decays to nothing and from this void emerge the dead and distant march rhythms that characterize the final scene.

The last movement is headed 'The pines of the Via Appia'. Do we really hear the rhythms of countless footsteps? It is doubtful. In the imagination the poet sees 'a consul approaching with his army amidst blaring fanfares and bright sunlight, on his way to the Via Sacra and a triumph on the Capitol'. The piece is one big orchestral crescendo; single wind instruments enter over the distant thump of the march rhythm in the basses. The fanfares of the approaching warriors sound, and finally the whole enormous orchestra is filled with triumphant jubilation. Respighi presents us with a truly intoxicating tone-poem in this finale.

FRENCH ORCHESTRAL MUSIC SINCE BERLIOZ

CÉSAR FRANCK — ÉDOUARD LALO — CAMILLE SAINT-SAËNS — PAUL
DUKAS — GEORGES BIZET — GABRIEL FAURÉ — CLAUDE DEBUSSY —
MAURICE RAVEL

The wave of enthusiasm for Berlioz which swept France after his
death soon faded. Even his immediate successors, amongst whom
Félicien David is perhaps worthy of mention, failed to establish
themselves in French musical life. The chief interest in France, as in
Italy, was opera, and many operas appeared which spread the fame
of French music throughout the world and have survived up to the
present time. Again, there are but few symphonic works of any
lasting value.

The first composer to mention is CESAR FRANCK (1822–90)
whose symphonic masterpiece, the *Symphony in D minor*, was written in 1889, one year before his death. Stylistically, Franck's music
is a strange mixture of French and German elements; the influence
of Wagner is unmistakable, which is perhaps due to the German
origin of Franck's mother. The *D minor Symphony* is in three movements. The broad first movement is very serious; the first theme, or
rather groups of themes, seem to be an interrogation of fate. It

starts in slow tempo, then races into a passionate allegro which is
again interrupted by a solemn lento only to break out once more
in wild animation. As a contrast to this first excited group, Franck
introduces a second thematic group which is equally extended and

which gives encouraging answers to the threatening questions of
the first group. A delicate violin cantilena emerges from a misty
pianissimo and swings up triumphantly into the bright harmonies of
the major key. The contrasted themes are brought together in the
long development section, and the first threatening group emerges
triumphant in the grandiose entry of the recapitulation. This feel-

ing dominates the end of the movement, too, after the light poetic melodies of the second group have had their say.

The middle movement of the symphony is peculiar: it seems to be a synthesis of andante and scherzo. First we hear a heavy melody in the cor anglais accompanied by *pizzicato* chords. The mysterious

weaving motion of the middle section gives it a scherzo feeling, and out of delicate colours emerges the melody from the opening. This makes some show of reaching a climax, but disperses again in misty vapour.

The opening of the last movement is magnificent and affirmative:

the energetic main theme is followed by a contrasted, expressive subsidiary idea. Both themes build up in the course of the move-

ment. The heavy melody from the second movement plays a decisive part in the development of this finale, but even this gets caught up in the mêlée and leads to a triumphant and joyful climax. Just before the end of the movement we hear a theme from the first movement like a threat, but it is overrun by the stormy finale theme and the work rushes to a victorious close.

Besides his *D minor Symphony*, Franck's *Symphonic Variations for piano and orchestra*, 1885, are frequently to be heard in our concert programmes. This work is very rewarding to the soloist. Franck dismisses the usual variation form; to start with, he states two

themes, and these are varied at random. We witness the birth of the
two themes in the slow introduction; the first theme, played by the
strings in unison, is answered by the piano with a memorable second
theme that is like a plaintive question. Gradually increasing the
tempo, Franck now runs through a series of variations, passing
freely from one to the next. The piano leads all the time and has a
very brilliant part. A middle movement is introduced when the
first section has died away to *pianissimo*; both themes are heard in
the 'cellos with lovely decorations in the piano part. *Pianissimo* trills
for the pianist lead to the final section which ends the work on a
note of brilliant virtuosity.

EDOUARD LALO (1823–92) wrote several concert pieces, of
which the *Symphonie Espagnole*, opus 21, 1873 (a violin concerto),
and the 'cello concerto are frequently performed. The *Symphonie
Espagnole* is a very gratifying piece for the violinist to play, and is
altogether very effective with its memorable melodic style and
rhythmic elements. The concerto has five movements and it is unfortunate that the third movement, intermezzo, is sometimes omitted on account of the exceptional length of the whole. The first
allegro is a powerful symphonic movement. The rhapsodic main
theme is introduced briefly by the solo instrument like a motto,
then taken up by the orchestra and later broadly executed by the
violin. The subsidiary theme is vocal and expressive, but slips more
and more into the background in the course of the movement. The
dramatic flow of the allegro depends almost entirely on the leap of a
fifth in the main idea, and on the brilliant passage work that springs
artlessly from the main theme. The violinistic climax of the work
is the scherzando, a dazzling piece of music with a distinct Spanish
tinge. The intermezzo can also be very effective. The andante is a
blossoming cantilena with virtuoso recitative-like passages for the
soloist in the middle section. The finale is based on a charming
rondo theme. Passionate counter themes are stated, but fresh
variants of the rondo theme carry the day and the work ends with
sparkling virtuosity.

The *Concerto for 'cello and orchestra in D minor*, 1876, is just as
effective as the violin concerto, and the thematic work is perhaps
even stronger. The first movement is one of the best pieces of
music for 'cello and orchestra, a genre that has not acquired a very
extensive literature. The slow, short orchestral introduction, tense
with expectation, forecasts some of the ideas that are to be worked

out in the allegro, and the same is true of the soloist's recitative that
follows with the striking melody of the main theme. The whole
dramatic movement is dominated by this steep, triadically ascending motif, and the lyrical second theme is forced into the background. The listener's attention is held by the effective, pathetic
melodic style and by the virtuoso treatment of the solo instrument.
The brilliant figurations are genuinely melodic, and not mere passage work. The middle movement is based on the contrast of a
melodious andantino and a temperamental scherzo. The last movement also opens with a short andante, followed by an effective
scherzo in $^6/_8$. This movement is particularly brilliant towards the
end and never fails to create its effect.

'Cellists are unanimous in their praise of the *Concerto No. 1 for 'cello
and orchestra in A minor*, opus 33, 1873, by CAMILLE SAINT-
SAENS (1835-1921). His symphonies and concertos, which were
so prominent in the concert halls at the turn of the century, are now
almost entirely forgotten, whereas his operatic masterpiece *Samson
and Delilah*, first performed in 1877, is still very popular. Besides
the 'cello concerto, Saint-Saëns' *Danse Macabre*, opus 40, 1874, is
one of the few pieces that have maintained their position in the
concert repertoire.

The *'Cello Concerto* is in one movement. Accompanied by *tremolos* in the strings, the soloist enters right away in the first bar with
the main idea of the work. This consists of a triplet figure ending
each time with a weighty pause. The flute repeats the theme, and
thereafter the violins. The soloist then leads over to the quietly
stepping second theme, but this is soon replaced by the flow of
triplets from the main theme. A march theme appears and disappears in the orchestra. The main theme is worked over in the
short development section, and we also hear the second theme in a
delicate blur. A scherzo section rustles by with ghostly effect. This
intermezzo leads to a restatement of the main theme, and after
a powerful climax this dies away on its moment of suspense, like
a sigh. The final section gives free rein to the virtuosity of the
soloist, who proceeds to display all the technical possibilities of his
instrument.

The *Danse Macabre* is a genial piece that is very direct in its effect.
A short poem precedes this symphonic poem by way of programme. Death plays a nocturnal dance on the violin and the
skeletons rise from their graves and join in the dance, until the

crow of the cock banishes the ghostly scene in the morning. The soloist who plays the *Danse Macabre* itself has to tune the highest string of his violin down from E to E-flat, and the open strings thus acquire a ghostly character. The sound of a bell in the harp, the clattering of skeletons in the xylophone, and the oboe's cockcrow are all very realistically done, and between them slides, with an air of total unreality, the obscure line of the *Danse Macabre*, now in the bare middle register of the flute, now in the strings in unison, now shrilly distorted in the piccolo, or in the strings *col legno*. At the wild climax we hear the cock crow, and the ghostly scene vanishes.

The Sorcerer's Apprentice, 1897, by PAUL DUKAS (1865–1935) is a very different proposition: the demonic elements of the *Dance Macabre* are humourously transformed in this brilliant orchestral scherzo, inspired by Goethe's famous ballad.

The slow introduction represents the apprentice considering his plan; the main theme is indicated by the woodwind. Anxiously he speaks the magic formula, expressed by muted horns and trumpets, and the orchestra boils over wildly. There is an uncanny silence. Gradually, low woodwind and timpani articulate the rhythm, and the bassoon strikes up the main theme. The magic formula works, the broom begins to fetch the water and the apprentice is very pleased with himself. The tempo increases, subsidiary themes are added and there is a general increase of excitement. As the horns and cornets take over the theme the atmosphere becomes more and more uncomfortable; the orchestra is boiling and hissing worryingly. The climax comes with the *fortissimo* reprise of the main theme: the apprentice realizes that he has forgotten the counter-spell! He resorts to violence and splits the broom with an axe. Wild tumult in the trumpets and horns, ending in the basses and bassoons; the spell seems to be broken. But gradually fragments of the theme emerge from the *pianissimo*, and finally the theme appears as at the beginning. This time, however, there are two brooms instead of one: the bassoon is the first broom and the clarinet the second, and they develop a fugato with the subsidiary themes in the violins. This builds up much faster than before; trombones are added, and the tempo quickens. At the final climax the sorcerer appears and speaks the powerful counter-spell. The orchestra plays *fortissimo*, and the brass hold long chords; the spirits are cowed. The theme appears timidly in the bassoons and clarinets, only to lose itself in the harp and piccolo. The piece ends with *fortissimo* orchestral chords.

GEORGES BIZET (1838–75), the composer of the immortal *Carmen*, 1875, is known to concert audiences for his two suites of music for Daudet's play *L'Arlésienne*. These suites have become amazingly popular. The prelude of the first opens with a powerful

march melody with the whole orchestra in unison; this is repeated in four simple variations. A peculiar andante follows with a sad, expressive saxophone melody accompanied by a sigh from the clarinet in every second bar. A minuet follows, and then a dreamy adagio. The last movement, 'Carillon', is the *bonne bouche* of the suite: horns, harp and violas introduce the bell motif, which is retained throughout the main section. Over this, the festive musical action of the piece takes place, and breaks off in *fortissimo*. The brilliant effect of the piece is heightened by the lovely contrast of the idyllic middle section.

The second *Arlésienne* suite also reaches its climax in the final movement, a farandole. First we hear the march from the first suite, but this time without the variations; this breaks off, and the quaver rhythm of the farandole is heard in the distance played by

the tambourine. The music grows constantly, with the quaver rhythm beaten out by tambourine, timpani and finally the whole brass section. The farandole is powerfully interrupted by the march, but reappears immediately; the two are combined and the music builds up to a pitch of wild ecstasy.

Bizet's *Symphony in C major*, written when he was seventeen years old, has been performed quite frequently in recent years. It is a student work, and the influence of the German romantics and Rossini is clearly traceable. However, the little symphony is utterly fresh and musical, and already indicates the melodic mastery that Bizet was later to develop. The adagio has a lovely soulful oboe melody, and the *perpetuum mobile* finale is very effective.

It would be inexcusable to leave a discussion of French music without mentioning GABRIEL FAURÉ (1845–1924), in particular his enchanting little *Requiem*. This work was written in 1888, and on the occasion of his death it was performed at the Madeleine Church in Paris. It is a profoundly religious work, but a very tender one; Nadia Boulanger, the distinguished Parisian teacher of composition, describes Fauré's religious feeling with great penetration: 'The Church may judge and condemn; the master has never expounded this view, any more than he has striven to follow the dogmatism of the text. It might be said that he understood religion more after the fashion of the tender passages of St John, following St Francis of Assisi rather than St Bernard or Bossuet. His voice seems to interpose itself between heaven and men; usually peaceful, quiet and fervent, sometimes grave and sad, but never menacing or dramatic.'

Köchlin, in his sympathetic monograph on Fauré, remarks that the Dies Irae of the *Requiem* 'appears as it were incidentally, and because it is obligatory'. The work is grave and gentle, touched

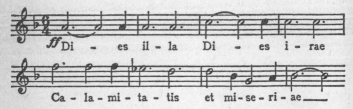

with austerity but never bitter. It is penetrated by the strongest human understanding, engaged to represent divine sympathy.

Fauré wrote few symphonic works, and those he did undertake —a violin concerto, a suite for orchestra, and a symphony in D minor—remained unperformed, for he was extremely self-critical. However, his *Fantaisie for piano and orchestra*, opus 111, written in the early years of this century, has enjoyed a quiet success. The transparency of texture in this work reminds one of Erik Satie, who was actually at work at the same time, but the work also contains some mild and pleasing *bravura*. The form is ternary, with a central allegro molto with dotted rhythms in 3/4, framed by allegro moderato passages in common time.

Fauré composed his famous *Dolly Suite for piano duet* in 1893. As was common with him, he did not orchestrate it himself, for he regarded orchestration as only a subsidiary art. Henri Rabaud is responsible for the orchestral version that we know. The Berceuse that opens the work is such a familiar melody to us now that it seems unnecessary to digress upon its beauties. The subtle relation between the semiquaver and quaver figures in the accompaniment, the effortless counterpoint that develops towards the end, the myriad touches of his exceptionally civilized musicality are in evidence everywhere. There follows an allegro vivo, 'Mi-a-ou'; Dolly's cat. No. 3, Dolly's Garden, is another tender piece with exquisite subtleties of figuration around balanced melodies. No. 4 is the celebrated Kitty-Valse. A luscious andante follows: 'Tendresse'. Note here the canon at the octave for horn and oboe accompanied by harp, in the middle section. The last piece is called 'Le Pas Espagnol'. This nicely-judged Spanish tinged allegro in $^3/_8$ makes much of the tambourine, and of the triplets on the accented second beat.

The name of CLAUDE DEBUSSY (1862–1918) is associated with musical impressionism. As in painting, musical impressionism is characterized by a heightened interest in colour as opposed to line. Debussy represents the culmination of a development that had started with the romantic composers. The constant refinement of the harmonic aspect of music by Schumann and Chopin which led to the dissolution of all previous tonal limits in Wagner's *Tristan*, the luminous orchestration of Berlioz and Liszt which led to a certain over-emphasis of the beauty of sound for its own sake, and the strong development of rhythmic possibilities—all these elements had brought about a completely new orientation in music. It was left to Debussy to take the final step and develop orchestral colour as an end in itself.

With his constant use of the whole-tone scale and the resulting augmented triads, supplemented by chords of fourths with a feeling of overlapping tonalities, Debussy evolved a strange new technique which is entirely his own. He writes programme music, but not in Berlioz' sense; Debussy is concerned with the representation of atmospheres, of moods, by means of the utmost refinement in the medium of sound.

Debussy made his name with the orchestral work *L'après-midi d'un Faune*, which he wrote in 1892, as a *prélude* to a poem by Mallarmé which speaks of an amorous faun and his play with the delicate, attractive nymphs. The close, sensuous atmosphere is created by a chromatic sliding motif for the flute, harp *glissandos* and muted string chords and *tremolos*. A glowing, reserved melody that appears first in the woodwind and later in the violins can be interpreted as the nymphs' song of invitation. The heat of the summer afternoon weighs heavily on the whole piece.

Nocturnes is the title of a suite consisting of three orchestral pieces: 'Nuages', 'Fêtes' and 'Sirènes'. In 'Nuages' the clouds are painted by the harp and flute, answered by the solo violin, in the most delicate, wispy colours; their contours are hardly visible, for it is a nocturnal skyscape. The moon glimmers through the shifting clouds.

The tone-painting 'Fêtes' is characterized by fiery rhythms. A triplet theme that rushes up in the woodwind is followed by strange chords in the horns. The surge of triplets carries the music forward. A beckoning gesture from the oboe, and then from the flute, form up into a little theme. Sensuous desire is audible through all the festive excitement. The scene changes: *pizzicato* chords with timpani accompany a slinky melody for three muted trumpets in thirds and sixths, and the music builds up to a climax where the whole brass section plays *fortissimo*. A sudden *pianissimo* takes us back to the mood of the opening, and the triplets again assert the mood of festivity. The scene disintegrates; the rhythms disappear in the distance and peace descends.

Debussy uses a women's chorus in the last piece, 'Sirènes', with the obvious intention of representing the sirens' song. The voices are treated purely instrumentally, however, and they blend marvellously with the loose, shimmering impressionistic orchestration. There is an air of secrecy about this tone-painting; the form is so vague as to be hardly noticeable, and the wave motion of the music dissolves very gradually into nothingness.

The rhythms and melodies of the Iberian peninsula had always had a strong influence on the music of France, and it is only natural that Debussy should follow suit. His suite *Ibéria* is an expression of his reaction to Spanish folk music. All three movements are characterized by Spanish rhythms with the appropriate percussion instruments.

The first movement is called 'Par les rues et par les chemins'. Tambourines and castanets give this fiery allegro its southern tinge.

The thematic work is fragmentary, and it is only after some time that the cor anglais manages a theme. This is then taken up by the violins and extended. There are constant changes of scene; excited climaxes are followed by passages of extreme monotony. Finally, the themes disperse, the castanets cease, and the piece is over.

'Les parfums de la nuit' is the title of the middle movement. Colours and sounds are in constant flux; only the rhythmic element has any profile, and this constitutes whatever structure the piece possesses. The final movement, 'Le matin d'un jour de fête', follows on without a break. March rhythms are heard in the distance, underlined by tambourine and drums. Bells sound over the solemn trombone chords. The march music approaches, and a rustic dance joins in, also the alluring, monotonous theme from the first movement. A steep build-up brings the piece to its tumultuous end.

Ibéria constitutes one part of a trilogy of orchestral pieces, which Debussy entitled *Images pour orchestre*. *Rondes de Printemps* (*Images* No. 3) had its première in the same year as *Ibéria*, in 1910, whereas *Gigues* (*Images* No. 1) was not produced until 1913. These three works are generally played separately even today. Just as *Ibéria* is an evocation of Spanish atmosphere so the *Rondes* and *Gigues* are evocations of French and English styles respectively. Though it was the last written, *Gigues* constitutes the first part of *Images*. Its Englishness is emphasized by the extensive development of the north country song 'The Keel Row', which is heard first in a whole-tone version. *Rondes de Printemps* depicts the joyful awakening of spring in the French countryside. The folk element is here provided by the old French children's song, 'Nous n'irons pas au bois, les lauriers sont coupés'.

Debussy's programmatic symphony *La Mer*, 1905, consists of three rather similar tone-paintings. The first movement is called 'De l'aube à midi sur la mer'. Quiet figurations in the winds play over the quiet lapping of the strings. After a complete hush, the music rises up again with *divisi* 'cellos and horns; the flicker and glitter communicates itself to all the instruments as the sun rises over the sea. 'Jeux de vagues' is the title of the second movement. Little waves spray and splash on the beach; the horns form a dissonant contrast to the flickering violins and harp *glissandi*. A slight wind gets up, but quiet returns, and we can hardly hear the murmur of the waves. After the anxious quiet of the opening, the third movement describes a storm: its title is 'Dialogue du vent et de la mer'. There is lightning in the trumpets and the rain rattles down.

Gradually, the storm passes over and a broad melody appears, spreading a lulling atmosphere of sleep.

Jeux is one of Debussy's most scintillating orchestral pieces. It was written in 1913 for the Russian Ballet, and the action of the ballet is printed above the score. A slow prelude gives way to a preparatory scherzando. A brief reference to the prelude follows, and then the scherzando proper sets off. The scene is still empty, but abruptly a tennis ball falls onto the stage, and is followed shortly afterwards by a young man in tennis costume, complete with tennis racket. He disappears, and then two girls appear at the back, fearful, but egged on by curiosity. The action of the ballet consists of the interplay between the young man and the two girls, first one, and then, when he notices her jealousy veiled by satire and mockery, the other, and finally both together. All the delicate and playful courtship is amorous in intent, and the climax of passion is reached when 'un triple baiser les confond, dans une extase'. The delicate sensuality of this work is reminiscent of the scented writings of Debussy's friend Pierre Louys. However, a second tennis ball falls onto the stage and the participants scatter in all directions. A reference to the slow prelude concludes the work. Musically the work demonstrates its internal formal coherence independently of the story, and despite the richness and fantasy of the orchestration each note proves its necessity: in fact, the work is a masterpiece of economy.

La Demoiselle Elue for two solo sopranos, women's chorus and orchestra, was written in the mid-'eighties, and was intended to impress the academic circles which had awarded him the Rome Prize in 1885. The text is a French version of Rossetti's poem 'The blessed damozel', and despite the distinctly personal touches in the score, there is an atmosphere of pre-Raphaelitism over the work.

The *Martyrdom of St Sebastian* was written a quarter of a century later, in 1911. It was intended as incidental music for a mystery play by Gabriele d'Annunzio, and although it has been performed several times in a concert version, it is only really acceptable in its original form, as an accompaniment to the play. Debussy wrote the music in a great hurry, as the première was only two months away when he began; in consequence the score is rather uneven, which escapes notice when it is used incidentally with a drama, but becomes obvious in a concert version. The play had some difficulty in Paris, for the Archbishop forbade Catholics to attend it. The reason for this is doubtless to be found in the martyrdom itself, which is treated with pagan sensuality. D'Annunzio described his play as a 'lyrical glorification not only of this splendid Christian athlete (St Sebastian) but also of all Christian heroism'. However, it is doubtful whether the commission would have appealed to Debussy if the feeling of the play was purely Christian; his own religious feelings were more pantheistic than Christian, and this was probably the reason d'Annunzio's commission attracted him. Besides, he may well have been flattered; d'Annunzio thought him the greatest French composer of all time, and used to refer to him as 'Claude de France'. Today, at last, many people agree with him.

The *Fantasy for piano and orchestra*, 1890, is an early work. The thematic work is extremely clear, and the piece achieves great unity through the thematic relations between the two outside movements. Flutes and oboes introduce the main theme in the dreamy, shimmering introduction, and when it appears in the allegro it is sharp and rhythmic, especially where the piano takes over from the oboe. The melodic second theme is very flowing, and played mostly by the piano, while the rhythmic main theme is entrusted to the woodwind. The climax is reached with the piano's restatement of the main idea. After a sort of *stretto* with an abrupt abbreviation of the main theme, the movement breaks off with a *fortissimo* run from the soloist.

The slow movement is like a nocturne: the main theme dreamy and languid. The middle section is whispering and mysterious and rising trills on the piano lead into the excitement of the final allegro. The basses play a variant of the main theme of the first movement, and first the oboes, then clarinets and bassoons add little motifs to this two-bar ostinato. The concerto ends rather suddenly in the middle of a climax.

After Debussy, MAURICE RAVEL (1875-1937) is the most important representative of impressionism. Orchestrally speaking, his work is perhaps even finer; his somewhat clearer thematic thinking gives his work a more solid substantiality than Debussy could achieve with his vague, undifferentiated forms. Of Ravel's early orchestral works the *Rhapsodie Espagnole*, 1907, is still very popular. It is really a dance suite in four movements, and is one of the most beautiful examples of French impressionism. The first movement, 'Prelude to night', is built on a four-note descending ostinato figure. We hear it first *pianissimo* in the violins and violas, then in

the oboes and later on in the horns. The figure is sometimes reduced to three notes, but it is never absent, not even for a single bar. A network of intoxicating colours rises above this endless monotony. The movement ends with delicate harmonies for 'cellos and basses.

The second movement is a lively dance in 3/4, a 'Malagueña'. The peculiar dance theme is introduced by muted trumpets after a

strange, dark introduction. The violins take it up, and then the trumpets again. There is a great surge from the full orchestra, but only for a moment. A benevolent cor anglais melody takes the stage and the ostinato figure from the first movement carries us back to the muted rhythms of the opening.

This is followed by a slow movement, 'Habanera'. Woodwind play a heavy, sensuous melody against the characteristic rhythms of the dance, related to the modern tango. The theme is extended by two solo violins and viola and expires in the sighs of the muted horns. The violins, all of them now, beckon us again, the rhythm becomes more pronounced, but the movement soon dies away to nothing.

The last movement, called 'Feria' after the Spanish festival, is preceded by a sizable introduction in an expectant *pianissimo*. Only the rhythm is recognizable; above it we hear occasional *glissandos* for harp or strings, and mysterious wind passages. The festival breaks out in a noisy C major dance tune. The middle section has a delicate cor anglais solo, answered by the clarinet, with the strings cloaking the whole in a shiny garment of slides and swells. Tension and expectation again herald the outbreak of the dance music which carries the piece to its racy end.

The fairy-tale *Mother Goose Suite*, 1908, is an orchestral arrangement of five pieces for piano duet that Ravel wrote for children. The forms are slight and the orchestra, too; the music contains charming tunes, magically orchestrated. The titles of the movements are sufficient to make the musical fairy-tales understandable: 'Pavane', 'Tom Thumb', 'Laideronnette', 'Beauty and the Beast' and, as a finale, 'Le jardin féerique'.

The ballet suites *Daphnis and Chloe*, 1911, on the other hand, are scored for the enormous orchestra that was customary in the early years of this century. And the suites have an intoxicating sound. The luminous colours and dancing swing of the music are perfectly straightforward in their effect, and the individual movements require no explanatory comment.

Bolero, 1928, had a sensational effect on the public: it raises the ostinato principle to the highest perfection. An eighteen-bar melody in a restrained bolero rhythm is repeated over and over in an unbroken crescendo. First we hear the rhythm alone, played by the drum *pianissimo* accompanied by the basses *pizzicato* (this is retained throughout the piece). The flute plays the melody *pianissimo*, and the clarinet repeats it. Then the bassoon plays a variant in the subdominant minor, and the E-flat clarinet repeats the variant. The dynamic is now an expressive *piano*, and the flute has come to the aid of the drum for the rhythm. This scheme of four eighteen-bar phrases is the first large period: theme, repetition, variant, repetition of the variant. The following periods follow this scheme exactly. Oboe d'amore, trumpet, and later the saxophone lead in the second period, and the drum's rhythm is supplemented by bassoons, horns and one trumpet. The third period is already *mezzoforte*; horns play the theme in overtone chords made up of celesta and two piccolos, with magical effect, then oboe and clarinet, and later the trumpet, take the lead.

The fourth period is *forte*, and horns, trumpets and *pizzicato* strings play the rhythm. The first climax is reached when the violins take over the theme, first as a single line and then in chords. The drum hammers relentlessly, with the C–G drone in the basses. The fifth period is a mighty *fortissimo* outburst. The theme is played only once, and leads directly to the variant, in which all the instruments participate, trombones included. It is a relief when the basses suddenly move to E major, and the music rises to a pitch of intoxicating ecstasy. The basses leap back to C major with equal suddenness, and with a cry the piece falls to the ground.

La Valse, 1921, a symphonic apotheosis of the Viennese waltz, is a great contrast to *Bolero*. The piece is planned in three scenes: the beginning is swathed in thick fog, penetrated now and again by a ray of light. Waltz rhythms emerge, and here and there we hear a fragment of melody. The fog gradually disperses and the waltz melodies take on a clearer form. This brings us to the second scene: a confusion of waltzing couples in a large ballroom. A waltz

theme reminiscent of the rhythmic structure of Richard Strauss'
Rosenkavalier waltzes heralds the final scene: a court ball in the
year 1855, where the festive multitude swing their partners in the
dazzling glare of a thousand candles.

The *Concerto for piano and orchestra*, 1932, is a dazzling piece of
work. The piano, favourite instrument of the impressionists, is
always in the foreground, and it is a gratifying show-piece for the
soloist. The concerto has three short movements. The playful main
theme of the first allegro is played by the orchestra and decorated
by the pianist with glittering figurations and *glissandos*. In contrast,
the second theme, played by the piano alone, is rather dreamy. But
this mood is soon dispelled, and the music hurries on with light,
accented rhythms until a bold, virtuoso run from the piano signals
the *fortissimo* return of the main theme. We hear the second theme
again and a large cadenza leads to a coda and one more exciting
climax.

The second movement is like a nocturne. The long theme is
played first by the piano alone, and after a short middle section it
returns in the orchestra, with the piano weaving rich arabesques
around it. The finale, *presto*, is written with a light touch, and leaks
cheeky themes at every seam, with brilliant effect.

The *Piano Concerto for the left hand* is thought by many to be
superior to the piano concerto. It was written in 1936, and dedicated
to Paul Wittgenstein, the brother of the philosopher Ludwig Wittgenstein. This transcendental one-armed pianist had already had
works written for him by Richard Strauss, and had arranged the
Chopin études for left hand for his own benefit! (In performing
this feat he somehow contrived to thicken the texture by convert-
ing single-note passages into passages in octaves, and so on.) Ravel's
work is in one movement. The orchestra opens *lento* with a statement of material, and then the piano enters with bravura passage
unaccompanied. Orchestra and soloist develop the material together
and the *lento* finally gives way to a $^6/_8$ allegro. This rhythmic movement proceeds unbroken, with astonishing coloristic vitality and
marvellous collaboration between soloist and orchestra right
through; it is snapped off in mid-flight as if by the flick of a switch
—to the restatement of the *lento* material. A complex, thundering
and yet expressive cadenza is supported at the end by the orchestra,
and the latter rounds the work off with five bars of $^6/_8$ allegro.

MANUEL DE FALLA

born Cádiz 1876
died Argentina 1946

The great Spanish composer is very closely related to French music. Falla was a pupil of Debussy for several years and the influence of impressionism is unmistakable. However, the conscious exploitation of Spanish folk themes and especially folk rhythms clearly distinguishes him from his French contemporaries.

In 1919 Falla achieved fame for himself and for the music of his country with his ballet *The Three-Cornered Hat* which he wrote for the Russian ballet. A suite of dances from *The Three-Cornered Hat* is often included in concert programmes, the most remarkable ones being the lyrical 'Miller's Dance' and the finale.

One of the most charming works of musical impressionism is Falla's *Nights in the Gardens of Spain*, three symphonic scenes for piano and orchestra, written in 1925. Although the piano part is difficult and virtuoso, the work cannot be regarded as a piano concerto; the solo instrument is much too submerged in the orchestra. Sound is the most important factor in the three charming movements; the thematic work is hardly significant.

The first movement 'In Generalife' is mysterious and reserved, but extraordinarily exciting. The burning sensuality of the southern night pervades the whole piece; we feel it in the thematic writing which circles round a few notes, and it trembles in the broken harmonies. The colours are clothed in shadow; only now and again does a strong note sound. When it does it immediately loses itself again in the darkness of the night.

The middle movement is entitled 'Dance in the distance'. A monotonous, but very impressive dance melody sounds from a distance, dies away, reappears, then builds up wildly and passionately and dissolves in the sighs of the night. The directly following final movement, 'In the Gardens of the Sierra Cordova', is vivid and happy. One dance theme follows another, each more fiery and passionate than the last. But even this sensuous intoxication and these glowing colours must fade, and night descends with a tender whisper.

Homenajes (Homages) (1922-33), is a symphonic suite of four movements for orchestra. The first movement is a brief fanfare for horns, trumpets and drums based on the initials (E F A) of E. F. Arbós. The second movement is an orchestration of the guitar elegy on the death of Debussy. After it, the fanfare is repeated in short-ened form. The solemnity achieved by these simple means is re-markable. The third movement is a short 'andante molto sostenuto' dedicated to Paul Dukas. The last movement, Pedrelliana, is more extended than any of the others. It opens with a solemn, distant

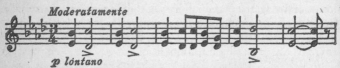

statement by the horns, but gradually the music picks up (*quasi allegro*), and the constant reversals of tempo in the sequel—*moderato, andante, deciso, allegretto scherzando, quasi vivo*—give an air of con-trolled animation to this lively finale.

It is debatable whether the *Harpsichord Concerto* (1926) falls within the scope of this book, but it is such an impressive work that it is imperative to mention it, at least. The score calls for flute, oboe, clarinet, violin and 'cello besides the soloist. It is reported that Falla turned to Domenico Scarlatti's sonatas for guidance in his dealings with this antiquated but spell-binding instrument. Scarlatti's in-fluence is most noticeable in the last movement, which is quite complex in texture and makes use of various ornaments and trills. The vitality that inspires every note of this vivace is amazing. The slow movement is marked 'jubilant and energetic' and it presents a wealth of figuration, in the form of scales and arpeggios. These appear sometimes in the wind parts, particularly the clarinet, with remarkable effect. There are moments of bold counterpoint in this movement which underline the extreme personal quality of Falla's music. The first allegro is the most straightforward movement; the harpsichord states the theme against rackety triplets and semi-quavers, with string accents on the off-beats. The material of this movement is developed with beautiful conciseness. The soloist leads all the time, and just before the end he plays alone the series of arpeggio chords that obviously exerted so strong an effect on Falla's imagination.

When he died, Falla left an unfinished oratorio *Atlantida*. He actually completed very little of this evening-filling, mystical work, though he had jotted down numerous sketches and ideas, particu-larly for the first half. Recently these have been collected together, edited, extended, and some performable music has been cajoled

into existence. This was played in 1961, and met with rather a
dubious reception, many people recording the judgement—a realistic one—that it was not the work of Falla. The poetic epic on
which the work is based is by Jacinto Verdaguer, and is written in
the Catalan dialect of the Barcelona area. The story, told by the
chorus, is of the lost continent of Atlantis, sunk off the western
coast of Spain; the former glories of the Hesperides are recounted
and the labours of Hercules who broke open the Straits of Gibral-
tar, dooming Atlantis to the sea.

RUSSIAN SYMPHONIC COMPOSERS

MICHAEL GLINKA — PETER TCHAIKOVSKY — MILY BALAKIREV — MODEST
MUSSORGSKY — ALEXANDER BORODIN — NIKOLAI RIMSKY-KORSAKOV —
ALEXANDER GLAZUNOV — ALEXANDER SCRIABIN — SERGEI RACHMANINOV

The year 1836 can be regarded as the birth date of independent
Russian music. In this year Glinka's opera *A Life for the Czar* had
its première, a work that marked the birth of Russian national
music. MICHAEL GLINKA (1804–57) strove consciously to free
himself from the overpowering influence of German and Italian music and to create a national style. He used two sources for
his purpose: the Russian folk song and old Slavonic church music.
He wished to preserve the character of Russian folk music unaltered, and this made it possible for him to develop a style that
was melodically, harmonically, rhythmically and metrically quite
different from the traditions of the West, even apart from the differences of phrasing and instrumentation. This was the starting
point of a grand development in Russian music. We hear only a
few pieces by Glinka in our concert halls, occasionally the overture
to his second opera, *Ruslan and Ludmilla*, and the brilliant orchestral
piece, *Kamarinskaya*. *Ruslan and Ludmilla*, 1842, is a fairy-tale opera,
based on a poem by Pushkin: the helplessly confused libretto is full
of fantastic adventures, knights and princesses, magicians and

witches. The music of the overture on the other hand has a beautiful clarity. The fiery theme appears after a lively swing-up in the
strings. The theme moves powerfully to its end with fanfares and
fortissimo drum strokes. This is followed by a lyrical, canonic version for the four woodwind. The second theme is an expressive
song for 'cellos and violas, but this soon gives way to battling
impulses. Mysterious magic forces are at work in the development
section; the long horn notes are particularly effective, with demonic
activity all around. The magic powers are banished when the main
idea reappears, and the brilliant piece moves to its effective close.

The orchestral fantasy *Kamarinskaya*, 1848, has become a model
for the national music of the later Russian composers. The original
title of the piece was 'Wedding song and dance'. The wedding song
is played by the strings in unison after a short introduction. It is
almost solemn, but is immediately followed by a pretty variation
for woodwind. Other parts are added, the melody appears in the
bass, and the violins play in counterpoint. After this short treatment of the wedding song, the dance melody appears in the first
violins, and the violas play a counter-melody. Then the second
violins take the dance melody with the counter-melody in the first
violins. Later the 'cellos play the melody, the woodwind join in,
and when the brass eventually decide to enter the noisy dance, it
is as though the watching crowd were underlining the rhythm
with stamping feet and clapping hands. The kamarinskaya (as this
dance tune is called) is taken up again after the reprise of the wedding song, and the slight changes of instrumentation and the constant dynamic effects make it difficult to realize how often we hear
the identical little theme. The strange magic of a monotonous
ostinato exerted a strong influence on Glinka, just as later it did on
Ravel.

With PETER ILICH TCHAIKOVSKY (1840–93), Russian
music became established throughout the world. There have been
more contradictory opinions about Tchaikovsky than about almost
any other composer; people criticize him as a sickeningly sweet
salon composer, and others find leather boots and stockwhips in his
music. But his exceptional and worldwide success is probably due
just to this strange mixture of a delicate sensibility and wild, un-
controllable temperament, of Asiatic wildness and western culture.
Without wishing to make a comparison, Tchaikovsky's music is
just as much his confession of faith as Beethoven's. Every melody

is felt, every movement really experienced, and the language of a supersensitive and great soul speaks to us in every work. Perhaps the sincerity and faith of his music are the secret reasons for its enormous effect.

Tchaikovsky was a reserved man, almost shy. His strange friendship with Frau von Meck is very characteristic of him. She entered his life in 1877, the year he began work on his *Fourth Symphony*, and they evolved a strange relationship which was to have a great influence on his later life and work. She gave him a regular income which enabled him to devote his whole life to his work. Thus Tchaikovsky, who was incompetent to carve his own way financially in practical life, found himself free of all worries, and this was probably the only possible solution for a man of his sensitivity.

The *Symphony No. 4 in F minor*, opus 36, was the first great work Tchaikovsky completed in this new situation. In gratitude, he dedicated the work to 'his best friend', Frau von Meck, and she, aware of his gifts and genius, continued to smooth his way in the world. The generosity of this extraordinary woman went much further: at Tchaikovsky's behest, she denied herself the pleasure of knowing him personally because he expressed the fear that this might bring disappointment. This fact served only to intensify their exchange of letters. Tchaikovsky wrote to her about everything that concerned him, and often gave her glimpses of his inner life and work. In a letter of 16 February 1878, he speaks exhaustively of the *Fourth Symphony*, 'our symphony' as they both called it. This letter still represents the best analysis of the symphony available, and I should like to quote the relevant passages about each movement.

He writes in answer to her enquiry: 'Yes, there is certainly a programme for our symphony; that is to say it is possible to express its content in words, and this I will do, but for you alone. The introduction is the kernel of the whole symphony. The main idea, first in the trumpets and then in the horns, is expressive of the idea of fate, that ominous power which prevents the success of our

search for happiness. This power hangs constantly over our heads,
like Damocles' sword. There is no alternative but to submit to fate.
The main theme of the allegro expresses feelings of depression and

hopelessness: wouldn't it be better to turn our backs on reality and
give ourselves up to dreams? The second thematic group, introduced by light woodwind runs and a delicate melody for strings,
is an expression of this dream-life. The intrusive first motif of the
allegro is pushed into the background. Gradually, the whole soul is
woven round with dreams, and all gloom and joylessness is forgotten. But these are only dreams, they scatter before the hard
theme of fate. The whole of life is but a constant traffic between the
darkness of reality and our unsteady dreams of happiness.'

Tchaikovsky writes of the second movement that 'it depicts
suffering at a different stage. It has that melancholy feeling of a
solitary evening at home, when the book that you have taken to
read slips from your hand, and a swarm of memories appears. How
sad that so much has already happened and melted away. You
remember happy times, too, when the blood was young, and
frothy and joyful. But that is all so far away, so far away. How
sad, and yet how sweet it is to brood over the past.

'The third movement expresses no particular feeling. It represents
the capricious arabesques performed by our imaginations. We give
free rein to our imagination and she turns some remarkable somersaults. Suddenly we see a drunken young farmer, hear a street
song . . . military music sounds from a distance. Just disconnected
images like those that appear in our mind's eye before we go to
sleep.'

The fourth movement depicts a national festival, and Tchaikovsky writes: 'When you can find no joy within yourself, look
around you, mingle with the people! See how they enjoy themselves. Hardly have you begun to forget yourself, than untiring
fate announces his presence in your neighbourhood. We hear again
the heavy theme from the first movement. But the other people
don't take much notice. They don't look your way at all, they are

too busy enjoying themselves. Find happiness in the happiness of others, and perhaps you will be able to go on living.'

So speaks Tchaikovsky; and there is little to add. The feeling and thematic work of the *Fourth Symphony* are very Russian. Russian folk melodies and folk rhythms appear in all the movements, and the finale is an orgy of Russian characteristics. But this most Russian of symphonies quickly found its way into the western world, whereas the first three symphonies are hardly ever played.

Tchaikovsky's most popular work is the *Symphony No. 5 in E minor*, opus 64, written in 1888. Again, it opens with a slow introduction, the significant theme of which appears in all the move-

ments, like a *leitmotif*. The low clarinets play the short phrase like the call of fate, and it is repeated several times, threateningly. The main theme of the allegro emerges from *pianissimo*, trembling slightly with excitement. The strings take the melody after clarinets and flutes have had their say, and it rises to a march-like climax.

A delicately rising melody for strings sounds like a warning, and a wind call leads to the vocal, enthusing subsidiary theme. This is

developed extensively and at the climax the excited first theme joins it in the brass. The music falls off into the transitional wind call, which now plays an important part in the development section. This ends with a gradual decay into *pianissimo*, which leads back to the reprise, with a somewhat stubborn statement of the first theme in the bassoon. The climaxes in this final section are perhaps even mightier than the elemental outbursts of the development. We hear the rigid rhythms of the fate theme from the trumpets, and this leads back to a mood of extreme calm. The movement ends in an uncanny silence.

The andante cantabile is a stream of lovely melody. The wonderful horn melody is unforgettable even after a single hearing, and is

followed by an emotional duet with the oboe. The main melody is played by the 'cellos and extended by the violins. There is some

discussion with the motif of fate in the course of the movement, but it ends happily with a fervent phrase for clarinet.

The third movement is headed 'Waltz'. The delicate waltz melody is passed round the various instrumental groups with several artful variations. The middle section brings anxious excitement into the amorous mood, jealousy too, which finds its way even into the reprise of the waltz theme. The theme of fate appears towards the end in low clarinets and bassoons.

Like the first movement, the finale begins with an andante maestoso. The theme of fate is in the major key, however, and has a triumphant sound. The joyful festival breaks out in the allegro vivace. After a wild excursion through dance melodies and excited rhythms we hear a broad flowing melody that is related to the love song in the second movement. The mighty theme of fate mingles with the festive confusion; the waves of festivity ride higher and higher; all the themes reappear, even the love melody, backed by stamping rhythms. The culmination of the work is the restatement of the fateful maestoso of the opening, which leads to a final *presto* section with all the main themes of the finale, ending with a grandiose augmentation of the theme from the first movement.

The *Symphony No. 6 in B minor*, opus 74, is Tchaikovsky's last symphony. He wrote it in the last year of his life, and lived to hear the first performance. Tchaikovsky himself thought this his best work, referring to it as his most honest and upright creation. In it he wished to portray himself, his own personality; there was certainly a programme behind the work, but, since it concerned himself alone, he never divulged it. The only relic of it is the title *Pathétique*—a symphony of passion—which was actually originated by the composer's brother, Modest, but approved of by Tchaikovsky.

The title is particularly suitable for the first of the four movements. This passionate expression of the most elevated sensibility is unsurpassed. Plaintively, the bassoon introduces the main idea of the movement in the short, gloomy introduction. First timidly,

but with increasing passion, this theme is extended in the allegro. After a first passionate climax the music sinks down to *pianissimo* with a longing question from the violas. The violins answer with the most wonderful melody of the piece; a consoling song of supernatural beauty. The reprise of this melody by the orchestra, *forte*, ends this hopeful episode; it dies away *pianissimo* in the clarinet. With a passionate stroke we are plunged back into the hardships and struggles of life, and Tchaikovsky develops a powerful and glowing tone-painting. The final word, however, goes to the beautiful, consoling melody, which has a transfiguring effect after

the stormy life of the movement, with its chorale-like tune as a tailpiece.

After this tremendous argument, it is only natural that the following movements should seem rather episodic in character. The second movement, 'allegro non grazia', is the most famous example in symphonic literature of the unusual metre of five crotchets in a bar. Though there are reflective moments, this movement strikes us as a lovely idyll after the storm.

The third movement, 'allegro molto vivace', on the other hand, is full of life and colour. A powerful march theme emerges from a host of gay tunes, at first only briefly; but in the end it presents

itself in its entirety like a triumphant assertion of health and vigour.

Life *can* be like that, but Tchaikovsky, writing the symphony of his own life, sees the darker side of life as stronger, and the *Pathétique* ends with the moving resignation of the adagio lamentoso.

This movement is the most beautiful part of the symphony. The will to live writhes passionately, but the final idea is expressive of defeat and resignation.

Although it lacks the scope and intensity of the symphonies we have discussed, the *Symphony No. 2 in C minor*, opus 17, is worthy of mention. The complete originality of Tchaikovsky's talent is apparent from the andante introduction to the first movement, with its unresolved horn melody left utterly exposed after the initial chord. The second movement is a martial andante over *ostinato* timpani. Again the confident delicacy of scoring is remarkable; every note counts, and nothing is drowned in an excess of mere noise. The scherzo is a dynamic movement with a peculiar trio in $^2/_8$, which fits over a rhythmic formula of $^3/_2$, as it transpires in the sequel. The electric effect of Tchaikovsky's *tutti* scoring is felt in the introduction to the finale, with its vigorous chordal writing for all the strings. This chorale-like statement is followed by an extremely light-footed development of the same melody, allegro brio. The movement builds up to a presto close.

The most important of Tchaikovsky's symphonic poems is the overture-fantasy *Romeo and Juliet*, written 1869 and revised in 1870 and 1880. Peculiarities of this masterpiece are the wonderful plasticity of the thematic work, the clarity of the form, and the intoxicatingly beautiful orchestral writing. The programme is sufficiently indicated by the title. The slow introduction is dark and premonitory. The main theme of the allegro paints the conflict

between the two families, and as a contrast we witness a delicate
love scene, with the pillow-talk of the muted strings accompanying the cor anglais' fervent melody. Flutes and oboes take up the

melody and it builds up into a painful, blissful song, with sentiment
and sighing horns. The action of the poem is constructed out of
these themes. The rhythm of the battling main theme dominates
the development section; neither the premonitions of the introduction nor the effective love melody can withstand it. A chorale-like
woodwind phrase signifies the lovers' release from earthly existence, and when the love motif is stated once more it is as though
we were witnessing the transfiguration of the unhappy lovers.

Of Tchaikovsky's ballet suites, the *Nutcracker Suite* (*Casse-
Noisette*), opus 71a, 1892, has achieved an unassailable position in
our concert halls. The 'Miniature Overture' dispenses with 'cellos
and basses, and thus achieves a marvellous lightness that forces one
to smile. This smile persists in the following 'Danses caracté-
ristiques': first a lovely little march that starts *piano* with trumpets,
clarinets and horns, and is graciously taken over by the strings.
Then comes the 'Danse de la fée Dragée' (Dance of the Sugar-
Plum Fairy) with the silvery celesta. 'Danse Russe' is wild and
coarse by contrast, and the 'Danse Arabe' is melancholy and monotonous with its fifths in the bass. The 'Danse Chinoise' combines the shrill register of the flutes with delicate *pizzicato* tones,
and the picture of little pagodas shaking their heads springs to
mind. 'Danse des Mirlitons' has the most beautiful tune of the
group, with its cheeky grace-notes, and withal so delicate and
graceful. The final section, the 'Valse des fleurs', is not quite up to
the standard of the others despite the harmonic beauties of the main
theme. Perhaps it is preceded by one too many delicious titbits.

Tchaikovsky also made concert suites from his music for the
ballets the *Sleeping Beauty* and *Swan Lake*. The *Sleeping Beauty
Suite* contains five numbers from the ballet (which originally consists of sixteen numbers), and these are not used in chronological

order. The suite starts with the Lilac Fairy, preceded by a new introduction—a high-spirited vivace. Then follows the Rose Adage, Puss in Boots and the White Cat, Panorama, and, to end, the celebrated Waltz. Undistracted by the grand scenic effects of stage performance, the listener will perhaps become more aware of the finesse of the music; for instance, the opulence of the harp writing, and the perfect balance of the accompaniments in general. The melodies defy description.

The *Swan Lake Suite* opens with the scene of the first appearance of the swan, from Act I of the ballet. Then comes the even more celebrated waltz from Act III with its fine rhythmic details. This is followed by the Dance of the Swan from Act II, and the beautiful *Andante non troppo* for violin solo and harp, also from Act II. The fifth movement of the suite is the Hungarian Dance, Czardas, from the last act. The suite ends with an agitato scene from Act II, with a lyrical interlude and resplendent coda.

We have the failure of the Moscow première of the ballet (1877) to thank for this concert suite. This failure was so decisive that the ballet was never performed again, in whole or in part, in Tchaikovsky's lifetime. In view of this, Tchaikovsky rescued the best parts in his concert suite.

Tchaikovsky wrote three piano concertos, but the first, *Concerto in B-flat minor*, opus 23, dedicated to Hans von Bülow, is the only one that has become really established. Perhaps the others have been forced into the background by the extreme popularity of this one, surely amongst the most frequently performed of all piano concertos. The *B-flat minor Concerto* is certainly a great and beautiful work with a lot of magnificent virtuoso writing for the soloist.

The introduction puts the spell on the audience straight away: violins and 'cellos play a broad, dramatic melody against the gigantic blocked chords of the soloist. The piano repeats the melody and goes off into an effective cadenza before the powerful repetition of the theme in the orchestra. An overwhelming introduction! The 'allegro con spirito' opens with the scherzando main theme played by the piano. The second theme is a dreamy melody reminiscent of Schumann, and a pressing third theme leads to an extended orchestral interlude. The following cadenza forms the bridge to the development section, which embarks on a symphonic build-up. The second cadenza is another climax of this movement, just before the brilliant ending.

The andantino semplice is dominated, as its name implies, by a simple, expressive melody, which is beautifully decorated by the soloist. The middle section is a virtuoso *prestissimo* for the piano against a banal waltz theme in the orchestra. The themes of the finale, 'allegro con fuoco', on the other hand, are strong, original and extremely memorable. The glowing melody of the second theme competes successfully with the self-willed main idea, and reaches a hymnic climax shortly before the end.

Tchaikovsky's *Concerto for violin in D major*, opus 35, 1878, is also one of the most popular works in its genre. One often hears Tchaikovsky's concertos criticized for their banality, and people maintain that he wrote them merely for effect. This criticism is completely unjustified; all the great soloists are only too glad to play them, and their audiences are appreciative and enthusiastic. Besides, the effect of Tchaikovsky's violin concerto is certainly not due entirely to its brilliant presentation; the noble directness of the thematic work has ensured the concerto's success. The symphonic and dramatic elaboration of the themes in the first movement is brilliant, and this movement is certainly the best part of the concerto. An orchestral introduction prepares the way for the first theme, which appears in the solo violin, confidently *piano*, proud and calm. This truly aristocratic theme is developed in enchanting

arabesques and leads to the second theme, a longing, insistent song. The long movement is controlled by the nicely calculated contrast of these two themes. An electrifying effect which occurs several times in the development section is the fiery bolero variant of the main theme. The reprise of the second theme is equally effective, played glowingly by the soloist on the G string. After the virtuoso fireworks, the quiet simplicity of the canzonetta is very effective, but the finale again is the last word in technical brilliance. The second theme really gets into your blood, while the other two themes are somewhat conventional. However, if played by a violinist who is technically equal to the challenge, this long movement creates a powerful effect.

The *Rococo Variations for 'cello and orchestra*, opus 33, 1876, is a very attractive work. The delicate theme passes through two free variations, and this constitutes the first section of the work. A slow variation follows with a lovely cantilena for the soloist, and then a gracious scherzo movement, which in the fifth variation leads back to the reprise of the rondo theme in the orchestra. After a short cadenza comes a variation in the minor, and finally a brilliant coda-variation where the soloist can let off all his technical fireworks.

In the 1860's, five young composers grouped together in St Petersburg with the idea of creating a really Russian national music. MILY BALAKIREV was the head of the group, which was contemptuously referred to as the 'mighty little dungheap'. He is chiefly remembered for his great oriental piano fantasy *Islamey*. The four other members were Borodin, Mussorgsky, Rimsky-Korsakov and César Cui. Glinka was the idol of this revolutionary group; Tchaikovsky they dismissed as being too 'westernized'. MODEST MUSSORGSKY (1839–81) is the most outstanding representative of this circle. His opera *Boris Godunov*, first performed in 1874, is one of the most significant works in operatic literature. He possessed great originality of imagination, and the realistic atmosphere of his harmony makes him one of the most important forerunners of impressionism. Mussorgsky wrote only one symphonic piece, the orchestral fantasy *A Night on Bald Mountain*, 1867. Liszt's *Danse Macabre* was the original inspiration for this piece, and Mussorgsky reworked it several times before finally abandoning it. It was left to Rimsky-Korsakov to resurrect this dazzling piece and decide on a final version. Rimsky dealt with Mussorgsky's papers after his death and revised several works by this great self-taught amateur before presenting them to the public.

A Night on Bald Mountain is preceded by a programmatic list of contents: 'Subterranean noise of spirits. Apparition of the spirits, later of Satan. Worship of Satan. Black Mass. Witches' Sabbath. The distant ringing of church bells in the village disperses the spirits. Daybreak.' The fantastic scherzo follows its programme quite clearly: a rustling and whistling, with abrupt changes from *pianis-*

simo to *fortissimo*, and shrill high notes from the piccolo, is followed by an uncanny silence. A monotonous theme for oboes and bassoon announces the approach of the spirits, and a grand climax introduces Satan. A wild dance begins, with impulsive rhythms in the

strings, and the winds pressing onward chromatically. Both themes are combined and the climax is reached with heavy strokes from the orchestra: homage to Satan. The witches' sabbath is continued in the reprise and breaks off in the middle of wild tumult. In the sudden silence we hear the distant sound of bells; the insistent chromatic motif is heard like an echo in the violins. Harp sounds, a pastoral tune in the clarinet—and early morning breaks.

Pictures from an Exhibition, 1874, was originally a cycle of piano pieces, but they are equally at home in an orchestral concert thanks to Ravel's dazzling orchestration of the work. The work consists of ten short pieces joined together by 'promenades', characteristic interludes in $^{11}/_4$ that represent Mussorgsky himself promenading from picture to picture in the exhibition. The pictures that the composer develops are highly varied as to subject-matter: 'Gnome' represents a dwarf waddling awkwardly on his little crooked legs. 'The Old Castle' is a reasonably conventional piece in $^6/_8$ with a long, melancholy melody. 'Quarrelling children in the Tuileries Gardens' is an impressionistic miniature. 'Bydlo' represents a Polish ox-drawn cart rumbling along dopily to the strains of a folk tune. 'Ballet of the Unhatched Chickens' is a scherzino. 'Samuel Goldenberg and Schmuyle' shows two Jews, the one fat and prosperous, and the other babbling away but unable to convince the other of the rightness of his argument. 'Market Place in Limoges' is a *perpetuum mobile* scherzo representing the haggling market women. 'Catacombs' is a gloomy largo. 'A Hut on Chicken's Legs' is Baba-Jaga's wild, broomstick journey, with a fascinating, stumbling trio section. 'The Great Gate of Kiev' is an extremely colourful impression of a religious procession to end the work.

ALEXANDER BORODIN (1834–87) is another important member of the St Petersburg group. Like Mussorgsky, he was an amateur composer, earning his living by other means. His most important orchestral work is the *Symphony No. 2 in B minor* which he finished in 1876. Four times, the strings in unison play a disquieting two-bar motif. This is answered by a folk tune in the high

woodwind, and the juxtaposition is preserved throughout, though

the questing main motif has the last word. This is balanced by the lovely pastoral second theme, heard first in the 'cellos. The develop-

ment section is built chiefly on the main motif: hesitant at first, it soon gets under way in a dancing variant, and both folk tunes are used in combination. The reprise is triumphant: the main motif gains constantly in power, and is victorious in the last bars, played by the full orchestra in unison. The torn, divided effect of the motif at the opening is thus perfectly balanced during the course of the movement.

The scherzo is amusing and original; the march theme appears first in the basses. The graceful trio is slightly oriental in feeling;

pastoral woodwind melodies arch over the delicate pedal-point of harp, horn and triangle.

The andante is also oriental in feeling; the music is a wonderful description of the depression and monotony of the endless breadth

of the Asiatic landscape. The clarinet plays a short expressive kernel-motif, and the horns develop the main theme from it. Peaceful and flowing, it is later taken over by the clarinet. Disquiet is apparent only when a chromatic descending figure appears in the basses, and thereafter seems worryingly ubiquitous. Unison woodwind introduce a counter-theme which gains in strength and leads to the final hymn of thanksgiving. The clarinet motif from the opening ends the movement.

The finale is a brilliant piece of merry folk life. Two typically Russian dance tunes are stated, and varied most amusingly. Unlike Tchaikovsky's finales, which carry an undertone of fate and seriousness, this finale is expressive of the purest *joie de vivre* and exuberance.

Borodin's *In the Steppes of Central Asia*, 1880, dedicated to Franz Liszt, is very frequently performed. The programme of this symphonic poem runs as follows: 'Over the sandy steppe we hear the peaceful sound of a Russian song. In the distance, strains of a melancholy oriental tune are audible, as well as the stamping of horses and camels. It is a caravan approaching. Protected by Russian watchmen it proceeds safely on its way through the endless desert, further and further away. The Russian song and the melody of the foreigners join together in common harmony, and re-echo in the distance.' The music is clearly characterized, and the listener should have no difficulty in following the programme. The whole piece is infused with the shimmer of the wide open landscape, and the high held octave in the violins symbolizes the glare of the sun.

The *Polovtsian Dances* from *Prince Igor* carried Borodin's fame well beyond the borders of his native Russia. They are an excerpt from the opera, which was first performed in 1890, and were originally intended as a ballet insertion with chorus. However, the purely orchestral version is just as effective. The rhythm is marvellously developed and all the themes are truly Russian in spirit, if not actually folk tunes. The types of dance vary between the shy games of the girls and the men's wild leaps. In the middle is the merry boys' dance. The themes are played off one against the other and combined. The climax comes in the middle section with the passionate syncopations of a wild dance in $3/4$ that is positively barbaric in its excitement.

NIKOLAI RIMSKY-KORSAKOV (1844-1908) was also an amateur to start with. But with great diligence he achieved a mastery of all forms of musical discipline. Mussorgsky and Borodin both owe a lot to him for his stimulus and substantial support, for Rimsky-Korsakov vetted their most important works and often made new instrumentations of them. Rimsky-Korsakov is a real magician in his handling of the orchestra, and he has a strange and beautiful feeling for harmony.

The symphonic suite *Scheherazade*, opus 35, 1888, is a dazzling example of his mastery of orchestral technique. Originally, it was a programmatic symphony; each of the four movements told a precise story. Later, however, he abandoned the programme and retained only the title *Scheherazade*, which is in itself eloquent and tells the listener a lot about the content. The story of *Scheherazade* is the frame for the *Thousand and One Nights*: the cruel sultan Schahriar has lost all faith in the fidelity of woman and vows to have every woman executed who spends the night with him. Scheherazade decides to cure the sultan of this malady. Her wonderful stories seduce him into postponing the order for her execution from one day to the next. She tells him a thousand and one stories, and lives with him a thousand and one days and finally convinces the sultan of her fidelity and purity. He abandons his vow and takes her to wife.

The main motifs of Rimsky-Korsakov's symphonic suite are determined by the two chief characters in the story: the sultan and Scheherazade. The sultan is characterized by the hard, assertive

theme with which the work opens, and Scheherazade's delicate motif played each time by the solo violin in fine, playful cadenzas

forms a contrast. The sultan's theme dominates the first movement, now threatening, now heavy and passionate, and now quiet and friendly, and in between are the episodes in which Scheherazade takes up her stories. According to the original programme she relates here the adventures of Sinbad the Sailor.

The second movement, introduced by the solo violin and Scheherazade's theme, paints a colourful picture. It is like an oriental market place or bazaar, full of the variegated forms and features of the oriental fairy-tale world. The tale is again interrupted by the sultan several times, now harsh and impatient, and then again gentle.

In the third movement Scheherazade tells a tender love story and the sultan listens in silence. But the last movement begins with a wild outburst from the thorny ruler. Scheherazade tells of a marvellous festival: whirling themes and dance rhythms are thrown about and the party borders on tumult. At the climax the trombones state the sultan's theme with great power, but no longer threateningly. The solo violin answers him again and the two themes unite.

A Russian Easter, opus 36, 1888, is another fascinating symphonic poem. Rimsky-Korsakov uses old Slav church themes with their monotonously flavoured modality hesitating between the major and minor keys. The allegro grows in confidence and hope after its gloomy beginnings in the mysterious, slow introduction. Fanfares announce the joyful Easter message. Mysterious music of the spheres follows, and the first bell is heard dulled by distance. Then a mighty build-up leads to the full-blooded jubilation of a Russian Easter Morn, with bells on all sides: small bells, large bells, all the instruments of the orchestra seem to be bells and at a wave of Rimsky-Korsakov's magic wand the air is filled, all space is filled with a great ringing.

The *Capriccio Espagnol*, opus 34, 1887, is a compendium of artful tricks of instrumentation. It is in five movements, played without a break. The main theme is a passionate and animated Spanish dance in $^2/_4$ that recurs three times in the course of the piece. The

counter-theme is an elegiac Spanish waltz, which goes through a host of instrumental variations. After the reprise of the main theme we come to the large middle section of the *Capriccio*, which is an extremely original gypsy scene. The constant crash-bang of tambourine, triangle and drum accompanies recitative passages for all the groups in the orchestra. They unite in a striking accompaniment rhythm over which rises a passionate gypsy melody for violins. The final movement is a fandango with an effective *stretto* of the main theme for coda.

A pupil of Rimsky-Korsakov's, ALEXANDER GLAZUNOV (1865–1936), also belongs to the St Petersburg innovators. His symphonies are in obscurity at present, but his *Concerto for violin in A minor*, opus 82, 1904, has always been quite popular. Formally, the concerto is peculiar, for the andante is built into the first movement as a sort of centre piece, and the rondo finale follows directly after the main movement.

The expressive first theme determines the fundamental mood of glowing passion of the first movement. This is introduced by the soloist, and so is the vocal second theme, which leads into the andante sostenuto. The soloist also dominates the andante, up as far as the repeat of the andante theme, which is entrusted to the woodwind. The interlude ends with expressive scales for the soloist accompanied by lovely harp sounds. The development section opens with a reprise of the main theme in bassoons and violas; the second theme follows quickly and the soloist presses forward to the recapitulation. The main theme is now passionate and wild, and the second theme, played darkly on the G string, also expresses disquiet. The climax comes with the big cadenza which leads straight into the finale. The violin takes over the trumpets' hunting theme and prolongs it with a great show of virtuosity: scales, arpeggios, runs in thirds and sixths, harmonics, everything. One noteworthy effect is the episode where the theme appears in bells and flute, with the soloist playing *pizzicato* like a guitar. The stream of ideas never dries up and the piece ends brilliantly.

ALEXANDER SCRIABIN (1872–1915) was a composer working outside the circle of the St Petersburg innovators. They demanded that Russian music should be national in character, whereas Scriabin obviously follows on from Chopin, and one can trace the influences of Wagner and Debussy. However, he freed himself of foreign influences and developed a musical language that is peculiarly his own. He is best represented by his late piano sonatas; his orchestral works, envisaged and thought out on a grand scale, never quite come up to scratch. Of his symphonies, *Poème divin*, 1903, *Poème du feu* (with colour keyboard) and *Poème de l'extase*, 1908, only the third is performed at all frequently in our concert halls. The dissolution of the theme is the most striking novelty in Scriabin's music. In its place we find the one-bar motif which combines with others to form ever fresh configurations. His dissolution of the theme led him to relinquish all pretensions to the strict forms of classical times, and so he really belongs among the impressionists. But his overlapping harmonies go far beyond mere tone-painting, hinting at unheard of fields of polytonicality, and such developments of the future. Scriabin's symphonies are really enormous *impressions*, and this is certainly true of the *Poème de l'extase*. Longing (first section) and suffering (middle section, *lento*) build up to the highest pitch of ecstasy (final section). The motivic work is highly chromatic and the rhythm is dominated by urgent syncopations. The orchestral writing is sometimes delicate, dissolving and blurred and sometimes extremely harsh.

SERGEI RACHMANINOV (1873-1943) is a dazzling musical phenomenon. The composer Rachmaninov was overshadowed for a long time by Rachmaninov the transcendental piano virtuoso, celebrated throughout the world. But his significance as a composer should not be underestimated. Rachmaninov follows on from Tchaikovsky; despite his Russian characteristics he is quite westernized. His piano concertos are of lasting value, and the *Concerto No. 2 for piano in C minor*, opus 18, 1901, enjoys enormous popularity.

Powerful rising chords from the soloist introduce the main theme, which is played with impassioned grandeur by the strings, decorated by sounding arpeggios from the pianist. The mood of this opening is decisive for the success of the concerto. The second theme also builds up to a powerful climax though it begins and ends in a quiet lyrical mood. The development section is no less rich in climaxes and crescendos, and the high spot of the movement comes with the reprise of the main theme as an opulent march.

The second movement has a lovely atmosphere but is somewhat long-winded. The piano writing is extremely effective; gratifying for the pianist and impressive for the audience. The finale is based on a fiery dance theme and its transformation, in combination with a lyrical second idea.

SMETANA AND DVORAK

It is a remarkable fact that national music in the various European countries only grew up with the advent of the romantic era. Musical races like the Czechs and Hungarians contributed a host of excellent practising musicians, but did not assert themselves in any independent creative activity. The Italian monopoly, and later the monopoly of the German classics, was too strong. The romantic era loosened these bonds, and the various peoples remembered their own folk music and began to use it for artistic purposes.

Bohemian music was pioneered by BEDRICH SMETANA (1824-84) who became the founder of Czech national music. Smetana's early symphonic efforts are completely under the influence of Beethoven and later Liszt. It was only when he turned his attention to opera that Smetana found his own style. He included folk elements in his operas and Bohemian music soon became an accepted part of the mainstream music of the West.

The Bartered Bride was a world-wide success after its première in Prague in 1866. The overture is characterized by the same fresh, Bohemian folk tune elements as the opera; it presents a picture of the happy life of the people. A happy fugato develops out of a gay, characteristic motif (note the excitement generated by the fact that

the *sforzati* of the theme occur at intervals of five beats, whereas the metre is $4/4$), and this leads to a rustic dance. The lyrical subsidiary theme in the oboe does not stand a chance against the general

animation; the excitement is irresistible and the music rushes forward to its fiery end. Technically, the overture is a very difficult piece to play, and it has become an orchestral show-piece of the first order.

Towards the end of his life Smetana turned back to purely instrumental composition. He wrote two symphonic poems, *Vyšehrad* and *The Moldau*, which were first performed in 1875 and scored an extraordinary success. In the following years he wrote four further symphonic poems and grouped them in a large cycle under the title *Má Vlast* (My Fatherland). Formally, they are all symphonic poems in one movement, somewhat in the manner of Liszt but much simpler, not so symphonic. Each piece is preceded by a short programme giving details of the content. The note for the first piece in the cycle *Vyšehrad* runs as follows: 'At the sight of the Vyšehrad rock the poet hears in his mind the harp sounds of the legendary singer Lumiv. Vyšehrad rises before his eyes in all its past glory. This was the stronghold of the dukes and kings of the Přemyslid line. But wild battles rage around the royal seat, and the splendid halls fall down in dust and ashes. The stronghold stands lonely and desolate, and only Lumiv's long-vanished song echoes mournfully from the ruins.'

The slow introduction is built on a melancholy motif played by the harp: the song of the mythical troubadour. The full orchestra

paints the glory of the castle, with a powerful version of the kernel-motif, decorated by figurations in the strings. The allegro depicts the battle for the castle, its siege and downfall. The final section is a song of mourning for all the vanished opulence and splendour. The noble main melody reappears, and the waters of the Moldau roll past the ruins. The knightly themes from the allegro are heard once more, with the strings of the harp trembling softly.

The second piece in the cycle, *The Moldau*, has become extremely popular, probably as a result of the pleasing melodic style and its clear, straightforward programme. The music depicts the whole course of the river Moldau in a series of finely differentiated scenes that merge one into the other. The Moldau is the most beautiful and mightiest river of Smetana's home country. The river rises in the bubbling of a spring; winds and strings play little wave motifs and the stream flows down, gradually gaining in strength. The woodwind state the Moldau melody, decorated by the strings, and a powerful river flows down through the rich fertile land. Colourful scenes are enacted on its banks: a hunt passes by with horns and fanfares, clarinets and violins strike up a polka, for a farmhouse

marriage is in full swing. The river winds its way through the night; moonlight plays on the water, the nymphs are dancing to little wave motifs, from which the Moldau theme detaches itself. The river wanders on. The climax is reached when we come to the rapids, with furious basses and shrill woodwind. The river rushes through rocks and gullies and then emerges into the broad plain, now a mighty river, calm and majestic. The Moldau song is heard in the radiant major key, and winds play the proud Vyšehrad theme from the first tone-poem; a greeting from the old castle as the broad river rushes by.

Of the other four pieces in the fatherland cycle, only *From Bohemia's woods and fields* has succeeded in gaining a foothold in our concert halls. This piece, like *The Moldau*, is a description of nature. There is a continuous rustling in the woodwind and strings, interrupted occasionally by long-held brass chords. The broad landscape shimmers in the midday sun. Oboes and bassoons play a merry tune in thirds. This passes away and there is complete quiet. We have entered a wood. There is a mysterious whispering from muted strings and the first violins play a delicate melody, joined by the other parts in fugal entries. Horns and clarinets intone a pious song which eventually rises to a pitch of solemn grandeur. The serious mood breaks off and we hear two bars of a fast polka. Pressing onward through the wood, we emerge to find a local festival in progress, where we give ourselves up to the uninhibited, stamping polka which triumphs with great enthusiasm over the more delicate feelings that are also expressed. We hear again the *piano* song from the wood, but the gaiety of the festival carries the day.

Smetana's real talent was for opera, however impressive his great fatherland cycle. ANTON DVORAK (1841–1904), on the other hand, was primarily an instrumental composer; his operas carry very little weight compared with his symphonies and chamber music. What the two composers have in common is their ardent nationalism—the fact that they both use Czechoslovakian folk elements.

Dvořák began his career as a viola player in the National Theatre in Prague, and later started teaching in the Prague Conservatoire. In 1892 he went to America as a teacher, and his stay there had a great influence on his work. In America he wrote his symphonic masterpiece, the Fifth Symphony in E minor, opus 95, generally known as the *New World Symphony*, and this has always been extremely popular on account of its melodic richness and the poetic content of the individual movements. Dvořák wrote the symphony in 1894 as a greeting 'from the New World' to his friends at home. He uses a few Indian and negro melodies, but the melodies and rhythms of his homeland are the life-blood of the symphony. They seem to express his homesickness for Europe and his beloved Czechoslovakia, and indeed after three years in America he returned to live amongst his own people.

The main theme, which expresses his longing for home, is preceded by a short, slow introduction. It is played first by the horn,

then the oboe, then the strings, and is finally developed in all the glory of the full orchestra. The second group of themes shows a different world. First there is a dance theme of a monotonous character, which may well have been derived from an American Indian

melody, then comes a sweet and memorable melody played by the flute to the accompaniment of the strings, *pianissimo*. In the course of the movement the two thematic groups are constantly juxta-

posed and artfully combined, and at the end the theme of longing emerges victorious.

I interpret the second movement as a landscape painting; wide open spaces, the solemn silence of nature, the loneliness of mankind, and a clutch of homesickness in the wanderer's breast. Mysterious wind chords precede the fervent melody for cor anglais. Various other moods are touched on and when, eventually, we return to this cor anglais melody, night is falling over the wide landscape.

The scherzo theme is wild and elemental, but there are two contrasted subsidiary themes. First an idyllic episode reminiscent of the cor anglais melody in the second movement, and then a rustic dance scene in Bohemia. The theme of longing recurs frequently in the transitional passages between these themes, and clearly underlines the fundamental character of the movement.

Whereas the themes of the first two movements are expressive of longing and expectancy, the theme of the last movement, introduced at the outset by the trumpets *fortissimo*, has an air of joyful decision. It is a really heroic theme and all other themes pale into

insignificance beside it. The longing themes of the previous movements appear and are combined, but all are overrun finally by the joyous strength of the finale theme.

The Fifth Symphony puts all the other symphonies in the shade, and the more we hear the *New World* the less chance the others have. Recently, however, the *Symphony No. 2 in D minor*, opus 70, and the *Symphony No. 4 in G major*, opus 88, have been given several hearings and the latter especially presents a glowing testimony of Dvořák's musicality and richness of melodic invention. The first allegro is full of lovely melodies. It is not a matter of two or three themes; here we find several groups of themes, each containing several beautiful and extended melodies. The symphony opens with a mysterious theme in the minor key, which moves to the major key to end. Then we hear the main theme like a bird-call

Allegro con brio

from the flute, and thereafter the flow of melody is uninterrupted. No ill-judged lapse mars the beautiful balance of the whole!

The opposition of moods in the adagio is very remarkable. There is a gypsy flavour in the thematic work with its self-willed end

Adagio

phrases and shining instrumentation, but the basic mood of the movements is one of melancholy. The scherzo has a lovely extended waltz melody to offer, which makes the delicate trio seem rather childishly naïve.

After an introductory fanfare, the finale emerges as a set of variations on a theme that is closely related to the main theme of

Allegro

the first movement. The variations are formed up into three groups, of which the middle group takes the form of a burlesque funeral march. A reprise of the fanfares for trumpets leads to the final group which ends in a brilliant *stretto*.

Dvořák's *Concerto for violin in A minor*, opus 53, 1880, is a very popular piece. It is gratifying for the soloist, and the strong national flavour in all three movements is infectious. The first allegro is dominated by two rhythmic, animated themes. There are several other melodic ideas in the course of the movement, but they are quickly submerged in the elaborate virtuosity of the soloist. The slow movement follows directly with a fervent melody played by the soloist with a simplicity that makes it seem like a folk song. The minor key section is a poetic dialogue between the solo violin and horn.

The dazzling virtuosity of the finale is perhaps even more effective. The enchanting, Bohemian, syncopated theme is introduced by the soloist with a delicate accompaniment in the violins. This refrain frames the extended subsidiary ideas, which are equally enchanting melodically. The movement sparkles to its close with unfailing richness of invention.

Dvořák's *Concerto for 'cello and orchestra in B minor*, opus 104, 1895, is even more frequently performed than the violin concerto. This is partly due to the fact that there are comparatively few great concertos for the 'cello. Dvořák's concerto supplies something that our concert literature urgently needs, and it is consequently seized on with enthusiasm. The concerto is laid out in the usual three movements: the first is an extended allegro, the second a dreamy andante, and the last a swinging, animated finale. One beautiful melody follows another in an unending stream; the 'cello takes up all the themes prepared in the orchestra and varies them in the most beautiful technical refinements. The themes of the first movement are powerful and dramatic, those of the andante sensitive and dreamy, whereas the final movement uses themes reminiscent of Bohemian folk tunes and dances.

LEOS JANACEK (1854–1928) was only thirteen years younger than Dvořák, but his music is in a totally different sphere. His later works dispense entirely with the romantic tradition in which he grew up, and he seems, indeed, to have been writing *against* his own time. A most original genius, comparable with Mussorgsky, his music is bold and powerful, particularly the rhythmic aspect, and his harmonic and melodic sense is unique, self-willed and unmistakably original. His most important work was in the field of opera; *Jenufa* brought him world fame. But he achieved this recognition only in the last years of his life, and it was around this time that he wrote the two symphonic pieces that appear in the concert repertoire. The first is the orchestral rhapsody *Taras Bulba*, 1918, a symphonic poem based on Gogol's famous Cossack novel. The three movements of the rhapsody are devoted to the three principal characters in the novel, the wild old warrior, Taras Bulba, and his two sons, Andrei and Ostap. Andrei (first movement) is the weaker of the two brothers; he falls in love with a beautiful Polish girl and through her he betrays his people; he is killed by his own father.

There are some delicate feelings in this movement, but the second
movement is stormy and warlike throughout, as it depicts the raw
Cossack existence of Ostap. The final movement, dedicated to the
old hero, Taras Bulba, rises in rhapsodic grandeur.

The *Sinfonietta*, 1927, is a work of Janáček's last period. The fact
that this dazzling work is so seldom performed is due to the enormous forces of wind instruments that the score demands. The outside movements require a supplementary chorus of trumpets in
addition to the five that he writes for in all the movements. The
extraordinary hymn-like sound effect is very affecting; behind all
the external opulence one feels the presence of simple goodness
and honesty.

GRIEG AND SIBELIUS

Although the Danish composer Niels Gade (1817–90) made a
considerable impression in Europe, it was left to EDVARD GRIEG
(1843–1907), a Norwegian composer of great originality and genius,
to put Scandinavian music firmly on the map. Under the influence
of the romantic movement spreading throughout Europe, Grieg
turned his attention to the indigenous musical elements of his
country and people. He was consciously opposed to the Mendels-
sohnian influence that characterized the music of Gade, and relying
on national resources, he was able to evolve a powerful musical
language of his own. He avoided the longer forms, concentrating
his attention on groups of short pieces like the *Lyric Pieces* for piano,
the *Norwegian Dances*, and song cycles. His idiom opens up a
musical world of surprising novelty; his melodic style is characterized by a constant, acid descent from the leading-note and sharply
accented dance rhythms.

Of Grieg's few orchestral works, his *Peer Gynt Suites*, opus 46,
in 1888, and opus 55, in 1891, achieved an unexampled popularity.
They are taken from the music he wrote for Ibsen's play, and they
consist of a series of short pieces with very little attempt to make
any extensive symphonic developments. However, the mood in
each case is so exquisitely created, so personal, and so strongly expressive that one hardly misses the symphonic scale; one is so
captivated by the directness of effect.

The first movement of the first *Peer Gynt Suite* is headed 'Morning'. Flute and oboe alternately play a pastoral theme expressive of

the glassy clarity of the mountain scenery in the early morning. The strings take over the theme and build up to the big climax of sunrise. The peaceful mood of the opening returns when the horn reverts to the main theme, and the movement dies away in soft flute trills.

The second movement is concerned with 'Ase's Death'. Peer Gynt's mother dies quietly and peacefully while her distracted son builds fantastic castles in the air for them both. This beautiful piece is in the rhythm of a funeral march.

'Anitra's Dance' is for strings alone, as is 'Ase's Death'. Here, the gracious tripping theme alternates with scurrying figurations. This seductive piece has a slightly oriental flavour.

The final piece, 'In the Hall of the Mountain King', is based on an uncanny four-bar motif played by basses and bassoons alternately. Then violins and oboes take up the theme and a grand

build-up leads to a *fortissimo* statement in the full orchestra, with the trombones stamping out the rhythm. The dance gets wilder and faster, always with this one motif. There is something fanatical, elemental, awe-inspiring or terrifying about the way the orchestra howls at the end of this dance.

The second *Peer Gynt Suite* has not achieved the popularity of the first. Only the final piece, 'Solveig's Song', has really caught on. Solveig is the love of Peer Gynt's youth, waiting faithfully for his return. His return to her brings peace to his troubled soul, but in the form of death. Consequently, the music is very serious in character, although there occurs a friendly major key section reminiscent of the happier days of youth. The gloomy ending is like a question that reverberates off into space, unanswerable.

The first movement, 'Ingrid's Lamentation', introduces a moving melody in the low register of the violins, preceded by a few

bars excited introduction. The 'Arabian Dance', scherzando, gets
its oriental character from the shrill sound of the piccolo. This
movement has a sensuous, seductive string melody in the middle
section. 'Peer Gynt's Return', the third movement, is explained by
its subtitle: 'A stormy evening on the coast'. An excited allegro
evokes the storm, and the score is characterized by the motif of the
open fifth, cascading dramatic runs, excited *tremolos* and shrill dissonances. In mood, this piece is dangerously close to Wagner's
Flying Dutchman.

Grieg's *Concerto for piano in A minor*, opus 16, composed in 1868,
is his most important symphonic work. The first movement is very
strongly dependent on Schumann's concerto, which seems to hover
before Grieg's eyes as an unattainable model, but the following
movements are pure Grieg. The work gets its extraordinary brilliance from the dazzling piano writing and the colourful instrumentation. Like Schumann, Grieg begins his concerto with a
powerful choral cascade followed by brilliant arpeggios. After this
opulent introduction, the pregnant main theme is given to the
orchestra. The second theme shows traces of Schumann in the
pretty harmonic writing. The pianistic climax of the movement is
the cadenza.

A lovely folk tune played by the strings is the soul of the slow
movement. The subsidiary idea is presented by the pianist with
delicate filigree work. The soloist takes the lead in the reprise and
lends grandeur and strength to the folk-song melody. The most
original movement of the concerto, the finale, follows directly.
The electrifying main theme passes through constant fresh variants,
and appears finally in $3/4$ as a sort of *stretto*. The idyllic second
theme on the other hand is grandly extended at the end and appears
in the full orchestra as a grandiose apotheosis surrounded by opulent
arpeggios for the soloist.

The Finnish composer JEAN SIBELIUS (1865–1957) is just as
consciously nationalistic as Grieg. He, too, builds on the folk songs
of his country and manages to achieve a peculiar, distinctive musical
language that mirrors the landscape of his country. As opposed to
Grieg, however, Sibelius is primarily a symphonic composer, interested in the larger forms. His style is accordingly weightier and
more difficult and his language presents more obstacles to the
understanding than the pleasing melodic style of Grieg. As a result
of this, Sibelius has found it more difficult to find his feet in the

musical world, but perhaps his influence will be the more enduring on that account.

Sibelius achieved his first successes with his symphonic poems, inspired by the mythology of his country. He wrote the tone-poem *En Saga* (A legend), opus 9, in 1892, when he was only twenty-seven years old, but his personal style was already formed. With this work he laid the foundations of a new Finnish music which has become accepted throughout the musical world thanks to his diligent and significant work over the decades. It would be mistaken to seek a programme for this piece, or attempt to fit the details of any particular legend to the music; *En Saga* is an expression of legendary Finland in general. It represents the mystery of the heroic grandeur of ancient times in relation to the primeval forces of nature. The architecture of the music is not easy to follow, however, for the themes are closely related as to mood and merge one into the other without any sharp differentiation. The motifs are repeated with constant variation, mostly reserved, but sometimes breaking out abruptly. The peace of nature rests on the long pedal-points in the basses and this feeling alternates with blistering fanfares. The listener must give himself up entirely to the atmosphere of the music if he wishes to get anywhere near the composer's secret world of sensibility.

The symphonic poem *The Swan of Tuonela*, opus 22, 1893, is based on a specific Finnish legend. The music is so clear that detailed explanations are superfluous. The lake of Tuonela lies between high cliffs and a lonely swan is dreaming there in the light of the midnight sun, sadly singing of vanished grandeur and faded beauty.

The heroic grandeur of the tone-poem *Finlandia*, opus 26, 1899, is very effective. Solemn fanfares alternate with heavy sounds from woodwind and strings. The monochrome, acid but beautiful land stretches away from us. The sound of a march is heard, with fanfares and solemn, festive music. A subsidiary theme has the character of a folk melody. The festive music rises now to a hymnic climax.

Sibelius wrote seven symphonies, and the first two became quite quickly successful. The *Symphony No. 1 in E minor*, opus 39, was written in 1899. The first movement (andante) opens strangely with a melancholy clarinet solo over a timpani *tremolo*. The allegro is like a great, gloomy heroic ballad. The themes are dry and powerful, but always shaded with sadness. There are melancholy undertones even in the greatest climax.

This undertone of melancholy is even more apparent in the andante. The strings play a monotonous melody which is prolonged

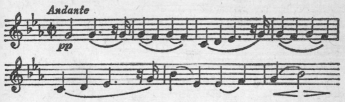

by the woodwind in a little fugato. The strings then take it up again in a painful variant. A delicate interlude precedes the second scene, which is a theme of depression played by the horn against a flickering string background. The landscape painting aspires to peaceful grandeur with the re-entry of the main theme, but the movement ends on a mournful note.

The scherzo is bitter and excitable, though there are softer notes in the trio. The finale opens with a powerful version of the longing clarinet melody from the beginning of the first allegro. The painful excitement of the main theme is then contrasted with the noble melancholy of the extended second theme, which, however, also shudders slightly with syncopations in the accompaniment. The ending is triumphantly executed, but it is no solution, no victory. The work ends on a note of bitter, gloomy grandeur.

The character of the *Symphony No. 2 in D major*, opus 43, 1902, is much lighter and more friendly. The first movement can be described as an idyll. The strings begin with a calm rising motion, answered by the woodwind with a pastoral tune; the horns echo the last phrase gently. This is like a sunny mood of summer, with changing feelings, but disquieting elements appear in the idyllic landscape with the arrival of the second theme: a slight wind gets up, and an angular phrase in the woodwind is representative perhaps of distant lightning. However, the peaceful mood is generally preserved. Further on in the movement the excitement really builds up: a big crescendo reaches its climax in one of the themes from the first group played by the complete brass section. Thereafter, the sunny mood of the opening dominates the music.

But the second movement is dark and bitter as it expresses the depression of the wide open spaces. The main theme is played first by the bassoon, and then rises steeply to the sound of harsh brass

chords. A melancholy melody for strings makes an attempt at reconciliation, but is impotent against the forces of nature.

The third movement is very clear in form. The oboe melody that constitutes the trio in the excited, ghostly scherzo may well be derived from a Finnish folk song. The scherzo is played twice, each time answered by the oboe theme, and the second time it leads straight into the final movement. This is dominated by a victorious

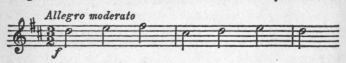

radiant theme, and the brooding character of the second theme makes little impression. The movement swings up boldly to its grandiose ending.

It is not easy to come to grips with Sibelius' musical language at a first hearing. Some details sound strange to our ears; the melodic style that evades the leading-note, the apparent perversity of certain harmonic sequences, the chains of falling fourths or fifths, and not least the constant changes of mood in the formal structure. Perhaps it is just these characteristics that give the listener the impression of an elemental strength behind the music.

Sibelius' *Symphony No. 3 in C major*, opus 52, was written in the years 1905–07. It is a short work of only three movements, of which the middle movement is a synthesis of slow movement and scherzo. The *Symphony No. 4 in A minor*, opus 63, though equally brief, has

more body: it is tragic and gloomy in contrast to the lightness of
the third. The first movement is a *quasi adagio* in sonata form! The
tritone motif stated at the outset dominates the movement, and
also sets the pace for the wealth of rhythmic subtleties and syncopations that characterize the movement. The second movement is
a scherzo with implicit trios; again the tritone dominates the harmony. The slow movement proper comes third, with crawling
phrases for winds over sustained strings. The longest movement is
the last, which again features the tritone; note the string D-sharp
after the arpeggio of A major in the first bar of the melody. Contrasts and developments of texture seem the main concern of the
movement, which presents a wealth of material. It ends *mf dolce* in
the strings, with psalmodic chords.

A letter of 1918 shows that Sibelius envisaged all three of his
subsequent symphonies in one spate of fierce conceptual activity:
'My new works—partly sketched and planned. The fifth symphony
in a new form—practically composed anew, I work at daily . . .
The sixth symphony is wild and impassioned in character. Sombre
with pastoral contrasts. Probably in four movements with the end
rising to a sombre roaring of the orchestra, in which the main
theme is drowned. The seventh symphony. Joy of life and vitality,
with *appassionato* passages. In three movements—the last an "Hel-
lenic rondo". All this with due reservation . . .' as we shall see.

The *Symphony No. 5 in E-flat major*, opus 82, was completed in
1919. It is in three movements, though they are obviously intended
to be played without substantial breaks. The first movement opens
with a long *molto moderato*, $^{12}/_8$, and then switches abruptly (by a
metrical modulation) to $^3/_4$ *allegro moderato*. This builds up in size
and speed though *presto* and *più presto*, and breaks off after long
climbing broken chords over sustained brass. *Andante mosso, quasi
allegretto* is the tempo indication for the following movement,
which begins with long held notes, *pp*, creating an impression of
adagio. *Pizzicato* crotchets for low strings set the real tempo, which
is easy-going and quite swift, as it turns out later. However, the
winds persist for a long time in their slow motion progressions of
minims and semibreves. The finale, allegro molto, opens with string
tremolo passages in which little melody is recognizable—it is more
like a diffuse progress. Soon the winds enter and lend their profile
to the blurred texture. The music slows down to end and builds up
in a big *largamente* climax; abruptly, six separated, hacked chords
for full orchestra end the work.

The *Symphony No. 6 in D minor*, opus 104, was not completed until 1924. Far from being 'wild and impassioned' the score is restrained, and even slightly modal in character. A great deal of important material is entrusted to the strings; it appears rather a mystery why he chose to include harp and bass-clarinet in a score that turned out so plain and even rather austere. The continuity and flow of music were probably preoccupying Sibelius at this point—there are certainly no Beethovenian contrasts such as his letter might have led us to expect. The two brass surprises in the third movement recall Haydn rather than Beethoven.

The first allegro (*molto moderato*) is an excellent example of the way Sibelius develops themes and motifs organically, one from the other, so that new material is acquired imperceptibly. Similarly, he sets off in the 'slow' movement (*allegretto moderato*) with an apparent walking $^6/_8$ (two in a bar). Only in the tenth bar do we realize what rhythm it is we are listening to, namely an allegretto $^3/_4$. Even after this awakening, the rhythmic colour of the violin theme comes as another surprise. The third movement, *poco vivace* (note the tempered tempi of all these first three movements), demonstrates admirably Sibelius' skill in juxtaposing running material with dotted-rhythm chordal material. The interruptions from the brass, mentioned above, enliven the interplay further. The last movement is *allegro molto* at last. The rhythmically accented theme is reduced at the end to a beautiful chorale-like string passage, with end-of-line pauses. A lovely effect of distance is created even before the violins' sustained D fades into silence.

The *Symphony No. 7 in C major*, opus 105, was completed in 1925, and contrary to his original plan, he attempted a one-movement form. Nor does this one big movement break up into three sections, but into four, although the first can be understood as introductory material to the second part, *allegro moderato*, thus making a three-part whole, without slow movement. Actually it is very difficult to make this cohere; indeed it is difficult to fit the work into a schema at all, for the $^6/_4$ metre is sustained for almost all the time, excepting the passages in $^3/_2$ at beginning and end. The $^6/_4$ is sometimes *moderato*, sometimes *vivacissimo*, once even the crotchets are transformed into sextuplet quavers to allow for an adagio over the top. And when the time comes to change back, they are changed back to half-speed crotchets! (This is what is meant by a metrical modulation.) It is easy to get lost in the score, since, as is often the case, the constantly available reference of the printed score is ultimately confusing. Obviously, the listener should be borne along by the music, and enthralled by each new change as it occurs. Sibelius certainly intended his formal vagaries to be followed by the listener, indeed they should constitute a large part of his pleasure, but they should be understood in linear succession, and not fitted into a total concept or overall system.

The *Concerto for violin in D minor*, opus 47, 1903, has special significance in Sibelius' œuvre. It is a good example of the personality and attractiveness of his style, and yet the internal laws of the concerto form are respected; the soloist has ample opportunity to show his virtuosity and powers of musical expression. The soloist is always in the foreground, leading the orchestra. He opens the work with generously extended melodic phrases over a *tremolo* in the strings and creates the basic mood of strength. A powerful cadenza leads to the lyrical counter-theme, and an extended orchestral interlude forms the bridge to a third theme, virile and accented. The movement, which is rather difficult to follow, is built on these three themes. The other movements are much more direct in their effect. There are wonderful transfigured climaxes in the fervent song of the slow movement, and the powerful, dancing finale is infectious in its brilliance.

GUSTAV MAHLER

born Kališt, Bohemia 7 July 1860
died Vienna 18 May 1911

Mahler studied in Vienna and during his life worked in various cities—Prague, Leipzig, Budapest, Hamburg—as a conductor, and after that became director of the Opera in Vienna. From 1908 onward he was a guest conductor in America.

It is customary to regard Mahler as a successor of Bruckner, whereas Richard Strauss continues the line of Brahms and Wagner. Certainly Mahler was greatly stimulated by Bruckner; the opulence of his orchestration and his gigantic forms are clear evidence of this. But these are externals; the ideas and expression of the two are worlds apart. Mahler found his own style as early as his first symphony; his aim and abilities were quite out of the ordinary and his symphonic œuvre is simply enormous, but he has had amazingly little influence over the generations following him and contemporary music. The young Schönberg built on Mahler's foundations, but his real music has nothing whatever to do with Mahler, and nor does the music of any of the younger composers of Schönberg's school.

Besides a few important song cycles, Mahler's œuvre consists of ten enormous works: nine symphonies, of which the eighth is really an evening's worth of oratorio, and the vocal work, the *Song of the Earth (Das Lied von der Erde)* which can also fill a whole evening. His symphonic work subdivides into four groups. First, the four first symphonies, which have in common their exploitation of folk song elements, then the symphonies five to seven, which are purely instrumental and unconnected with song. The third group consists solely of the *Symphony of a Thousand* (the eighth symphony), and the final group comprises the *Ninth Symphony* and the *Song of the Earth*. Almost all the symphonies are enormous both as regards form and size of orchestra, and this is taken beyond all limits in the *Symphony of a Thousand*. The extraordinary difficulty of performing these works has hindered their becoming very widely known; the most popular are the first four symphonies and the *Song of the Earth*.

The *Symphony No. 1 in D major*, completed in 1888, is a symphony of nature. The introduction to the first movement paints the mysterious awakening of nature. Distant wind fanfares, the sound of the cuckoo, and a simple morning song for the horns emerge above the strings' delicate harmonics. An urgent motif mounts from the depths and opens out into the allegro. The theme is a

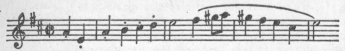

fresh walking melody taken from the song cycle 'Lieder eines fahrenden Gesellen'. The words run 'I went walking in the fields this morning', and this mood of a carefree morning walk dominates the whole movement. The themes are all very closely related; they seem like folk songs symbolizing nature and they combine easily. Indeed, the lack of strong contrasts makes the form seem rather blurred.

The scherzo is unproblematic. A jolly *ländler* melody is played over the rustic, stamping basses. The atmosphere of the Austrian Alps is retained throughout, even in the idyllic trio.

Mahler prescribes a pause after these two major-key movements, and the following movements are in the minor key. Above dull timpani strokes we hear a little canon for muted basses, 'cellos and

Solemnly, measured

violas which, with its countless repetitions, evokes an image of end-less monotony. The canon is a version of a well-known folk tune. This tired uniformity is relieved by parody: sobbing wind melodies in thirds accompanied by *col legno* string chords with drums and cymbals. The middle section is a delicate, melancholy melody, again taken from the 'Lieder eines fahrenden Gesellen'. However, this dreamy interlude is but a short respite; the anxious, funereal canon returns and finally reverberates in the dull timpani strokes.

The stormy finale follows immediately. Partial motifs in the winds emerge from wild string passages and form up into a power-ful march theme. This is immediately developed with elemental power and the entry of the second theme, *pianissimo* in the violins, is like a release from bondage. Again, this interlude is but a brief respite; the storms break out with renewed passionate strength, and after a mighty argument we return to the original key, a radiant D major. The final section uses ideas from the first movement; the themes of nature in new forms build up to an ecstatic ending.

Mahler's second symphony, in C minor, was completed in 1894. It is generally known as the *Resurrection Symphony* because of the text of the last movement. After some initial difficulty on account of the enormous scale of the work, the *Resurrection Symphony* had considerable success, which has lasted up to the present day. The lofty ethical feelings expressed by the work ensure its place in the repertoire, but the necessity of a large orchestra supplemented by a chorus of equal dimensions has had the effect that it is not per-formed very frequently.

The first movement is headed allegro maestoso. Urgent figures push up from the basses, and slowly the form builds up into some sort of shape, restlessly oscillating between *pianissimo* and *fortissimo*, without actually achieving the clarity of a proper theme. A sudden twist introduces the quiet rising cantilena of the second theme. This dreamy mood often tries to assert itself in the course of the move-ment, but it is ever and again slapped down by the might of the main thematic group. The development section is exclusively dominated by the wild hammering rhythms of the first group. A chorale-like theme appears in the horns and builds up to an enormous climax: fate, inexorable death, appears before us! This mighty movement breathes the grandeur of Bruckner, but the thematic work is Mahler's own.

The turmoil of the first movement is followed by a comforting andante moderato. In the score, Mahler advises a pause of at least five minutes before the second movement, which is justified by the extraordinary contrast between the two movements. The idyllic second movement is like a dream of life, as opposed to the vision of death presented by the first movement. A remarkably naïve and old-fashioned dance melody awakens melancholy memories. A little interlude introduces a *pianissimo* triplet motif and the reprise of the main melody follows, all in the most delicate colours.

The 'cellos play an enthusiastic counter-melody. The triplet motion reappears in *fortissimo* interruptions, while the winds try to assert the song-like melody. The conflicting energies gradually exhaust themselves and the music sinks back into the andante of the opening.

The scherzo is very earthy. Coarse, primitive themes alternate with gay and sometimes grotesque ideas, the whole enveloped in the unbroken semiquaver motion of the strings. A dreamy melody glimmers briefly in an interlude, but the rhythms of the main section sweep it away. The final movement follows directly; it is a solo song with words from *Des Knaben Wunderhorn*, an anthology of old German poetry. 'O Röschen rot! Der Mensch liegt in grösster Not' (O little red Rose!) are the opening words, and fulfilment comes with the words 'Ich bin von Gott und will wieder zu Gott!'. The death wish is expressed by the alto soloist with moving simplicity and delicacy.

Mahler himself has provided an interpretation of the meaning of this enormous finale. The orchestra shudders expectantly; a horn call sounds in the distance, and a delicate chorale melody from the

first movement emerges from the stillness. This represents the song
of the dead at the Last Judgement. As a contrast we hear a radiant
theme in the trombones, but this is transitory for the time being,
for the big battles are yet to come. A march develops and progresses inexorably forward: the dead are marching to the Last
Judgement. Above this we hear festive trumpet flourishes, proclaim-
ing the Resurrection. The enormous climax is answered by the
light sound of an orchestra in the distance. The noise breaks out
again and elemental forces clash above our heads, but the Day of
Judgement is essentially past. Delicate sounds take over; a longing
melody rises in the 'cellos, and the horns' call, the trumpets' flourish
and an imitation of the songs of birds all help to create a mood of
perfect unreality, which gradually fades into silence. Then we hear
the low, dark sound of the chorus: 'Auferstehn, ja auferstehn.' The
chorale marches rigidly forward while the solo soprano separates
and floats above. The orchestra joins in, the rigidity softens and the
alto soloist sings 'O Glaube', followed by the soprano with 'hast
nicht umsonst gelebt, gelitten!'. Now the chorus sings 'Bereite dich
zu leben' with an air of mystery, and gradually the forces and feelings involved unite and build up to the powerful climax of 'Sterben
werde ich, um zu leben' in unison. 'Auferstehn, ja auferstehn',
repeats the chorus with profound emotion, and the full organ bursts
out, bells ring, trumpets play the Resurrection motif and the orchestra shines out in all its glory.

Mahler's *Symphony No. 3 in D minor*, written in 1896, possesses a
complete programme, written by the composer while he was
sketching the work and sanctioned by him when it was finished.
According to this programme, this is again a symphony of nature.
It subdivides into two main sections: the enormous first movement
comprises the first section, and the remaining five movements the
second.

'Pan awakens. Summer marches in with a singing and a ringing,
and buds and blossoms appear on all sides. And yet how completely
strange and painful it is, the way lifeless nature lies dull and motion-
less, resisting the advent of life.' With these words Mahler indicates
the meaning of the first movement. A powerful, decided motif for

the horns in unison opens the movement, but even while it hurries

on we hear a harsh trumpet call against it. Other themes are introduced, but none receives any extensive development; the music
just 'sings and rings on all sides'. Finally, all the elements combine
and form a triumphant march: summer has come in. This movement lasts forty-five minutes, and Mahler always followed it with
the main intermission.

The five movements of the second part are very easy to understand. For the graceful minuet Mahler chose the title 'What the
flowers say'. There are moments of disquiet in this movement too,
but the grace of the minuet theme sweeps away all obstacles. The
third movement is headed 'What the beasts of the forest say'. The
main theme of this scherzo is the song 'Kuckuck hat sich zu Tode
gefallen'. The trio, amazingly, is a solo for post horn which blends
very well with its scherzo frame.

The three last movements are played without a break. The fourth
movement, 'What man says', is an alto solo to Nietzsche's words
from Zarathustra: 'O man, take heed! What says the deep midnight'; this is the slow movement of the symphony. The fifth
movement, 'What the angels say', tells with happy naïvety how
Jesus forgave Peter his sins. The verses are sung by a female chorus,
while a boys' chorus imitates the sound of bells, to a delicate
orchestral accompaniment. In the sixth movement we hear again
the theme of the first movement. Perfect equilibrium seems to be
the aim of the slow build-up; darker passages are quickly overcome
and brought into line with the clean major-key harmony of the
whole. The work ends with a glowing chorale.

Like the *Resurrection*, Mahler's *Third Symphony* is performed but
seldom on account of the enormous orchestral apparatus involved.
If the composer's instructions are followed, the orchestra alone
consists of one hundred and twenty musicians. Compared with
this, the *Symphony No. 4 in G major*, completed in 1900, presents no
difficulties at all; Mahler even dispenses with trombones!

The first movement opens with little bells like sleigh bells. The
naïve and graceful melody of the main theme is played by the
violins. The subsidiary themes, rich and plentiful here, as always in

Mahler, have a similar naïvety, and the gay mood of the whole movement is interrupted hardly ever.

In the scherzo the solo violin tunes his instrument a whole tone higher than usual. The dance melody is almost exclusively merry; only occasionally does Mahler introduce uncanny or fantastical turns of phrase.

The adagio of the symphony, a set of variations, is characterized by its measured step. The emotion builds up gradually, and culminates in prayer. The movement becomes more flowing, and quite unexpectedly Mahler inserts a scherzando section, only to fall back into the reserved mood of the opening. Suddenly, a brilliant *fortissimo* pours over us; trumpets and clarinets play the theme of Paradise from the movement, ringed with arpeggios in all the strings. Shining like a message from heaven, the movement ends in the highest register of the orchestra.

The final movement introduces a solo voice. After a short introduction the solo soprano enters with the song of 'heavenly joys', a poem taken from *Des Knaben Wunderhorn*, that describes with naïve satisfaction all the pleasures awaiting us in heaven. The idyllic first stanzas, ending with the amusing words 'Saint Peter in Heaven is watching' (Sanct Peter im Himmel sieht zu!), are followed by

the realistic details of the middle stanzas, with bells as in the first movement. The final verses, which tell of the music in heaven, are set to a lovely fervent tune. Extremely fine, extremely delicate, hardly sounding at all, are the final words of the naïve and happy message.

Mahler's first symphonies stem quite clearly from the circle of ideas of *Des Knaben Wunderhorn*. The *Symphonies Nos. 5, 6 and 7* are purely instrumental; they are enormous in size and tragic in content, and form a harsh contrast to the folk-song qualities of the early symphonies. Mahler's style underwent a strange metamorphosis in these works and they met with very little success. In 1910 he was able to have the première of his *Symphony of a Thousand* in Munich, and the work had an exceptional success which might have heralded a proper appreciation of his other symphonies, for up till then only the *Resurrection Symphony* had been received with any real warmth. But six months later the composer was dead.

Mahler's eighth symphony, the *Symphony of a Thousand*, is a choral work. Two large mixed choruses, a chorus of boys, eight vocal soloists and an orchestra of at least one hundred and twenty musicians are necessary for a proper performance of the work, and hence its title. The symphony divides into two parts: for the first part Mahler chose the words of the old Latin hymn, 'Veni, creator spiritus', a Whitsuntide hymn celebrating God as the source of all

love. As a complement to these medieval words comes the mysterious final scene of Goethe's *Faust*, in which the poet speaks of the final transfiguration and liberating power of love.

The work opens with a mighty double chorus 'Veni, creator spiritus' accompanied by the organ. The cry 'veni' is repeated stormily. The second main idea is stated by the solo voices with the soprano leading, and the 'imple superna gratia' is set with great delicacy. The chorus joins in and timidly takes up the plea for heavenly grace. The first section ends with the strong reprise of the 'Veni, creator spiritus'. A short orchestral interlude takes up the main theme, but after a powerful climax it breaks off abruptly. 'Infirma nostri corporis' pleads the chorus, and the solo voices join in with a depressed 'virtute firmans'. The voices cease, and another excited interlude hurries past. The middle section is a development of enormous intensity: both themes are used constantly, combined one with the other; the orchestra also participates in the thematic

development. The theme to the words 'accende lumen sensibus, infunde amorem cordibus' forms the climax of the middle section. The voices press forward with fugato entries, and the striking main themes sound out in the bright jubilation of the boys' chorus. Above the powerful pedal-point on the dominant everything seems to press onward to the great final climax, culminating in the ecstatic reprise of the 'Veni, creator spiritus'. The recapitulation is brimming with enthusiasm and rejoicing, and the end of the movement is no less tremendous.

The first part consists of a single line, one long crescendo of feeling with transitory interruptions. The allegro motion of the movement is maintained consistently. In this respect the second part forms a complete contrast. The changing moods of the final scenes of *Faust* are treated individually and grouped into larger sections according to the formal laws of music. Mahler investigates the smallest details of the poetry, and traces the slightest emotional events. The mystical character of the poem is decisive for him, and inspires his composition from the first note to the last.

A mysterious orchestral introduction prepares the way for the first scenes. The 'accende' theme from the first part is played *pizzicato* by the basses, at first like a warning but later concentrated into a chorale. Thematic connections of this kind occur frequently in the course of the movement. The first adagio contains the scenes of the Anchorites and the songs of the three Fathers. A short allegro follows, 'Gerettet ist das edle Glied', and the scherzando of angels, 'Jene Rosen'. The chorus' 'Uns bleibt ein Erdenrest' is almost a note-for-note transcription of the 'infirma' chorus in the first part. The pious song of Doctor Marianus, 'Hier ist die Aussicht frei', forms the end of this section. The final words are: 'Jungfrau rein, im schönsten Sinne Mutter, Ehren würdig. Uns erwählte Königin, Göttern ebenbürtig.' The chorus accompanies very delicately, with harmonies that seem to descend from a higher sphere, and the apparition of the 'mater gloriosa' sways past, accompanied by a delicate theme for violins, the all-forgiving love melody which

surrounds the following choruses and songs of the penitents. Gretchen's song 'Neige, du Ohnegleiche' is also dominated by the 'gloriosa' melody. Gradually, the light and festive colours pre-dominate, both instrumentally and harmonically, and everything dissolves in a *pianissimo*. The high *tremolo* of the celesta over the dark kettledrum roll creates an unreal light in which we hear the voice of the 'mater gloriosa', 'Komm, hebe dich zu höheren Sphä-ren'.

Everything trembles in adoration. The sounds become lighter and ever more delicate, and the 'gloriosa' theme is heard in both chorus and orchestra, finally losing itself in the music of the spheres. Then the *chorus mysticus* breathes 'Alles Vergängliche ist nur ein Gleichnis' to a theme based on the chorale melody of the instru-mental introduction. The theme of the 'eternal feminine'—the 'gloriosa' melody—joins in with the words 'Ewig, ewig!'. All the voices are seized with immense enthusiasm; trumpets and trom-bones and the brilliant 'Veni, creator spiritus' join together, the organ sounds, bells ring, and the work closes in majestic grandeur.

Before starting work on his next symphony Mahler completed the *Song of the Earth* (1908). He was only forty-eight years old at the time, and yet this work seems overshadowed by some premonition of his untimely death. The *Song of the Earth* is a cycle of six songs for alto and tenor alternately. Mahler referred to the enormous work as a symphony, but this description is even more incompre-hensible here than for the *Symphony of a Thousand*; in character the songs are lyrical throughout; only their orchestral garments are symphonic. Mahler chose Hans Bethge's exquisite translations of Chinese lyrics for the text of his songs. They are enchanting poems, descriptive of a melancholy dream world of unreal beauty. Mahler's melodic writing is accordingly fragrant; the orchestra is handled sometimes in a chamber music idiom, with a slightly oriental flavour in the ornamentation, and the texture is largely polyphonic with an interplay of delicate, blurred lines.

The first song is called 'Das Trinklied vom Jammer der Erde' (Drinking Song of Earth's Sorrow) and has a gloomy refrain, 'Life is dark, and so is death' (Dunkel ist das Leben, ist der Tod). The

Very peacefully

Dun-kel   ist   das   Le-ben,   ist   der   Tod.

orchestra enters powerfully and the tenor's introductory recitative is also strong. The sequel is dark, delicate, but passionately expressive. The climax is reached with the question 'But thou, O Man, how long livest thou?' (Du aber, Mensch, wie lange lebst Du?), and the great song collapses with the dull resignation of 'Life is dark and so is death'.

The contralto song 'Der Einsame im Herbst' (Autumn loneliness) is also resigned. Striking figurations in the muted violins and a monotonous oboe tune set the scene for the soloist, who sings of the mists of autumn, of tiredness of heart, of loneliness. The death wish is ubiquitous and penetrating. The music erupts briefly at the words 'Sun of love, will you never shine again' and then sinks back into the monotony of the opening.

The three shorter songs that follow are devoted to more lively scenes; they treat of youth, beauty, spring and all the joys of life. A soft triangle stroke, quiet motion in the woodwind and the bell-like tones of the horn prepare the way for the delicate grave of the

melody, and the soloist sings of a tiny porcelain pavilion set in the middle of a lake.

The following song, 'Von der Schönheit' (Of Beauty), has a strange, flowing style of declamation. The melody is enveloped in a web of accompanying voices. For the time being the scene is pleasant and idyllic, a dream of youth and beauty, of young, innocent girls picking flowers and surrendering themselves to the sun and nature. A new scene is introduced with great excitement in the orchestra—fanfares, harp *glissandos* and a powerful march. The contralto explains: 'See now, a company of lovely lads comes riding along the bank on prancing horses.' The march comes nearer and the youths ride past, trampling the flowers. The music returns to the peaceful mood of the opening; the virgins are alone again, but in their breasts stirs an unknown excitement, a dull longing.

'Der Trunkene im Frühling' (The drunkard in Spring) tells of the joys of drinking. The middle section is a complete surprise after the exuberance of the opening; the orchestral writing is expressive of a delicate awareness of the coming spring. Soon, however, the drinking song takes over again and ends the song with frothy excitement.

After these scenes of gaiety, the effect of the final song is extremely heavy, almost depressing and yet the finality of its renunciation of life is in a way liberating. 'Abschied' (Farewell) is Mahler's title for this song, farewell to life, to the world. The first part is expectant; recitative alternates with great vocal climaxes, and the orchestration is quite impressionistic in its painting of nature and delicate emotional responses: 'O Beauty, O world of endless loving, world of endless life' (O Schönheit, O ewigen Liebens, Lebens trunkene Welt). There is a bitter change of mood after this hymnic climax, as the heavy sounds gradually form up into a funeral march. We recognize a strange motif in thirds from the beginning of the movement; the march swirls up to a mighty vision of death and then dissolves. The voice sings the final words almost voicelessly above the gloomy bottom C; the tired sound of the gong intrudes, as well as the melancholy motif in thirds from the funeral march. And yet, the earth blooms again in eternal beauty, even when—for us—the end has come. The thought of the immortality of beauty is consoling, and the music ends with light and clear harmonies.

Mahler's *Symphony No. 9 in D minor* (1909) is a colossal work of almost two hours' duration. In it, he returns to the purely instrumental conception of the symphony that had preoccupied him in the *Symphonies Nos. 5, 6 and 7*, and it has found a place in our concert repertoire somewhat more easily that its heroic predecessors. Of the four movements, the second and third are the only ones that recall the traditional symphonic form. The second movement is in the style of a rustic *ländler*, but it is enormously extended formally, with several trio ideas. The third movement is entitled 'rondo-burlesque'. In rhythm and structure this movement is energetically conceived; it grows out of a fierce iambic main idea that falls over two quavers into a powerful down-beat, and a complementary theme of rising minims followed by a descending scale of accented crotchets. Interest is maintained by beautifully varied orchestration and by fine contrapuntal exploitation of the material.

The outside movements are both slow, and both grow slowly out of nothing and finally return to silence. The first movement, andante comodo, opens with a low A thrown quietly between 'cellos and horns; then the harp states the regular four-note motif, F-sharp

A B A, which is to dominate and penetrate the texture of the whole enormous structure. Gradually, themes form up and rise to passionate heights. To eulogize is useless; this movement is a whole world, and the only entrance is through the ear. The final movement comes under the same edict of unspeakability. *Molto adagio*, unison violins state a two-bar recitative which dies away into a *streichersatz* that is often affectionately referred to as 'abide with me' on account of its similarity to the hymn tune in melody and harmony in the first three notes. The working-out of this melody, together with the strong exploitation of the 'turn' motif from the recitative, builds up a huge intensity of emotion from which one has to awaken at the end, as though from some long absence in— or dream of—some other world, peopled by titans. There are moments of phenomenal lightness and extremely delicate extended scoring, and the prolonged warmth of the whole stuns the audience with sadness.

The *Symphony No. 10*—as much as exists of it—seems to continue the story of the adagio: a long unaccompanied line for strings precedes the entry of a far-flung melody of such richness that it feeds the whole twenty-five minute movement. This monolith is all that Mahler completed of the symphony, but alone, with its enormous, shattering climaxes and the endless, ever-increasing beauty of the thematic development, this movement is a symphony in itself. Ernst Krenek scored a further movement, a scherzo that was to occur later in the symphony, from a complete set of sketches left by Mahler, and this is often played as a sort of coda after the adagio. The sketches for the remaining movements were incomplete, yet an enterprising Englishman, Deryck Cooke, ventured to create a full score from them, and this version has been broadcast by the BBC. Mahler's widow, it should be added, frowned on this attempt, and one can understand her point of view, for it is hard to follow the existing monumental adagio with material which must be denied the final benediction of real authority.

Of Mahler's many songs for voice and orchestra, three collections stand out as particularly significant: *Lieder eines fahrenden Gesellen* (Songs of a wayfarer), *Des Knaben Wunderhorn* (The youth's magic horn), and the *Kindertotenlieder* (Songs on the death of infants). Novelists often fall into the routine of producing a volume of short stories after every novel, as it were a collection of material left by the wayside. Mahler, on the other hand, evolved his symphonies out of his song melodies, and this is what makes his song cycles interesting for the concert-goer.

The *Lieder eines fahrenden Gesellen* were written in 1883 and are associated with the *First Symphony*. In general mood, they represent the disappointed lover's gloom and desire to pass on into solitude. The first song, characterized by constant changes of tempo, opens 'On my love's wedding day, all will be merry there, but my day will be sad'. The second song describes the cheerful start of the wayfarer's travels: 'Through the field I took my way' with a bold, striding melody. But 'There is a gloomy dagger in my breast. Oh pain! Oh grief! it cuts so deep' cries the singer in the third song, which is fast and wild. The fourth and last song is a march, *pianissimo*, with an expression of mysterious melancholy: 'The blue eyes of my darling have sent me out into the world.'

In 1886 Mahler was captivated by the anthology of lyrics published by Arnim and Brentano, under the title *Des Knaben Wunderhorn*. Mahler's two *Wunderhorn* song cycles date from 1888–1900 and are spread over the period of the *Symphonies Nos. 2, 3 and 4*. Familiarity with them will illuminate our understanding of these symphonies, but not by means of knowing exactly which theme in which symphony is a reference to which song. Rather, if we feel at home in the climate of these simple songs, then we have at least a conception of the world in which Mahler moved, or wished to move, in his symphonies. Suffice it here to list the English titles of the songs: in the first set 'Sentimental night song', 'Labour lost', 'Solace in sorrow', 'Up there on the hill', 'Earthly life'. In the second set: 'Antonius of Padua's first sermon', 'Rhine legend', 'Song of the prisoner in the tower', 'Where the shining trumpets are blowing' and 'In praise of lofty intellect', which refers to the donkey's lofty intellect in preferring the cuckoo's song to the nightingale's!

The instrumental *Symphonies Nos. 5, 6 and 7* do not derive in any straightforward way from a set of songs, but there are certainly thematic connections between these symphonies and the Rückert songs written between 1901 and 1904. Mahler's settings of Friedrich Rückert's poems fall into two cycles, of which the second, the *Kindertotenlieder* (Songs on the death of infants), is by far the most popular. These songs anticipate the death of Mahler's own eldest child by three years. The first song is soft and very simple: 'Once more the sun would gild the morn, as though the night's darkness had wrought no harm.' The second song is more romantic, but still calm: 'Ah now I know why oft I caught you gazing, pure childlike love with sweetest sadness mingling, ye bright eyes, ye bright eyes.' Resentment and anger begin to appear in the third song: 'When your mother opens the door, it is not on her face that my eyes first fall, but lower, where they would fain trace thy sweet infant face.' The fourth song opens forlornly, 'Often, I think they have simply gone on a journey, and that soon I shall see them safely returning', but this half-world of self-deception breaks down into beautifully ambiguous resignation: 'They have only gone on ahead a little; they will not want to return home.' The last tempestuous song 'In such a tempest' bears the same message, and, sinking gradually back to *pianissimo*, it ends 'No ills can now betide them, for God's own hand will guide them. All safe they rest, as on their mother's breast.'

RICHARD STRAUSS

born Munich 11 June 1864
died Garmisch 8 September 1949

Richard Strauss was the son of Franz Strauss, the horn player in the court orchestra. While still a boy he showed great musical talent: Hans von Bülow and Alexander Ritter took care of his musical education, and Strauss came to know Brahms and Wagner, whose music was to be the fundamental inspiration of his own creations. Strauss worked as a conductor in Munich from 1886–89, in Weimar and later on in Berlin and Vienna, in the years 1919–24. From then on he lived exclusively for his compositions, and only appeared rarely as an honoured guest-conductor.

Richard Strauss turned his attention to all sorts of different fields. His prodigality enriched the repertoire of a variety of genres in the early years of his life. Later his activity concentrated itself into two main streams, symphonic music and opera. His style became the general musical language of his time, and went on to dominate the music of the first twenty years of this century; Mahler's influence was small by comparison, and the effect of Schönberg, for example, made itself felt only much later.

The specific novelty of Strauss' music lies in its harmony: he burst the bonds of traditional harmony as he knew it without ever letting the colouristic exploitation of this field become an end in itself. His shimmering harmonic brilliance became a general asset and was used by all his contemporaries, and for us, now, it is a hallmark of this musical epoch. Strauss' melodic style is characterized by radiant, ascending phrases and long lines. Melody was for him the primary element in music and this is what differentiates his music from that of the French impressionists, for whom the exploitation of harmonic colour became an end in itself.

The formal significance of Strauss' thematic work is very important for a survey of his music. The way he states and develops his themes, varies and exploits them, brings the whole range of musical expression within his reach. The poetic idea is transformed into absolute musical form in his symphonic poems, and this constitutes a completely new approach to programme music.

Don Juan, opus 20, was a stroke of genius made possible by his 'classical' *Symphony in F minor*, opus 12, and the programmatic symphony in four movements *Aus Italien* (From Italy). *Don Juan*, written when the composer was twenty-four years old, gives a clear idea of Strauss' originality and strength. This work represents a breakthrough to something completely new, and yet the expression is so perfect that its musical language was immediately comprehensible. Hereafter, Strauss' symphonic poems are all in one movement, but the subdivisions are various and dictated only by the poetic idea. This basic poetic idea is the decisive factor in the form and structure, and makes any particular programme completely superfluous.

Don Juan symbolizes the abundance of life; he is the prototype of the assertive feelings of youth. He enjoys women and conquers them, and in fact, eroticism is such an elemental fact in his life that he finally succumbs to it.

The thematic and formal layout of the piece is extraordinarily clear: the bold, storming themes of the virile conqueror are contrasted with the lyrical melodies characterizing various women and the erotic episodes connected with them. In the course of the work two themes appear that characterize the virile strength of will of Don Juan. The first of these appears in full knightly regalia after a few stormy bars of introduction, and proceeds to dominate the

whole of the first part, with various lyrical episodes in contrast. The last of these is an innocent oboe melody expressive of unsoiled

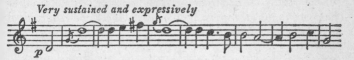

femininity. This lovely song is rudely interrupted by the second of Don Juan's themes: magnificent, bold and heroic, it is played by horns accompanied by a high *tremolo* in the violins. A scherzo

section representing a gay masked ball follows, and then breaks off with a cry. There is a paralyzed silence, but only for a few moments. Timidly at first, but with increasing vigour the music storms ahead reaching its climax in the reprise of both the heroic themes. Here the music breaks off and we hear a *pianissimo* chord; one more brief flare-up and the piece is over. However, the impression one retains of this piece is one of joy and power; the gloomy ending is no cause for regret.

The tone-poem *Death and Transfiguration*, opus 24, was completed in 1889, and became popular relatively quickly. This success hastened the public's understanding of the bold, new language of the young composer. One contributary factor for the work's success was the poem which is printed along with the score even in modern editions. These histrionic verses were written by the composer Alexander Ritter, who was a friend of Strauss', and they attempt to give a programmatic description of the individual sections of the symphonic poem. Nowadays the music of Strauss has become so familiar to us that we no longer need such a programme. After all, it is not as if Strauss based his work on Ritter's poem! His point of departure and inspiration was simply the title *Death and Transfiguration*.

Accordingly the work is divided into two parts. The first part is written mostly in the minor key and depicts the struggles of life re-experienced in the shadow of death. The end of this section with the short reprise of the first theme represents death's entrance. The second part is in the major key and represents the transfiguration;

it contains the reprise of the second theme and an extended coda. The thematic work is extremely consistent, and the structure, however complicated in detail, is correspondingly well-knit. The introduction is dominated by an apprehensive syncopated motif, and it

is against this rhythmic background that the main themes of the work are introduced. The main section begins with a sudden *fortissimo*, representing perhaps the heroic struggles of life. The contrasting flute melody can be interpreted as a memory of the happier days of youth. The idyllic mood is short-lived, however, and the delicate theme receives a powerful working-over. An extended development section follows, in which the syncopations of the introduction play a warning rôle. Passionately, the hero lives his life through to the end. Before death's entry, however, we hear the radiant transfiguration theme twice, like an apparition. Then

comes the passionate *furioso* of the death theme, interrupted by the paralyzing syncopations from the introduction. Finally the life force ebbs away *pianissimo*. The sound of the delicate subsidiary melody emerges as if from the misty distance; gradually coalescing, it leads on to the transfiguration theme. This builds up magnificently and then reverberates away to nothing in the high register.

Till Eulenspiegel's merry Pranks, opus 28, is a genial orchestral scherzo. The musical impact of the work is absolutely direct. The content of the tone-poem is adequately indicated by the title; no exhaustive programme is required.

Strauss' tone-poem tells of the jokes and adventures performed by this famous knave. Eulenspiegel is characterized by the little melody with which the work begins. It can be sung to the words

'Es war einmal ein Schelm' (Once upon a time there lived a rascal...) and this melody, or rather this rascal, undergoes an enormous variety of transformations and adventures in the course of the piece. It is answered by a racy horn theme, and between the

two of them, these tunes of Till's dominate the whole work. The second theme proper is a prosperous melody probably intended to characterize the landed gentry!

Till Eulenspiegel is a masterpiece of rare perfection. Written in 1895, it has lost nothing of its charm and freshness in the following decades; on the contrary, its audience grows steadily from year to year.

Thus Spake Zarathustra, opus 30, a tone-poem based on Nietzsche's writings, aroused a storm of protest at its première in 1896. Contradictions and misunderstandings were rife. 'Philosophy set to music' has never been much in demand, and Strauss' work was regarded as such, quite unjustifiably, as it happens. Strauss gives expression purely to the idea of *Zarathustra*. However, the score contains a series of subtitles taken from Nietzsche's work and these confuse rather than elucidate. Moreover, there is no clear demarcation of the individual sections of the tone-poem, which lasts a full half-hour, and the listener cannot possibly follow the programme in detail without an exhaustive knowledge of the score. However, Strauss' tone-poem is sufficiently explained if one remembers the basic ideas behind Nietzsche's *Zarathustra*, namely the theory of the free man, aware only of his own high spiritual standards, and free from *Weltschmerz*, who pursues Joyful Wisdom, with one sole desire and ambition—to achieve spiritual wholeness and union with nature.

The two motivating poles of the work can be interpreted as representing nature and man. The trumpet opens the work with the theme of nature, an ascent to the octave via the dominant.

Mighty chords swing from major to minor and then back, and the orchestra is presented in all its brilliance. This is Strauss' manifestation of nature. The mighty *fortissimo* of orchestra and organ dies away and we hear the steeply ascending theme of longing played

by 'cellos and basses *pizzicato*, followed by a pious, simple string passage. The most important ideas of the work have now been stated; in the midst of the massivity of nature man is set down, pursuing his beliefs and doubts, with his joys and his thirst for knowledge.

The themes of nature and of human longing dominate the work in a variety of guises. Another important theme is the trombone motif that resists the joyful flow of the music. Strauss called this the motif of 'satiety'; the two falling diminished fifths are expressive of rejection and resistance. It appears once after the episode of the joys and passions, and again after the fugue representing dry science and empty clerical work. Man finds release in the dance represented by a lively scherzo. At the end of the work, the two themes are combined; not only the two themes but also their respective keys: C major and B minor! *Zarathustra* ends on a note of irresolution; the problem is unsolved, the question unanswered.

Strauss chose the variation form for his *Don Quixote*, opus 35, written in 1897. The work bears the subtitle 'Fantastical variations on a knightly theme', and title and subtitle are sufficient to explain the work. As in the case of *Till Eulenspiegel*, Strauss refrained from publishing a detailed programme, but he sanctioned the brief notes on each variation that are generally printed in the concert programme.

The work opens with a long introduction. We hear a large variety of themes: Don Quixote has buried himself in romantic novels of chivalry, and his imagination has been captured by the various adventures he has been reading about. Don Quixote's theme is heard at the beginning like a chivalrous fanfare in the woodwind; it reappears immediately in the violas and is considerably extended. Next comes Dulcinea's melody in the oboe; Dulcinea is the lady for whose hand Don Quixote wishes to fight. A number of battling themes appear in the subsequent course of the introduction, always in association with Don Quixote's own motif, of course, which is finally blared out by the trumpets in augmentation: he has made his decision! He is going out into the world to fight like the heroes of his romantic novels.

The solo 'cello leads with an exhaustive statement of the Don Quixote theme, transposed into the minor key; this theme is hence-

forth always given to the solo 'cello. Sancho Pansa is to accompany the hero on all his travels; his portrait is drastically painted by bass clarinet and tenor tuba with the solo viola completing the theme. The first variation begins with a combination of both themes;

Sancho Pansa and Don Quixote ride out together in search of adventure. Dulcinea's lovely melody is like a guiding star encouraging Don Quixote in his trials.

It would be a mistake to try and follow the separate adventures in detail. Failing a thorough acquaintance with the score, the trail will soon become obscure. There are several realistic details, for example the battle with the windmill, but these are really unimportant compared with the symphonic line of the whole. Nor is it worthwhile counting the variations; there is often no very clear demarcation between them. The best thing to hold on to is the clear thematic work: Don Quixote characterized by his theme for solo 'cello, and Sancho Pansa portrayed by the solo viola. The fifth variation is a clear point of rest: an enchanting nocturne for solo 'cello, accompanied by the remaining 'cellos. The tenth variation represents Don Quixote's last stand: he is beaten and, according to

his promise, he is forced to abandon his life of adventure and return
to his home in the village. His theme disintegrates, falls apart dramatically. The finale shows him looking back over his life: themes
from the introduction appear and disappear, and finally even his
own 'cello theme dissolves. It is a truly moving epilogue.

In 1898 Strauss completed his tone-poem *Ein Heldenleben* (A
hero's life), opus 40. This work is often considered very difficult to
understand, on account of its enormous proportions. However, the
ideas, the form and structure of the work are of such clarity that I
find it much easier than, for example, *Zarathustra*. The composer
himself is the self-professed hero of this epic. The individual sections of the work are characterized by six brief subtitles.

The first animated section is headed 'The hero'. An extremely
powerful theme spanning several octaves expresses the creative
personality of the hero. This short allegro is planned as a single

crescendo and breaks off with a full orchestral *fortissimo*. After a
general pause the second section begins: 'The hero's adversary'.
This is a grotesque scherzando representing the envy and criticism
of the hero's antagonists in unmelodic, fragmentary bleating, chat-
tering and whistling. The heroic theme asserts itself powerfully in
the face of these light-weight figurations. The entry of the solo
violin heralds a new section: 'The hero's wife', a section that plays
capriciously with a variety of moods before developing into a love
scene with wonderful long melodic phrases.

Distant trumpets herald the following section: 'Battle with the
adversary'. The big development section begins with fanfares and
noises of war; coarse augmentations of the adversary motifs reappear. The hero is, of course, victorious and the full orchestra plays
his theme. In the following section, 'The hero's achievements',
Strauss combines *Heldenleben* themes with motifs from his most
important previous works. The wonderful horn-call from *Don*

Juan appears, as well as themes from *Death and Transfiguration*, *Zarathustra* and other pieces. A general pause precedes the final section, 'The hero's retreat and ending'. After one more outburst, the hero retires into loneliness; the cor anglais plays a pastoral theme and the end is near. The work ends in a beautiful simple melodic style.

In 1903 Strauss completed his *Sinfonia Domestica*, opus 53, which was to be his last symphonic work for some years, for in 1905 *Salome* had a sensational success and Strauss was launched on his operatic career. No other work of Strauss' met with so much initial resistance as the *Sinfonia Domestica*. People took offence at the privacy, the homeliness of the programme, and consequently over-looked the purely musical beauties of the work.

Strauss dedicated his *Sinfonia Domestica* to his wife and child. He outlined the work in words as follows. First part: the themes of the man, his wife and their child; second part: scherzo, childish games, lullaby, the clock strikes seven o'clock in the evening; third part: adagio, waking and thinking, love scene, the clock strikes seven o'clock in the morning; fourth part: finale, waking up, joking quarrel (fugue), reconciliation, happy end.

The work begins without preliminaries with the man's theme rising 'steadily' in the 'cellos, 'dreamily' answered by the oboe

melody. The clarinet, 'slightly annoyed', interrupts this beautiful idea, and the violins introduce a genuine 'fiery' Strauss theme that forms the climax of the man's thematic group. The steady 'cello theme ends the group with its typical grace-note figure to the sixth above. The woman's group is much more lively. An emotional melody for solo violin joins in with the excitable main idea. This

builds up merrily, until the man's theme appears in the bassoons and calms it down. The short motifs in the themes of man and wife are in complete contrast. They are like mirror images of each other: for instance, the jump of a sixth upwards in the man's theme and the jump of a sixth downwards in his wife's. A gay little development works over these themes in combination, and then, in a sudden *pianissimo*, comes the delicate theme of the little boy, played

by the oboe d'amore. A small coda takes up the rhythm of the main theme.

The scherzo represents a happy playtime with the child. The theme, played again by the oboe d'amore, is a merry metamorphosis of the little boy's theme. This theme occurs later in its original form. After further play, we hear a flimsy melody in the solo violin. Apparently the child is tired; he is crying and it is no easy matter to reassure him. The end of the movement is a lullaby for two clarinets in thirds and sixths. The violins take it up and drop it, and the soft strokes of the glockenspiel announce the time. The man's second, dreamy theme is played in this gentle twilight atmosphere and folk-like melody leads to the third part, adagio.

The adagio starts off using the man's themes; the woman's themes are only introduced later, in a variety of new guises. The themes combine and build up to a hymnic love scene. At the end of this wonderful movement we hear the little folk-song tune in the woodwind, a fervent version of the woman's theme in the violins, and the man's theme in the 'cellos. A disquieting interlude follows that can be interpreted as the 'dreams and troubles' that accompany sleep. This episode is dominated by the child's theme. At last we hear the seven strokes of the clock. Against woodwind trills, the 'cellos and horns present powerful abbreviations of the child's theme, used this time as the main theme of a happy double fugue. The counter-subject is based on one of the woman's motifs. The chaos of the fugue subsides only gradually and finally the woodwind play a simple folk tune as a gesture of peace. A flowing 'cello theme leads then to the second section of the finale, the happy ending. All the main themes reappear, some in their original form, some artfully transformed. Towards the end we hear the delicate voice of mama, and an energetic aspect of papa, but the child has the last word.

Strauss' largest symphonic work, 'An Alpine Symphony' (Eine Alpensinfonie), opus 64, was written in 1915, after a silence of twelve· years in this field. The work, which lasts almost an hour, is in one continuous movement; its form—this genial simplicity is characteristic of Strauss—is that of an enormous sonata movement, containing all four movements of the conventional symphony. The introduction and exposition is followed by a long development section from which the scherzo and adagio movements emerge quite clearly; the reprise and coda constitute the finale. All that is necessary to win the utmost pleasure from this great experience is a constant awareness of the general idea of the symphony, namely a climb to the peak of a high mountain in the Alps, and a surrender to the sonorous beauty of the score. Strauss wrote a lot of explanations in the score, without which it is easy to lose one's way, but whether or not the listener understands all the references is really quite unimportant. Many episodes are very clearly described and provide the necessary footholds for the great climb.

It is night when the symphony begins. A descending motif is followed by sustained, unmoving tones, and an inexplicable and mysterious mood is created. A solemn wind motif rises in the rustling twilight, and the sun rises. As it rises, the allegro begins. A fresh hiking tune appears in the strings, ascending powerfully; horns and trombones play a striking counter-theme. Hunting horns are audible in the distance as we enter the forest, and horns and trombones play a big, vocal melody. Walking beside a stream that ripples and splashes in woodwind and strings, we come eventually to a waterfall with steep descending arpeggios and, later, showering glissandos in harp and strings. An oboe theme emerges from the ceaseless rushing of the water followed by an impressive, visionary horn melody that is to appear later in the symphony at various important points. We come out in a meadow full of flowers, with the 'cello leading with a walking theme. The idyll of the Alpine meadow is intensified by the distant sound of cow-bells. The stormy climb begins, on wandering byways through thickets of undergrowth. A fugato presses forward with artful combinations of the various themes. At last we reach the glacier, where there are some dangerous moments, with sharp dissonances in the strings and an angular motif in horn and trumpets that has already occurred in combination with the hiking theme. Finally we reach the top. Majestically, the trombones play a hard motif of rising fourths, the oboe sings its idyllic song and we hear the visionary horn motif again. This is the climax of the adagio and of the whole work. All the main themes are heard again in solemn grandeur. Now it becomes foggy, the sun is darkened, and the climber is filled with sadness. The storm breaks and the descent begins, to the recapitulation, or finale. All episodes are repeated in reverse order, as we hurry back past the meadow, the waterfall and the forest. The strings plunge chromatically the while, and massive clouds gather in horns, trumpets and trombones. The kettledrums roll *fortissimo* with side drum and wind-machine, the organist pulls all his stops, and flutes and clarinets join in the plunging chromatic descent. The storm lessens but breaks out afresh. Then comes peace, and with it, sunset. In augmentation we hear the majestic mountain motifs and the theme of the sun. The organ plays a harmonic theme like a prayer, and horns and trumpets prolong it. In the marvellous peace that follows the music climbs up and up towards transfiguration. It is night again and, as at the beginning, the tones halt in their descent and remain static. The lights go out, and nature breathes peacefully in her sleep.

Strauss made a suite out of the music he wrote for Molière's *Le Bourgeois Gentilhomme*, opus 60, which contains some of the most charming music he ever wrote. It is scored for a small orchestra, with only two horns, one trumpet and one trombone, with the important addition of a piano. The suite consists of nine pieces: the Overture, with a drastic characterization of the ridiculous Monsieur Jourdain, ending with the enchanting rococo Ariette; a magical Minuet for the hero's dancing lesson; 'The Fencing Master', with his artful thrusts and feints contrasting with Jourdain's clumsiness; 'Entrance and Dance of the Tailor' (an elegant polonaise); Minuet by Lully, in the spirit of the baroque, and yet genuine Strauss; Courante; 'Cléante's Entry'; the marvellously amorous A-flat major Intermezzo; and finally, the 'Dinner', with its charming descriptions of the various courses.

Strauss wrote two horn concertos, an oboe concerto, a concertino for piano, bassoon, strings and harp, a violin concerto and a piano concerto. Of these, only the last has become quite popular. It is called *Burleske for piano and orchestra*, and was written in 1885, Strauss' earliest period. It is in one movement, and displays the

complete mastery achieved by the twenty-one-year-old composer.
He was already ploughing his own furrow, speaking his own personal language. The *Burleske* opens with a theme for kettledrums
alone and the orchestra answers with a rough rhythmic motif of

thirds. The kettledrum speaks again, and this time the orchestral
answer is more extended and leads to the soloist's entry. The motif
of thirds is transformed with gripping power, the orchestra plays
in the background, and the kettledrum is heard again. The first
thematic group ends with an interplay of piano and kettledrums.
After a general pause, the piano picks up the last notes of the drum
and develops an extended second theme from them. In the development section the kettledrum comes more and more into the foreground, finally hammering out an ostinato against the piano's
chromaticism. Quiet ensues, and a lyrical third motif is stated. The
subsequent development and the reprise are constructed as usual.
The brilliant cadenza makes a brief scrutiny of the third motif before disintegrating into a waltz. One more powerful outburst and
the kettledrum theme reappears, but this time timidly, and with
pauses between. The work gurgles to its end in the piano, like some
grotesque hobgoblin.

Strauss continued to compose right up to the end of his long life,
and many critics consider the late works among the best he ever
wrote. Certainly, the *Rosenkavalier Suite*, selected from the opera,
cannot be denied this praise, since it contains some of the finest
music from his finest and most popular opera.

The *Four Last Songs* date from as late as 1948. The title of the
third song 'Beim Schlafengehn' (On going to bed) and its first
line 'Now the day has wearied me' seem like Strauss' farewell after
his long and industrious life. The poems of this and of the first two
songs 'Spring' and 'September' are by Hermann Hesse, and his sad
and gentle lyricism is beautifully captured in the music's perpetual
andante: 'In half-light I waited, I dreamed all too long', and again
'These mournful flowers, raindrenched in the coolness, are bend-
ing'. Never has a composer chosen texts more apposite for a set of
'last songs'. The final song 'Im Abendrot' (Evening Twilight) is a
setting of an Eichendorff poem, again andante.

The impact of the *Metamorphosen*, of three years earlier (1945), is perhaps more purely musical, with a strong musicality untempered by nostalgia. This work for twenty-three solo strings was written for Paul Sacher and the Collegium Musicum, Zürich, in 1945. It is scored for ten violins, five violas, five 'cellos and three basses. The work is in a single movement, but one that grows continuously from the initial adagio to a forceful and passionate allegro. The sound brings to mind an image of a string quartet enormously enriched and more flexible. Shortly before the end, the tempo (*adagio*) and the material of the opening returns. Richard Strauss' circle has been very quiet in recent years. Strauss' work continues to attract enthusiastic audiences, but his associates have gradually faded into the background; Hausegger, Schillings, Georg Schumann and Graener are all unfamiliar names. EMIL NIKO-LAUS VON REZNICEK (1860–1945) is remembered for a single work, the *Donna Diana* overture. Quite a few masters have succeeded in gaining popularity by means of one piece, for instance Reger with his *Mariä Wiegenlied* or Rachmaninov with his famous *Prelude in C-sharp minor*. The *Donna Diana* overture is an enchanting piece, and it has carried its composer's name to the furthest corners of the earth. The chief characteristics of Reznicek's style are all represented: the lively southern temperament, the formal plasticity, the depth of feeling and endearing humour. The overture is based on two sharply contrasted themes, the one dancing and impulsive, the other delicate and reserved. These vibrate and sparkle with all the animation of the carnival that the piece is supposed to represent.

Strauss' language had become general by the turn of the century and continued to hold sway in the first two decades of the twentieth century. In the 'twenties this language was supplanted by the stylistic novelties of New Music, but it did not disappear entirely. The explosive vitality of EDWARD ERDMANN's *First Symphony* (1920) is testimony to the aliveness of Strauss' influence at this stage.

The first four symphonies of MAX TRAPP (born 1887) are also written in the shadow of Strauss' world of expression. Trapp's powerful musicality was equal to the task of extending and developing Strauss' ideas. His *Concerto No. 1 for orchestra*, opus 32, was not only a turning point in Trapp's career, it signalized the birth of a new symphonic style. The validity of Trapp's expression was generally recognized, and this work really covers new ground, even though it seems primarily to consolidate and establish a position already gained.

The concerto is somewhat loose in its tonality, but the *Symphony No. 5*, opus 33 (1937), is clearly in F major and explicitly melodic in style. The *Concerto No. 2 for orchestra*, opus 36 (1939), is stricter in form than the first; but his *Concerto for 'cello and orchestra*, opus 34 (1937), is his most interesting work, formally. The piece is really in one movement; it is divided into three sections of which the first presents an exposition of the two thematic groups. The slow middle section contains a development of the thematic material, and the finale (allegro) represents the recapitulation. The effect achieved is one of extraordinary unity.

Trapp breathed new life into the tradition of Richard Strauss. The stylistic upheaval of the 'twenties is certainly documented in his music, but whereas the avant-garde of the New Music stormed forward without respect for tradition, Trapp seems more reflective and backward-looking. His symphonic œuvre consolidates the past, forming an effective synthesis of what had gone before; thus he represents the culmination of a great stylistic epoch.

MAX REGER

born Brand, Bavaria 19 March 1873
died Leipzig 11 May 1916

Reger perfected his genius early and at the time of his premature death he had already written hundreds of works of all kinds, and was just about to embark on his first symphony. Reger's contrapuntal facility is amazing—in this respect one can almost compare him with Bach—and he combined this with a very personal feeling for harmony. His melodic gifts were meagre compared with these enormous talents. Reger's favourite instrument was the organ, and he wrote his most important works for it. He also wrote a great deal of chamber music, which is to his credit, for this genre was badly neglected at the turn of the century. Only after writing eighty-nine works for organ, voices of instrumental combination did he decide to write an orchestral work, the *Sinfonietta*, opus 90 (1905). Neither this work nor the subsequent *Serenade for orchestra*, opus 95, achieved much success. The critics had a lot to say about his expansive forms and heavy instrumentation, and neither work has managed to gain the public's affection, right up to the present.

Reger had long been recognized as a master of organ music and chamber music, but it was only with his third orchestral work, the *Variations and Fugue on a theme by Johann Hiller*, opus 100 (1907), that he found approval for his orchestral style. With Brahms, Reger is undoubtedly the greatest master of variation technique since Beethoven. The variation form imposes certain restrictions; these had a good influence on Reger's endlessly sweeping imagination. The theme was an excellent choice: a very melodic and rhythmically fertile song by the eighteenth-century composer Johann

Adam Hiller. The gay and graceful mood of this melody communicates itself to the whole work. Reger himself spoke of his Hiller variations as a piece of 'enormously lovable music'.

Variation form had undergone a great deal of extension and development in the nineteenth century, and had retained very little in common with the variation movements of the classical and preclassical symphonies. In the eighteenth century a 'variation' was considered a slight transformation of a characteristic theme, and this theme was always clearly recognizable. Each variation altered only one aspect of the theme, either the rhythm or the metre or the harmony; or the melody could be decorated or ornamented. The variations in romantic music were handled with much greater licence; completely fresh structures were built up over the basic pointers of the original harmony. Reger's variations go a long way beyond this; they are really free fantasias on all elements of the theme, and a great deal of study is necessary to discover in the enormous score all the threads that Reger has spun in conjunction with the theme. Such study is worthwhile, for the refinements of the thematic relationships in almost every bar are quite amazing. But it is useless for the layman to attempt the disentanglement of such a complicated score as the Hiller variations at a first hearing. There are eleven variations, or eleven movements, and these present an enormous variety of moods; sometimes the music is gay and happy, sometimes reflective, sometimes passionate and stormy. The charming theme is always present, now rhythmically altered, now metrically, often decorated, but always recognizable if one has paid sufficient attention to the statement at the beginning. The final movement is an extended fugue in which the theme appears in the trombones after a mighty build-up.

Reger's *Orchestral Variations on a theme by Mozart*, opus 132 (1913), is his most frequently played orchestral work. It had its première in February 1915 in the Berlin opera house concerts, under the composer's baton. As a master of variation technique Reger takes all the romantic liberties with the theme, but—perhaps out of respect for the spirit of Mozart's melody—he also relies to a large extent on classical variation technique, and the theme is always recognizable in something approaching its original form.

The theme that Reger chose was also used for variations by Mozart, in the A major piano sonata with the famous 'Turkish march' as a finale. The theme is genuine rococo, and possessed of

rare charm. The oboe and the clarinets play it first in a gracious, rocking $6/8$. It is continued by the strings and is then taken over again by the woodwind. The two groups unite in a delicate build-up, and the ending is clothed in the simple beauty of the strings alone.

The first variation is an exact repeat of the theme with charming figurations in the individual orchestral parts. The second variation retains the $6/8$ motion, and also the kernel of the theme; but the tempo is increased and a crescendo is set in motion. The tempo of the third variation is animated, and we hear a simplified version of the theme in the minor key. The fourth and fifth variations have a scherzando character, and the relaxations of tempo that were introduced at the ends of phrases in the first variations now become very important.

The theme almost disappears in the scherzo variations, but in the sixth and seventh variations it comes into the foreground again. The flowing sixth variation simplifies the rhythm of the theme, but the seventh is in the original tempo and the theme is almost exact, played chiefly by horns and 'cellos. The cycle of variations is really complete in this seventh variation; the two final movements, adagio and fugue, are completely free.

The so-called eighth variation is a substitute for a symphonic slow movement, and it could be described as an extended free fantasia on Mozart's theme. It presents a host of fresh melodic ideas and rises to a sublime climax, only to die away again on a note of transfiguration. The final fugue opens in extreme *pianissimo*: the

first violins are answered by the seconds, who are followed by the 'cellos and basses. The mysterious *pianissimo* is retained. Wind parts take up the fugue subject, and the motion is kept up with the regularity of a pulse beat. Gradually the subject builds up to radiant orchestral *fortissimo*. Just as gradually, the voices cease one by one; the tide has turned and is running out. An expressive theme introduced by the flute seems to give the fugue subject a lyrical twist, but only temporarily. The fugue subject again takes the lead and builds up to a mighty climax with the Mozart theme over everything *fortissimo* in the trumpets. A very effective ending, but one that estranges some people on account of the blaring presentation of Mozart's delicate little melody.

The *100th Psalm* is easily the greatest of Reger's choral works. The work is expressive of great faith and rejoicing, and overflows with vigorous life. The organ joins in at the big climaxes, and in the final fugue Reger writes for a second band of trumpets and trombones for the execution of the chorale. This large orchestra should be balanced by a strong choral body, so as to achieve the maximum of sonorous expressiveness as Reger intended it. The work is clearly divided into four movements corresponding to the movements of a symphony, with the dramatic outside movements enclosing an 'andante sostenuto' and an 'allegretto con grazia'.

The first part begins with a choral unison 'Make a joyful noise unto the Lord, all ye lands', with a rejoicing motif presented by strings and horns. The second theme is bathed in delicate colours. The chorus sings timidly, sometimes unaccompanied and sometimes with a gentle accompaniment of strings and organ, 'Serve the

Lord with gladness'. The joyful mood is twice interrupted by feelings of depression, but the 'joyful noise' of the reprise is introduced by an enormous *crescendo* supported by a drum roll and culminating in a reverberating cymbal clash.

The andante sostenuto expresses the idea 'Know ye that the Lord he is God'. The sudden *fortissimo* outburst at the first mention of the word 'God' is elementally effective. The movement as a whole is expressive of peace and confidence, despite the occasional appearance of slightly threatening voices. Happiness through faith is the keynote of the 'allegretto con grazia'. The words of the text are 'Enter into his gates with thanksgiving', and the song is decorated with lovely melodies for woodwind and violins. The idyll mounts up to a powerful manifestation; the chorus sings with increasing urgency 'Be thankful unto him, and bless his name'. An effective climax is reached and a march-like transition taken from the first movement prepares the way for the powerful entry of the final section. This part contains a wonderfully clever fugal structure to the words 'For the Lord is good; his mercy is everlasting; and his truth endureth to all generations'. The two subjects of the double fugue generally appear together. The first is the more expressive— it is introduced by the tenors—whereas the second, introduced by the sopranos, is more an accompanimental ornament. The stream of fugal writing is several times interrupted by calm, homophonic passages. The final climax is crowned by the apparition of the great Luther chorale 'Ein feste Burg ist unser Gott'.

Reger wrote concertos for violin—in A major, opus 101—and piano in F minor, opus 114 (1910)—but these are rarely heard outside Germany and Austria.

HANS PFITZNER was born in Moscow in 1869 of musical German parents. He studied in Frankfurt and was active as a conductor in Berlin, Munich and Strasburg, where he died in 1949. Besides his work as a composer and conductor, he devoted much of his time to teaching and writing about music.

In contrast to the overwhelming sonorities of Strauss' music, Pfitzner's music shows an almost ascetic reserve. The purity of emotion and lack of artificiality in the ideas are the hallmarks of Pfitzner's music. He speaks a language that is very much his own, with a peculiar air of detachment that derives from his use of the church modes. His conscious avoidance of the sensuous attractiveness of music, and also of the element of dance, gives his music a brittleness that is often criticized. In view of this it is understandable that his music—the same applies to Reger's—has not been heard very much outside of Germany and Austria. Nevertheless, both Reger and Pfitzner can boast a hard core of devoted admirers who genuinely appreciate their work.

The musical legend *Palestrina* is Pfitzner's greatest masterpiece. The preludes to the three acts of *Palestrina* appear sometimes in concert programmes as a suite—unfortunately, only too seldom. *Palestrina* made a great impression at its première in 1917, and that impression has been consolidated and reinforced by subsequent performances. Quite apart from the high ethical principles of the drama, the work shows clearly Pfitzner's preoccupation with the synthesis of the dramatic aspects with the formal concepts of absolute music. The three acts of *Palestrina* make a musical triptych as well as a dramatic one, and in consequence the three preludes make a satisfactory symphonic trilogy, without any detailed explanations of the story. Nevertheless, it is as well to remember the outline of the plot. The creative solitude of the artist (Act I) comes into conflict with the worldly activity of the Tridentine Council (Act II). In the third act, the artist, who has been threatened and almost broken by the world—after he has presented the world with the invaluable fruits of his talent—retires quietly and triumphantly into his creative solitude.

The prelude to Act I **is** similar in function to the *Lohengrin* and *Parsifal* preludes; it elaborates the basic ideas of the work. The rising

first theme is played gently by flutes and solo violin. The second idea is more decided; it is played first by the flute alone. Both

themes symbolize the mystery of creativity and its development. The third theme is more mundane, but is combined with the two main themes.

The prelude to the second act represents the big world of the

Tridentine Council, and forms a brusque contrast with the illumination of the creative artist. This prelude is introduced by a wild motif for horns, which constantly interrupts the further development of the stormy music. The prelude calms down at the entry of the mighty brass chords that form up into a new powerful theme. This episode probably represents the radiant power of the Church. The movement ends with the agitated horn motif.

The prelude to the third act takes us back into Palestrina's world. The musical structure of this introspective prelude is built on two themes: the first expresses the most shattering grief, heroically controlled, and the second is the earnest clarinet melody in seconds that represents Palestrina's son, Ighino, and thus provides symbolic

consolation. The form of this prelude is ternary: the mood of the opening builds up to the highest intensity of feeling, and then sinks back into introspective peace.

Pfitzner's overture to Kleist's play *Das Käthchen von Heilbronn* is played more frequently. The composer wrote a few words describing the connection between the music and Kleist's drama: 'A general background of the age of chivalry, with knights and jousting tournaments, soon gives way to a particular scene. This is set in the "Circle of ruins, where a greenfinch is building a nest in a sweet-scented elderberry bush"—Käthchen's favourite spot. Strahl, against his own true sentiments, feels obliged to reject Käthchen, for he has not recognized the profound internal relationship of their two souls, as decreed by Fate.' The music of this part is very clear. The introductory knightly theme is followed by a delicate theme of nature, first in the violins and then in the piccolo. This dissolves into the twittering of birds. The following thematic group is indescribably beautiful and inspired. The next large section depicts the feverish night when Strahl learns in a dream that Käthchen is the daughter of his Kaiser, and recognizes the obscure relation between himself and the girl. An urgent, searching theme in the bassoon rises over a restless bass figure, and this is repeated canonically by flutes, oboes and finally trombones. A radiant climax caps the irresistible *crescendo* of feeling. About the final section, the reprise, Pfitzner writes as follows: 'Strahl, for whom life has regained its freshness, is now in a position to proclaim to the world that "Käthchen is the first among the people, a position accorded to her by God long ago". Now Strahl can take Käthchen to his heart without fear of the Kaiser's or the world's disapproval.' The knightly themes from the opening reappear, and in a hot exuberance of feeling we hear the wonderful melodies that sublimate Käthchen and Strahl's love.

Pfitzner's *Symphony in C major*, opus 46 (1940), is in three movements played without a break. It contains a profusion of ideas, but the form is brief and concentrated. The work is dominated by an urgent will to live, and this is expressed particularly strongly in the passionate and stormy third movement. The main thematic idea of the symphony is introduced in the first bars of the first move-

ment. It is a clear virile theme played first by the horns and then by the trumpets, and its strong, affirmative character sets the tone for the whole symphony. This theme is followed by more delicate themes, but it again comes into prominence in the development section. The idyllic secondary themes then lead—with a gradual quietening down of the general mood—to the slow movement. The cor anglais plays a wonderfully vocal melody over a *pianissimo* kettledrum roll. This longing, melancholy song is taken up by the violins and prolonged, and is later supplanted by a canonic duo for

oboe and clarinet. The cor anglais has the final word, and the plaintive melody dies away with a sigh. A *fortissimo* stroke introduces the big last movement. This impulsive finale is inspired by a driving triplet rhythm. The stormy triplets rush up to steep climaxes, and in the ensuing quiet they are still present in the charming interplay of the individual orchestral voices. Finally, in a radiant C major, the tonic key of the work, we hear the wonderful main theme of the first movement played victoriously by the trumpets, and surrounded by stormy triplets in the whole orchestra.

After the First World War, the impact was felt of an important stylistic crisis that had its origins as far back as the turn of the century. The multiplicity of new directions became known under the general heading of 'New Music'.

Primarily, the new music was a reaction against the romanticism of the nineteenth century. Then it was really a radical, revolutionary phenomenon, although we can trace its roots back to Debussy, Mussorgsky, even to Wagner. The influences of Strauss, Mahler, Scriabin, Ravel and so on were also important. However, this evolutionary aspect seems unimportant compared with the decisive and powerful *break* with tradition. There is no doubt that the romantic attitude had been pushed to extremes, and that there was little room for further development in this direction. On the one hand we see the gradual degeneration of impressionism through Debussy and Scriabin, and on the other the hypertrophy of vitality in Strauss and Mahler. The exaggeration of these final phases of a great musical epoch positively demanded some reaction, and when it came it was of extraordinary vehemence and radicality.

The first stage was the fundamental reformation of all the stylistic elements: melody, rhythm, harmony, tonality, metre. Melody was denuded of its strong garment of feeling: composers wanted more reserve after the exaggerated feelings of the romantics, they aimed for realism and objectivity as opposed to an over-cultivated subjective expression.

The continual refinement of harmony is one of the most notable characteristics of the romantic development, and the young composers of the new music were anxious to dethrone it. More importance was attached to horizontal or contrapuntal writing; two or more melodic lines were superposed without particular regard for the resulting harmony, and the resulting sourness and simplicity forms a great contrast to the opulence of romantic harmony.

Rhythm now came into the foreground, and was not only promoted to a position of equal importance with harmony and melody, but was raised to such heights that melody and harmony were often forced into the rôle of mere necessary accompaniments. Folk songs had been an important stimulus early in the romantic period; now, folk dances lent their elemental, driving force to the new music. The peculiar rhythms of slavonic dances and the constantly changing metre of Rumanian and Hungarian dances came to be accepted in art music. Jazz also found its way into new music, bringing with it a host of rhythmic innovations, extreme syncopation in particular. The rhythmic element was studied and refined to such an extent that it sometimes became an end in itself. 'Polyrhythm', or the simultaneous use of various different rhythms, was practised with great virtuosity.

These rhythmic refinements led to a complete disregard of a constant metre. The regularity of a certain number of beats in the bar had been one of the fundamental laws of traditional music, though there are isolated examples in the nineteenth century of odd bars with a different number of beats. Another fundamental law of traditional music was the retention of one tonality, one key. The introduction of the whole-tone scale and circles of fourths had already paved the way for the dissolution of tonality, and the new composers consciously accelerated this development towards 'atonality', which means music with no central key. Atonality is one of the most striking features of new music, but atonal music does not embrace all the music of the period under discussion.

Several other features are characteristic of the rejection of all romantic ideals. As opposed to the enormous orchestral apparatus of Strauss and Mahler, the new composers wrote for small combinations of instruments. They cultivated the chamber orchestra and wrote intimate and often brittle music. The brilliance of string sounds was neglected in favour of the wind instruments. Percussion instruments assumed an important position as the rhythmic department of the orchestra. Even the piano, the darling of the romantics, was stripped of its poetry and handled purely as a percussion instrument.

Other influences came from jazz, the grotesque effects that are common in new music, for instance, and the motoric and mechanistic elements. The glorification of technology and the big city brought crass naturalism and the harshest dissonance in its wake. Motoric elements resulted in the extensive development of the *ostinato* principle, and this easily degenerates into monotony.

The linear style of writing resulted in a re-examination of the music of the seventeenth and early eighteenth centuries. The strict contrapuntal forms, like the fugue, the canon, the toccata, the passacaglia, and even the concerto grosso, were revived. Depersonalized titles were a further feature of the new music; the composers were striving for objectivity and general validity, and they called their pieces 'concerto for orchestra', 'music for wind instruments', and so on. The romantic era was dominated by nationalism; new music tried to be international, or rather 'super-national'.

The most important pioneer of new music was ARNOLD SCHÖNBERG (1874–1951). His style derived originally from Wagner and Mahler, and his earlier pieces, the string sextet *Transfigured Night* (*Verklärte Nacht*) and the *Gurrelieder* for chorus and orchestra, are really products of high romanticism. But with his piano pieces, opus 11, 1909, the *Five Orchestral Pieces*, opus 16, 1908, and particularly the melodrama *Pierrot Lunaire*, opus 21, 1912, he turned his footsteps into territory that was completely uncharted. Consciously, he turned away from tonality; his melodies slide over one another without regard for the laws of harmony, and the resulting chordal formations are purely intuitive. He follows the implications of Wagner's *Tristan* to the end. With his 'Method of composition with twelve tones related only to one another', Schönberg invented a new system as a substitute for the constructive properties of tonality. A fixed series of intervals using all the twelve notes of the chromatic scale provide the material for a work, and all the melodic and harmonic elements of the structure are derived from this series. However artificial and constructed this may sound, it proved a very successful solution, and Schönberg's innovation created a revolution in music, and his compositional principle soon attracted a whole school of composers.

Schönberg's *Chamber Symphony* (*Kammersinfonie*), opus 9, 1906, is scored for fifteen instruments, with ten woodwind and five solo strings. Purely externally, this is the direct opposite of the enormous scores by Mahler and Strauss that were appearing concurrently. The *Chamber Symphony* is a transitional work; Schönberg's aims and ideas about musical expression are already present, but he has not yet made the breakthrough into complete atonality. Clear themes are readily distinguishable and harmonic relationships occur very frequently; consequently the *Chamber Symphony* does not sound nearly so strange as the later *Five Orchestral Pieces*. However, it is genuine Schönberg, and not, like the *Gurrelieder*, an echo of late romanticism.

The one movement of the *Chamber Symphony* is clearly subdivided: a scherzo is inserted between the exposition and development section, and an adagio is inserted between the development section and the reprise (finale). The horn theme of towering fourths introduces a stormy opening section. Then a vocal violin melody adds a more reflective note, but the animated section returns quickly. Then follows an excited scherzo, and the reprise of the theme of fourths forms a mysterious climax. The network of parts becomes progressively thicker and the mood more restrained, under the influence of the second theme played this time by the oboe. There is another stormy outburst towards the end which leads the work to its powerful, accented close.

The *Five Orchestral Pieces*, opus 16, 1908, are completely atonal, and there was a storm of protest at their première. In these pieces Schönberg plays with ostinatos probably finding them the handiest device for organizing the form of the pieces without resorting to tonality. They are very brief, and this too resulted from the abandonment of tonal means for the composition of forms. The work was originally scored for a very large orchestra, but when the composer came to revise the score later in his career he reduced the size of the orchestra to normal. The five pieces are entitled: 'Presentiments', a wild tune on a rising ostinato figure A-flat, C, D with ingenious cross rhythms; 'The past', which is very near tonality, but moves away from it in the contrapuntal middle sections; 'The changing chord (colours)', which stems from a conversation with Mahler, when they discussed the possibility of a 'Klangfarbenmelodie', or a melody consisting of a single note played successively by different instruments; 'Peripetia' (a sudden reversal in dramatic action); finally 'The obligato recitative', which is a long flexible mass of complex counterpoint building up to a big homophonic climax. The orchestration throughout is daring and brilliant and the musical logic seems clear to us now, but it is worth remembering that Schönberg felt himself bound to think up the titles for the individual movements in order to facilitate an understanding of the work. He did so only after the work had been performed and completely misunderstood.

The *Variations for Orchestra*, opus 31, 1925-28, were given their first performance by Wilhelm Furtwängler. This work is a clear example of Schönberg's new twelve-note style, and was written after a break of almost twenty years in this genre. During that time he wrote several important experimental chamber works. The orchestral variations are a sort of genial proof of the flexibility of the new compositional system, which was based really on the transformation, or constant variation of a melodic kernel, namely, as Schönberg would say, the chosen series of twelve notes. After a short introduction the theme is stated by the 'cellos with slight

indications of bass notes and accompaniments. This theme is built strictly on the chosen series.

The variations are not always easy to follow. The first presents an inversion of the theme in the basses, which passes on to the horns and finally to the trombones. Practically all the other parts get involved in the subsidiary themes which spin a fine, strictly thematic web. The second variation is much easier: the characteristic motif is given to the solo violins, with woodwind accompaniment. The third variation bandies a powerful dotted version of the theme almost amongst the instruments with a rhythmic accompaniment. The fourth variation is in waltz tempo: a theme for flute is joined by a languorous counter-melody for muted viola. After the lively fifth variation the interplay of themes gets closer and closer and reaches its climax in the extended finale. It is not possible to follow all the thematic subtleties in the sound, though the score is highly aesthetically pleasurable to read. But nor can one follow all the voices of a double fugue at first hearing. Nevertheless, a lively performance of this work makes an indelible musical impression.

The *Violin Concerto*, opus 36, 1936, and the *Piano Concerto*, opus 42, 1942, are two very important works of Schönberg's later period. Classical forms are imaginatively transformed quite unschematically. These long Schönberg movements have little in common with the traditional relations of thesis and antithesis, exposition, development and recapitulation. In the *Violin Concerto*, however, there is a pregnant 'head-theme' in the first allegro that

reappears at the end of the movement and also at the end of the work. More important than this for the understanding of the forms, however, is the variation technique applied to the beautiful formation of the twelve-note melody. The solo part is very brilliant and full of virtuosity, without deteriorating into mere showing-off. Every passage and figuration is determined thematically, and the style of the work thus achieves a most convincing consistency. This new method of composition really requires a new technique of listening; late Schönberg is especially demanding, since the composer is dealing now with completely new musical concepts.

The *Preludes to Genesis* and the *Survivor from Warsaw* are two short orchestral pieces that are characteristic of late Schönberg. Both works use a chorus only at the end; this device is extremely effective, and seems to give profound human significance to the preceding music. The scoring of the *Survivor from Warsaw* in particular is harsh and brilliant, and yet extremely lucid. The snare drum (side drum) is used very effectively as a symbol of the militarism against which the piece protests. The music throughout accompanies a declaimed description by a survivor of the atrocities in Warsaw in the Second World War. The patent genuineness of the text combined with the harsh, unemotional score, and the unison male chorus at the end make this piece one of the most directly effective that Schönberg ever wrote.

Two posthumous works of Schönberg's should rank high in his total œuvre. The oratorio *Die Jakobsleiter* (Jacob's Ladder) was begun as early as 1913. The existing fragments have yet to be published, and the present author has not had the opportunity to become acquainted with them. The text consists of philosophical and theological reflections by Schönberg himself; his negotiations with Dehmel for a libretto evidently came to nought, despite the latter's friendliness and encouragement, and willingness to co-operate. Shortly before his death, Schönberg sent the existing musical fragments to his old friend and pupil Karl Rankl to orchestrate, but he declined and the only available concert version is an orchestration by Winfred Zillig. The work was planned in three large sections, with a large symphonic interlude, purely orchestral, in the centre position. Schönberg's sketches go a little distance into this orchestral passage—685 bars in all. (These facts are gleaned from Josef Rufer's excellent publication of Schönberg's literary estate, available in English translation from Faber & Faber.) The world première of the work, in Hamburg in 1958, presented only the first 180 bars; the whole existing fragment had its première in Vienna in 1961.

The opera *Moses and Aaron*, begun in 1931, threads its way in and out of his career, and when he died he had completed only two of the projected three acts. Again, Schönberg wrote the text himself, and essentially it deals with the contrast of personality and calling exemplified by the two brothers Moses and Aaron. Moses, the inspired idealist, is set off against Aaron, who is sensitive to what is known as 'the climate of opinion', and has a fluent public manner, and who feels himself called upon to pacify the people of Israel with false gods while Moses is receiving the tables of the law on Mount Sinai. The awkward Moses is a speaking part, whereas Aaron is a lyric tenor. The only part of the opera that is suitable for concert performance is the 'Dances round the Golden Calf' from Act II. This section is an orgy of sound, a brilliant piece of orchestral writing. It subdivides into numerous separate dances; for instance, a dance of the slaughterers, and a dance of the six naked sacrificial virgins. Despite sharp contrasts, the music builds up cumulatively in a wild crescendo of bestiality. In the opera, the spell is broken by Moses' return with the tables of the law, which he smashes in disgust.

Of Schönberg's two great pupils, Berg and Webern, ALBAN BERG (1885-1935) has reached a wider public. His activity was tragically curtailed by death, and he left his second opera, *Lulu*, unfinished. The period of his most intensive study with Schönberg was the years 1905-10 and in this period he wrote the *Sieben frühe Lieder* (Seven early songs) that mark the beginning of his career. In the mid-twenties he orchestrated the songs, thus providing us with an opportunity to study his early development unmarred by any dimness of orchestral technique. Brahms, Schumann, Wagner, Mahler, Debussy may be named as traceable influences in this sensuous music, but in the light of Berg's later work the songs are all unmistakably his own. The seven poems are by various poets, all in a lyrical vein, with that profound emotional interpretation of nature that is characteristic of the German poetry of the early years of this century. The titles are: *Nacht* (Night), *Schilflied* (Song amongst the reeds), *Die Nachtigall* (The Nightingale), *Traumgekrönt* (A crown of dreams)—this magical Rilke poem inspires Berg to orchestral writing that is truly representative of his personal blend of opulence and delicacy—*Im Zimmer* (Indoors), *Liebesode* (Lover's Ode), and *Sommertage* (Summer Days).

Shortly after completing his orchestral version of the *Sieben frühe Lieder*, Berg wrote his only true concert aria *Der Wein* (1929) based on three translations by Stefan George from Baudelaire's *Fleurs du Mal*. The three songs follow on without a break, though they are separated by orchestral interludes. They are 'The soul of wine', 'Lover's Wine', and 'The solitary's wine'. This brief work has a clarity and conciseness that is unusual in Berg's later works; it is his first attempt to find a usable adaptation of Schönberg's twelve-note system. Unlike Schönberg, who must have felt that his system would solve at least some of his problems, Berg seems to approach it with extreme circumspection; his twelve-note works are characterized by an *increased* emphasis of tonal relations, whereas the system was intended to relieve the paralysis attendant on the abandoning of tonality. *Der Wein* begins and ends at least in D minor; perhaps, however, this was merely a concession to the singer to whom he dedicated the work: 'Madame Ruzena Herlinger, the first interpreter, with heartfelt devotion.' The work is not difficult to listen to, and forms a useful bridge to an understanding of the opera *Lulu*, to which it is similar in many ways, for instance in the constant use of piano and saxophone sonorities in the orchestra.

The *Altenberglieder*, opus 4, are an earlier set of orchestral songs and represent Berg's alignment with the current trend towards brevity that became such an important feature of Webern's style. The small temporal dimensions do not reflect on the scale and richness of Berg's orchestral style, and this discrepancy probably contributes largely to the songs' somewhat baffling impact.

The *Three Orchestral Pieces*, opus 6 (1914), provide a good introduction to the orchestral style of Berg's first opera, *Wozzeck*, which he wrote in the following years. In this period Berg's writing is distinctly 'atonal', and the music seems to progress by metamorphoses of texture rather than tonality. The elaborate formal thinking that exists buried deep in all of Berg's work is reminiscent of Joyce's technique in *Ulysses*. The first of the three orchestral pieces is called 'Präludium'; it grows from and dies away into a quiet texture of percussion instruments, and percussive rhythms are constantly discernible in the orchestral writing between. The second piece is called 'Reigen': this polyphonic pile is sustained by the pronounced rhythms characteristic of Berg's dance movements— the music floats away over heavy down-beats. The final march accounts for half of the whole work. This alarming piece contains brusquely contrasting elements and many amazing passages of orchestration. The climaxes are fierce, and the *pianissimos* eerie, especially so just before the starkly fragmented end.

Twenty years later, Berg wrote his last non-vocal orchestral work, the *Violin Concerto* (1935). Though this is a twelve-note work, it is a great deal easier to listen to, and this is often attributed to the following facts: the twelve-note series on which the work is based consists of ascending thirds, making up dovetailed triads of G minor, D major, A minor and E major. The remaining three notes follow on to form a whole-tone tetrachord: (B) C-sharp, D-sharp, E-sharp. Apart from the sequential possibilities inherent in these triads, it should be noted that the respective tonics line on the open strings of the violin. This formation of open fifths forms the basis of the ten bars of introduction to the first movement; the sureness of touch with which Berg leads us from the arid quality of the open fifths into the world of pathos that characterizes the whole work is miraculous. The first movement proper (andante) uses the triads in their sequential exposition and the series is its melodic form—an unbroken ascent (or descent)—in the solo part.

The work contains two movements, but these are so disposed as to accommodate a four-movement symphonic form. The first movement embraces an allegretto scherzando that should be construed as a displaced scherzo with trios. This section is light, expressive and delicate. The second movement opens with an accompanied cadenza (allegro) that grows to a frenzy of rhythmic ostinato, followed by a calmer unaccompanied cadenza, of legendary technical complexity—it contains a four-part canon! More accompanied cadenza material follows, culminating in a shattering climax that subsides swiftly into the second half of the movement—adagio.

This adagio is an elaborate chorale-fantasia or variation movement on Bach's chorale 'Es ist genug' which begins with an ascent over a whole-tone tetrachord; in other words it begins with the last four notes of Berg's twelve-note series. Of all twelve-note composers, Berg had the strongest feeling for the direct expressive symbolism of the contrapuntal devices of inversion and retrogression. This final adagio—which is extremely moving and shows no trace of pastiche—surely bears comparison with the greatest contrapuntal masterpieces of Bach and such works of Beethoven as the great *Hammerklavier Fugue*.

The *Violin Concerto* is dedicated 'to the memory of an angel'; a young girl known to the Bergs had recently been killed by a painful disease.

Before leaving Berg—who wrote no other purely concert music unless we include the somewhat academic *Chamber Concerto* (1925) for piano, violin and fifteen instruments—we should mention that he made concert pieces out of each of his two operas. The *Suite of three excerpts from Wozzeck* was compiled after the completion of the opera, and Berg's intention was to draw attention to the opera itself and thus further its stage performances. Luckily for us, he completed his *Lulu Symphony* while still working on the opera, which he did not complete before his death. The 'symphony' has six movements: rondo, ostinato (this is the music that in the opera accompanies a screened portrayal of events in Lulu's life over one year), *Lied der Lulu* (a deliciously transparent song in which Lulu, harlot and murderess that she is, pleads that she is what she is, and refuses to admit the right of anyone to assert that she could be anything different—this subtle defiance is brief and beautiful, and extraordinarily effective in the opera), Hymne, Variations, and Adagio, making up the final music from the incomplete third act. Opinions as to the satisfactoriness of this symphonic version of *Lulu* are divided; various conductors rearrange it to suit themselves. Robert Craft, for instance, omits Lulu's song and includes the Hymne (which is not included in the printed score). He also decides against the rondo on the grounds that the developmental music is 'too full of references that fail to refer'. Apart from the question of the work's symphonic self-sufficiency, however, the music is beyond question some of the best that Berg ever wrote, and as such well worthy of performance.

One further arrangement by Berg of a work of his own is his string orchestra version of three movements from the *Lyric Suite* for string quartet. The quartet was written in 1926 and the string orchestra version in 1928. The quartet comprises six movements, and Berg adapted three of these: the andante amoroso, the allegro misterioso with its inset trio estatico, and the adagio appassionato, in other words the second, third and fourth movements of the quartet. The work presents only minor elaborations on the string quartet version, but the gain in dynamic range—especially in the *misterioso* and *estatico* passages, which are amazing *tours de force* of orchestral writing for strings—is indisputable. And although the missing movements are interesting and significant music, the shortness of the orchestral version facilitates our comprehension of the music. In this work Berg made his first tentative experiments with the twelve-note system, using it only sporadically, but constantly preoccupied with its possibilities.

ANTON WEBERN (1883–1945) was also a pupil of Schönberg. Webern is the most controversial composer of the twentieth century. Doubtless much of the controversy is due to misconceptions, misconceptions that are bound to develop when so little is known about a composer's actual work. Until 1950 he was dismissed, though listed by musicologists as a composer of delicate miniatures—so small as to be invisible, and in any case unremarkable. Since then, many critics, encouraged by Stravinsky's confessed admiration for this 'tireless cutter of exquisite diamonds', have taken his work seriously, and perhaps we have them to thank for the relative profusion of performances that have been promoted in recent years. The public is largely responsible for the selection of classical works that appear in our concerts: but in modern music it is often the composers who decide what shall be played. We have also to thank therefore Stockhausen, Nono and Boulez—each of whom, for his own ends, became passionately interested in Webern in the late 'forties and early 'fifties—for Webern's present accessibility. After a decade of public performance a few of Webern's works are beginning to take shape in our minds as pieces of music of a highly personal character. As yet, only the chamber works have had the benefit of consistent and acceptable interpretation. In his orchestral works Webern made few concessions to facility of rehearsal and performance, and renderings are at best uneven.

Webern's opus 1 is a *Passacaglia for Orchestra* that derives more from Brahms, with its formal accumulations, than from Mahler, whose insight into the expressive possibilities of instruments seems to bear even further intensification in Webern's mature work.

The *Passacaglia* was written in 1908, four years after his first meeting with Schönberg. In 1909 Webern wrote his *Five Pieces for String Quartet*, opus 5, and these belong in his first period proper. In 1930 he made a score for string orchestra, and, since conductors have the excellent interpretations of celebrated string quartets to guide them, performances of this version are often of a high standard. The exhilaration and excitement of the first leaps is quite breathtaking; this must be the most forceful and compelling gesture of Webern's career. And quickly, before you have got your breath back, he trips you headlong into the crackling, icy needle-shower of his extraordinary string writing. Whiplash *col legno* chords and a wide range of *pizzicato* and *ponticello* effects and harmonics rivet the attention again and again. The extreme fluctuations of tempo and dynamics that are characteristic of most of Webern's music are already clearly in evidence. The ear is never lulled with continuous rhythms or dulled with thick volume; it is constantly stimulated. The form, consequently, is clear and concise, in fact concentrated. The gesture from the opening reappears towards the end and the piece is over. Despite the revolutionary brevity of these pieces, it has never occurred even to the most obtuse critic to associate this with any paucity of invention. The musical ideas are packed into these pieces like sardines in a tin—but each sardine is alive, mobile, and free to breathe.

The second piece is very slow with melodic writing over sustained chords. The third piece is motoric in character, with a low C sharp *pizzicato* by the 'cello *ppp* for six bars, with a crescendo in the last bar. The lines and contrasts of the music flare over this rhythmic bass. This is complemented in the ending by a three-note ostinato in quavers for the 'cello.

The fourth piece is again slow and the refinement of sound is extreme—the loudest sound is *pp* with a *diminuendo*. The last piece is headed 'with delicate movement' and opens with an undulating 'cello melody under high *tenuto* chords.

The success of this composition—for as a composition it is a complete success, and always has been, irrespective of its general acceptance—may have encouraged Webern to undertake a work for large orchestra. The *Six Pieces for Orchestra*, opus 6, were scored originally (1910) for quadruple winds, six each of horns, trumpets and trombones, tuba, two harps, a great deal of percussion and strings. In 1928 he reduced the size of this orchestra to normal. Despite the enormous forces involved, the length of the work is not more than ten minutes, like the five pieces for string quartet. Apart from the *Passacaglia*, opus 1, this is the only work of Webern that could actually become accepted as part of the standard orchestral repertoire (in the revised version, that is). In London, these six pieces have actually been programmed with the *Emperor Concerto* and Beethoven's *Ninth Symphony*. If this ever becomes a general practice, it will be on the strength of the funeral march (the fourth piece), which presents an enormous, slow build-up of sound, and leaves an unforgettable impression.

The *Two Rilke Songs*, opus 8, are scored for soprano and a skeleton orchestra of eight instruments: clarinet, bass clarinet, horn, trombone, celesta, harp and string trio. Beautiful though they are, they are unlikely to feature in orchestral concerts, and indeed they are not really material for orchestral musicians. The same is unfortunately true of the *Five Pieces for Orchestra*, opus 10 (1913), which demand an almost unattainable sensitivity in delivery. Of these pieces the third is probably the first to make an impression, with its soft tinklings of harp, celesta, mandoline, guitar and cowbells in brilliant contrast to the hair-raising ending of the second piece. The fourth piece is a cool six bars of quiet and, mostly, flowing music. The last few bars of the fifth piece are remarkable for their *alla breve* rhythmic style; this page of score might have come from Webern's orchestral variations, written almost thirty years later.

The *Four Songs with Orchestra*, opus 13, are more easily assimilable, and extremely lyrical. The vocal line gives the music an easy continuity, and the beauties of the sound seem to float by effortlessly. The texts of the four songs are 'Wiese im Park' by Karl Kraus, probably the most significant man of letters in Vienna at this time, and a personal acquaintance of Webern; 'Die Einsame', from *The Chinese Flute*, a collection of German translations from the Chinese by Hans Bethge; 'In der Fremde', from the same collection; 'Ein Winterabend', by Georg Trakl, the great Austrian lyric poet killed in the First World War. The settings of these lyrics are of such seductive beauty that singers have to guard against a sentimental interpretation. In a clean performance the sensuousness of sound is unparalleled.

This is not the place to discuss Webern's route to the twelve-note technique. Suffice it to say that the next work that we have to discuss—the *Symphony for Chamber Orchestra*, opus 21, written in 1925—shows Webern's mastery of the new technique, and also his awareness of its implications. This work is scored for strings (no basses), harp, clarinet and bass clarinet. There are two movements. The first is slow, and approximates to a sonata movement in some not very easily definable way. The exposition is repeated (as in Haydn and Mozart), and the music after the double bar grows in intensity (long notes with crescendos, and so on). However, the texture is purely canonic. The second movement is rather livelier in tempo—a set of sharply characterized variations, each one a short palindrome.

The *Concerto for Nine Instruments*, opus 24, is again scored for a skeleton orchestra, with piano. There are three movements—fast, slow, fast. This is definitely a chamber work, and amongst Webern's chamber works probably the most difficult to grasp. The principle of syncopation is carried to such lengths in the last movement that the listener often has the impression that the players are all counting time furiously, and making sounds only when they have nothing to count, instead of—as is customary—playing their parts, and counting bars when they have nothing to play.

In 1935, Webern scored Bach's six-part Ricercare from the *Musical Offering* for orchestra. The score demands single winds and brass, timpani, harp and string quintet. This score is a remarkable piece of work: the subject of the fugue is broken down in a specific way, and at each entry this specific break-down of the subject is repeated, but in accordance with the new context. The opening is a good example: the subject is distributed with great subtlety between the brass instruments, with certain notes reinforced by the harp. The 'answer' is distributed amongst the winds, but the harp again reinforces, and in the same places as it had before. The counter-subject, meanwhile, is distributed in the strings. The score makes remarkable use of *pizzicato* strings and harp harmonics. The harp, in the situation just described, finds itself in a sort of pivotal position in the orchestra, and maintains it admirably. The timpani are used with discretion and to great effect. However, this is not simply a work of instrumentation; Webern interprets it completely, right down to fluctuation of tempo and expression marks.

Das Augenlicht, opus 26, is a five-minute cantata for chorus and orchestra to words by Hildegard Jone, the poetess who supplied the lyrics for all Webern's vocal music after 1934 (*Three songs*, opus 23). The work is scored for chorus and small orchestra, and consists of a single movement. Contrapuntal choral writing alternates with homophonic passages of considerable harmonic richness. All the characteristics of Webern's late orchestral style are in evidence here—the strange intensity of the unison wind phrases, the soloistic use of timpani, the expressive grace-notes enlivening the otherwise extremely lucid rhythmic texture, the prevalence of triplets in all note values, and so on. Apart from the *Passacaglia*, this is the first work of Webern's in a single extended movement, and the effect is one of breadth and consistency.

In his *First Cantata* proper, opus 29, Webern again handles a form
made up of several separate pieces. It was written in 1939, and is
scored for soprano solo, chorus and small orchestra. The first
movement is choral and opens with a motto of three slow chords.
The general tempo proves lively, however, and when the chorus
enters, it does so extremely energetically. The second movement
is a lyrical song for soprano and orchestra in Webern's 'semiquaver'
style—the metric unit is a semiquaver, which makes the score look
rather complicated, but creates an impression of fluidity in performance. The first line of the poem begins 'small, winged maple
seeds, floating in the wind'.

The third and last movement is for soloist, chorus and orchestra,
but the soloist joins in only briefly in the final section, and sings,
appositely, of 'the heart's gift of perfection'.

The *Orchestral Variations*, opus 30, which were written in 1940,
were heard by Webern at a performance in 1943. This was
probably the only occasion in the last seven years of his life
that Webern heard his work performed in public, since in Germany and Austria it was banned by the Nazi régime. The work
was published in 1956. Despite the title 'Variations', Webern
does not indicate a theme and specific variations; 'variations' is
rather a description of the sort of technique employed in the composition. However, it is not difficult to segment the work into an
introduction, followed by something approaching a theme, with
strummed accompaniment (beautifully scored), four variations and
a coda. But these divisions are differently interpreted by different
commentators. One reasonable analysis sees what I have called the
first variation as a bridge passage leading to a second theme (variation 2), followed by a 'recapitulation' of the first theme, or rather
a working-out of it, or contrapuntal 'variation' on it. Variation 4
is then supposed to be a further treatment of the material of the
introduction and the bridge passage. However, no such construc-
tions are necessary for the appreciation of the sequence of ideas.
One is tempted to think of it thus: all of it is Webern's music, and
we can only wish there were more of it. The work is scored for
small orchestra; after opus 6, Webern never again wrote for a large
orchestra.

Webern's last work, the *Second Cantata*, opus 31, was written in
1943. He was surely working in the last two years of his life, but
he did not complete an opus 32. This cantata has six movements
and is scored for soprano and bass soloists, chorus, and small

orchestra. The first movement is a bass solo, and the accompaniment makes use of those '*blocs sonores*', which Pierre Boulez sees as indissoluble chordal complexes in which the individual note—of such paramount importance for Webern—surrenders its individuality to become part of a sonorous whole. Counterpointed with these chords, the last of which ends the movement with all twelve notes of the chromatic scale, are short phrases for solo instruments, and the long cantilena of the soloist. Perhaps it is appropriate to consider the first movement as a sort of recitative, for the second movement is definitely arioso in style, with several strophes punctuated by a recurrent twice-repeated bell-note on middle C. This is followed by a swift dramatic movement for soprano solo, female chorus and orchestra. The chorus opens with a wild, energetic canon, and this dovetails into an extravagant statement by the soloist: 'Let all the bells and the hearts of the people be ringing, O mankind.'

The fourth movement is one of Webern's most beautiful songs for soprano and orchestra. It is very brief, and again we are tempted to think of it as a preamble to the fifth movement, in which the soprano joins forces again with the chorus. The last movement is a piece of fast contrapuntal choral music with the orchestra doubling the voices. The music is repeated three times for the three verses of the poem. The sound is reminiscent of nothing so much as a joyful round! And this is approximately what it is. The writing is strictly canonic, and the cross accentuation that results is evocative of that vocal writing of preclassical times that had been Webern's chief preoccupation at the musicological outset of his career, before his meeting with Schönberg.

Webern's music will never move millions of men and women. Doubtless with time a large public will be impressed with the strength of his diction to the extent that they will realize that his was a genius of the first order. But he will speak explicitly only to a small audience, not necessarily an audience of musicians, but probably one that can share his almost religious reverence for the humble materials of music.

Stravinsky has had a much more immediate effect on our musical life and he stands as the second most important key-figure in twentieth-century music. IGOR STRAVINSKY was born in 1882 in Oranienbaum near St Petersburg. His early works show clearly the influence of his teacher Rimsky-Korsakov and of impres-

sionism. The most striking aspect of his style, and his most important contribution to the music of our time, is the rhythmic differentiation in his music. The turbulence of Borodin's *Polovtsian
Dances* is intensified to a pitch hitherto unheard of, by means of
countless repetitions and the use of rhythms that were considered—
until he used them—completely unusable. There is a constant interchange of metres, two, three, five, or seven crotchets or quavers in
the bar. In the early years of this century Stravinsky occupied
himself chiefly with Diaghilev's Russian Ballet, and his development
of the rhythmic aspect of music is a natural consequence of this.
Melodically and harmonically the early ballet suites are coloured
by Russian folk lore.

Stravinsky's first great success, the *Firebird Suite* (*L'Oiseau de
Feu*), 1910, has retained its place in the public's affection right up
to the present day. No other work has achieved such popularity.
The suite contains five movements. The firebird's dance breaks
brightly into the dark mystery of the short introduction. It flickers
brilliantly in the piano and woodwind, and the orchestra vibrates
with excitement. The 'Dance of the Princesses', on the other hand,
is purely melodic. The oboe plays the folk-like theme with a delicate counter-melody in the violins; the little andante is gracefully
stepping, and gently flowing. The dance of the magician Kastchei

is wild, rhythmic and uncontrolled. The fourth movement is a
lullaby with beautiful sounds and nocturnal character. The finale
follows directly with a powerful theme played first by the horn

and then developed to a mighty climax as an effective ending to
the work.

The music for the ballet *Petrushka*, 1912, is wilder, coarser and
still more rhythmic. There is a strong tendency towards the gro-

tesque, and its accompanying sharpness of characterization. The scene is a Russian fairground, with an old conjurer and his three mechanical dolls, Petrushka, the Ballerina and the Moor. Stravinsky creates the atmosphere of the fairground with breathtaking accuracy and originality. The music is very realistic in parts; we hear the music of the carousel, the vendor's trumpets and so on, combined in an extremely effective manner. And the elemental strength of the dance pieces breaks through all the noise. At the end of the first part there is a stormy 'Russian Dance', and an exceptionally

colourful dance in the finale. A portrait of Petrushka is inserted as

a middle section between the two big fairground scenes. Petrushka's human aspirations and activities are banal and ridiculous and yet his automaton existence contains an element of bizarre tragedy. Stravinsky parodies him, but with great affection.

Petrushka had a mixed reception, but the next ballet suite, the Rite of Spring (Le Sacre du Printemps), provoked an explosion of disapproval. The brutality and strength, and mountainous dissonance of this score were something undreamt of. Polytonality, which means the simultaneous presentation of several keys, resulted in the juxtaposition of elements that have little to do with one another and the result, though completely logical, is extremely dissonant. But again, the most significant aspect of the Rite of Spring is its rhythm. The rhythm becomes an elemental natural force, but one that borders on the mechanical! This is the motoric element in twentieth-century music; it can be powerful and exciting, and at other times it has a peculiarly soulless effect. Without the actual ballet, the Rite of Spring music is not easy to understand, and the titles of the individual sections have very little to say about the actual content of the music. The basic symbolic idea is the triumph of spring over winter, and this is expressed in the cult dances of the original inhabitants of Russia. Reserve alternates with the wildest animation, and new ideas are constantly pushing their way into the

foreground. Quieter sections form impressive interludes, like the
'Rounds of Spring' played first by the clarinets, then by oboes and
flutes, or the 'mysterious circles of adolescents' in the second part,
a delicate little andante for strings with a lovely graceful theme.

Mostly, however, the rhythm is triumphant and self-sufficient;
melody and harmony are left standing. The instrumentation is an
extraordinarily novel phenomenon, a text-book in itself. The best
way to enjoy the music without acquaintance of the action of the
ballet is to surrender yourself to the elemental power of the rhythms
and enjoy the magic of Stravinsky's world of sound for its own
sake. It has hardly been possible to reconstruct the formal development of the ballet since the work is not constructed symphonically.

The next ballet that Stravinsky wrote for Diaghilev, *Pulcinella*,
1919, caused a sensation of dismay and amazement. The simplicity
of the work was a complete surprise and it was thought that the
composer of the *Rite of Spring* was pulling his public's leg. The
Pulcinella melodies were written by Pergolesi (1710-36), the
master of the charming opera *La serva Padrona*. Stravinsky leaves
the melodies almost untouched, harmonises them with a correct
feeling for the style and dresses them up in beautiful orchestral
sound. He does not hesitate to use jazz effects where he considers
them appropriate. The ballet consists of nine short movements,
with titles like Serenade, Tarantella, Gavotte, Minuet, a suite of
charming *delicatessen*. Was this return to the early eighteenth century purely a coincidence, dictated by a whim of Diaghilev's?
Whatever its cause, it was a turning point in Stravinsky's career
and signified the beginning of the neo-classical movement in music.
The characteristic element of the new style was the search for unconditional objectivity and radical depersonalization. The most
amazing feature of the neo-classicism is its explicit reactionariness;
there is hardly any trace of the old revolutionary Stravinsky. As in
the Pergolesi suite, Stravinsky hides behind the masters of earlier
times; in the case of the *Baiser de la Fée* it is Tchaikovsky, and in
the dance suites he consciously and ironically turns to the world of
Johann Strauss. The most extreme example of this retrospective,
radical objective style is the ballet *Apollo Musagetes*, 1928. *Oedipus*

Rex, 1927 (an opera), and the *Symphony of Psalms*, 1930, are the most important works of this period.

Oedipus Rex is actually described by Stravinsky as an opera-oratorio. Stravinsky collaborated with Jean Cocteau on the scenario, which is based on Sophocles' tragedy. The sung text is in Latin and the spoken text is in French. It is symptomatic of Stravinsky's and Cocteau's consciously sophisticated intention that the whole text was written in French, and then the vocal parts were *translated* into Latin by J. Damelon. E. E. Cummings has made for Stravinsky an English version.

The participants in the drama are Oedipus (tenor), Jocasta (mezzo-soprano), Tiresias (bass), a shepherd (tenor), a messenger and Creon (both sung by a single baritone soloist), and a male chorus and a speaker. The orchestra is a standard large orchestra (triple winds) and the duration of the whole is close on an hour. The work was revised in 1948. The presentation is extremely formalized; even the speaker—though not hidden by the heavy and immobile masks worn by the others, who are supposed to look like living statues—is instructed to wear a black suit and tell the story in a completely detached fashion. So much the more powerful is the impact of the music, even though it too strives towards formal monumentality. The speaker introduces the work by saying that he will be giving a scene-by-scene report on the events narrated in the Latin text. Act I begins with the chorus of Thebans bemoaning mightily the plague that has fallen on them. They call on Oedipus to deliver them and he promises to do so. His brother-in-law Creon has been sent to consult the oracle and returns to say that Laius' murderer is hiding in Thebes and must be found. Oedipus consults Tiresias, the fountain of truth. The latter is persuaded to speak with difficulty, and announces that the king's assassin is a king. The first act ends with an exciting *gloria* chorus.

The second act begins with a repeat of the gloria chorus. Jocasta pours scorn on the pronouncements of oracles: Laius was killed by robbers at a crossroads; how, then, could he have been assassinated by a son of hers? Oedipus listens and reflects; he remembers killing an old man at the crossroads. Could that have been Laius? After this complicated scene, the speaker speaks over timpani roll: the witness to the murder appears. A messenger announces the death of Polybe (whom Oedipus had supposed to be his father), and reveals that in fact Oedipus was only his adopted son. Jocasta understands and kills herself. Finally, the truth strikes Oedipus. A messenger recounts the death of Jocasta. Oedipus puts out his own eyes. He wishes to show himself for what he is: incestuous beast, parricide, madman. He is hunted, very gently, by the populace: 'Adieu, poor Oedipus.'

The *Symphony of Psalms* is scored for chorus and orchestra and Stravinsky uses verses of the psalms in the Latin version of the Vulgate for his text. The orchestra uses no violins and violas, but adds two pianos and harp. The three movements are played without a break, but they are clearly defined, and, as always with Stravinsky, the forms are free and independent of the classical and romantic conventions. Despite the absence of thematic contrasts, development and reprise, however, the movements are perfectly consistent and beautifully rounded formally.

The chosen verses from the psalms give a clear picture of the mood of each movement. Stravinsky does not go into the details of the text; the words serve merely as a vocal basis for the music. The tone of the first movement is given by the words from the 39th Psalm, 'Hear my prayer, O Lord, and give ear unto my cry'. After a sharp orchestral chord, the oboes and bassoons start up a relaxed semiquaver movement, occasionally interrupted by further chords. When the voices enter, the motion falls back into steady quavers. This motion is constant and unfailing, and produces a feeling of monotony. Finally it spreads over the whole orchestra with hammering octaves for the piano. The psalm rolls on in grand, steady tones.

The second movement is a slow-stepping fugue on an expressive subject exploiting the tension of the major seventh. Oboes and

flutes execute the first four entries and a short episode follows. The chorus enters with a new subject, with the original subject in the bass. The text here is taken from the 40th Psalm, 'I waited patiently for the Lord; and he inclined unto me, and heard my cry'. The chorus also sings its entries strictly and follows up with a *stretto*. Both subjects are combined in a short orchestral postlude, and this ends the first section of the movement. The second, much shorter section is homophonic and is a setting of the words 'And he hath put a new song in my mouth, even praise unto our God'.

The final movement uses the text of Psalm 150, 'Let everything that hath breath praise the Lord. Allelujah'. It is built in six sections, with a recapitulation of the second section, a powerful and urgent piece of instrumental music, preceded by a short solemn introduction. At the repetition the chorus joins in with unison statements of 'Laudate Dominum'. After an ecstatic build-up, a vocal interlude leads to the final section. The chorus rises in calm grandeur over the pedal-point of fourths, F, B-flat, E-flat, in harp, timpani and piano. The endless monotony of this final passage is like a hymnic river, and confirms the general elevation and solemnity of the movement.

The *Symphony of Psalms* is a marvellous synthesis of Stravinsky's two styles. The smooth coldness of *Apollo Musagetes* seethes with the glowing temperament characteristic of his early ballet scores. The urgent rhythms, sharp dissonances and harsh juxtapositions are combined with sublime and radiant voice-leading and the result is a work of truly classical grandeur. But this cornerstone in Stravinsky's œuvre should not blind us to the beauties of the works that preceded it.

Les Noces was written in the 1920's and is a superb example of Stravinsky's gift for sonority. It is scored for soloists, chorus, four pianos and considerable percussion, and describes a Russian peasant marriage celebration.

The *Symphonies of Wind Instruments* was written in 1920 and revised in 1947. It is scored for triple winds, four horns, three each of trumpets and trombones, and tuba, and is dedicated to the memory of Debussy. This short work in one movement is considered by many to be Stravinsky's most interesting piece. It is strongly characterized by its bony sonorities and the clear-cut antiphonal form of the opening. Sinuous melodic lines for the woodwind soloists are contrasted with the incisive rhythms of the ensemble. Stravinsky performs miraculous feats of registration throughout, but the sober, solemn chords at the end in particular make an impression that will outlast that created by his more grandiose works and pieces of *delicatessen*.

The *Concerto for Piano and Wind Instruments* (1924) is of a heroic nature. There are three movements, of which the first opens with an orchestral largo that uses dotted rhythms and displays the horn particularly prominently. The following allegro introduces the soloist with driving insistence. The second movement—largo—incorporates an extended cadenza for the soloist. Woodwind soloists and horn consort with the soloist; a short instrumental interlude follows, and a further (shorter) cadenza for the soloist shortly before the end. The third movement is again allegro, the same tempo as the first. Kicked by an orchestral burst, the piano introduces a harmonized fugue subject. The semiquavers of the codetta are continued to form a decorative counter-subject against the orchestra's answer. After a time the piano states a new theme intimately related to the first theme. This is developed, notably in augmentation in the winds, while the semiquavers persist. A *lento* passage recalls the introduction to the first movement, and then, with a brief *stringendo,* the work ends.

In the following works—*Dumbarton Oaks,* the *Violin Concerto,* the *Symphony in C* and the *Jeu de Cartes* ballet—Stravinsky presented his audience with a string of fresh surprises. He seemed a different man in each work, and both the critics and the general public had a hard time keeping up with him.

In 1938 Stravinsky wrote a concerto in E-flat for chamber orchestra entitled *Dumbarton Oaks.* The score of this little work demands flute, clarinet, bassoon, two horns, three each of violins and violas, and two each of 'cellos and basses. The second movement—allegretto—is an enchanting flight of fantasy. The violas state a delicate, chromatic, accented melody, to the *pointilliste* accompaniment of 'cellos and bassoons. Later, flute and clarinet broaden the outlook with shrill rhythms, but the chromatic melody returns. A further attempt succeeds in establishing a completely different texture of low string *tremolos* and *ostinatos,* and the upshot is, that when the chromatic melody returns, it is subordinated to a concertante flute part. Slow chords end the movement. Features of the third movement are its rhythmic attack and the delicious writing for strings. That is misleading; the writing for *all* the instruments is a joy, and the scoring, as distinct from the instrumentation, is faultless.

Stravinsky's *Symphony No. 2 in C,* though much larger than the work we have just discussed, again impresses one as a small work that approaches perfection. It was written in 1940, and comprises four movements: 'moderato alla breve', preceded by a largo introduction, larghetto, allegretto, adagio. The refinement of the accompaniment and the simplicity of presentation in the melodic material suggest Mozart as a possible model; however, Tchaikovsky is usually named as Stravinsky's inspiration. The work ends with quiet chords reminiscent of the ending of the *Symphonies of Wind Instruments*.

Jeu de Cartes, 1937, which was originally a ballet score, has retained its popularity in the concert hall. It contains three big movements, each preceded by the same pathetically-ironic intrada. The first movement is vocal and lyrical, whereas the second movement is a variation movement of a relaxed, dancing character. The final part is a light parody.

The *Symphony in three movements*, 1947, is again something of a synthesis of the composer's work over the preceding decade. In form and structure the work is exceptionally clear, though again the classical formal concepts are absent. However, the symphony does have a main theme that occurs in many variants in the first movement and reappears in the last movement. The symphony opens with a striking theme in unison, *fortissimo*, after which the horns intone the *leitmotif*. This is then relegated to the bass in a sort of development section. The writing gets progressively thicker, and the motif appears in a host of variants, now in the top part now in the middle, until it finally gets lost in the fine web of parts.

The andante is beautifully transparent. A comedy theme in the style of Rossini seems like a caricature in this context. A short transitional passage leads straight into the finale, which is closely related to the first movement, and a fugato begins in trombones and piano, building up to a strong climax. The tension is maintained right up to the cataclysmic final chord.

In the years since 1945 Stravinsky has written three significant choral works of a religious nature. The *Mass* of 1948 is scored for mixed chorus; boy's voices are recommended for the upper parts, which speaks for Stravinsky's liturgical intention, as does the brevity of the work, which may be sung in a church service, with a double wind quintet consisting of two oboes, cor anglais, two bassoons, two trumpets and three trombones. The Kyrie opens homophonically, but the texture is in the main contrapuntal, with a directly imitative 'Christe' passage. The Gloria is a single complex movement that juxtaposes treble and alto soloists with quiet *tutti* passages. The Credo, which is introduced by the priest's intonation, is psalmodic throughout, with a contrapuntal Amen. Sanctus and Benedictus are grouped together in one movement, with related but not identical 'Hosannas' in a faster tempo. The Agnus Dei is a piece of antiphonal writing in which the vocal chorus alternates with the wind chorus, but is never accompanied by it.

The *Canticum Sacrum*, 1955, is dedicated (by tenor and baritone soloists with trombone accompaniment) 'to the city of Venice, in praise of its Patron Saint, the Blessed Mark, Apostle'. The orchestra lacks violins and horns, but includes harp and organ.

The chorus enter in the first movement proper: 'Go ye into the world and preach the gospel to every creature.' Three animated choral statements with full orchestra are separated by two gentle interludes for organ and bassoons. At this time, Stravinsky was preoccupied with problems of serial procedure, and his approach to a solution can be clearly traced in this work. The second movement is a highly contrapuntal and lyrical tenor aria 'Surge Aquilo' (Awake, O North Wind) accompanied by flute, cor anglais, harp and three solo double basses. This idea of chamber music interludes in orchestral works is an essential feature of Stravinsky's recent style. The third movement deals separately with the three cardinal virtues, charity, hope and faith. Each section is preceded by a twelve-note series in octaves. Charity is expounded contrapuntally by trebles, altos and tenors, with trumpets providing a fourth voice. Hope is set as a series of duets for tenor and baritone soloists, and choral trebles and altos. Faith is expressed by the chorus in octaves, with a hypnotic rocking motion, 'I believed, therefore have I spoken', followed by a contrapuntal setting of 'I was greatly afflicted'.

The fourth movement dwells further on the subject of faith; it takes the form of a dialogue between baritone solo and chorus: 'Jesus said unto him, If thou canst believe, all things are possible to him that believeth (baritone). And straightway the father of the child cried out, and said with tears (chorus), Lord, I believe; help thou my unbelief (baritone).'

The fifth movement 'And they went forth and preached everywhere' is a recapitulation of the first ('Go ye into all the world'). All the texts are in Latin, taken from the Vulgate Bible.

Threni (1957–58) is a large-scale work for six soloists, mixed chorus and large orchestra. The texts are taken from the lamentations of the Prophet Jeremiah, again in Latin. In this work Stravinsky has mastered very thoroughly the principles governing 'composition with twelve notes related only to one another', although the latter half of this definition will always be understood by Stravinsky in a modified form. Every note that Stravinsky hears is related to a key, to a harmonic function grounded on a bass. His treatment of the twelve-note system is not liable to be confused with that of Berg, Schönberg or Webern, though from the latter he seems to have inherited a passion for brief statements. His formal technique relies on the recurrence of sharply contrasted textures, and this places him directly opposite Webern, whose striving throughout was for *continuity* of thought, rather than formal assembly. Also in instrumental technique the two masters are poles apart; their transparency is comparable, but Stravinsky's transparency subserves a certain *efficiency* of sound, or effectiveness, whereas Webern's subserves expression alone. It is clear that effectiveness and expressiveness are not different worlds; the difference is one of approach. The gulf between the two masters is readily appreciable if one compares their approaches to religious music. The choice of text is symptomatic: Stravinsky takes passages from an Old Testament prophet in an archaic language, Webern takes lyrical and personal verses by a contemporary poetess writing in his native language. The list of antitheses can be prolonged indefinitely.

The Hungarian composer BELA BARTOK (1881–1945) is the next most important figure in new music. Bartók found his own style early on in his career and arrived quite independently at some of the same conclusions as Schönberg and Stravinsky. His strong ties with Hungarian folk music safeguard him from extreme constructivism. His melodies are primitive but highly characteristic, his style polyphonic, his rhythms elemental and compelling.

The *Dance Suite*, 1923, is a striking example of these characteristics. Five dance themes that are probably based on folk tunes are developed one after the other, with a graceful interlude—Bartók calls it a ritornello—between each one. The finale goes back over all five themes. The first dance opens quietly and develops intermittently with constant increases of tempo. The monotonous theme circles around four neighbouring semitones; it is played first by the bassoon, then by the cor anglais, then the oboe, and dies away in tuba and trombone. The music returns to the original tempo at the end, and the bassoon plays the final phrase. The drums roll and the piano hammers, and the strings produce a constant stream of fresh effects around the monotonous theme. The ritornello for violin accompanied by the remaining strings in delicate

harmonies is refreshing after the harsh dance. The second dance is
a fiery allegro on a motif based on the constant repetition of a leap

of a third, the ritornello entrusted this time to the clarinet. The
third dance is a typically Hungarian four-bar theme that builds up
electrifyingly in constant repetitions. These wild dance themes are
followed by two quieter melodies: first, a recitative-like number
for woodwind interrupted by veiled string chords, and then an
orientally gliding melody over a lifeless pedal-point. The finale
starts with a steep build-up on this last theme; then the other dance
melodies appear. The ritornello achieves a transitory peace and then
the finale picks up again and storms on to its wild end.

Although we tend to think of Bartók's *Dance Suite* as an early
work in his career as an influential composer on the international
contemporary musical scene, it should be remembered that he
wrote it in his forty-second year and that there are many earlier
works that cast valuable light on his development, besides being
admirable pieces of music in their own right.

Bartók's two stage works date from 1911 and 1919, and both
can be heard in concert versions. The symbolical tale of *Bluebeard's
Castle* (1911) owes much to the impressionist technique of orchestral writing, without of course impressionistic intent; the story
of Bluebeard's seven dead wives and the locked doors of his weird
apartment lends itself rather to expressionistic treatment.

The *Marvellous Mandarin* (1919) is far less operatic, and we see
already the nascent developments in rhythm that are to characterize his mature works, such as the second piano concerto or fourth
string quartet. The stage version tells of a group of tramps in a
hovel who persuade a girl to dance so as to lure victims into their
clutches. The element of dance is predominant. The main dance
concerns the strange mandarin who falls under her spell, and who
then casts his spell on her, finally uniting with her only to die
immediately from the wounds inflicted by the robbers. The concert version, however, concerns itself mainly with the first two
victims, one young and one old, and breaks off soon after the entry
of the mandarin.

In 1907–08 Bartók wrote a concerto for the Hungarian violinist

Stefi Geyer, to whom he gave the manuscript. This did not come to light until the violinist died, and the concerto was discovered among her papers. It was premièred in 1958. This beautiful work opens with a flowing melody for the soloist, joined later by the first violins and second violins contrapuntally. The andante is concisely constructed around the opening motif of rising thirds, and the orchestration is rich, yet clear. The soloist leads almost continuously.

The second movement, allegro giocoso, begins with a declamatory theme for the soloist with orchestral comments, and this material is developed fully. However, there is a great profusion of subsidiary material; noteworthy is the passage in triplets for the soloist, two harps and woodwinds, with strings accompanying.

Another early work of Bartók's that is not often played is the *Rhapsody for piano and orchestra*, opus 7. Bartók used to play the solo part himself quite frequently. A heroic adagio begins the work, but the soloist takes over in double tempo very soon with a grandiose display of virtuosity. This procedure is repeated and varied, and then the pianist states the opening material, *piano*. The main body of the piece is a *vivo* passage in $^4/_8$ that is introduced allegretto, *molto capriccioso*. This $^4/_8$ movement undergoes frequent fluctuations of tempo, and finally the opening material is re-introduced. A duet for horn and piano concludes the work, with strings building up in chords at the very end.

In the years between the composition of the *Dance Suite* and the *Cantata Profana* (1930) Bartók had devoted his energies chiefly to chamber music, and concertante pieces such as the *Piano Concerto No. 1* and the two *Rhapsodies for violin and orchestra*, which we will examine shortly. The *Cantata* shows a great advance in formal thinking over the *Dance Suite*, and also a great development in the use of counterpoint. The work is scored for tenor and baritone soloists, double chorus and orchestra, and the words are taken from a Hungarian folk song about a father who taught his nine sons nothing but how to hunt in the high distant mountains. The boys, on the trail of a giant stag, are magically transformed into nine stags and wander in the mountains. The father trails them and is just about to shoot when the eldest speaks to him. The father pleads that they come home to their weeping mother, but they reply that their antlers cannot pass through the doorway, that their slender feet cannot tread the pavings, only the leafy mould of the open.

Bartók plans his cantata in three movements. The main section of the first movement is an allegro fugue that grows out of rhythmic ostinato. This part tells of the boys out hunting. A *moderato* passage tells of how they reach the haunted bridge, cross over it, and are all transformed.

The second movement, andante, follows without a break, and shows the worried father setting out in pursuit. A climax is reached where he is about to shoot at his own sons. The favourite son calls out agitatedly (tenor solo) and in a frenzy threatens to smash his father on the rocks below. The father (baritone solo) pleads with them, and the following interchange is treated almost operatically. The chorus has a passive, narrative rôle that acquires definition in the third and last movement, which follows on without a break. In this movement the story is recapitulated in succinct, undramatized, almost moral form. Finally the tenor solo joins in with the choruses, pointing out the beautiful pathos of the stags' fate, their mouths unable to drink beakers of wine, only the clear waters of the woodland springs.

The *Music for stringed instruments, percussion and celesta*, 1936, is a masterpiece. In this work Bartók's strange, bitter style seems richer in expression and more profound, perhaps because he had to dispense with the harsher orchestral effects. All the same, we hear some strange sounds; the work is scored for two string orchestras, piano, celesta, and a formidable percussion section.

The first movement is introductory in character. It consists of a long fugato for strings on a slinking theme using a strange gypsy gamut. The voices enter regularly at first, and then at shorter and shorter intervals. The climax comes with the closest possible *stretto* and all the strings, *fortissimo*, change over to an inversion of the theme. This falls off gradually and dies away *pianissimo*.

The second movement, allegro, is in sonata form. The first theme is energetic and rhythmic and the contrasting second theme is scherzando. Both motifs are artfully worked over in the long development section. The reprise is announced by both string orchestras playing the powerful first theme, underlined by the timpani.

The adagio is improvisatory, written in gypsy style; Bartók masterfully creates the impression of a complete gypsy band, with cimbalom and all, by means of the cunning exploitation of the xylophone, with *portamentos* and *glissandos* for strings, harp, piano, celesta and even timpani.

The finale, allegro molto, is dominated by a powerful, urgent rhythmic movement. Excited syncopations alternate with the hammering regularity of the march rhythms. The coda is again a gypsy piece: the themes are shaken up together with a constant interchange between adagio and presto. The fugato theme from the first movement also has an important part to play here.

In 1939 Bartók wrote another work for strings, this time a *Divertimento* for a straightforward string orchestra. The work has three movements: allegro non troppo, molto adagio, allegro assai. The first movement is an elaborate developmental movement; the adagio is drawn-out and passionate, with wide-ranging dynamics. The final allegro is the most exciting movement: the incessant cumulative rhythms give way in a central passage to a short cadenza passage for solo violin in a freer tempo. But the driving rhythms return, and wriggling triplets begin to infiltrate into the hammering quavers, softening their profile and yet heightening the excitement.

The five movements of the *Concerto for orchestra*, 1944, form a large symphonic arch, and Bartók finds employment for increased orchestral forces. The piece is scored for twelve woodwind, eleven brass, two harps, extensive percussions and a large body of strings. The first allegro is preceded by a slow introduction. A theme of fourths rises in the basses and is answered by a mysterious rustling in the high strings. The motif of a fourth acquires the character of an accompanying figure as the tempo increases; a trumpet signal joins in and climbs steeply into the allegro. This allegro is domi-

nated by a fiery theme stated by the violins; the woodwind continue it and it loses itself in the flute. As a substitute for a second theme the oboe plays a bucolic melody over open fifths in the strings. This is repeated by the clarinet, but as an idyll it fails to make its mark and a striking canon for violins and 'cellos on the main theme supplants it. The development section is also dominated by the main theme in several variants. The thematic work in this movement is amazingly consistent; every subsidiary phrase is derived from the principle motifs. The pastoral second idea is given fuller treatment in the reprise, but the main theme in its original form takes over again at the powerful ending.

The second movement, allegretto scherzando, begins with snare drum rhythms, from which a happy march develops with the bassoons in sixths. The oboes, following in thirds, are interrupted by blustering basses, and shrill clarinets in sevenths. At the climax, muted trumpets in seconds are heard over delicate string *tremolos*, Then comes a new scene: the brass wind play a steady idea, interrupted by the rhythms of the drum. The bassoons reappear and introduce the reprise.

The third movement is an elegy, and seems to express Bartók's homesickness for Hungary. The colour of the movement is given by the flickering rhythm, the cimbalom sounds of the harps and strings and the wild outbursts.

The intermezzo is like the second movement, light and playful. A gentle theme for the oboe sets the tone and all the further melodies result from this constant interplay between 2/4 and 5/8. A

cheeky street song attempts to assert itself but soon sinks back into the graceful play of the opening. The finale is very effective and brilliant. The stormy, excited main theme is contrasted with dancing subsidiary ideas.

In Bartók's work, the piano concertos seem to represent turning points in his style, as though he turned to this form when his thought was problematic. Thus, though they rank among his most difficult works, they are also his most rewarding, in that they express a great tensity of thought and feeling. The *Piano Concerto No. 1* (1927) is still somewhat of a bravura concert piece for the concertising virtuoso that Bartók was, and yet we find glimpses of the harmonic 'hardness'—or dissonant quasi-diatonic writing—that finds its strongest expression in his second concerto.

The *Concerto No. 2 for Piano and Orchestra* (1931) is an excellent example of the brave, uncompromising Bartók of the fourth string quartet and the piano sonata. Here there is little trace of the resignation evident in his last works, the third piano concerto or the viola

concerto, nor of the playfulness of the concerto for orchestra. The
work is laid out in three movements in a reasonably conventional
way: there is a cadenza for the soloist shortly before the end of the
first movement; the second movement abounds with the coloristic
effects that Bartók prefers in his slow movements; the finale is
based on a repetitive dance melody with a great deal of ostinato
treatment. The writing for the piano is throughout of such toughness and endurance as to leave no doubt about Bartók's capacity as
a pianist.

Bartók's *Piano Concerto No. 3* is the one that is most frequently
played. He finished it in 1945 shortly before his death, and it is a
magnificent work both in the total conception and in the details. The
virtuoso treatment of the solo part betrays the composer's exceptional pianistic gifts; he is constantly wrestling new technical possibilities from the instrument. The first movement (allegretto) is
built on the contrast between the sharp rhythmic profile of the
first theme, played by the soloist in powerful octaves, and the vocal
subsidiary ideas in the woodwind. The middle movement is headed
'adagio religioso'. The soloist plays the chorale-like main idea supported by the strings. In the reprise, the woodwind take over the
theme, with simple two-part imitations in the piano part. The last
movement relies on dancing rhythms and brilliant passage work.
The concerto is in E, and it is the constant interchange between the
major and minor modes and their frequent juxtaposition that gives
such exotic charm to the work as a whole.

Bartók actually left the score of his *Piano Concerto No. 3* incomplete by seventeen bars. These he was unable to orchestrate before
the doctors abducted him into the hospital where he died. A bitter
end for a man who, for the five years that he spent in America before his death, felt himself to be a wild, free savage in a cold and
hostile land. These seventeen bars were completed by Tibor Serly,
Bartók's trusted friend and pupil. The *Viola Concerto* that he was
working on concurrently did not exist in full score at all, and we
have to thank Serly for the whole of the orchestration of this work.
It was dedicated to Primrose and was premièred by him on the
completion of the orchestral score.

Bartók's second violin concerto, 1938, generally known simply
as his *Violin Concerto* since the earlier one was lost, is one of his most
mature and significant works. The vitality of the main movement
is followed by a middle movement in romanza style. This conceals
a scherzo at its centre, like a sweet kernel. The fiery last movement,

allegro molto, is the climax of the concerto. The dancing élan of
the main theme breaks through constantly and dominates the
movement. The subsidiary ideas are always interesting, and so is
the shimmering orchestration and the virtuoso writing for the
soloist.

The violin concerto is certainly Bartók's greatest contribution
to the concert literature of this instrument. However, it is important to remember the works that prepared the way for it. The posthumous violin concerto of 1907 has been discussed above, but there
are two further scintillating works in this genre, both written in
1928. These are the two *Rhapsodies for violin and orchestra*, the one
dedicated to Joseph Szigeti and the other to Zoltán Székely. Both
are divided into two parts: 'Lassu' and 'Friss', and both derive
largely from folk melodies. The first part in each case is rhapsodic,
whereas the second part is dance-like and animated. The writing
for the solo violin is particularly brilliant in the second rhapsody,
revised by Bartók in 1944. The first rhapsody is remarkable for its
cunning exploitation of the popular Hungarian instrument, the
cimbalom. Bartók states that each movement of these works can
be played on its own, as a separate concert piece.

Bartók's compatriot ZOLTÁN KODÁLY, born in 1882, should
also be mentioned. His folkloric orchestral works attracted a lot of
attention—the *Hary-Janos Suite*, the *Maroszeker Dances* and the
Dances of Galanta—but have not retained their popularity. The
Psalmus Hungaricus, a choral work, is generally considered his most
important work.

The growth of new music is inconceivable without PAUL
HINDEMITH, born at Hanau near Frankfurt, in 1895. With
Stravinsky, he is the most important contributor to neo-classicism.
Hindemith was closely connected with all the stormy develop-
ments of the 'twenties, and played a decisive part in them.

The young Hindemith seemed to stand all traditions on their
heads; the cheeky, juvenile desire to shock the bourgeois then gave
place to the more reserved and peaceable attitude of the later Hindemith. His journey towards neo-classicism was not a matter of count-

less twists and turns and surprise corners, however; he moved steadily along his chosen path, with a sleepwalker's sureness of his destination.

The most striking element of Hindemith's style is his straight-line polyphony; far from shirking the resultant dissonances, one sometimes has the impression that he courts them. His melodies tend to avoid the profound expressiveness of the romantics, without deteriorating into an empty aphoristic style. They sweep on unendingly, defined by rhythmic units, dynamic differentiations and harmonic colour, but never by a uniform periodicity. The most important element of his style, besides linearity, is his powerful musicality; he is unconcerned with over-cultivation; his forms and rhythms stream out, healthy and carefree, from a never-failing well of invention.

The *Concerto for orchestra*, opus 38, 1925, is overflowing with musicality. The swing of the main theme played first by the strings

and later by the wind is contrasted with a concertante trio of violins, oboe and bassoon. The second movement is an electrifying and turbulent scherzo. Instead of a slow movement, Hindemith inserts a peculiar march for woodwind alone. The finale is a big ostinato movement. The one-bar bass figure supports a swift fugato

on a swinging theme. This soon disappears in a maze of parts, but reappears towards the end like a bright fanfare for the full orchestra.

It is usual to define a second period in Hindemith's work beginning in 1931 with the oratorio *Das Unaufhörliche* and reaching its first great climax in the opera *Mathis der Maler*, 1934. At this time Hindemith began to discard his more bumptious attributes and turn towards a new classical style. However, we are too close to these events to be able to draw sharp boundaries in an artist's work. Generally speaking the artist moves continuously along his true path without sudden somersaults and jumps, and this is true of Hindemith.

The *Mathis der Maler* symphony consists of three instrumental
pieces out of the opera. Hindemith found the inspiration for this
work in the wonderful masterpiece of the painter Matthias Grünewald, the Isenheim altar. Grünewald's life and work became the
subject of the opera, and the symphony depicts three scenes from
the Isenheim altar. The first movement deals with the 'Concert of
angels'. Three trombones, with delicate figurations in the strings,
play an old-fashioned carol tune after the solemn opening chords.
The clarinets and later the flutes and glockenspiel take up the carol,
and the whole forms a delicate introduction to the real 'concert of
angels'. The words of the carol are 'Three angels are singing' and
consequently the main movement contains three themes. The first
is a joyful song, while the second seems calmer and more reflective

by contrast. The third is a childlike, jubilant flute theme accompanied by gentle motion in the high strings. The angels' communal

concert now begins: to begin with, the first two themes are com-

bined and succeed one another in strict fugal entries. The carol from
the introduction also joins in, again played by three trombones.
The second angel's theme acquires greater and greater prominence,

only to die away again. The third theme is introduced again at this point, and the mood of jubilant musicality carries the movement through to the end.

The second movement is headed 'Burial'. The flute plays a mournful melody against the gloomy funeral music of the muted strings. The oboe takes up the sad melody and the music builds up steeply to a frantic outburst of sorrow. The mighty climax collapses with a cry, and the melody appears timidly in the woodwind. The piece ends with a consoling phrase in the horn.

The last movement shows the 'temptation of St Antony'. The altarpiece is a monstrous, fantastical vision and the music is similar; an uncanny, frightening orchestral recitative precedes the wild, stormy allegro. The unrelenting urgency of the rhythms dominates the music. Finally, strength ebbs away, and strings play lines that seem to plead for peace and calm. The winds answer with renewed excitement and disquiet, and a lively fugato for strings leads to the final passage. The hymn 'Lauda Sion Salvatorem' builds up over a four-bar ostinato in the horns based on a melody that was played by the clarinet in the fugato. Finally the brass play a jubilant Allelujah with all their might and the work ends on this invigorating note.

The suite *Nobilissima Visione*, 1938, is very easy to understand. The first movement is headed 'Introduction and rondo' and the second movement 'March and pastorale'. The music is fresh and carefree, particularly the middle section of the second movement, a lively jumping dance in $3/8$. The last movement is a solemn passacaglia on a six-bar theme. This appears first in the bass, then—in the middle section—in the top part, and for the final climax it is given to brass and basses in combination.

The *Symphony in E-flat major*, 1940, is unfortunately not so easy to understand, but the *Symphonic Metamorphoses on themes by Weber*, 1943, provides a very good starting point for the layman who wishes to become acquainted with Hindemith's style.

. The first movement is dominated by a quick march with a czardas-type ending. The scherzo is built on a somewhat larger scale, with a light exotic theme from Weber's *Turandot* music, a melody that is repeated seven times, building up gradually to *fortissimo*. A triplet figure forms the transition to a merry fugato on a variant of the theme. With the entry of the strings the theme takes on its original form, and this builds up to the climax of the movement over a four-bar ostinato version of the theme. The timpani

take over at the end; they intone the theme more and more hesitantly until it finally disappears.

The third movement is an andantino, in which the metamorphoses of the regular sixteen-bar melody take the form of two
fragrant variations. An extended march closes the work. Weber's
melodies are sweet and memorable, but the whole is unquestion-
ably the work of Hindemith. Actually, the former facilitates the
comprehension of the latter.

The *Harmonie der Welt* symphony, completed in 1951, is a counterpart to the *Mathis der Maler* symphony. This work again consists
of exerpts from an opera, this time devoted to the life and work of
the great astronomer Johannes Kepler. According to the composer's
introductory words the titles of the three movements refer to the
three classes of music beloved of earlier authorities; thus 'they draw
attention to all previous attempts to recognize a harmony of the
world, and understand music as its sounding equivalent'.

The first movement is headed 'Musica instrumentalis' and contains, according to Hindemith, 'Music from the scenes where the
heroes' activities are hindered by external difficulties'. The movement consists of three sections, each with its own theme and tempo.
The first theme is stated by the trumpet and developed by the other
instruments in a polyphonic structure. The second part is like a
march, and the third part is 'fast, loud, and brutal in its unbridled
wildness'. In this last part the themes of the first two parts are also
involved, first the march theme and finally the weighty theme from
the opening.

The second movement, 'Musica humana', uses themes representing (in the opera) 'the spiritual relations of the actors'. Two large
melodies, the first in the violins and the second in the oboe, are
stated, interrupted and combined, before they finally die away in
the distance.

The third movement, 'Musica mundana', is an attempt 'to symbolize the postulated harmony of the world in musical form'. A
solemn theme is treated fugally at the beginning, and then follows
the main section of the movement, a passacaglia whose nine-bar
theme is derived from the fugue theme. To start with, the melodic
and rhythmic structure of this theme is left unaltered, but in the
subsequent variations it is gradually dissolved, and reappears only
in fragments. Slowly the thematic texture resolves and the solemn
theme from the opening emerges powerfully in the brass to end
the work.

Hindemith's numerous concert pieces for one soloist and orchestra are his most accessible works. His musicality finds particularly happy hunting grounds in this genre, and it is disarming to see how he sets himself problem after problem and solves them all impeccably.

Of his early concertos, the first *Violin Concerto*, opus 36, no. 3, 1925, is still frequently played. Despite its harshness and the occasional formal obscurity, this work is dazzlingly effective. It is even rewarding for the player if he is really on top of it technically! The concerto begins with a short introductory orchestral movement entitled 'Signal'. The following allegro is dominated by a bold rising theme with a reserved second theme in contrast. The slow movement is headed 'Night-piece'. The soloist plays the atmospheric theme calmly against a delicate string accompaniment. The final appearance of the theme is very effective; it is played by the solo instrument at the top of its register. The fourth movement is a sparkling scherzo that changes suddenly into something ghostly and uncanny. The following finale is a *stretto* in the form of a scurrying *perpetuum mobile* for the soloist, *pianissimo*. Against this, the orchestra plays a remarkably obstinate melody that emerges finally as a ghostly waltz!

The thematic writing in the *Concerto for 'cello and orchestra*, 1940, is extremely dry. The large line of the main theme is answered by an anxious, retreating subsidiary theme played first by the woodwind and then by the soloist. The main theme rises powerfully in the development section and a big cadenza for the soloist leads into the reprise, which presents the themes in reverse order.

The second movement is a peaceful canzonetta, with a stormy allegro tarantella as a middle section. The canzonetta theme reappears in flute and clarinet, while the soloist hastes away with the tarantella. Hindemith describes the last movement as a march. The striding main section is met by a charming trio written mostly for high woodwind, celesta and percussion, *pianissimo*. The *fortissimo* entry of the main section is very coarse by contrast. A brief *stretto* effectively ends the concerto.

Hindemith was an outstanding viola player himself, and wrote three viola concertos for his own use, so to speak. The first *Viola Concerto*, opus 36, no. 5, was written in 1927, at a time when the composer was exuberantly active in the musical world. This exuberance finds its happiest expression in the outside movements of

the concerto, a toccata at the beginning and a set of variations on a
Bavarian march as a finale.

The *Concert Music for viola and chamber orchestra*, opus 49, 1930,
is more of a virtuoso piece, and generally more elegant and gracious. Again, the finale is the most impressive movement. The
third *Viola Concerto*, 1935, is based on old folk tunes.

The *Theme with four variations*, representing the four tempera-
ments, for string orchestra and piano can be regarded as a piano
concerto. Like the theme, each variation is in three parts, or rather
in three continuous movements. The ternary form may be the only
recognizable similarity between the theme and the variations, however. The best procedure is to surrender yourself to the flow of the
composition, without worrying about the refinements of variation
technique.

The theme is a memorable melody in moderate tempo played
by the orchestra alone. The piano's entry is very lively: now merry
and now excited, the orchestra participates freely in the game. The
third section, in a rocking ⁶/₈, is again chiefly orchestral.

The first variation, 'Melancholic', starts with heavy chords for
the soloist, with the sighing, plaintive voice of the solo violin
against them. The middle section is a mysterious whispering con-
ference in the orchestra, and the final section is a strange march.
The second variation, 'Sanguine', is a waltz. The 'Phlegmatic'
variation has a charming scherzando in its third section, but the
final variation 'Choleric' is the most amusing. After a recitative-like
introduction with constant changes of tempo between fast and
slow, we hear a fine rhythmic *vivace* leading to a powerful *appassionato* and finally to a *maestoso* that closes the work on a note of
magnificence.

The decisive battles for the establishment of new music were fought
in Germany and France. There were heated arguments in Berlin,
Frankfurt, Munich and Vienna, but in France, as usual, all the forces
were concentrated in Paris. A group of young composers had
collected after the First World War, who wanted to get away from
romanticism and impressionism, and who also wanted to free
themselves from German influences and seek a national French
style. *Le groupe de Six*, as they called themselves, consisted of
Milhaud, Honegger, Poulenc, Auric, Durey and Germaine Tailleferre. Their hero was the revolutionary composer Erik Satie. Satie
was against hypertrophied chromaticism, and in favour of sim-

plicity in melody and harmony, of bitonality and motoric elements. He also used grotesque elements, and the influence of jazz is traceable in his music. The six soon split up, as was only natural, for some of the personalities were so strong that they had to go their own ways whether they wanted to or not. Milhaud and Honegger quickly achieved world fame, and Poulenc and Auric made names for themselves at least in France. Durey and Tailleferre, however, fell into obscurity.

As an influence on his generation it is impossible to underestimate ERIK SATIE (1866–1925). Not only must *Les Six* be traced back to him, but many elements in Stravinsky's neo-classic style. Satie was also active in furthering the cause of this sort of music, as his letters to 'Grand Maître' Stravinsky show. Perhaps he used this title satirically when writing to his friend; however that may be, he wrote articles and got favourable reviews printed, and thus contributed to easing Stravinsky's abandonment of the grand Diaghilev style. Composition seems to have been rather a matter of conscience for Satie. He can have had little inclination for extended work—'Socrate', an impressive cycle for soprano and piano, is probably his largest work, and this is extremely spare and repetitive—and yet he conscientiously produced a variety of small-scale pieces, each entered meticulously in his diary, with the number of hours he spent on them.

Parade is a ballet score that has achieved fame. Piano duets for four hands must have been his favourite medium; *Parade* is more often performed by enthusiasts in this intimate arrangement than as an orchestral piece. It contains all the elements of his style, the non-expressive melodies, the satirical registrations and constant surprises.

Trois petites pièces montées for orchestra (as usual his title is difficult to explain) deals with scenes from Rabelais. The first is entitled 'De l'enfance de Pantagruel': muted violins and violas provide movement with a gentle accompaniment figure. The melodies are extremely simple, and the orchestration is a marvel of economy; no single unnecessary note is included. The second movement is 'Marche de Cocagne', and begins with martial duet for two trumpets. A melody for first violins with hack accompaniment provides the feminine element, and a *tutti* restatement of the trumpet duet in slower tempo rounds off the piece. The final piece 'Jeux de Gargantua', subtitled 'Polka corner', shows extreme subtlety in the way melody and accompaniment are fused and grow out of one another. Brusque *fortissimo* cadenzas are interjected without warning, and blatant comic relief is provided by the duet for clarinet and bassoon just before the end.

DARIUS MILHAUD, born in 1892, is the most versatile member of the group, and has been active in all fields of music. His symphonic œuvre comprises five symphonies and numerous suites. These last have found their way into concert halls throughout the world, particularly the dance suite *Saudadas de Brazil*, 1919, based on Brazilian folk dances, the *Suite Provençale*, 1936, and the *Suite Française*, 1946. These suites are clear in form; the movements are brief, and the melodies are national in origin. The articulation of the little movements betrays the hand of an extremely subtle musician. Milhaud is a master of bitonality, or the combination of two melodies in different keys, and this lends his music its harmonic spice. His instrumentation is very careful; he holds his listeners' attention by a constant interchange of orchestral colours, with subtle use of percussion instruments to underline the highly differentiated rhythms.

Milhaud wrote his ballet music *La Création du Monde* in 1923. The work subdivides into an overture and five scenes. The use of trombone *glissandi*, saxophone and a large selection of percussion testify to the composer's preoccupation with the jazz idiom of that time. The music itself—the melodies, harmonic language, and rhythmic declamation—is explicitly 'bluesy', without having anything whatever to do with 'the blues'. Any jazz idiom dates very quickly, which may be the result of the fact (or the reason for it) that it is not written down comprehensively. Milhaud's exploitation of the jazz materials is mechanical, and very dusty. It is difficult to enjoy, except for a sophisticated minority of devotees of 'the period'. However, the score is by no means devoid of instrumental finesse.

ARTHUR HONEGGER (1892–1955) was an important figure in the further developments of new music. His symphonic poem *Pacific 231*, and *Rugby*, 1928, are orgies of machinery. The 'motoric' element is carried to lengths undreamed of even by Stravinsky. *Pacific 231* had a sensational success at the time as being the last word in machine music. Honegger has expressed himself at length about the work; he says that he wished—being a passionate lover of locomotives—to express the peaceful breathing of the stationary engine, the effort of starting, and the gradual picking-up of speed. The climax of the work comes when the engine is racing through the night at seventy-five miles per hour. This work is a real song in praise of machinery; a *furioso* is reached with extreme precision, and, under an expert baton, the resulting excitement can be breath-taking.

Actually, *Pacific 231* was more of a sensation than a success, and despite its symptomatic significance, it could not hold the public's attention for long. The oratorio *King David* had a more lasting impact. Honegger calls this work a symphonic psalm in three parts, based on a drama by Renée Morax. In concert performances it is best to include some spoken words of narrative to facilitate com-prehension of the action. However, even without explanations this imaginative and suggestive music is direct and appealing, and demands the audience's appreciation. Childlike solo songs such as David's shepherd song alternate with powerful, excited choruses. Honegger expresses his ideas in short forms, and the texts are mostly taken from the psalms. The songs accompany individual episodes in David's life: the fight with Goliath, his visit with King Saul to the witch of Endor, Saul's death. The first part ends with a great song of mourning for Jonathan and Saul; with a few strokes Honegger achieves a very strong effect.

The second part is the climax of the score: David has been made king, and the multitude rejoices, praising the Lord. David dances and the chorus cries with increasing strength 'Great God, come to us'. And God reveals himself to his people; an angel announces to David that the Redeemer shall be born of his seed. This promise is accompanied by a breathless silence, and the tension is not easily relieved in the following timid exchange of Allelujahs. The mood gains in confidence with the entry of the male voices, but an atmos-phere of reserve in the face of such a miracle is preserved up till the end of this part.

The same Allelujah theme dominates the final part, 'David's death'. In his last hour he is again assured of his proud rôle as ancestor of the Messiah, and again we hear the happy and yet reserved Allelujahs. This time, however, they build up to a pitch of mighty strength and the work ends with bright jubilation.

Honegger's dramatic oratorio *Jeanne d'Arc au Bûcher* (Joan of Arc at the stake) is a setting of the poem by Paul Claudel that tells the story of Joan and all her inward and external conflicts, culminating in her final apotheosis at the stake. The work is scored for large orchestra with six soloists, mixed chorus, and chorus of children; it lasts an hour and twenty minutes. The chorus is the most important protagonist, setting the atmosphere of the different scenes, and expressing the sense of paradox and amazement that Joan feels at the judgement passed on her. The chorus is ever-present at the work's long climax, now with her, now against her. The image of Joan (a speaking part) is that of a young country girl, virginal and of humble origin, led on by a sense of wonder, and baffled and incredulous at the sight of the vindictiveness she encounters in the world. The music is like a pageant; the different scenes that succeed each other in quick succession build up cumulatively, and involve us in the drama that is being played out, right through to its devastating climax, and so to the consoling words that end the work, sung by Margaret and Catherine, the Virgin Mary and the children's chorus: 'Greater love hath no man than this, that he lay down his life for a friend.'

Of Honegger's later works, the *Symphony No. 2*, 1941, quickly found a welcome. The symphony is scored for strings, with the accent on the low register. A rich dark sound is peculiar to this symphony. The first allegro is the main movement, and receives its powerful impulse from an energetic rising theme. The delicate

longing of the subsidiary theme cannot maintain itself against this energetic motif, and is consistently overrun by it. The ending of the movement is effective: after the reprise of the lyrical theme, the main idea is heard once again, this time in a whispered unison, *pianissimo*.

The adagio is rich and polyphonic. It radiates endless peace, and thus forms a particularly good preparation for the racy last movement. A fiery scherzo, the last movement is spontaneously appealing, with its amusing rhythms, its virtuoso writing for strings, and its exciting bitonality. The waves subside only towards the end, where the first violins play a chorale tune, supported by a trumpet *ad libitum*, and lead the symphony to its triumphant ending.

Honegger calls his *Symphony No. 3*, 1946, a liturgical symphony. This work is again in three movements, but the orchestra employed is a large one. The first allegro is subtitled 'Dies Irae', and boils with profound internal excitement. The thematic work is clean-cut and primitive and the rhythm stormily impressive.

The profound faith that inspired the adagio 'De Profundis' is immediately effective, and some stylistic features of the writing are reminiscent of Bach. The finale, 'Dona nobis pacem', expresses the struggle for inner peace by means of a single crescendo spanning the whole movement. The music breaks off abruptly at its *fortissimo* climax, and a delicate adagio for strings follows, filled with profound sensitivity. The mood created is one of unending peace and transfiguration. The flute rises to spiritual heights, supported by throbbing strings.

JEAN FRANCAIX, born in 1912, attracted attention even before the Second World War with his gracious and amusing orchestral works.

OLIVIER MESSIAEN, born in 1908, created a considerable stir after 1945 and was destined to have a much greater influence on subsequent musical developments in France. Messiaen was originally an organist, and the Catholic faith is the starting point of his music. He incorporated elements from the Far East into his style, for instance the strange sonorities of Gamelan music and its finely differentiated rhythms. Messiaen's most important work is the *Turangalîla* symphony which lasts about two hours. (It was first introduced by Leonard Bernstein in 1949.) Fragments of this work are sometimes played under the title 'Trois Tâla'. In addition to an extensive percussion section Messiaen employs the 'ondes martenot', an electronic instrument. Messiaen's music gets a novel and strangely penetrating odour from the combination of Catholic mysticism and Javanese cultism. The frequent repetitions of brief melodic fragments and ostinato techniques of various kinds give the music a character of excitement, and even ecstasy, and the suggestive effects of the strange sounds are inescapable.

Technically, Messiaen is continually breaking new ground, but the 'advanced' feeling of his recent works, *Oiseaux Exotiques*, *Chronométrie* and others, is not to be attributed to a desire to 'keep up' with the avant-garde. Rather, he thinks his ideas through to their conclusions, and follows his lines of research—Hindu rhythms, birdsong and so forth—as far as he can; the result is an extreme modernity that is very far removed from sensationalism.

The breakthrough of new music in Switzerland took place under the influence of French music. Honegger was born in Switzerland, but became so French that we can hardly regard him as a Swiss composer. The most famous Swiss composer of that generation is

FRANK MARTIN, born 1890, whose musical language is convincing and original. His style shows the influence of the twelve-note system. Besides his most important work, the scenic cantata *Le vin herbé*, he has written a violin concerto and a 'cello concerto that have both secured their place in the concert repertoire.

This same generation in Italy is represented by GOFFREDO PETRASSI, born 1904, and LUIGI DALLAPICCOLA, also born in 1904. Dallapiccola uses a strange variant of the twelve-note system: his twelve-note melodies are accompanied by indications of harmony.

Soviet music occupies a peculiar position within new music generally. Stravinsky, one of the chief fathers of modern music, did not return to Russia after the revolution of 1917. His music, which was originally so closely bound up with Russian folk lore, gradually shed these bonds, and the national Russian composer became the leader of the internationally orientated new music. SERGE PRO-KOFIEV (1891–1953) also emigrated to the West after the First World War and soon achieved international fame. In 1935 he returned to Russia and henceforth subscribed to the Soviet musical ideals, namely that music should be easy for the general populace to understand, clean-cut formally, and closely related to folk music. New music was rejected on account of its experimental character; the Soviet Union condemned it as 'formalistic', alien to the people, and undesirable.

Prokofiev wrote five symphonies, and numerous suites and instrumental concertos, all of which are evidence of his stylistic brilliance, his spirit and sense of humour. His *Symphonie Classique*, opus 25, the first in order of his symphonies, has achieved a certain popularity. In this work, written in 1921 and therefore at the same time that Stravinsky was concerned with neo-classicism, Prokofiev comes to terms with the classical style. The outside movements are both in sonata form, the slow movement is ternary and the third movement is a gavotte. All the movements are perfectly clear, but the classical forms are executed in the modern spirit. The rhythm and harmony are of our own time. An original creative imagination with considerable charm is at work here, whether in the syncopations that interrupt the regularity of the classical forms, or in unexpected dissonances and sudden harmonic jumps that show the musical draughtsmanship in a new light.

Of Prokofiev's five piano concertos, the *Concerto No. 3*, opus 26, written at the same time as the *Symphonie Classique*, has become generally accepted. The première took place in 1921 in Chicago with the composer as soloist. Brilliance and animation are the features of this work; the climax is reached in the middle movement, an extended set of variations.

By far the most widely known of Prokofiev's works is the musical tale for children *Peter and the Wolf*, opus 67, written in 1936. Each character in the story has a particular musical instrument and a particular melodic fragment to describe him. Peter is characterized by the string quartet, the bird by the flute, the duck by the oboe, the cat by the clarinet, the grandfather by the bassoon, the wolf by three horns, and the rifle shots that are featured at the end of the story are mimicked by the timpani. A narrator tells the story while the music develops the main characters appropriately; the piece is enchantingly effective.

DIMITRI SHOSTAKOVICH, born in 1906, suffered under the same decree as Prokofiev. He was receptive to the ideas of new music and its spirit was observable in his own music, and this was severely frowned on by the Soviet authorities. Shostakovich felt he should submit to official pressure and his later works show a tendency towards a 'people's' neo-romanticism.

His *Symphony No. 1*, opus 10 (1926), certainly shows his awareness of the musical climate of the 'twenties. The four movements are straightforward and vital. The first movement, allegretto, presents several themes and develops them clearly. The second movement, allegro, makes striking use of the piano as an orchestral instrument, with a predilection for the glittering high register. Shostakovich's rather static bass-line is particularly noticeable in this movement, which functions as a scherzo. Under the expressive melodies of the following slow movement, however, the slow basses serve their purpose admirably. The piano is again prominent in the last movement, an allegro molto, preceded by a *lento* introduction. The sliding chromatic figure introduced by the clarinet builds up finely to homophonic climaxes, and although tempo changes are frequent, this movement has a satisfying drive and weight.

Shostakovich's breakthrough to world fame came in 1937 with his *Symphony No. 5*, opus 47, written shortly after he had turned away from the 'formalistic' style of his earlier works. Shostakovich is a musician of great expressive strength, one who speaks his own musical language with great conviction. The four movements are long, but they are full of intense, dramatic life, and continually varied as to orchestral sound, so that the tension is not allowed to flag. The thematic work is bold, and the development linear; he writes mostly in two parts and this results in transparency of texture throughout, even in the biggest climaxes.

This symphony is best described in the composer's own words: 'The subject of my symphony is an individual in the making. The symphony is conceived in a lyrical vein. The finale of the symphony resolves the tense tragedy of the early movements on an optimistic plane. The question is sometimes raised whether tragedy should have a place in Soviet art, confusing tragedy with doom and pessimism. I believe that Soviet tragedy as a genre has every right to exist. But its contents must be suffused with a positive idea as in the life-asserting pathos of Shakespeare's tragedies.' Shostakovich considered his *Fifth Symphony* as 'The artist's reply to just criticism'. His *Fourth Symphony* (1935–36) had had to be withdrawn when already in rehearsal, because it was not considered compatible with Soviet musical ideals. More recently, this work has been revived and performed in England, but no printed score is available as yet.

Shostakovich's Seventh Symphony, opus 60, 1942, is entitled the *Leningrad Symphony*. The peaceful life of the people, the threat of the enemy, the uprising of the people, and the victory over the enemy is the content of the four movements, of which the two outside movements are unusually long. The musical language is simple; the peaceful life of the people is represented by songs and dance-tunes over which the horrors of war pour in. The structure is clear and direct; for instance, the enormous climax in the first movement is achieved by twelve repetitions of the same melody culminating in an enormous outburst. This technique is similar to that of Ravel's *Bolero*, and it is just as effective, even though Ravel's technical refinements are missing.

The *Symphony No.9*, opus 70, 1945, represents a complete break with the attitudes of the preceding symphonies. This symphony is happy, brief and instrumentally transparent. Two-part writing is characteristic of this work too, but there is some harmonic friction and even occasionally a bitonal turn of phrase.

Shostakovich has written concertos for violin, 'cello and piano. The *Piano Concerto*, opus 35, is the most important, as it dates from before his return to the Soviet musical fold. This twenty-minute work is actually a concerto for piano, trumpet and strings. There is no actual cadenza writing for the trumpet, but the part is important and gratifying to play. A spiky curtain raiser of three bars for the soloists precedes the theme of the first movement, with its sim-

ple ostinato accompaniment, and slightly un-European rhythmic articulation. This is developed quite subtly by piano and strings before a common chord theme in the relative major appears in the bass with a new, more military tempo. This arpeggio theme is ideally suited to trumpet, and this instrument now plays an important part in the development. The first theme reappears, and the two soloists end the movement alone. The strings begin the slow movement with a long melodic statement. The piano answers and builds up an enormous climax. The trumpet sing the tune in a middle section; then the piano takes over again and ends the movement with strings accompanying. The third movement is brief, with running passages for the pianist, and leads straight into the finale, *allegro brio*. This last movement is of rare vivacity, and the piano *glissandi* and trumpet fanfares make the ending brilliant and effective.

Shostakovich's *Concerto for 'cello and orchestra*, opus 107 (1959), is dedicated to the great Russian 'cellist Rostropovich. Quite in keeping with the personality of this superb player, the solo part seems to *drive* the orchestra in front of it. The first movement, allegretto, gives the soloist little chance to rest. From the quiet, energetic opening to the brusque ending, the soloist is ever-present, setting the tempo, getting things moving, supporting the orchestra. Woodwind solos are not infrequently juxtaposed with the solo part, but after a while it becomes clear that the horn is the main protaganist apart from the 'cellist, and the two players combine in a strong duet just after the restatement of the first theme.

The horn again plays an important melodic rôle in the $^3/_4$ passage at the beginning of the slow movement (moderato), but the 'cellist soon takes over. The $^4/_4$ 'cello theme recurs at the end in harmonics, in conversation with the celesta. This movement contains some bravura material for the soloist, but the real cadenza comes in the

third movement which follows on without a break. In this movement, which is unaccompanied, the tempo builds up by degrees to
the allegro con moto finale, which again follows on without a
break. A central section in $^3/_8$ relieves the drive of the main part,
which is predominantly $^2/_4$. When the $^2/_4$ returns it is slightly
slower, partly because it has to allow for a restatement of first movement material and partly to accommodate an increasing wealth
of figuration. The solo part builds up to a climax of triple-stop
virtuosity (against the orchestra's thematic interjections), before
being supplanted by hammering timpani in the final bar.

Besides Prokofiev and Shostakovich, the only Soviet composer
who has found his way into our western halls is the Armenian
ARAM KHATCHATURIAN, born in 1903. His is a really music-
making temperament, he writes the music of his heart without
worrying about the stylistic problems of our time. It is perhaps in
consequence of this that his music sometimes sounds rather derivative. Among two symphonies and several concertos, his most successful work is the *Violin Concerto*, a virtuoso piece that is very
gratifying for the soloist. The themes are easy to grasp, and memorable. The storming main idea is contrasted with a lyrical subsidiary
theme of an attractive oriental flavour. The thematic work is clever
and effective; the main theme of the first movement reappears to
form the brilliant ending of the finale. The middle movement is
song-like and the cadenzas are brilliant; no attractions are lacking.
And yet, unwillingly, one has to admit that it *is* a lack that the
work shows no personal connections with the musical language of
our time.

England has also been active in the development of music in recent
years. EDWARD ELGAR (1857–1934) is reckoned the father of
English symphonic music. He wrote two symphonies: *Symphony
No. 1 in A-flat major*, opus 55, in 1908, is dedicated to Hans Richter;
the *Symphony No. 2 in E-flat major*, opus 63, of 1911, is dedicated
'to the memory of King Edward VII'. Elgar's reputation was
established at the turn of the century: his oratorio, the *Dream of
Gerontius*, for three soloists, chorus and orchestra based on a poem
by Cardinal Newman, had its première in Birmingham in 1900,
and was twice performed in Germany in 1902 where it was immediately recognized as a great work (Richard Strauss paid tribute to
it in a public speech). Elgar's overture *Cockaigne (In London Town)*,
opus 40, written in 1900, endeared him to English audiences, and

he was enormously revered in England right up to his death. His most celebrated work is the *Enigma Variations*, opus 36, 1899. The

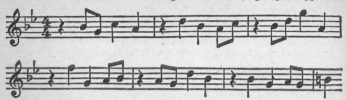

theme of this work is supposed to combine in counterpoint with a melody familiar to everyone. Elgar never revealed what this tune was, and this is one of the reasons for the title 'enigma'. His *Violin Concerto in B minor*, opus 61, 1910, dedicated to Fritz Kreisler, con-

tains another enigma: on the title page Elgar wrote a quotation from *Gil Blas*: 'Herein is enshrined the soul of . . .' The last of the three movements of this concerto is perhaps the most interesting: it is an allegro molto in which the soloist acquires more and more prominence, and which culminates in a long accompanied cadenza. Of the four movements of the *Concerto for 'cello in E minor*, 1919, the second is the most exciting. The moderato first movement is restrained, and so the rude contrasts of this scherzo—it could be described as a recitative and gallop, but it is lightly and beautifully scored—are very effective. However, brilliant though Elgar's works are, they cannot by any stretch of the imagination be seen as part of the tendency towards new music. Firstly, Elgar belongs clearly among the late romantic composers, and secondly—the *Dream of Gerontius* and the *Enigma Variations* excepted—his works have not managed to assert themselves on the continent of Europe.

FREDERICK DELIUS (1862–1934) was born at Bradford, the son of a wool merchant. It was not until 1884, when he was living in Florida, that he began seriously to teach himself the violin and study harmony. Two years later he moved to Leipzig to attend the Conservatoire, where, encouraged by Grieg, he began to compose.

He settled in Paris, and later at Grez-sur-Loing, where he remained until his death.

Delius' operas *A Village Romeo and Juliet* and *Fennimore and Gerda* were originally performed in Germany, and his work was first accepted there. In England, during the first decades of this century, Sir Thomas Beecham's devoted enthusiasm and repeated performances of his work gradually won the attention of the English music public. The orchestral interlude from *A Village Romeo and Juliet*, 'The Walk to Paradise Garden', is typical of Delius' romantic, impressionist music, that seems to shimmer and constantly dissolve, like the reflections on water in a painting by Monet. *On Hearing the First Cuckoo in Spring* (1912) is one of the most frequently performed of his tone-poems for orchestra, which include the companion piece *Summer Night on the River* and the fantasy, *In a Summer Garden*. *Brigg Fair* is an orchestral rhapsody on an Lincolnshire folk song. Delius also composed several concertos for piano, violin and 'cello.

The orchestral and choral works of RALPH VAUGHAN WILLIAMS (1872–1958) are admired and performed in England, but are little known elsewhere. Vaughan Williams was interested in the work of the American poet Walt Whitman, and the work that established his reputation was a setting of a poem of Whitman's and appeared in 1907 under the promising title *Towards the Unknown Region*. The *Sea Symphony*, 1910, is a choral symphony, and also uses Whitman poems. Vaughan Williams' melodic style is partly derived from local folk tunes and this popular feeling is most strongly expressed in his *London Symphony*. Of his later works, the *Antarctica Symphony*, his seventh, is worthy of mention. It is based on music that Vaughan Williams wrote for a film about Scott's expedition to the South Pole, and is a happy expression of the composer's pictorial talent.

WILLIAM WALTON, born 1902, and MICHAEL TIPPETT, born 1905, are the leading figures of the younger generation. Walton's was an exceptional and progressive talent and he achieved fame at any rate in England when he was only twenty-one with *Façade*, an entertainment which he undertook in collaboration with Dame Edith Sitwell. Two orchestral suites from this entertainment appeared later, and were used as ballet music in 1931. The music is lively and satirical. Walton consolidated his reputation with his mellow *Viola Concerto*, 1929, *Belshazzar's Feast*, 1931, an exciting choral work, and, in 1955, his opera *Troilus and Cressida*.

Michael Tippett lacks Walton's facility, but instead of lapsing somewhat as he gets older (as Walton has done), Tippett's work continues to attract attention and provoke discussion, at least in England. His early preoccupation with the snappy, irregular rhythmic style of the madrigalists of Elizabethan England found expression in his *Double Concerto for strings*. In recent years he has turned his attention to opera, and *The Midsummer Marriage* and *King Priam* show a further preoccupation, this time with the problems of Jungian deep psychology.

The Midsummer Marriage has yielded one scintillating concert piece: the *Ritual Dances* from Act II. These are four dances woven together in a complex series of 'preludes', 'preparations' and 'transformations'. The work opens with a prelude which is to recur at the end as a postlude. This is an ornate movement that contrasts the woodwinds' agility with the stable horns. This is followed by a 'transformation' introduced by celesta and with ascending scales for the woodwind. Brass calls are heard in the second half of this brief interlude. Next comes a vigorous 'preparation for the first dance'. The first dance 'The earth in autumn. The hound chases the hare' is based on a hesitant bass line, ornamented by low strings. This builds up, and is superseded by new 'transformations' material which then lapses into the material for the first transformation and leads on to the 'preparation for the second dance' which is also a restatement. The second dance is called 'The water in winter. The otter chases the fish'; the music relies on quiet viola figures and passages for two clarinets. It is unnecessary to describe the further structural layout of the work in detail, since each dance is strongly characterized, and all the preparatory sections are related to previous material. The third dance is called 'The air in spring. The hawk chases the bird' and opens with a gracious passage for four solo violins answered by woodwinds. In the preparation for the fourth dance 'Fire in summer. The voluntary human sacrifice' we hear the chorus (optional in the concert version) singing 'Fire! Fire! St John's fire! in the desert in the night. Fire in summer' and the fourth dance begins. This is a vigorous affirmation of the power and value of carnal love, underlined by the chorus 'Rejoice exceedingly'. At length, the first choral statement returns, with strange effect: 'Fire! St John's fire! in the desert in the night'. Then the postlude gradually reduces the tension up to the ending, with three quiet, familiar, and yet immutable chords for horns, muted.

Tippett's *Piano Concerto* was first performed in 1953 by Louis

Kentner with the Birmingham Symphony Orchestra under Rudolf Schwarz. The opening recalls Schönberg's piano concerto with its cantabile piano writing and harmony of piled-up fourths. The wealth of figuration is also functionally conceived. The movements are long and elaborate, and one easily has the impression that one is swimming in a bath of a particular kind of sound, and the composer has no particular desire to make any drastic changes. Thus, in the second movement (*molto lento* and *tranquillo*), the complex polyrhythms of the orchestra and elaborate figuration of the piano part seem to prolong themselves autonomously. A climax *is* actually reached, but it does not seem important, and after a while we feel that it simply represents a new texture, with soloist and orchestra placed antiphonally. The last movement is a gigue-type vivace; interludes in a slightly slower tempo help to clarify the form, and this movement—the least ambitious—is probably the most successful. The concerto is permeated with a feeling of vagueness and unreality.

BENJAMIN BRITTEN, born in 1913, has achieved an international reputation. Since the sensational success of *Peter Grimes* in 1945 his works have been performed throughout the world. Britten's gifts are quite exceptional, and his musical language is only moderately modern but highly original. The early orchestral work *Variations for string orchestra on a theme by Frank Bridge*, opus 10, 1937, is a good example of his abilities. Frank Bridge was one of Britten's teachers. The theme of this work is idyllic in character, and the ten variations are executed with great delicacy. They are rich in contrasts; an Italian aria is placed next to a Viennese waltz, and a funeral march next to a. *perpetuum mobile*. The work is crowned by a fugue.

The *Variations and fugue on a theme by Henry Purcell*, opus 34,

1945, has been described by Britten as a 'Young Person's Guide to the Orchestra'. He wrote this humorous piece for the children of a friend, in the hope of developing their understanding of the nature of the various orchestral instruments. The beautiful Purcell theme is played first by the full orchestra, then by the woodwind, the brass and the strings, and finally by the percussion section alone. Then come the variations; each instrument has a variation to itself: the flute begins, and then come oboe, clarinet and bassoon. The strings follow: first the violins with a brilliant polonaise, then by violas, 'cellos and basses. The harp concludes the string group with virtuoso *glissandos*. Then comes the brass, with the horns in fanfares, the trumpets bright and cheeky, the trombones solemn and serious. Timpani, drums, triangle, tambourine, xylophone, cymbals and many others are represented in the percussion variations. The final fugue puts the whole machine together again. Starting with the piccolo the instruments enter with the merry fugue subject in the same order as in the variations. Finally the winds play the beautiful Purcell theme decorated by the fugue subject in the strings.

The *Serenade for tenor, horn and strings*, opus 31, 1944, is a charming and original piece. The magic of night is depicted in a series of songs to texts by various poets. The songs are framed by a characteristic horn solo. The central song is particularly effective: it is a burial song consisting of a single six-bar phrase repeated nine times by the soloist accompanied by march rhythms in the orchestra.

Space forbids that we analyse all of Britten's major works; they are too numerous. The early *Sinfonietta*, published in 1935 and dedicated to Frank Bridge, is a characteristic work that still sounds fresh. Britten's feeling for instruments appears already highly developed. There are three movements: presto agitato, variations, and tarantella.

His audacious setting of Rimbaud's *Les illuminations* for high voice and strings, opus 18, 1939, forecasts the later *Serenade* described above. The poems he chose are 'Villes', 'Phrase', set together with 'Antique', 'Royauté', 'Marine', 'Being beauteous', 'Parade' and 'Départ'. The final phrase of Parade 'I am the sole possessor of the key to this savage parade' (J'ai seul la clef de cette parade sauvage) is used by Britten to introduce the work in a number entitled 'Fanfare', and also as an 'Interlude' between 'Marine' and 'Being beauteous'. The predominant material of these movements is instrumental. The writing is fine and evocative throughout, though the registration sometimes strikes one as commonplace.

The last piece, for instance, 'Assez vu, ... Assez eu', is introduced by Britten with sostenuto repeated chords of E-flat major in the middle register; Rimbaud expressed his weariness in wilder ways.

The *Sinfonia da Requiem*, opus 21, of two years later is a requiem without words. The three movements have titles: Lacrymosa, Dies Irae and Requiem Aeternam. The second movement is the most exciting, and generates considerable rhythmic drive, culminating in powerful homophonic attacks, and some of the most ambitious orchestral writing that Britten has undertaken. The last movement is an 'andante molto tranquillo' with a walking bass line in the harps.

The *Spring Symphony*, opus 44, 1949, is scored for three soloists, large orchestra and chorus. The arrangement of the text is very subtle, as we have come to expect from Britten. The symphony is divided into four parts. The first part begins with an introduction 'Shine out fair sun', an anonymous sixteenth-century lyric. The music makes constant use of fugato techniques both chorally and orchestrally. This is followed by Spenser's 'The merry cuckoo' set for tenor solo and three trumpets. 'Spring, the sweet spring' by Nashe follows, set for the full complement of instruments and voices, with a concertante string quartet. This is the number that contains—besides the notorious initial melody, which seems more appropriate to the words 'Swing, my sweet swing'—the amusing cadenzas where the soloists imitate the various bird songs *ad lib*. The next number juxtaposes the soprano soloist with a choir of boys 'The driving boy', and the first part ends with Milton's 'The moving star' for chorus and orchestra. The alto soloist sings the first song of part two, 'Welcome maids of honour' by Herrick, and the next lyric, 'Waters above' by Vaughan, is entrusted to tenor solo and violins. W. H. Auden's 'Out on the lawn I lie my bed' (as characteristically English a poem as one could find in this century) closes the second part, a night-piece for alto solo and orchestra with wordless chorus.

If the songs of part two seem like varied expositions of slow movement material, it is equally true that the third part presents a collection of scherzos. The impetuous stanzas of 'When will my May come' by Richard Barnefield, for tenor solo, give place *attacca* to the gracious allegretto of George Peele's 'Fair and fair', a duet for soprano and tenor. As before, the chorus lends a hand to finish part three, with Blake's cute lyric 'Sound the flute, now it's mute'. Light brass repeated chords in a snappy rhythm accompany the tenors and basses. The sopranos and altos bring in the woodwinds: 'Little boy, full of joy' and the boy's choir sets off the strings: 'Little lamb, here I am. Come and lick . . .' The finale (part four), a lyric scene to words by Beaumont and Fletcher, is all of a piece and requires no detailed analysis. The tenor soloist rhetorically presents London with the merry month of May, and this is the cue for lyrical excursions in all directions. The theme of rising and falling thirds of the beginning becomes more and more prominent and acquires a healthy stretch; it is admirably suited to roundelay treatment.

In 1960 Britten composed a further large-scale choral work for the 500th anniversary of the University of Basle. The *Cantata academica carmen Basiliense*, opus 62, is based on Latin texts taken from the charter of the university and other orations in praise of Basle. The work is scored for four soloists, chorus and orchestra and is subdivided into separate numbers like an oratorio. The first part begins with a chorale for chorus and soloists with orchestral interjections of a festive kind. The other movements in order are: Alla rovescia (chorus), tenor recitative 'But who was the author of this heavenly gift to Basle?', arioso for bass, duettino for soprano and contralto, tenor recitative, scherzo for soloists and chorus. Part two begins with a 'Tema seriale con fuga' which presumably refers to the fact that the theme contains the twelve notes of the chromatic scale in the first four bars, firmly anchored in E-flat major none the less. The baroque fugue that follows has a scale subject answered in inversion. This is followed by 'soli e duetto' for contralto and bass, 'arioso con canto popolare', for soprano solo and male chorus, tenor recitative 'O citizens of Basle', 'Canone ed ostinato' for soloists and chorus which leads straight into a recapitulation of the opening chorale material to the words: 'A free academy may thrive in a free community, for ever the ornament and treasure of illustrious Basle.'

At the time of writing, Britten's *War Requiem* (1961) naturally looms large as the most recent and most monumental of his choral and orchestral works. It was commissioned for the festival celebrating the completion of the new cathedral at Coventry, and had its première there on 30 May 1962. The work uses the Latin text of the Mass for the Dead, and in addition several War Poems by Wilfred Owen. This double stream of text is followed up in the Latin texts, sung by a mixed chorus, boy's choir and soprano solo, and in addition, a twelve-piece chamber orchestra to accompany the poems in English, sung by tenor and baritone soloists. This expedient allows the listener to shift the weight of his attention, as it were, from one foot to another, in the course of the work's eighty-five minutes. Each of the six movements contains one or more of these lyrical insertions or arias: in the Requiem Aeternam, the tenor solo 'What passing bells for those who die as cattle' is inserted before the final Kyrie section. The Dies Irae contains no less than four poetic insertions, shared between tenor and baritone soloists. The Offertorium uses the bitter biblical parody, 'So Abram rose, and clave the wood' with its desperate ending (the angel is speaking): 'Offer the Ram of Pride instead of him (Isaac). But the old man would not so, but slew his son—and half the seed of Europe, one by one.' The Sanctus text is followed by 'After the blast of lightning from the East' for baritone solo. In the Agnus Dei the tenor soloist's stanzas are integrated with the Latin choral refrain in a rather Bartókian slow motion *perpetuum mobile* of rising and falling five-note scales. This, the only concise movement in the work, acts as a prelude to the three-part finale Libera Me, which sets out as a march for percussion instruments. The long dreaming poem 'It seemed that out of battle I escaped' is set as a recitative passage in the centre, and finally all the forms combine, with the chorus 'In paradisum deducant te angeli' with orchestra, while the two male soloists elaborate 'Let us sleep now', with chamber orchestral accompaniment.

The American contribution to European concert programmes was restricted, until recently, to the occasional appearance of the *Rhapsody in Blue* of GEORGE GERSHWIN (1898–1937) and maybe some curiosity or other by the 'bad boy of music', GEORGE ANTHELL (1900–59). Today the situation is very different. After the Second World War we came to know a whole series of American composers whose work was obviously very serious, and yet often more original and open to suggestion than much of the music

of the musical countries of Europe, with their often restrictive traditions. The most important names are WALTER PISTON, born
1894, VIRGIL THOMPSON, born 1896, AARON COPLAND,
born 1900, WILLIAM SCHUMANN, born 1910, and SAMUEL
BARBER, born 1910. All of these write progressive music in a
tonal framework; often a French influence is notable, perhaps because many Americans studied with Nadia Boulanger in Paris in
the 'twenties.

Aaron Copland is the most famous of her American pupils. He
returned to America when his *Dance Symphony* won a prize there
in 1930, and since then he has been an active administrator in the
interests of the more conservative sort of American music. Actually
his earlier music is more progressive and more interesting, particularly the piano variations on a theme of obsessional brevity.
This work can be heard in the concert hall in an orchestral version,
under the title *Variations for Orchestra*. Copland has been active in
a wide variety of fields: he has written ballet music—*Appalachian
Spring* (for Martha Graham) and the popular *Billy the Kid*—and
music for several films, notably *Quiet City*, which exists in a concert
version. His *Piano Concerto* owes a lot to jazz, and folk elements
from neighbouring countries have played a large part in his more
recent music, witness *Danzon Cubano* and *El Salón México*. He is
at his best on a small scale and his most incisive orchestral works
are the *Short Symphony* and the *Statements*.

Samuel Barber's *Essay for Orchestra*, 1928, and his second *Orchestral Essay*, 1942, are two enjoyable pieces. The first is a lively
scherzo preceded by a broad, solemn introduction, and the second
is pastoral in character, interrupted by the brilliant fireworks of a
fugato. Of Barber's symphonies, the *Symphony No. 2*, 1944, attracted
considerable attention. His first *Symphony in One Movement*,
opus 9, 1936, was lyrical in style and reminiscent of his earlier
work, whereas the second, in three movements, is quite experimental. It is very dramatic and passionate, and powerful and personal in expression.

Three composers who have been more influential on the radical
side of American music are CHARLES IVES (1874–1954), HENRY
COWELL, born 1897, and ELLIOT CARTER, born 1908. Charles
Ives experimented with polytonality and microtonality, and his
music is rich both in banality and in extraordinary effects. He wrote
five symphonies, but in Europe we are more likely to encounter
his symphonic poems *Three places in New England*.

Henry Cowell has done as much or more for radical American music as Copland has for conservative American music, and his task was much more difficult. He has written a symphony, but we are more likely to meet his *Hymn and Fuguing Tune* in European concerts. Cowell was an outstanding pianist, and his experiments with clusters of notes and playing on the strings like a harp have had considerable influence on recent literature for the instrument.

Elliot Carter is another Boulanger pupil. His chief claim to fame is his development of the technique of 'metrical modulation', a process whereby one tempo is changed by means of imperceptible metrical transformations into another (enharmonic changes in harmony are the tonal equivalent). He has written several orchestral works—a double concerto for piano and harpsichord, and an oratorio, *The Bridge*—but his reputation this side of the Atlantic is based largely on his monumental string quartet, a work which exploits the metrical technique outlined above.

The general rejection of Richard Strauss resulted in a new musical orientation in Germany, and the great consistency of the romantic period was followed by an alarming diversity of styles.

KARL AMADEUS HARTMANN, born 1905, is a somewhat heavy-handed musician, but one of extraordinary vitality. His *Symphony No. 3*, 1951, is in two big movements; a fiery fugato followed by a long adagio. The strength and significance of the work appears in the adagio, which is expressive of deep suffering. The fugato is rather an *al fresco* construction. The *Symphony No. 5* is in complete contrast to the third. Hartmann calls it a concertante symphony, and accordingly dispenses with the large expressive line in favour of an element of playfulness. The outside movements are a toccata and a rondo with swift characteristic themes distributed between the two trumpets. In the middle is a slow interlude entitled 'melody' with a scherzo inset.

WERNER EGK, born 1901, is possessed of real musicality. Primarily, he is a composer of opera, but his orchestral works are not without interest. His three peasant pieces for orchestra, *Georgica*, 1934, and his *Fiddle music with orchestra*, 1936, are both inextricably connected with Bavaria. Even in modern German music it is thus possible to find an exploitation of national folk elements parallel with that carried out in almost all other countries in the nineteenth and twentieth centuries. Egk, however, contents himself with certain typically Bavarian melodic touches and the exploitation of the local dance rhythms with their characteristic alternation of $^2/_4$ and $^3/_4$. He recreates the atmosphere of Bavarian peasant art, and the result is sometimes primitive, but generally extremely refined. The 'fiddle music' is a full-blown violin concerto, with a virtuoso part for the soloist. Egk's most popular orchestral work is the *French Suite*, 1949, based on themes by Rameau. Each of the five movements is an increase over the last, and the climax is reached in the march-like finale.

BORIS BLACHER, born 1903, achieved a significant success with his *Concertante Music for orchestra*, 1937. His exceptional talents are well displayed in this early work: his sure feeling for form, his absolute mastery of orchestration, his rhythmic subtlety and the powerful dramatic force in his music. Two important themes are stated in the brief introductory bars: a two-bar ostinato for bassoon, and over it a cantilena for horn. The allegro is built on a bitonal main theme, and in the middle section the ostinato is introduced in the violas and also an extended version of the cantilena which builds up enormously and leads to the reprise of the allegro, in its thematic inversion. The work is crowned with a long extension of the cantilena melody in the violins and woodwind against the characteristic rhythms of the allegro intoned by the brass. This creates a fascinating effect.

Blacher's orchestral *Variations on a theme of Paganini*, 1947, have achieved considerable popularity. The sixteen sections are to be understood as variations in the broadest sense. The score is a master-piece, and rich in enchanting details. His *Orchester-Ornament*, 1953, is composed with variable metre. Variable metre is a system in-vented by Blacher that has had considerable success. Complexes of bars of different lengths are combined and repeated in such a way that serial formations appear, and metre and rhythm are seen in a new light. This system demands great concentration from the con-ductor, but the flow of the music is such that the audience hardly notices the complexity. The piece hurries on like a *perpetuum mobile*, relieved by a slow interlude and then rushing to its brilliant end in a wild *furioso*. The constantly changing rhythm is breath-takingly exciting to listen to.

Blacher's personality is very well expressed in his piano concertos. The piano *Concerto No. 1*, 1948, is almost romantic in the slow sections. The piano *Concerto No. 2*, 1952, is again composed in variable metre. The slow middle section is reflective and delicate, and the excitable disquiet of the fast movements is fascinating.

WOLFGANG FORTNER, born 1907, earned well-merited praise for his *Violin Concerto*, 1946. This work placed him high on the list of leading German composers. It was one of the best violin concertos to appear for a considerable time; it is full of lively, sparkling ideas and is dazzlingly violinistic at the same time. The slow movement has a dry, sensitive grandeur; it is built on a characteristic ostinato, with a bitonal flavour. The final rondo is brilliant and full of life. The basic character of Fortner's *Symphony*, 1947, is equally lively and affirmative. This work is in classical form and the four movements are terse and economical. Fortner achieves great unity by means of the relationships between his main themes. A trumpet fanfare, for instance, recurs constantly in different guises. The stormy allegro is followed by an adagio that begins reflectively but builds up into passionate feeling. The scherzo uses ostinato basses, and the animated finale excels itself in clever imitations. Fortner's musical language is dissonant, and swings free of tonality. Recently he has moved towards the twelve-note technique.

The twelve-note system has been warmly welcomed by the younger generation of German composers. HANS WERNER HENZE, born 1926, is the strongest personality amongst these, and despite his youth, he has a large number of works to his credit: three symphonies, instrumental concertos and various suites. Henze's style is very much his own, with a high degree of differentiation in the sound, supersensitive particularly in the lyrical passages.

HANS JELINEK, born 1901, is the most notable of Austria's twelve-note composers. His music is powerful and expressive, sometimes almost romantic. A comparison of Jelinek and Henze will show the enormous differences that are possible within the twelve-note system. The main thing, as ever, is the personality behind it, and it is natural that, of the many young composers who seek salvation in Schönberg's system, only a few should ever get beyond an experimental stage. Indeed, the tendency towards experimental music is almost as strong in Germany as it is in France.

CONTEMPORARY MUSIC

by Cornelius Cardew

In the decade 1950 to 1960 three European composers have created a musical revolution that seems likely to have as far-reaching repercussions as did that created by Schönberg and Webern in the second decade of this century. They are the Frenchman PIERRE BOULEZ, born 1924, the German KARLHEINZ STOCKHAUSEN, born 1928, and the Italian LUIGI NONO, born 1926. The starting-point for this revolution was the discovery of Webern as a composer totally different from Schönberg. Webern, they saw, was a composer who exercized the greatest control over the tiniest details of the musical materials he was handling. He recognized that Schönberg had 'invented' a new musical substance, and that this substance demanded new forms, new procedures, and new ways of thinking about music. Boulez, Stockhausen and Nono are often lumped together as our musical avant-garde, but their approaches to these problems and their solutions are widely divergent. All three have written orchestral works, and though these appear only rarely in English concert programmes, I shall examine some of them in detail. I hope in this way to make clear the differences of personality that exist between these composers. If an audience can identify the musical personality of a composer, it will be more ready to receive the experience that only the music itself can communicate.

Boulez wrote two extended cantatas early in his career, and has recently produced a long work for soprano and orchestra called *Pli selon pli*. The first cantata, *Le soleil des eaux*, was written in 1948, and presumably revised for publication in 1959. It is scored for soprano, tenor and bass soloists, mixed chorus (soprano, tenor, bass) and standard orchestra (double winds) with full complement of percussion: xylophone, vibraphone, glockenspiel, chromatic timpani, gong, tamtam, cymbal and harp. The texts are two poems by René Char: *Complainte du lézard amoureux* and *La sorgue (Chanson pour Yvonne)*. The voices are handled with great refinement; there are special notations for spoken language, spoken in pitch—a singing attack decaying into speech, and 'almost sung'. The writing is motivic throughout and the orchestration is reminiscent of the Schönberg of *Erwartung* and the *Five Orchestral Pieces*, with its frequent use of solo strings, and precise indications of modes of attack. Yet one has the impression that all the artifice is employed solely for the purpose of a clear articulation, rather than for mere effect. There is very little sectionalization of the individual orchestral groups, no passages for strings alone, or winds or brass, and very little counterpointing of the sections. It is impossible to hear all the refinements of orchestration, but the resultant *mélange* is vital and exciting.

The first movement, *Complainte du lézard amoureux*, is in the form of a free dialogue between the solo soprano and the orchestra. The soloist's lines are for the most part unaccompanied, and the orchestral interjections are short-winded but extremely concentrated. The second movement opens with a flowing orchestral introduction with the chorus sopranos humming 'like an instrument in the orchestra'. This fluid texture seems like an illustration of the first word of the poem: *Rivière*. But when this word comes, it is shouted by the male voices, and the music is correspondingly *martellato*. The movement now follows the course of the poem without any sizeable orchestral interludes. The interplay of the three soloists and the choral voices is subtle and complex, and the orchestral texture is varied and contrapuntal. The voices sing the final words alone, or rather tenors and basses share them, so that one part is singing the words while the other hums an accompanying line. Against this the sopranos speak: 'et ami des abeilles de l'horizon', and then a measured two-part progression of quavers wanders down through the orchestra from violin harmonics to the bass clarinet, and a low harp *bispigliando* fades into silence.

Boulez' second cantata, *Le visage nuptial*, was written at about the same period. It was published in 1954 but is not yet available to the public. The poems are again by René Char, and the five movements have individual titles: 'Conduite', 'Gravité (L'emmuré)', 'Le visage nuptial', 'Evadné', 'Post Scriptum'. The work is scored for soprano and alto soloists, female chorus and large orchestra.

'Conduite' is built on alternating phrases between the soprano and alto soloists. The second movement—'Gravité'—introduces the difficult quarter-tone intervals that are a feature of the work. The two soloists are juxtaposed with the chorus and the strings, since it was an accepted fact in those days that only strings and voices could execute quarter-tones. In the course of the movement the string band splits up into a multitude of complex lines, each independent of the others. The lines amalgamate into a weird thick, soft texture against which the voices sing their exotic lines; the function of the woodwind is to hold long, sustained notes. The complexity of this texture is set off by two crotales—tiny solid cymbals that give out a high bell-like note—that play constantly throughout the movement. At one point the orchestra and voices break off and after a general pause the high crotale plays two notes *pianissimo*; there is another short pause and then the voices burst out *fff*, 'j'ai pensé de tout mon désir'. After this it is the chorus' turn to divide into numerous parts, and the held notes pass from woodwind to strings. These long, held notes are a strong characteristic of the work as a whole; they are like the music's subconscious: the music progresses and seems to take no notice of them, and yet they colour and influence the musical events irrevocably. There is a static quality of uneasiness about this movement that prepares the way admirably for the central piece of the cantata, the 'Visage nuptial' itself.

This central section is marked *rapide*, and the vocal style is declamatory, with all the voices singing—or speaking—together. Here, the scoring is much more 'orchestral' in the impressionistic sense; the long-held notes have been converted into trills and at the climaxes the full orchestra plays as one body. The percussion section, which is subdivided into skin instruments, metal instruments, and wooden instruments, becomes more and more important as the movement progresses. A big build-up starts when the tempo reverts to *lent*, and bongos, maraccas and metal blocks play incessant and irregular rhythms while the long-held notes build up obsessively. This reaches a climax, and thereafter the music moves through various juxtapositions of the established textures. The effect of this colossal movement is hypnotic. The sound seems to

acquire a scale, a size, that makes of it an autonomous organism.
It envelops the listener, as if it were an element, like water or fire.
It is my experience that the faculties of appreciation, critical judgement and so forth, are submerged when the sound reaches this level.
The will seems embodied in the sound, and one loses all *concepts* of
form in experiencing its actual evolution. In this situation it is
immaterial what exactly the singers are singing about, for instance;
it is sufficient that the words gave rise to this enormous creature of
sound.

The fourth movement—'Evadné'—is a lyrical, spoken statement
of the poem by the female chorus. Here, the words are the most
important factor. Except for brief outbursts the music is restrained,
though as always extremely complex and refined. Boulez indicates
that the sonority of the spoken words should be on a different plane
from the orchestral sound. The sensuous, recollective quality of the
poem is summed up in the final words: 'La terre nous aimait un
peu, je me souviens.' The 'Post Scriptum' is marked *très lent* and is
scored for soloists, chorus, percussion and strings alone. Quarter-

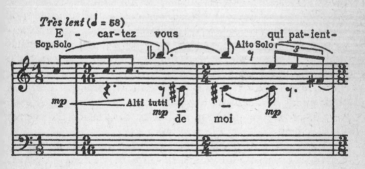

tones are again exploited throughout. The voices start, and then twelve 'cellos and eight basses enter as accompaniment; each instrumentalist has his own complex part. After a short choral interlude accompanied by percussion, the violins take over the accompaniment divided into thirty individual parts. A second interlude with percussion leads to a passage with fourteen violas accompanying. A bar of silence, and then the soprano and alto soloists sing quarter-tone melodic lines accompanied by a string orchestra of twenty-four solo parts, all muted. The complexity of the writing for strings can hardly have been equalled before or since. Not only do they have to intone quarter-tones, they have to enter at complex rhythmic points, and with constant changes between *col legno*, *pizzicato*, rebounding *pizzicato*, *sul tasto*, harmonics, *spiccato*, and a host of other possible modes of articulation.

Again, the correspondence between the complexity of the score and the acoustical differentiation is debatable; what is achieved is an unparalleled organic vitality within the mass of sound, and a convincing *impression* of enormous sensitivity and refinement. Boulez is consciously forging ahead in the tradition of Debussy in his treatment of sound, and he is probably the only musician with an orchestral genius equal to the task. His complexity is not systematic, as can be objected to certain complexities in Stockhausen and Nono, and even Webern and Messiaen; the musician's hand is observable in every nuance.

The revolution we are examining is a very different sort of revolution from that which took place in the early years of this century. Here there is no trace of commentary on the tradition that is being supplanted, or enlarged. There is no explicit or ironic reaction against the foregoing, perhaps because there was very little to react against. Stravinsky and Schönberg had been in America since the early 'thirties and nobody in Europe had time to write music during the war. Webern was working, but very few people had access to his work. Only after his death in 1945 was there an increase of interest in Webern's work.

Two important organizations were inaugurated after the war: the summer school for new music at Darmstadt, organized by Wolfgang Steinecke for the purpose of propagating in Germany the music that the Nazi movement had suppressed, notably Schönberg's and Webern's, since theirs seemed to symbolize a spirit of research and experiment which it was wrong to suppress. This institution soon attracted a swarm of young composers from all

over the world, and these came there every year to exchange ideas.
Darmstadt became a sort of international new music 'bazaar'. The
other organization was more exclusive—a series of concerts in Paris
called the *Domaine Musical*. Boulez was the musical director of these
concerts and designed his programmes around the work of Webern
(Schönberg he criticized for his adherence to classical forms after
inventing a system which was equivalent to a new medium, and
which therefore established its own formal conditions. Boulez'
article 'Schönberg is dead' temporarily estranged the older generation of contemporary musicians), Messiaen (his teacher), himself
and his friends, Stockhausen and Nono. Boulez alone was responsible for the choice of the programmes, and he directed his efforts
towards producing an environment that would benefit the music.
That is, he tried to achieve some homogeneity in the programmes,
so that, for instance, the brevity of Webern's *Orchestral Pieces*,
opus 10, should not render them totally incomprehensible, but that
the listener should in some way be already in Webern's world when
the music began. The obvious way to do this is to precede the work
by another of Webern's, say the string orchestra version of the
Five Pieces for string quartet, opus 5, which are more direct and gripping in their effect. However, this sort of consistent programme
design is rare, and many concert organizers believe that a variety of
styles in the same programme is beneficial. Notable examples of
this attitude are Stravinsky in his 'Evenings on the roof' concerts in
Los Angeles, and the 'Thursday concerts' at the BBC. There is
much to be said on both sides, and when one considers the hazard-
ous and incalculable quality of 'being in the right mood to listen
to a certain piece of music', the discussion seems irrelevant. Sooner
or later, a piece of music has to stand on its own; it has to create its
own imaginative world and sustain it unaided.

Anyone who has enjoyed a Mahler symphony will known the
feeling of settling into his musical world in the first few minutes,
of getting acclimatized. Similar considerations may have led Boulez
and Stockhausen to write their lengthier works. If the listener
knows that the work will last for half the concert, he will take more
trouble to get acclimatized and reflect perhaps that if he wishes
to understand the world of this music at least he has ample time to
do so. Boulez' *Poésie pour pouvoir* for electronic sound and orchestra
lasted forty-five minutes (it was said to be incomplete: Boulez'
works are generally in a state of flux, either they are appearing in
a new edition, or being withdrawn, or added to, or revised) and

the instrumentalists and equipment took up so much space in the hall at Donaueschingen that only four hundred people could hear it at a time. Consequently it was decided to play it three times, each time with a different audience. Stockhausen was impressed with this procedure and envisaged continuous programmes of electronic music like cinema shows, where people could come in at any time, sit down and listen for an hour and a half, and then, if they were astute enough to recognize it, 'this is where we came in' and they would leave. This idea ties in with his conception of his recent pieces as part of a 'Process', which contains itself as it were in each moment, and is thus just as comprehensible from moment to moment as it is as a whole. Another idea of Stockhausen's—this one decidedly influenced by John Cage—was that the concert hall should be like a gaming room. The prospective listener comes in and there are little groups of musicians sitting around engaged in various musical activities. One group might stop and go out for a meal, or a conductor might step up and conduct some of the musicians, or some people, apparently audience, might get up and join in. From each fragment, supposedly, one could get the *impression* of a coherent process, which of course need never end.

Boulez' longest work to date is a collection of his three *Improvisations sur Mallarmé* for soprano and various instruments, preceded by an introduction 'Don' and followed by a postlude 'Tombeau'. The whole bears the title *Pli selon pli—portrait of Mallarmé for soprano and orchestra*. In its present form it lasts a good hour. There is a gap of at least ten years between this piece and the cantatas we have already discussed, and Boulez has gained enormously in assurance. There is a certain flamboyance in the easy way he combines works that were written separately and for separate purposes. At the time of writing this (1962) only the first two improvisations have appeared in print.

The first improvisation is a setting of Mallarmé's poem 'La vierge, le vivace et le bel aujourd'hui', scored for soprano, harp, vibraphone, tubular bells and four percussion players. The vocal lines are reminiscent, not so much of Webern as they were in the

earlier cantatas, but of Messiaen, with their oscillation between and
around certain recurrent pitches and their curious kicking grace-
note rhythms. In character, the music is really improvisatory; one
feels that Boulez is exploring the possibilities of a specific set of
sounds or pitches. But the nuances of scoring are carefully controlled, and the score is a model of notational accuracy. The same
is true of the second improvisation, 'Une dentelle s'abolit', although
this piece is much freer in style and the musicians are actually free
on occasion to place their phrases where they wish within defined
time-limits. Piano and celesta are added to the ensemble, and the
characteristic sound of this piece is cloudy and lush. A novel feature
of the vocal line is the occurrence of long phrases of equal-length
notes all to be executed in one breath. According to how the in-

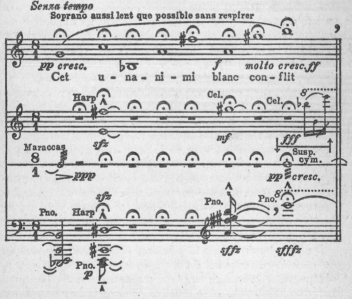

dividual singer times her notes, the other musicians have to follow
suit, and insert their accompaniments appropriately. This sort of
smooth, long-winded vocal technique forms a strong contrast with
the gracious hiccoughs of Boulez' usual vocal style. The two styles
have a highly salutory influence on each other in the later stages of
this second improvisation, particularly at the words 'tristement

dort une mendore' where the over-sophisticated grace-notes are omitted, but without sacrifice of rhythmic profile.

The third improvisation is a setting of 'A la nue accablante tu' scored for a remarkable orchestra: three flutes and also flute, trombone, two xylophones (played by four players! it is a shocking effect when this double xylophone duet sets up its clatter), glockenspiel, tubular bells, percussion, three harps (two of them tuned a quarter-tone flat and sharp respectively), mandolins, guitar, five 'cellos and three basses. For the purposes of *Pli selon pli* Boulez also orchestrated the first improvisation, again for a curious combination including two saxophones, four horns, a high F trumpet, eight violas and six basses. This time the three harps take the stage for a full performance. This is quite something to behold, and lends an air of resplendence to live performances of this work. Stockhausen shares Boulez' enthusiasm for flamboyant presentation: his *Momente* requires a Chinese gong measuring eight feet in diameter. In front of this he enthrones—six feet off the ground—his full-bodied vocal soloist, with the ranks of chorus disposed at her feet.

Boulez has certainly been influenced by the ideas set out in Mallarmé's celebrated *livre*, witness the interchangeability of the movements in his third piano sonata, and the idea of an unending skeleton of a work that can be amplified at various points, or not. He is a composer who is generally susceptible to literary inspiration, without ever becoming the slave of a system of concepts. He sometimes describes his music as a labyrinth, with many possible courses open to the interpreter, amongst which he must choose. He is also fond of the stock-piling image in Kafka's *Der Bau* (The Burrow), where the animal is constantly shifting and redistributing his resources. Boulez is never seduced by such affinities, but they are illuminating for anyone interested in understanding the origin of his music and the way it works. He is, rather, an instinctive musician; he has a great, inborn musical talent which earned him high honours in harmony and counterpoint at the Paris Conservatoire. Now he has reached the point where he is the complete master of his style, he can control it perfectly; his audience has simply to wait and see what he will do with it.

Karlheinz Stockhausen is less settled, and more receptive to direct influences, in particular that of John Cage. The latter has had little or no influence, however, on Stockhausen's two big orchestral works, *Gruppen* for three orchestras, and *Carré* for four orchestras. To understand the origin and technique of these pieces, it is perhaps useful to make a brief survey of certain facets of electronic music.

A studio for electronic music was fitted out in Cologne in the late 'forties by Dr Herbert Eimert. The line of investigation was the development and extension of electronic musical instruments like the trautonium, the inventor of which was also working on the project. Stockhausen, together with Boulez, had been studying with Messiaen in Paris for a year. Among other things he had acquired from Messiaen an interest in the question of duration as opposed to rhythm. That is, instead of having a regular pulse which could be subdivided in a variety of ways, Messiaen had begun to construct the rhythmic element in his music out of smallest units, say demisemiquavers, strung together to form 'durations' of two, three, four, five or more demisemiquavers. The Hindu rhythms that Messiaen had been concerned with could also be notated with these quantitative rhythmic configurations. In his *Modes de valeur et d'intensité*, a piano piece, Messiaen used both his durations and his dynamic values ('intensities', that is, *pp*, *p*, *f*, *ff*, and so on) in much the same way as serial composers (as composers in the twelve-note system had come to be called) used their series of notes. I conjecture that Stockhausen—just as he may well have seen Webern's music as breaking down the melodic and harmonic elements in music to their atomic components, and discovering in the process that they were one and the same substance—saw Messiaen's experiment as leading to a similar discovery of the atomic components of rhythm. The concurrent experiments in Musique Concrète in Paris—which must not be confused with electronic music since it deals with the electronic manipulation of actual 'concrete' sounds, and not with the electronic construction of sound—may have contributed towards awakening in Stockhausen an interest in the atomic components of tone-colour or timbre, namely the individual sinus-

432   CONTEMPORARY MUSIC

tones that, heaped up in a variety of different configurations and
relative intensities, go to make up the instrumental timbres that we
identify as flute, clarinet, piano and so on.

The fact that one can generate pure sinus-tones electronically
and combine them in any way one likes almost inevitably gives the
impression that there are unlimited numbers of new timbres to be
constructed, in fact that one can construct a timbre for each note
in a piece, compositionally. The first electronic pieces were constructed out of fragments of tape, spliced together and superimposed. Recorded on the fragments of tape were the required
'sounds' or mixtures of sinus-tones. Two other sound sources besides the sinus-tone were quickly enlisted: the electrical 'impulse',
a click of no particular pitch, in fact a random oscillation over the
whole pitch range, and 'white noise', again a random oscillation
over the whole pitch range, but continuous. These sounds could be
filtered to give individual pitches or areas of pitch with a 'noise
quality'. Strips of tape material constructed from these elements
could be transformed electronically with filters, frequency boosts,
reverberation chambers, and ring-modulators (machines that give
the combination and difference tones of the material on tape). Both
Stockhausen and Gottfried Michael König achieved musical results
with this type of work, and Stockhausen decided to take a final
course of study with Werner Meyer-Eppler, the late authority on
acoustics, communications, and information theory in Bonn.

In his *Gesang der Jünglinge*, 1956, Stockhausen recorded a boy's
voice singing part of the text of the Benedicite and used it in combination with electronic sounds. This piece introduces a second
phase in electronic music, because in it Stockhausen was already
leaving behind the concept of the absolute compositional control
of the tiniest components of duration and timbre, and turning his
attention to random textures of electronic sound, irregular flocks
of impulses heaped together and controlled statistically, and so
forth. One can view this tendency as the externalization of the
internal features of white noise and filter processes. Instead of working in the studio for a solid month splicing together a complex texture of white noise lasting, say, three seconds, a loop of tape with
white noise on it would be ring-modulated with the impulse gener-
ators and put through a variable filter. A second loop of the required
duration would be set in motion, and with one hand on the controls
of the impulse generator and the other on the variable filter, the
composer could superimpose as many as twenty or thirty different

sequences of impulses by moving the controls at random, or as desired. The result would be recognizable by its group features instead of by its individual pitches; a particular group might comprise a flock of impulses moving down two octaves in pitch over five seconds, and getting denser and denser on the way down.

It was soon after electronic music had reached this stage that Stockhausen wrote his first important orchestral work, *Gruppen* (Groups), for three orchestras. Each orchestra comprises about thirty musicians, with woodwind, brass and strings represented in the usual proportions, and a large percussion section added. The three orchestras are placed on three sides of the audience, which is thus all but enclosed in the sound, with its back to the wall. The work was first performed in Cologne in 1958 with the composer, Boulez and Bruno Maderna conducting. The critics responded for the most part with invective, but the audience was enthusiastic; many must have felt that this was the most exciting and invigorating thing they had ever experienced in the concert hall, though perhaps not the most moving or profound. One musician of note found it the 'greatest orchestral experience since the première of the *Rite of Spring*'. This time, however, no rotten eggs were thrown at the performers.

The work, which lasts twenty minutes, consists of six passages where the three orchestras are counterpointed, and play short groups in different tempi that overlap. Interspersed between these passages are five sections that handle the orchestra as a whole. The same chord is thrown from one orchestra to another like a ball, or all six trumpets and later the trombones play a spiky counterpoint that rains in on the audience from three sides, or the three percussion sections start a battle, or again the strings send up trembling clouds that swing to and fro hovering between the orchestras and then suddenly move with decision into one or the other. It is in these sections that the main climaxes of the work occur, but the musical content resides now quiet, delicate, now vicious and energetic in the 'group' passages. Not only does each little group have its own tempo, while the other orchestras are playing different tempi, but within each group there is a fine interplay of different rhythms. Some of the groups have a limited pitch range, say a major tenth, and the effect of so many instruments subdividing the beat in septuplet, quintuplet, semiquaver, demisemiquaver and triplet figurations all at the same time, with occasionally some note or chord singing out, is very beautiful at times, even when rude interruptions are shouted in your left ear while your right is trying to appreciate the subtleties of the orchestra on that side.

The subdivision of the orchestra into three spatial units was an expedient here, intended to facilitate the appreciation of music in several strata simultaneously. The idea of sounds moving around in space was exploited only as an afterthought in the interspersed sections. The expression 'music in space' caught on quickly, however, and was soon circulating independently. It found its way back into electronic music, and the four-track tape-recorder came into general use, and in concerts of electronic music the audience was completely surrounded by loudspeakers with sounds whiffling round at an alarming rate, now one way, now the other. Not content, as were the composers of earlier times, with wringing our hearts, bringing tears to our eyes, and generally playing havoc with our emotions, Stockhausen (perhaps even by-passing this sort of musical reality altogether) now set about playing havoc with our ordinary orientation in space. His next big orchestral work, *Carré*, for four orchestras, four choruses and four conductors, surrounds the audience completely, and at certain points the sounds begin to circulate, sometimes at an alarming speed. At the première in Hamburg the audience did not fall out of their seats, however. Nor did they experience feelings of nausea or bleed at nails and ears as one always imagined the first astronauts would. As 'music in space' it was an anticlimax. In fact, the piece took effect at something much nearer the conventional level than Stockhausen had achieved in his earlier pieces. Chiefly, perhaps, because of the clear presentation of the harmonic aspect, the piece had something like the emotional impact that one associates with great music, whereas *Gruppen* could easily be misunderstood as an experience similar to a firework display.

Each orchestra in *Carré* comprises four woodwind, four brass, eight strings (no basses), eight voices (four-part) and two percussionists; the work lasts thirty-five minutes. One fundamental idea of this piece is that the music should be static, at rest, but stirring with inner life. The work opens with a long low E-flat sung by the basses. It is heard first in the third orchestra; after a time it moves to the second orchestra, and then to the first, without perceptible breaks. Although there are agitated passages, most of the time one listens to long held chords, which then, suddenly or imperceptibly, alter. Some organic change takes place; one or other of the notes slides up in pitch, swells dynamically, or is taken over by another

instrument. Banal though a chord may sound when it is first introduced, the slow insistence of the musical treatment breathes
significance into it. At other points a chord will suddenly dissolve
into impalpable complexes of harmonics or flickering figurations.
The overall form of the piece corresponds to this type of structure.
As the piece progresses it gets larger; it builds up in volume, and
in the scope of its ideas. It becomes more complex and yet more
sure-footed as it steadily walks on toward the end; in some Proustian
sense, it expands as it acquires a past. The obviously spatial sections
are like diversions in this grand progress. Little eddies of sound
played by all the instruments or by individual groups float round
the hall, accelerate, slow down, change direction, get sent off on a
new tack by some sudden percussive attack. As in *Gruppen*, the big
climaxes occur in these diversions, but the most lasting impression
is made by the slow progress of the harmony, the gradual metamorphosis of one chord to another. When he had sketched the layout
of the whole piece, Stockhausen delegated the actual writing of it
to another composer.

Seeking a line of demarcation between Boulez and Stockhausen
we stumble on the fact that Boulez always uses a text, furthermore
a poetic text, however firmly the musical ideas come later to stand
on their own. With the possibly allowable exception of his fragmented version of the Benedicite in *Gesang der Jünglinge*, Stockhausen has never used words as a means to holding his music
together. In *Carré* the choruses sing nonsense syllables notated in
phonetic script, and in *Momente* the singers look and sound as
though they had something to say, but actually they have not.
Luigi Nono is a composer who relies to a large extent on words for
the continuity of his music, and the texts he uses are very significant.
However, his *Incontri* is one important exception.

Incontri was written in response to a commission from the South-
west German radio in 1955, when the composer already had several
important works behind him. The extraordinary attacking quality
of this little work—it lasts only six and a half minutes—placed him
firmly on the map of European music as a unique, forceful and
unmistakable personality. It acted as a curtain-raiser on his career.
The work is scored for double wind quintet, trombone, trumpet,
timpani and double string quintet, a standard small orchestra. It
consists, to use traditional terms, simply of an exposition and a
recapitulation. However, there is considerable difficulty in the way

of appreciating it like this, for the recapitulation runs backwards, completely backwards, and there is no break to indicate where it begins. The piece has often been criticized (most often by composers, it must be admitted) for presenting such a mechanically symmetrical picture, but this I consider unfounded, for musically it sounds very different backwards. For instance, the end of each note is now its beginning, and consequently a very different rhythmic pattern emerges in the retrograde version. However, certain features of the repetition are clearly recognizable and the listener can hear a ternary A–B–A form, with fast, loud repeated notes sticking out at the beginning and end, with a high, dissonant passage for flute, piccolo and string harmonics as a B section. It is

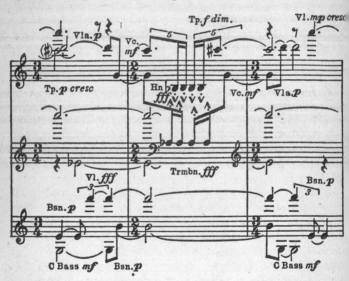

in this passage that the change of direction occurs—a brusque reminder of the opening. The general impression of the piece is that its composer is a very strong, almost wilful personality with a taste and technique for hard, earsplitting sound.

The sterling qualities of *Incontri* recall the early works of the solitary genius EDGAR VARESE, born 1885, contemporary of Stravinsky and Schönberg. Varèse, a Frenchman, lived in New York in the 'twenties, and the performances of his works *Intégrales* for chamber orchestra, and *Ionisation* for percussion must have formed a strange contrast to the high jinks of the famous Jazz Age. *Intégrales* in particular is extremely harsh and shrill, exploiting the extreme registers of the wind and brass instruments employed. Rhythmically ('motorically') the work is equally tough, and the obsessive repetition of hard, concise phrases gives the music its unforgettable quality. Varèse wrote a few works for large orchestra, such as *Amériques* and *Arcana*, but they are rarely played. Around 1930 he decided that music could progress no further except electronically, and since no electronic equipment was available he stopped composing. Recently, electronic sound equipment has been put at his disposal and he has started composing again. His *Déserts* for tape and orchestra is rather a disappointment after the early works. A certain tensity of aural imagination seems to be lost. However, the early works stand with the permanence of a Stonehenge as testimony to the greatness of his imagination. Varèse invented no new theories or musical techniques, he simply 'heard' a music that was completely new, primitive and overwhelming in its effect.

Nono too is gifted with a unique and accurate aural imagination; his music is also characterized by a grand simplicity of line. The mechanical formulae of serialism that he uses in his compositions seem rigid and uninteresting, but the accuracy of his aural judgement combined with his humanistic commitments give his music an emotional attack that makes technical considerations seem out of place.

Il Canto Sospeso (suspended song) was commissioned by the West German radio in 1956. Of the nine movements, numbers one, four, and eight are purely instrumental; the rest are settings of fragments of letters written by European resistance fighters condemned to death during the Second World War. The texts are taken from a book of such letters published in Germany in 1954 under the title *The flame shall never singe you*, with a foreword by Thomas Mann, in which he remarks that these international Resistance fighters were not only resisting the Nazi rape of their countries, but fighting for a better human society, for ideals.

The work is scored for soprano, alto and tenor soloists, mixed chorus and a large orchestra that includes six horns, five trumpets, and a large percussion section. The opening movement consists of eight large orchestral phrases that expand from a point of rest like a vibrating string, swell up and fall back to a new point of rest, from which the next phrase takes its departure.

The second movement for *a cappella* chorus follows without a break. The words are from a letter by a Bulgarian teacher and journalist: 'I die for a world of such light and beauty that my sacrifice is as nothing. Millions have died for this world in the war. I die for justice. Our ideas will triumph.' The words are treated in a fragmentary fashion and are rarely audible, but the symbolic impact of the human voices singing alone is difficult to miss. The third movement is scored for the three soloists and orchestra. Three fragments of text are used here, fragments of letters from three Greek students aged fourteen, nineteen and twenty-two. Musically, this movement is more clearly defined, and the words are set in a more linear style, as opposed to the ecstatic penetration of the text by means of clouded fragments of words in the second movement. Number four starts with trembling *pianissimo* notes for wind and percussion, with the strings gradually building up a chromatic cluster of harmonics. The music builds up to *fortissimo* and dies away again as it began. A short pause precedes the fifth movement, for tenor solo and orchestra. The texture of this movement is almost Webernian, and the juxtaposition of the two harps with a reiterated four-note

figure like a refrain creates a lyrical atmosphere. The soloist sings
an expressive line that is also reminiscent of Webern; the words
were written by a fourteen-year-old Polish farm boy: 'If the sky
were paper and the sea ink, I could not set down the horrors that I
see around me. I say farewell to all, and weep...' This amazing
lyricism is well represented in the music, which seems to skate over
dangerous depths of intensity.

'The doors open, and there stand our murderers, dressed in black.
They drive us out of the Synagogue. How hard it is to say goodbye to such a beautiful life, for ever.' These are the words of number six, and the music is correspondingly black and dramatic. The
chorus starts on a unison E-flat with irregular rhythmic entries, and
then divide gradually and chromatically. The music never rises
above the G above middle C, and the accompaniment uses only
the low instruments of the orchestra. A second section starts at the
words 'How hard it is...' This is lighter and softer; the voices
hum, and the accompaniment is scored for strings and one trumpet. The seventh movement is scored for soprano solo, female
chorus, a reduced body of strings with flute, celesta, glockenspiel,
marimba and harp.

'Farewell, mother. Your daughter Ljubka is going down into
the damp earth.' Nono lets the voice and instruments speak for
themselves, and they do so eloquently and movingly. The following movement shatters the mood of transfiguration; it is scored
chiefly for brass, and features the rude repeated notes familiar from
Incontri. In the final movement, scored for chorus and timpani, the
use of the drums is extremely restrained; their occasional short
thunder lends an impressive perspective to the text, which tells of
firmness in the face of death, and faith in the sense of dying.

Varianti for solo violin, strings and three each of flutes and clarinets is dedicated to Rudolf Kolisch. It was written in 1957. The formal simplicity of Nono's music allows of very cloudy and blurred effects in the material itself. Here he exploits the effect of several instruments, say five violas, playing the same notes, but entering and leaving off at different points. The rhythmic profile is thus extremely blurred, while the pitches remain distinct. In Nono's next piece the procedure is reversed: *Coro di Didone*, 1958, is a setting of poems by Giuseppe Ungaretti for mixed chorus (eight each of sopranos, altos, tenors and basses) and a percussion section comprising eight suspended cymbals, four tamtams and bells. Here, it is often the pitch that becomes blurred; the singers sing sometimes in chromatic clusters, and the accompaniment of suspended cymbals increases the element of indistinct pitch. This music is very evocative, almost impressionistic, especially the final section with its incantatory reiterations of 'il mare, il mare'.

Nono wrote his opera *Intoleranza*, 1960, at a time when theatrical music, or musical theatre, was very much in the air. Several composers were writing pieces where the music did not stand on its own, but 'had to be seen to be believed'. MAURICIO KAGEL (born 1932) indicates several possible procedures for the beginning of his work for orchestra, *Heterophonie*. The piece proper is preceded by a section headed 'Accordez Messieurs!' in which the oboe plays an A-sharp and all the instruments join in with odd phrases at random centred on A-sharp. It sounds just like an orchestra tuning up! The players are then instructed to practise their parts. In the middle of this chaos the conductor starts to beat time, and gradually the music sorts itself out and the piece is under way. Stockhausen's *Momente* is more explicitly theatrical, with the enormous gong and a singer enthroned in front of it—at first glance it might almost be an oriental night-club entertainment. The music itself begins on a very theatrical note: as the audience applause is dying away, the conductor signals to the chorus and they begin clapping. This engages the audience in a fresh outburst of applause, now mingled with annoyance or hilarity. It takes some time for the music to get going. Stockhausen also wrote a piece specifically for the theatre. The title was *Original* and a number of local practising artists took part in the performance: paintings were painted, actors acted, happenings happened, even the composer's little son had a rôle. Such experiments as these would have been unthinkable without the influence of John Cage.

JOHN CAGE was born in 1912. He studied with Schönberg for a time, but the composer who caught his imagination was Henry Cowell. Cage's adventurous spirit took over where Cowell left off: Cowell had written pieces to be played inside the piano, and pieces with extensive use of clusters; Cage wrote pieces where the lid of the piano is slammed shut, and the strings are prepared with screws, rubbers, toys and other objects. The invention and development of the prepared piano in the 'thirties and 'forties was an important phase in Cage's career. He had written extensively for percussion instruments of all kinds, and the prepared piano was like a small percussion band in the hands of one player. Cage's early music for prepared piano was rhythmic and 'motoric' in character, and he wrote a concerto for a piano literally bursting with preparations. Later he discovered that it was possible to prepare the piano manually in the course of performance, and the amount of previous preparation began to diminish. By the time he wrote his *Concert for piano and instruments*, in 1958, he had come to take a total view of

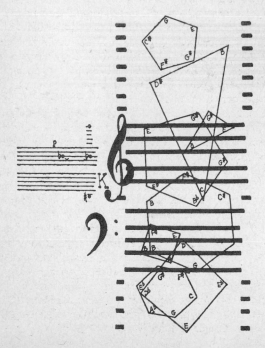

the piano as a resonant body with which one could do *anything*. His writing at this time left a lot to be decided by the interpreter on the basis of enigmatic musical notations. The accompanying orchestra for this later piano concerto often sounds enormous, but consists actually of a small number of players, generally between five and twelve. Besides his own instrument, each player can have a number of subsidiary percussion instruments or common objects for making noises. Each musician has an independent part, and Cage does not specify any points in common for the players; in other words there is no full score. The conductor stands in front of the players and moves his arms like the second hand of a clock, in a circle. The conductor is, in fact, a clock, but one that changes speed, and the musicians arrange their parts according to the temporal fluctuations of this clock. The pianist has a more complex part than the other musicians, and plays independently of the conductor. The calm, serene behaviour of the conductor contrasts strangely with the wild, primitive sounds that fill the air when his hand begins to move. Generally, the music is full of hard, percussive sounds, and wandering microtonal *glissando*, and is often evocative of the howls and screeches of a tropical jungle, or the car horns of modern city life. For Cage, this is all in order; if people were able to hear the music in the sounds of daily life they would no longer need to go to concerts, and Cage's work would be over.

Since this piano concerto, Cage has written a further orchestral piece called *Atlas Eclipticalis*, 1961. This consists of ninety-six parts for musicians, but not all the parts are necessary for a performance; the piece can be played by any number of musicians up to ninety-six. Each instrument is amplified electronically, and the effect is probably even more hair-raising than that of the piano concerto. Of his specifically theatrical pieces, the titles *Water Music* (for pianist), *Music Walk, Theatre Piece*, and *Water Walk* should be mentioned; these pieces are apt to engage the performers in activities in various parts of the concert hall, and the constant commuting contributes substantially to the theatrical air.

Cage is a great pioneer and adventurer in music, and many composers and others have followed in his wake. The mixture of Cage with the Beat movement has produced a whole series of musical 'happenings' in New York. Composers like TOSHI ICHYANAGI (also an exceptional pianist), GEORGE BRECHT and LAMONTE YOUNG have carried Cage's ideas to extremes of absurdity, which can be both amusing and disturbing. LaMonte Young has a real

talent for sensation, and his pieces have a unique atmosphere. To
date, he has not written for anything so organized as an orchestra,
but it is conceivable that he will find a way of doing so.

Outside this movement, which, though it originated in Cage,
continues to flourish rather in spite of him, are three composers
who studied with Cage and then branched off on paths that were
very much their own. EARLE BROWN worked with Cage on
experiments in electronic music in the late 'forties, and since then
has worked as a recording engineer for a record company in New
York. He is a musician of outstanding ability, and his recent
orchestral piece, *Available Forms*, has attracted attention in Europe.
This piece gives the conductor an active rôle in the creation of the
musical form; he can vary and control the order of sections, and
often mould the actual sound—and radically—in the course of the
performance.

CHRISTIAN WOLFF, the youngest of this trio of composers,
has concentrated on the smaller forms so far, and has written a
considerable amount of chamber music. In a sense, Wolff is an
amateur of music; he is intent on an academic career.

MORTON FELDMAN is also an amateur, and his music avoids
the complexity and labour that characterizes the full-time modern
composer. As a result of the Second World War Cage is said to
have resolved to write only quiet music thenceforth. Feldman
seems to have taken this very much to heart; a great deal of his
chamber music is so soft as to be audible only with an effort on the
part of the listener. The orchestral work that I have in front of me
is also 'very soft throughout'. Its title is *Structures for Orchestra*,
1960, and the score is written in a perfectly straightforward manner.
In the latter half of the pieces there are solo passages for horn and
alto flute. Two isolated three-note harp phrases separated by an
orchestral chord, that occur soon after the horn solo, reappear at
the end, separated by the long pauses so beloved of Feldman. The
progress of the music is steady and solemn, and the chords have an

enigmatic and yet persistent, searching quality that forms a strange counterpart to the wild, battling insistence of Varèse's music. Both composers are in a sense trying to penetrate—to see through—the tangling predicament of contemporary music, and move towards some new simplicity and clarity, whether harsh or sweet.

Meanwhile Messiaen and particularly Stravinsky add to their past achievements. Messiaen has become rather isolated, and his recent pieces seem more like catalogues of birdsong. *Oiseaux Exotiques* has an extended preface giving a list of sources, including details of plumage, colouring, habits and so forth. This work was written in response to a commission from Boulez in 1955. It is scored for piano and chamber orchestra with percussion. The piano writing is extremely brilliant and the instrumentation is hard and virtuosic.

Although Stravinsky must have discovered Webern before writing his ballet music *Agon* in 1954 to 1957, this piece does not betray his fascination. *Agon* is a tight progression of short sections, each one fresh and delightful in sound. The orchestra is used like a cabinet; drawers with different combinations of instruments are pulled out, rather like the stops of an organ. The full orchestra is never used. Stravinsky has said that of the composers working now, Boulez is the one that interests him most. It is remarkable that Boulez used a similar procedure of instrumentation in his chamber work *Le marteau sans maître*. Here also, each movement is characterized by its own particular 'sound' or combination of instruments.

Stravinsky's *Movements* for piano and orchestra, 1959, is relatively difficult to grasp. The style is miniature, brittle and complex, and the work is Stravinsky's closest approach to the 'pointillist' style of early Boulez and Stockhausen.

A sermon, a narrative, and a prayer, 1961, shows Webern's influence clearly. The second movement, which tells the story of the stoning of St Stephen from the Acts of the Apostles, is again built up in brief, tight sections; it is evidence of Stravinsky's mastery that the dramatic flow of the story does not suffer from this. The movement is full of masterstrokes, but its greatness comes from the fact that the music is entirely an interpretation of the story. It is as though Stravinsky were simply putting his understanding of the drama at the service of his audience. Such humility is a true measure of Stravinsky's stature.

Recently a school of thought has emerged that may perhaps be seen as a counterpart to the futurist composers of Italy in the early years of this century, whose fate has been total obscurity. It is possible that these composers envisage a synthesis of Boulez' orchestral genius, Nono's simplicity of form and Stockhausen's schematicism. The names that have attracted attention so far are GYORGY LIGETI, a Hungarian whose *Articulation* is probably the liveliest piece of electronic music to date (and liveliness is no mean achievement in electronic music), FRIEDRICH CERHA in Vienna, and PENDERECKI in Warsaw. These composers have an uncanny gift for weird orchestration and extraordinary atmosphere, but the music seems to me essentially unsophisticated; the composers are engineers of sound, building enormous, gleaming, twilight machines without function. Nevertheless, some of this music has that trance quality, characteristic of the best science fiction, that makes us ask, with hope and dread in our hearts (assailed by a strange nostalgia for the future), 'Will my generation live to see it?' We had best enjoy the nostalgia, for the generation that does see it will in all probability think nothing of it.

I have an uneasy feeling that although its unreality does not debar this music from arousing interest, it does debar it from possessing permanent validity. Stockhausen, Boulez and Nono on the other hand, each speaking with his own voice, have between them created a coherent contemporary language that is solid and real. 'Coherent' in this context means that the language will be comprehensible in as much of perpetuity as we can envisage; 'contemporary' means that it is capable of presenting a true reflection of the world at this juncture.

Appendix A

THE ORCHESTRA AND ITS INSTRUMENTS

Over the centuries the symphony orchestra has had to undergo a number of changes and reformations before emerging in the shape we know today. And the orchestra, being one of the main media of music, will presumably be able to sustain all further changes, corresponding to the continual developments of the music itself.

The extraordinary size of the modern orchestra was unknown in baroque times. For us, the purely orchestral works of Bach and

Handel, their suites and concertos, seem to have been conceived simply as chamber music, to be played by a small orchestra. The harpsichord, playing the figured bass, was used as a harmonic support for the single strings and wind. A larger orchestra was quite exceptional, as, for instance, in Handel's *Water Music*, where not only the strings but the oboes too were used 'chorally' (that is, in groups) and, with the addition of flutes, horns and trumpets, the orchestra amounted to something over fifty players. But even for his oratorios Handel used a relatively small orchestra. The chorus was also extremely weak by modern standards: Handel had only eight singers to a part, but they were mostly trained, professional singers. In the larger performances he arranged when he was at the peak of his fame Handel probably augmented the orchestra considerably to balance the larger chorus. In cases where the performance was in church the increased forces were supported by an organ.

Even in classical times the orchestra was very thin, and retained the character of chamber music. The individual groups were more clearly differentiated; besides the strings, there were oboes and bassoons, and later horns and trumpets began to be used fairly regularly. The harpsichord (hitherto the indispensable harmony instrument) lapsed and in its place we find flutes, and then clarinets, used as regular orchestral instruments. Add the timpani, and the trombones, and we have assembled Beethoven's orchestra in its entirety.

In the romantic era, Berlioz introduced further extensions of the classical orchestra. Cor anglais, bass clarinet and double bassoon were accepted as permanent members of the orchestra. The harp was generally adopted; the percussion section was considerably extended; Wagner introduced the tubas. The multiplication of the strings followed naturally on the heels of this large extension of the wind groups. Then the high romantic period brought with it an exaggeration of all this; Richard Strauss' *Festive Prelude*, for example, is scored for the following gigantic orchestra: five each of flutes, oboes, clarinets and bassoons, eight horns, ten trumpets, four trombones and bass tuba; eight timpani, percussion and organ; twenty each of first and second violins, twenty-four violas, twenty 'cellos and twelve basses. Mahler's eighth symphony is another example of this, and earned its name, the *Symphony of a Thousand*, on account of the enormous forces employed. A reaction had to come after this exaggeration: New Music discarded the giant orchestra, and reinstated the chamber orchestra, in the most varied forms. On the other hand, new instruments constantly found their way into the orchestra, for instance the saxophone, as a result of the influence of jazz. The saxophone had, of course, had a part in the orchestra of Berlioz' times, but had lapsed since then. The piano also has a significant place in the modern orchestra, not as a harmony instrument, as the harpsichord had been, but more as a percussive instrument.

In the orchestra we differentiate between strings, wind and percussion; the wind are then subdivided into woodwind and brass. Thus the modern orchestra consists of four groups: woodwind (flutes, oboes, clarinets, bassoons), brass (horns, trumpets, trombones, tubas), percussion (timpani, bass drum and snare drum, triangle, cymbals, tamtam, bells, tambourine, xylophone, glockenspiel, and in addition celesta and piano), and strings (first and second violins, violas, violoncellos and double basses). The harp stands alone, though it too, like the piano, is used as a percussive instrument in recent scores. This is the order in which the instruments are written in the score, but with the harp just below the percussion. The flute is at the top, and the double bass at the bottom; vocal parts are written above the strings, or between the violas and the 'cellos.

The strings are always used 'chorally', unlike wind instruments, who work as soloists, and generally consist of fourteen first violins, fourteen second violins, twelve violas, ten 'cellos and eight basses. The strings form a large family, generally handled like a chorus in four voices; this is why one speaks of 'the quartet of the orchestra', for in the classical orchestra the 'cellos and basses almost always played the same part, in octaves.

All the strings are strung with four gut steel or strings, and the bow which strokes the strings, setting up the vibration, is strung with horsehair. The four strings of the violin are tuned in fifths, and the music is written in the treble clef.

The lowest of the four strings, the G string, is bound round with silver wire. Its rich, dark sound is very striking, and is often specifically prescribed for its characteristic effect. The most important ways of bowing are *legato* (very smooth playing), *staccato* (the opposite of legato—thrusting playing, as though each note were bowed separately), *tremolando* or *tremolo* (fast repetition of the same note, often used to create an excited mood), *arpeggiando* (like a harp), used to designate broken playing of chords, as opposed to simultaneous chords on three or four strings. *Vibrato* means a slight swaying of the note, which is achieved by means of a shaking motion in the violin hand and finger stopping the string. *Pizzicato* is a more important effect; the string is not bowed, but plucked with the finger, as on the zither or guitar. *Coll'arco* or simply *arco* (the Italian word for 'bow') means that the notes should again be bowed. *Col legno* (with the wood) means that the string must be struck with the wooden side of the bow, which produces a quite original sound.

The violin has a range of about three and a half octaves, which can be extended upwards by means of harmonics. Harmonics are artificial notes, the partial tones of the bowed strings, and have a strangely delicate, vibrant sound. The violin is an extraordinarily mobile instrument, and is capable of amazing runs and technical passages. 'Double-stopping' (two parts sounding simultaneously as the bow rests on two strings) is also quite possible. Mainly, however, the violin is to be regarded as the ideal exponent of the melody, the expressive *cantilena*. The addition of a mute (clamped onto the bridge of the violin) gives another special effect; the sound becomes dulled.

The viola is tuned a fifth lower than the violin. It is larger, and can be thought of as the contralto of the string section, though in the orchestra it rather tends to take the tenor part. The sound of the viola is somewhat veiled. All the techniques available to the violinist, *legato, staccato, pizzicato*, and so on, are also available to the viola player. The music is written in the alto clef, but the treble clef is used for the high register; the viola's range is about three octaves.

The violoncello, generally abbreviated to 'cello, is held between the knees, unlike the violin and viola which are held with the arm. The 'cello is considerably larger than the viola, and has a fuller and more powerful sound. The higher reaches of the 'cello are quite particularly suited to expressive *cantilena*. The four strings are tuned an octave lower than the viola, and the music is notated in the bass clef, helped out by tenor or treble clefs in the higher registers.

On account of its size, the double bass, or simply bass, can only be played standing up, or sitting on a high stool. The four strings are tuned in fourths, and sometimes a fifth string is added extending the range down to the C three octaves below middle C. Bass parts are written an octave higher than they sound. The double basses, the orchestra's foundation, mostly take the quiet bass part, but runs and passage work can also be very effective. A *pizzicato* in the basses is particularly characteristic.

The flute is the highest of the woodwind instruments. It is not played straight, as the other woodwind instruments are, but across the mouth (*a traverso*). The flute, with its range of three octaves, is blown directly, without the intervention of any sort of mouthpiece, and this has an important effect on the sound, which can easily be distinguished from all the other wind instruments. It has a soft and noble note; high up it tends to shrillness, and in the low register it makes a strangely dulled sound. Often you can hear the breath of the player together with the sound of the note. The flute is perfectly suited both to expressive *cantilena* playing and to mobile virtuoso passages and runs. It is often used merely to double, or reinforce, the first violins. Beethoven's orchestra requires two flutes; nowadays three or even four are necessary. Besides the big flutes, a small flute, or piccolo, is to be found in most orchestras, and this is generally played by the second flautist, who alternates between the normal flute and the piccolo. The piccolo sounds an octave higher than the flute, and has a very sharp note; this extremely individual timbre is ideally suited to certain special purposes, for instance the imitation of military music. The piccolo is immediately recognizable in the orchestra, if only on account of its high register and shrillness.

When played *forte*, the sound of the oboe is nasal and tends to suggest pressure, but *piano* it has a pristine delicacy. The oboe is charmingly effective in lyrical moods. There are usually two, or nowadays three, in an orchestra. The cor anglais provides an extension downwards of the oboe; it sounds a fifth lower. The cor anglais—again, the second oboist generally alternates between oboe and cor anglais—is a solo instrument in its own right and is particularly suited to pastoral moods (the shawm). The character of its sound is veiled and extremely melancholic. Anybody who has ever consciously heard the cor anglais, in, for example, the long solo at the beginning of the third act of Wagner's *Tristan and Isolde*, will never forget the distinctive character of this instrument.

The clarinet is more mobile than the oboe, and its sound is more flexible than that of the flute: exciting and suggestive in the low register, polished and noble in the middle register, and up high, powerful, penetrating and finally somewhat crude. It is especially suited to *cantilena* playing, but it can also execute fast runs and passage work. The clarinet, like the cor anglais, is a transposing instrument, which means that the notes sound differently from the way they are written in the parts; they sound a second, a third, and so forth, higher or lower according to the indications. Besides the usual clarinets in B-flat and A, you sometimes come across the E-flat clarinet, whose shrill sound is used chiefly for grotesque effects. The sound of the bass clarinet is extremely noble and respectable.

The bassoons form the bass of the woodwind group, together with the double bassoon, which goes down an octave lower. The bassoon has an extraordinarily wide range of about three and a half octaves. The full, powerful sound of the low notes gets progressively thinner and softer as you take the instrument up over its range; the character of the middle register is remarkably like a horn. The bassoons—there are at least two in most orchestras—are extremely adaptable; they can be used as melody, accompaniment, or bass instruments, and are capable of expressive *cantilena* playing, mobile passage work, and also grotesque effects.

Among the brass instruments, the horns form a closed group. In the orchestra they always appear in fours. Their flexibility was not yet fully developed at the time of the classical symphonists; they could only produce a series of overtones and a fundamental bass; this explains the somewhat passive rôle of the horns, and also of the trumpets, in classical music. Some of the remaining notes were achieved artificially; certain series of notes became typical of the horn, because they could be comfortably played, for instance hunting fanfares, and so forth. It was for the purpose of overcoming these limitations that horns were built in many different keys, and thus it is that they are also transposing instruments. The invention of the valves obviated all these limitations, for the trumpets as well as the horns. Since then the horns have been used in all sorts of different ways, particularly by the romantic composers, and their sound has, indeed, become typical of the romantic orchestra. It is exceptionally noble, rounded and full, and is suited to the delivery of spirited melodies. The horn's 'attack' is difficult, and slight accidents, such as the so-called 'split' notes caused by over-blowing, can befall even the best players. The horns are often called the pedal of the orchestra, because they can produce the effect of resonance by means of long sustained notes, similar to the effect of the pedal on the piano. The thick orchestral sound which is apt to appear as a result of this is also typical of romantic music. Modern composers deliberately avoid it.

The trumpet is the descant of the brass section. Its bright, luminous sound is resplendent and heroic when played *forte*, and as such it is ideal for capping the climax of a long build-up. *Piano*, it can also be used as a melody instrument in a variety of ways. The introduction of a mute into the bell of the instrument—this applies to horns as well as trumpets—produces the strange effect of 'stopped', or muted sounds. *Piano* it gives a mysteriously dulled effect, but *forte* it is suitable for grotesquerie. There are always two trumpets in our orchestras; but recent composers often write for three or even four.

Sublime grandeur and solemnity are the hallmarks of the trombones. In the orchestra they appear in a group of three: two tenor and one bass. The bass tuba is often added as the lowest voice of the brass section, and makes a quartet with the trio of trombones. The majestic sound of the trombones is unmistakable; it gives the orchestra an extraordinary splendour, and can be used with most impressive effect. Their *forte* can be used only very economically, for it represents the most extreme display of strength of which the orchestra is capable. The trombones playing *piano* are especially suitable for the expression of religious moods. Richard Wagner had special tubas constructed for the *Ring of the Nibelungs*, and hence their name 'Wagner tubas'. He treated them both as an independent group and as reinforcement for the sound of the horns, extending their range downwards. Bruckner also used them in his last big symphonies.

The saxophone, named after its inventor, Sax, is occasionally seen in the orchestra. Although it is made of metal, its reed mouthpiece and the technique of playing it prove it a member of the clarinet family. Berlioz used the saxophone occasionally, and on account of its peculiar sound it is found in recent symphonic music. It is available in all ranges—soprano, alto, tenor, baritone and bass. When played *forte* it can easily degenerate into vulgarity, but when it is cleverly employed the saxophone is capable of very pretty and original effects.

The percussion section provides the spice in the orchestra, and must be used sparingly in consequence. We distinguish between percussion instruments of definite pitch and those of indefinite pitch. Timpani, bells, glockenspiel, xylophone, celesta belong to the first group, and the second includes drums, triangle, cymbals, tamtam, tambourine, castanets, and so on. The most important instruments in the first group are the timpani, or kettledrums, of which there are always two and sometimes three. A kettledrum consists of a brass 'kettle' with calfskin stretched over it. The tension in the calfskin can be regulated by means of metal taps, and this tunes the kettledrum higher or lower. The sound of the timpani can be varied by means of various sticks, with heads made of wood, leather or sponge. The 'timps' mix admirably with orchestral sound. Primarily, the drum is a rhythmic instrument, but it can be very effective in setting a mood; *piano*, it has an uncanny sound, and *forte* it is wild and powerful. The kettledrum roll is one of its special effects.

Besides the timpani, classical music uses only the triangle and the cymbals. The triangle with its light, happy ringing lends particular charm to orchestral pieces of the gayer sort. The cymbals, two round metal plates which are struck against one another or rubbed together, make a splendid bright sound, and are used mostly to support the climax of a long crescendo.

The bass drum is generally used together with the cymbals; its *tremolo* makes a sound like thunder. The snare drum, or side drum, is rhythmically extremely sharp, and its roll has a powerful effect. The tambourine is also an instrument of the drum family; it is a little wooden band, with skin stretched over one side only; little bells are set in the wooden ring, and these tinkle in sympathy when the diaphragm is struck with the hand, or shaken in a *tremolo*. These noises, and also the clack of the castanets, are used chiefly to characterize pieces with a Spanish or Italian flavour.

Low bell notes are produced by tuned metal tubes which hang free. The silvery, ethereal sound of the celesta, a little steel piano, has a magical effect, whereas the xylophone's clatter is coarser and more grotesque. The xylophone is a system of tuned blocks of wood. The sounds of the tamtam and gong—large metal discs struck with the kettledrum stick—are sombre and solemn; a soft vibrato on the gong creates a mood of mystery.

The harp has a special rôle in the orchestra; it is one of the oldest musical instruments, much loved in the Renaissance, but thereafter lapsing into oblivion. Even the classical composers completely neglected the harp; Beethoven uses it only once, in his ballet *Die Geschöpfe des Prometheus*. But since Berlioz, the use of the harp has again become general, particularly in French music. The harp has such a striking sound that it can hold its own against a large orchestral body, despite its relative quietness. The low notes have a bell-like effect, and towards the high register the sound gets progressively brighter. Harp harmonics have a magical delicacy, a positively unreal character. The best-known effect on the harp is the *glissando*, when the fingers glide swiftly over the strings. *Forte*, this has an intoxicating swing, and *pianissimo* it is as ephemeral as a light breeze.

The piano is to be met with more and more frequently in recent scores. The harpsichord, precursor of the piano, was considered quite indispensable in baroque music; it played the continuo part or figured bass, the harmonic foundation of the orchestra. The gradual filling-out of the orchestra in the second half of the eighteenth century left the harpsichord without a function and it disappeared from the orchestra. In classical and romantic music the piano only appears in the rôle of a brilliant solo instrument, co-starring with, or playing opposite the orchestra, in the piano concerto. But the way it is used in the modern orchestra completely eschews its romantic magic; it is used very characteristically as a percussive instrument, for rhythmic support, and in powerful octaves to obtain the effect of bells, and so on. Indeed, the range of possibilities for the utilization of the piano in the orchestra seems unlimited, for on the one hand, it has a sound which can always make itself heard, and on the other, the sound mixes admirably with most orchestral sonorities.

The orchestra's effectiveness of sound depends to a large extent on the seating or layout of the players. The principles governing the layout of the concert orchestra are the same the world over, with only minor deviations. An amphitheatral structure has become generally accepted; a wooden podium with raised steps going up towards the back has proved the best sound-board for the music. The conductor's desk is on a raised platform at the front in the middle. The first violins sit on the left, and the seconds on the right. The violas are accommodated behind the second violins, while the 'cello desks are set up in the middle, directly in front of the conductor. The basses are usually off to the left and slightly raised, with the harp close in front of them. The woodwind sit, also raised, in two rows behind the strings; from left to right, the flutes and then

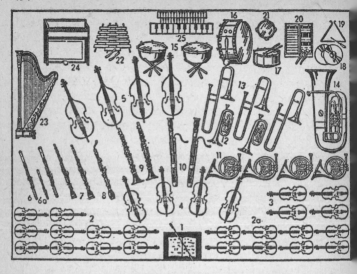

THE ARRANGEMENT OF THE ORCHESTRA

1   Conductor's score and   12   Trumpets
      baton   13   Trombones
2   First violins   14   Bass tuba
2a Second violins   15   Kettledrums
3   Violas   16   Bass drum
4   'Cellos   17   Snare drum
5   Double basses   18   Cymbals
6   Flutes   19   Triangle
6a Piccolo   20   Celesta
7   Oboes   21   Tambourine
8   Cor anglais   22   Xylophone
9   Clarinets   23   Harp
10 Bassoons   24   Harmonium
11 Horns   25   Organ

the oboes, and behind, the clarinets and then the bassoons. The trumpets, timpani and trombones sit on the top step, and the horns are off to the right.

Occasionally this familiar seating arrangement is changed. American and some English orchestras, for instance, prefer to bring the higher strings together and the lower ones together, so that on the conductor's left you have the first violins and behind them the seconds, and on his right the 'cellos, with the violas and double basses behind them. This layout has the advantage that the two main parts, the melody and the bass, are evenly distributed. Visually however, this layout disregards the symmetry of the two violin sections facing each other. As opposed to this, the Viennese layout is excellent from a visual point of view: the seating is as usual, except that the basses—and the Vienna Philharmonic boasts ten of these—are placed in a line on the topmost step, thus forming a powerful shelter for the whole orchestra.

In large choral works, the chorus is usually grouped around the orchestra. The male voices take their place on the highest step, the tenors on the left and the basses on the right, and the women's voices are distributed at the sides, coming right down to the front, with the sopranos on the left and the contraltos on the right.

Finally a few words about the conductor, the responsible leader and the driving force of the orchestra. In the seventeenth and eighteenth centuries the conductor always participated in the performance; either he played the harpsichord, thus holding the whole ensemble together, or he played the first violin. This situation underwent a permanent change in the nineteenth century; the orchestra by this time had become much too complicated to be able to dispense with a director. An early model of the modern conductor was Carl Maria von Weber; Wagner admiringly took him as a pattern. Then Wagner and particularly his pupil Hans von Bülow were in a position to develop the art of the sovereign mastery of the orchestra, which we all admire so much in the 'virtuoso conductors' of today.

The conductor plays on the orchestra like an instrument; he is able to exert his power of suggestion over the orchestra by means of his signs and gestures, and his mental picture of the work he is to play takes on musical form. Beating time, the motion executed by the conductor with his baton, is not the most important part of his job; these motions can be learnt, and it is mainly a matter of making a down-beat on the accented part of the bar and an up-beat on the unaccented part of the bar. These basic forms undergo subdivisions in the more complicated metres; and in addition to this, each conductor varies his scheme of beats according to his taste. But beating time, as we said, is only the foundation of the language of gestures by means of which the conductor expresses his will and his ideas about the musical form. Through his gestures and carriage at the desk, he can exert an enormous suggestive influence on the orchestra, and also on the audience.

The main movements involved in beating time can be shown graphically as follows:

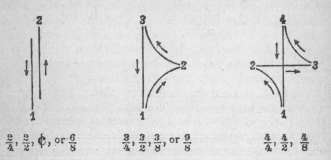

$$\frac{2}{4}, \frac{2}{2}, \not\!\!C, \text{ or } \frac{6}{8} \qquad \frac{3}{4}, \frac{3}{2}, \frac{3}{8}, \text{ or } \frac{9}{8} \qquad \frac{4}{4}, \frac{4}{2}, \frac{4}{8}$$

All music requires the medium of an interpreter before it can come alive for the listener. Understandably enough, there came a reaction against the exaggerated stress laid on the subjective interpretation demanded by romantic music and the cult of the virtuoso. The reaction proceeded to demand objectivisation, or complete exclusion of any personal interpretation, and this extreme view implies that finally music will have to be absolutely mechanical. Happily we have not got to that point yet!

The exaggeration of the cult of virtuoso conducting has led, too, to the widespread practice of conducting from memory. It is certainly a bad thing, to quote von Bülow's famous remark, 'to have your head in the score, instead of the score in your head', but, as a no less significant contemporary conductor has said, 'the score, because it is the final referee, belongs on the conductor's desk'.

THE BASIC CONCEPTS OF MUSICAL THEORY

Music can be divided into many categories; for instance, we can differentiate between folk music and art music, or between serious and light music. We have not dealt with folk music as such in this book; folk songs and folk dances have been mentioned several times, but only in so far as they were a significant inspiration to art music. Light music has also been excluded from our considerations, for the simple reason that its easily comprehensible forms require no comment. Art music, or 'serious music', has been the subject under discussion. 'Serious music' is a misleading expression, since the music we have discussed contains a great deal that is gay and happy. As yet, however, nobody has discovered a better formulation for the opposite of light music. In Germany, at the time when wireless transmission introduced serious music to hundreds of thousands of people, the phrase 'opus music' became current as a joking and rather derogatory designation of art music. *Opus* is Latin for 'a work', and almost all composers since Beethoven have used this word to number their works in order of composition. 'Opus music' aptly expresses that horror of the many strange words, like a sort of secret language, that surround the foreign world of great music, so difficult to understand.

Every art has its own collection of special expressions, its technical vocabulary, just as does every science and every craft. What makes it more difficult in the case of music is that the majority of these technical expressions are taken from Italian, Italy being the birthplace of occidental art music. On the other hand, this very difficulty makes for the general international intelligibility of even the technical terms, for almost all the Italian expressions have been taken over by all musical peoples, and so turned into a truly supernational language of music.

There are further distinctions between sacred music (church music) and secular music, and between vocal music and instrumental music. Vocal music includes all music for voices, whether with or without accompaniment. Unaccompanied vocal music is designated by the phrase *a cappella*. Vocal music can be further subdivided into sacred and secular vocal music. Masses, Passions, sacred oratorios, chorales, motets (usually for several voices *a cappella*) come under sacred vocal music. Operas, secular oratorios, choral songs, ballads and just plain songs are the main forms of secular vocal music.

Instrumental music can best be subdivided according to the combinations of instruments involved: orchestral music, piano music, organ music and chamber music. Chamber music is any music that can be played by a small number of musicians in a small room. The categories of chamber music are duets (for two players), trios (for three players), quartets (for four players) and so on up to nonets (for nine players), all using string or wind instruments, with or without piano.

Now a few words about the notation of music, which is probably—in its present perfection—one of the most beautiful manifestations of Western culture. In ancient times there was no particular notation for music. The seven fundamental notes were designated by the first seven letters of the Greek and later the Latin alphabet: A B C D E F G.

The first real notes were the *Neumes*, but these only indicated the approximate movements of the notes, up or down. By the addition of a line, and later four lines, and finally five, this early medieval notation was constantly expanded. The absolute pitch was established by writing a letter of the alphabet at the beginning of the stave, as a clef. The credit for this master-stroke goes to Guido von Arezzo (c. 995–1050), the monk of the Benedictine order who, with this innovation, laid the foundation of our modern musical notation.

Mensural notation followed in the twelfth century; this made it possible to determine the temporal values of the individual notes. A further addition was the time signature, and the introduction of the barline in about 1600 completed the development of a musical notation that is still valid today.

It is only necessary to use the indications for the seven fundamental notes, A B C D E F G, to name all the tones which are musically perceptible to the human ear. Beginning with the eighth note, this sequence repeats itself in a higher register. This eighth note, which has the same sound as the first, is called the octave, and this is the name given to the span of eight notes. The complete range of musical notes is subdivided into octaves, and we will differentiate between these octaves as follows, taking 'middle C' as our point of reference: the fourth, third and second octaves below middle C, the octave below middle C, the octave above middle C, and the second, third and fourth octaves above middle C. In this way we can refer to any particular note, for instance the F in the third octave above middle C that the coloratura soprano has to sing in the aria of the Queen of the Night in Mozart's *Magic Flute*, or the E in the third octave below middle C, which is the lowest note on the double bass. These octaves are not divided according to the sequence of notes beginning with A, but according to that beginning with C (each octave runs C D E F G A B C) which represents the fundamental sequence of our (modern) musical sensibilities, the C major scale.

In our five-line system, the notes are written either on or between the lines, and the clef at the front determines the absolute pitch of the individual notes. The most usual clefs are the treble clef and the bass clef. The treble clef fixes the G on the second line (that is why it is sometimes called the G clef), the G above middle C; the other notes then follow on above and below this. The bass clef fixes the F on the fourth line (it is sometimes called the F clef), the F below middle C. Among other things, the treble and bass clefs are used for the notation of piano music, and the notes that are not encompassed by the two sets of five lines in our staff system are accommodated on leger lines above and below the staves. Beyond these, and to facilitate reading, the sign *8va* (*octava alta*) is written above the notes, or *8va bassa* below them, and this indicates that they are to be played an octave higher or lower.

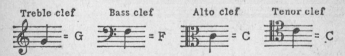

Treble clef = G   Bass clef = F   Alto clef = C   Tenor clef = C

There are two C clefs in general use besides the treble and bass clefs; the alto clef (fixing C on the third line) is used for writing viola parts, and is sometimes called the viola clef, and the tenor clef (fixing C on the fourth line) is used for the higher registers of the 'cello, bassoon and trombone.

According to their duration, notes are written as breves, semibreves, minims (half-notes, that is, half a semibreve), crotchets (quarter-notes), quavers (eighth-notes), semiquavers (sixteenths), demisemiquavers (thirty-seconds), and hemidemisemiquavers (sixty-fourths).

There are rests corresponding to all these note-values, signs which indicate how long any particular part should keep silent. When everybody keeps silent, when there is a rest held by every part, this is called a G.P., or General Pause. The sign ⌢ written above a note or rest is called a 'pause sign'; this indicates a point of rest and means that the note or rest above which it is written is to be held for a length of time, not predetermined, but significant.

Where a dot is placed after a note or rest, this means that its length is increased by half again.

A metrical order is introduced into the movements of the notes by means of the subdivision of the music into bars; the sequence of notes is distributed in a regularly recurring succession of accented and unaccented parts of the bar. The individual bars are separated by barlines, and there is a distinction between simple-time bars (with two beats to count) and compound-time bars (with three beats to count). The two-beat, simple-time bar breaks down into one heavy (accented) part of the bar, and one light (unaccented) part. Compound-time bars (with three beats) have an accented first beat, while the two remaining beats are unaccented. Bars of $^6/_4$ and $^6/_8$ are also simple-time bars, but with compound subdivisions. The $^5/_4$ bar, which has its origins in Russian music, appears to us as a hybrid bar made up of $^2/_4$ and $^3/_4$. *Alla breve* means that although the bars are written in crotchets, they are counted in minims, so it amounts really to an indication that the tempo is doubled. The sort of bar that is to be used in a piece of music, and also every change of bar-length, is indicated by the 'time signature', which is usually written as a fraction, indicating the number and the value of notes; for instance $^2/_4$ (two crotchets), $^3/_2$ (three minims), $^5/_4$, $^6/_8$, and so on. The sign C is written for $^4/_4$ and ₵ for the same, but *alla breve*, or $^2/_2$.

The scale (from the Italian *scala*, a ladder) with seven steps was the basis of musical theorizing even for the Greeks. They built their different scales out of various combinations of tones and semitones, and these passed over later into the church modes of Western music, which have had a great influence on the final form of our system of keys. Our musical sensibilities are naturally adjusted to the subdivision of the octave into semitones, as opposed to the different subdivisions used by other races. The church modes were built on the various successions of tones and semitones, and retained their old Greek names like Ionian, Dorian, Phrygian, Aeolian, and so on. In our present system of keys, the scale divides into two halves, each constructed the same way: two rows of four notes, called tetrachords, C D E F and G A B C. In each half a step of a semitone follows two steps of a whole tone. Thus, in our basic scale the steps C–D, D–E, F–G, G–A and A–B are whole tones, while

E–F and B–C are only semitones. The step of a semitone has a special tension; it demands a continuation, a resolution, particularly the step B–C, which leads to the fundamental or key-note (tonic), which is why B carries the name of 'leading-note'.

'Accidentals' are necessary for the construction of scales corresponding to the scale of C, but starting from other notes. The semitones which lie between the whole tones are shown by means of accidentals. A sharp (♯) in front of a note raises it by a semitone, and a flat (♭) lowers it by a semitone. Notes altered in this way are referred to as, for example, C-sharp (C♯), E-flat (E♭). A natural sign (♮) is necessary to neutralize either a sharp or a flat. Other accidentals are the double sharp (x) and double flat (♭♭); these raise or lower the note by two semitones.

The relation between two notes is called an interval. The intervals are designated by cardinal numbers according to the distance of the higher note from the fundamental. Thus there are seconds, thirds, fourths, fifths, sixths, sevenths, octaves, ninths, tenths, and so on. The interval from the first to the second step of the scale is a second, for example C–D; that from the first to the third step is a third, for example C–E. When the individual steps are chromatically altered, the distance between them alters too. For this reason the size-relationships of the intervals are differentiated; there are perfect, major, minor, diminished and augmented intervals. With seconds, thirds, sixths and sevenths there are two different forms to be distinguished, with a difference of a semitone; for example, the major third is C–E and the minor third is C–E-flat. Fourths, fifths and octaves have one form and are therefore called 'perfect'. Besides this, all intervals can be chromatically either extended or compressed, and this gives rise to the augmented and diminished intervals, for instance the augmented fourth C–F-sharp (the so-called 'tritone', or step of three whole tones), the augmented fifth C–G-sharp, or the diminished seventh C-sharp–B-flat.

The stepwise succession of tones is called a scale. A sequence consisting of only the basic notes is called a 'diatonic scale', as opposed to the 'chromatic scale' which consists entirely of semitones. Notes are called 'enharmonic' when they sound identical on a keyboard instrument such as the piano, but are written differently and have different names, for instance F-sharp and G-flat. So far as frequency relationships are concerned, F-sharp and G-flat are different pitches originally. 'Tempered tuning' was the result of the recognition of the need to adjust this discrepancy. The twelve semitones of the octave were submitted to an even tuning relationship, and this made it possible to start a scale on any note of the chromatic scale. All the chords built on these scales display a relative purity sufficient to satisfy our accustomed ears perfectly. The end of the seventeenth century saw the final solution of this problem, and the solution has proved decisive in the development of our music. Johann Sebastian Bach came out in favour of the new system with his famous work *The Well-tempered Clavier*; the two series of twenty-four preludes and fugues (written in 1722 and 1744) provided striking proof of the perfect utility of tempered tuning.

The system of major and minor keys evolved from the church modes quite unconsciously. The Ionic mode is the precursor of our major scale, and the Aeolian mode corresponds to our minor scale. Major (in German *dur*, from the Latin *durus* meaning hard) and minor (in German *moll*, from the Latin *mollis* meaning soft) can be thought of as the two sexes of a key. The major scales are constructed like the series of basic notes: two tetrachords each consisting of two tones and a semitone. Each major scale has a corresponding minor scale—its 'relative minor' scale—consisting of the same notes as the major scale but starting two notes lower, and this changes the position or sequence of whole tones and semitones. The minor scale corresponding to the major scale of C therefore begins on A; it starts with a step of a whole tone from A–B and this is followed by a semitone B–C; then another whole tone C–D. The step from the seventh note to the octave is also a tone, and the seventh note has to be raised so as to give it the character of a leading-note. Thus we arrive at the 'harmonic' minor scale, which then has a step of a whole tone *plus* a semitone between the sixth and seventh notes. So as to bridge this gap, the sixth note can also be raised, and this results in the 'melodic minor' scale.

A major or minor scale can start from any one of the notes of the chromatic scale, and is constructed according to the fixed sequence of tones and semitones. Thus the major scale starting on D runs as follows: D E F-sharp G A B C-sharp D. Instead of writing the accidentals beside the individual notes every time, they are placed once and for all on the stave at the beginning, just after the clef. In the case of D major, there are two sharps to be written, and these are called the 'key signature'. The twelve keys built on the twelve notes of the chromatic scale are obtained by progressing in perfect fifths upwards and downwards from C: upwards G D A E B F-sharp, and downwards F B-flat E-flat A-flat D-flat G-flat. With each step upwards you add one more sharp to the key signature, until, with F-sharp major, you have six sharps, and with each step downwards you add one more flat to the key signature, until, with G-flat major, you have six flats. Because F-sharp major and G-flat major sound the same enharmonically, you have thus obtained all the twelve keys of the so-called circle of fifths.

As we said, every major key has a corresponding minor key starting two notes (three semitones) lower. These two keys—both have the same key signature—are called 'relative keys'; C major is the relative major of A minor, A minor is the relative minor of C major, and C minor is the relative minor of E-flat major and vice versa.

The church modes maintained their position in baroque music during the seventeenth century and the first half of the eighteenth, but in classical music all feeling for the peculiarities of the modes was completely submerged; the system of major and minor keys held complete sway. Romantic composers also used the system of major and minor keys. It is only towards the end of the nineteenth century that a tendency towards other sorts of scales became apparent. The pentatonic scale of exotic peoples, a scale consisting of five notes without any connecting semitones, for example C D E G A, and the 'Gypsy' scale containing two steps of an augmented second, for example A B C D-sharp E F G-sharp A, came into general use. The use of the whole-tone scale had a greater influence than these; it consisted of six steps of a whole tone, completely dispensing with chromaticism, for example C D E F-sharp G-sharp A-sharp. The whole-tone scale goes a long way towards dissolving tonality, which can be described as a feeling of being bound to a home key. Whereas 'polytonality' provides the possibility of using two or more keys simultaneously, 'atonality' represents a radical break with tradition. Schönberg's twelve-note system, for instance, no longer recognizes any connection or relation to a home key.

Melody, rhythm and harmony can be viewed as the basic elements of any musical configuration. If we define melody as an expressive sequence of notes, this formulation already indicates something of the great multiplicity inherent in the interpretation of this concept. It is impossible to set up a norm for the value or beauty of a melody; tastes differ too widely. A melody which one person finds beautiful may seem banal to another, and a melody that this other person would describe as noble, says nothing whatever to a third person.

The smallest closed unit of a melody is called a motif; the motif is thus the germ cell, or kernel, of a melody. We call a melody a 'theme' if it stands as an indissoluble whole, and as such can be a basis for further working and development. When we speak of a 'figure', or 'figuration', this means a melody based on the successive notes of a chord. A 'run' is a scale-like series of notes. Figures and runs are also called 'passages' or 'passage work'.

The simplest way of extending a melody is to repeat individual motivic sections. When a motif is repeated on a different step of the scale, this is called a 'sequence'; sequences (particularly those that rise a step at a time) can be used to create the effect of a strong build-up. A theme can also be augmented or diminished, which means transferring it into larger or smaller note-values. Pre-classical music and classical music made great play with the ornamentation of a melody. The ornaments and the way they should be played depend on the style and period of the particular piece of music. The best-known ornaments are the *appoggiatura* and the *acciaccatura* (relatively long or very short notes preceding the appropriate note of the melody), the 'glide' (a step-wise series of notes preceding a note of the melody), the 'mordent' and the 'inverted mordent' (a fast trill of the main note with the note below or above it) and the 'trill' with the upper note, which lasts for the whole length of the note. The trill is the only one of the baroque ornaments that is still in constant use.

Without rhythm, the melody is dead and expressionless; it is the rhythmic movement that breathes life into the melody. The rhythm indicates the temporal course of the series of notes; it determines their relations to one another in time. There must be a clear distinction between rhythm and metre. The metre is given by the sort of bars, and the beats to be counted in them; whether, for instance, a melody or a whole piece is in $^2/_4$ time or $^3/_4$ time. The accentuation, on which the rhythm leans, is determined by the bars: accented–unaccented or unaccented–accented are the basic forms of accentuation in simple time, and long accented–short accented is the basic form in compound time. The reverse of this (short unaccented–long accented) includes the up-beat; the up-beat is the light unaccented part of the bar that leads to the heavy or accented part.

There are just as many rhythmic possibilities as there are melodic possibilities. Every epoch in the history of music has produced new differentiations and refinements in rhythm, and the twentieth century in particular. We can mention only a few rhythmic peculiarities in this chapter. The continuous use of note-values extended by the addition of a dot, together with the correspondingly shorter completion of the beat, for instance ♩. ♪♩. ♪ or ♩.♩♩.♩ etc. are called dotted rhythms. They occur in many different forms; when the music is fast, they have an excited character, and are somewhat insistent. Syncopation also has an exciting, disquieting character; the accent is shifted from the heavy to the light . part of the bar. A 'triplet' is three notes taking the time that would generally be taken by two or sometimes four notes. The continuous use of triplet motion generally has a balancing, calming effect; but triplet rhythms can also carry considerable excitement, when they are strongly worked up. Quadruplets are groups of four notes taking the time of three notes according to the time signature; and it is similar with quintuplets (five in the time of four), sextuplets, and so on. 'Polyrhythms' are the simultaneous use of various different rhythms in two or more voices. When these rhythms complement each other, they are also called 'complementary rhythms'.

Harmony is the ordered sounding together of several notes at once; a theory of harmony is thus a theory about chords, the connection of different notes. 'Consonance' is a combination of notes which leaves no tension, and does not require to be resolved. The counterpart of this is a 'dissonance', a chord which contains some tension which demands to be resolved into a consonance. Unfortunately 'dissonance' is a word with many false connotations.

'Triads' are the basis of harmony; a triad is three notes sounding together. Every triad consists of a fundamental note (the root), plus the third and the fifth above it. It is thus made up of two superimposed thirds. According to the sizes of these thirds we distinguish between the major triad (a major third plus a minor third), the minor triad (a minor third plus a major third), the diminished triad (a minor third plus a minor third) and the augmented triad (a major third plus a major third).

Major triad	Minor triad	Diminished triad	Augmented triad

Triads can be constructed on any step of the scale. The triad on the fundamental note is called the 'tonic triad', since the fun-

466 THE BASIC CONCEPTS OF MUSICAL THEORY

damental note is called the 'tonic'. The fifth note and the triad
on it are called the 'dominant', and the fourth note and the triad
on it are called the 'subdominant'. The tonic, dominant and
subdominant determine the key, and there is a complete finality
about the sequence of chords subdominant–dominant–tonic that
gives rise to its name: 'full close', or 'perfect cadence'. A 'half close'
is a cadence on the dominant, 'half' because the final resolution onto
the tonic is yet to come. When the dominant resolves onto the sixth
note of the scale instead of onto the tonic, this is called an 'interrupted cadence', by reason of its unsatisfying effect. Ending formulae which unambiguously determine the key of the music are
called 'cadences'. Cadential writing is a typical feature of classical
and romantic music, but is, of course, completely foreign to atonal
music.

The construction and designation of chords is always based on
the fundamental note (or root). By placing either the third or the
fifth at the bottom instead of the root, we get the two 'inversions'
of the triad. The first inversion is sometimes referred to as the 'sixth
chord', and the second inversion as the 'six-four chord'.

Inversions of C major triad

Root position   1st inversion   2nd inversion

The sixth chord, or first inversion, is rather undecided and intan-
gible in character; it is noble and brilliant, but incomplete. The
radiant six-four chord, or second inversion, has a definite tendency
to finality; it demands resolution and a cadence. A peculiar tension
inhabits the augmented triads; they seem filled with longing. The
augmented triad is typical of music of the high romantic period
(Wagner and Liszt), and in French impressionist music it is the
chief vehicle for the harmony, for it is the only triad that can be
constructed out of the whole-tone scale.

By adding the seventh note to triads, we get 'chords of the
seventh', consisting of three thirds one on top of the other. The
'dominant seventh' is built on the fifth note of the scale and is the
most important of the seventh chords; it demands a resolution onto
the tonic. By adding the ninth (major or minor) chord to a seventh
chord we get the 'chord of the ninth'. The ninth chord, too, with

its mysterious, blurred quality, was a great favourite with the later romantic composers.

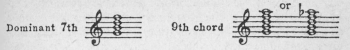

Dominant 7th ⋯ 9th chord ⋯ or ♭

The 'chord of the diminished seventh' is a very striking version of the chord of the seventh and is closely related to the chord of the

ninth; it, too, contains something of mystery and excitement. Any of the notes of a chord can be raised and lowered, or 'altered' to use the technical expression. Altered chords tend to intensify the tension which is already present in the chords in their original form.

In classical harmony all chords are based on superimposed inter-

vals of a third. 'Chords of the fourth' are obtained by piling up fourths. Chords of the fourth tend to push outwards from the home key; they seem unsettled, indeterminate; they tend to dissolve the tonality. The use of these chords leads easily to 'polytonality', sustaining two or more different keys simultaneously. Polytonality is to be met with quite often in recent music, and also the simultaneous use of major and minor keys, which often gives rise to false relations. One speaks of a 'false relation' where a chromatically altered note comes face to face with the unaltered note, but in different voices in a series of chords.

As opposed to the freely flowing melody of baroque times and also of modern music, classical melody is laid out harmonically. Every note of the melody stands in relation to a harmony, even if the harmony is not actually sounded. There are also notes which are foreign to the harmony, and these are heard as dissonances; for example, the 'passing' note constituting the connecting link between two notes of the harmony, sometimes called an 'unaccented dissonance'. The 'suspension' is more arresting and expressive; this is a note retained from the preceding chord, and hence 'suspended' over the new harmony before going on to resolve onto a note of the new harmony.

An 'anticipation' is the opposite of a suspension; here the melody uses a note of the harmony that is to come next; the anticipated note enters too soon, predicting the chord to come.

'Modulation' is the name for the transition from one key to another. In classical and romantic music, the end or destination key of a modulation is clearly defined by a cadence, and it is only after this clearly marked manœuvre that a modulation is considered closed. The later romantic composers and the composers of the twentieth century were not so particular about their modulations; the frequent transitions and modulatory deviations without any particular relation to any particular tonality are quite characteristic of modern music. The music easily slips into a series of unpredictable flares, or else smoulders longingly. But in this sort of music there is the danger that the constant to and fro of modulations will give an impression of molluscoid lack of strength.

Melody, rhythm and harmony can be considered the three basic elements for the construction, or composition of music. In playing or performing music, tempo, dynamics and expression are the primary considerations.

Tempo means the time-measure, or speed of a piece of music. In ancient times there were no very precise indications of tempo; it was only in the baroque that the Italian expressions became current, and they are the ones that have been retained up to the present day. The most important indications for fast or slow have become so accepted over the years that they have become permanent expressions designating pieces of music, or at any rate individual movements of pieces of music in the corresponding tempo. Thus 'allegro' is the generally accepted name for a fast movement, and 'adagio' or 'andante' for a slow one. We give here a list of the most important subdivisions in the scale of tempi, together with their meanings:

largo	broad
larghetto	fairly broad
adagio	slow
andante	walking pace, or moderately slow

andantino	not too slow
moderato	moderate movement
allegretto	with considerable movement
allegro	fast moving
vivace	lively
presto	fast
prestissimo	extremely fast

Besides these, there are numerous further subdivisions and differentiations. Since the romantic period German, French and even English tempo indications have sometimes been used instead of the Italian expressions, but it must be admitted that this has more often made them more difficult to understand than easier.

The indications for increases and decreases in tempo are extremely important: *accelerando* means 'get faster', and *ritardando* 'get slower'. A gradual increase or decrease is indicated by *poco a poco accelerando* or *poco a poco ritardando*. *Più mosso* means 'with more movement', 'onwards'; *meno mosso*, 'less movement', 'hold back'. If the main tempo is reinstated after a tempo change, this is indicated by *tempo primo* or simply *a tempo*.

The metronome, an apparatus constructed by the Viennese mechanic Mälzel in 1812, serves for the exact determination of tempo. This instrument consists of a clockwork-driven pendulum which swings constantly to and fro, and the speed of its swing can be accurately adjusted by means of a little weight that can be slid up and down on the pendulum (effectively changing its length). The minute is the standard time for the measurement of tempo: ♩ = 60 means that a crotchet should last one-sixtieth of a minute, or one second; ♩ = 120 indicates a tempo twice as fast, with one hundred and twenty crotchets to the minute.

Metronomic indications are abbreviated to MM (Mälzel's Metronome). The weight on the pendulum can be accurately adjusted to the required number of swings per minute. The determination of musical tempo is in a way dependent on our purely physical time measure, namely the mean pulse beat, which is approximately eighty to the minute. We consider this as a medium tempo, and everything below it is as slow, and everything above it as fast. Thus we think of ♩ = 60 (or one crotchet per second) as slow, or perhaps *andante*, and MM ♩ = 120 as fast, or *allegro*.

'Dynamics' in music means the scale of loudness, which is a very important means of expression. The decisive indications are *piano*, soft, and *forte*, loud, and what follows is a list of the various differentiations, together with their abbreviations:

pianissimo possibile, *ppp*	as soft as possible
pianissimo, *pp*	very soft
piano, *p*	soft
mezzopiano, *mp*	half-soft
mezzoforte, *mf*	half-loud
forte, *f*	loud
fortissimo, *ff*	very loud
triple forte, *fff*	as loud as possible

The following dynamic indications are also important:

crescendo	get gradually louder
decrescendo or *diminuendo*	get gradually softer
sforzato	sudden accentuation of individual notes
marcato	bring out (mark out, by playing louder than the context) individual notes
morendo	dying, fading away

The dynamics of transition, *crescendo* and *decrescendo*, were introduced by the composers of the Mannheim school in the middle of the eighteenth century, the direct predecessors of the Viennese classical composers. Before that, the gradual crescendo was completely unknown. Baroque music used 'terraced dynamics', the stepwise increase or decrease by means of the addition or subtraction of whole groups of parts. Brusque contrasts of *forte* and *piano*—echo effects—were also typical of baroque music.

However exactly a composer may define his tempi and dynamics, a sensitive interpreter undertakes many more subdivisions and refinements in his playing. These slight fluctuations, hardly perceptible, and yet decisive, of tempo and dynamics are called 'agogic treatment'. *Rubato* means a very free interpretation of the tempo, which is very necessary in playing certain pieces of music of a romantic or nationalistic character.

The right phrasing is of paramount importance when playing a piece of music. 'Phrasing' means the sensible and right grading of every melodic unit. To facilitate the recognition of the right phrasing, composers make use of phrase-marks, which distinctly group the individual phrases of a melody together. But phrase-marks are by no means identical with the marks for *legato* (which look the same), and this has caused a lot of confusion in the interpretation of music. However many indications of interpretation and expression marks there are, they never can and never will be more than indications or pointers for the interpreter. A gifted interpreter carries within himself a sensitivity for the right way to play. Nevertheless, the indications for expression, which are often combined with the tempo indication, are not to be ignored. Indications like *dolce*, sweetly, *espressivo*, expressively, *leggiero*, lightly, have become part of our everyday vocabulary. *Maestoso*, majestically, or *marciale*, warlike, are also frequently employed. Many other Italian expressions, among them *appassionato*, passionately, *con fuoco*, fiery, *animato*, lively, *agitato*, excited, *con brio*, 'with a swing', have become part of a general stock of expressions which it is hard to dispense with when describing music. In the presentation of the individual works in this *Concert Guide* we have transcribed these foreign expressions wherever possible.

At the beginning of this appendix we divided music into several departments: folk music and art music, vocal music and instrumental music, and so on. The distinction between homophonic music and polyphonic music also makes a significant division throughout all music. Originally 'homophonic' meant little more than music in one part, or unaccompanied music. As the antithesis of polyphony, or music written in several lines or voices, we can define homophony as a way of writing whereby *one* voice takes precedence, and is accompanied by the other parts with simple harmony. The distinction between homophonic and polyphonic music corresponds to that between harmonic and contrapuntal music.

Counterpoint (from the Latin *punctus contra punctum*, note against note) is the art of leading several independent voices simultaneously, but maintaining a subtle and satisfying interdependence between them. Melodic imitation is one of the main devices in counterpoint, and this is also the basis of the difficult forms of canon and fugue. Whereas the music of the Middle Ages was very polyphonic, there was a tendency towards homophonic writing in the seventeenth century. In Bach, the two forms are ideally balanced. Both the classical and the romantic composers preferred the homophonic style, though all the great masters without exception paid homage to the contrapuntal principle. In recent times composers have consciously rejected the homophonic style and devoted themselves to a 'linear' style, as polyphony is called in the modern jargon. The linear, or horizontal, principle (that is, the simultaneity of various melodic lines, as opposed to the sort of music where the harmony is recognizable in vertical section) has thus become a characteristic of the music of our time.

INDEX OF MUSICAL TERMS

New Journal of Music, (Schubert) 171, (Schumann) 177, 227

ninth, chord of, 466

ninth, interval of 9 notes

nocturne, notturno (It.), name given particularly to slow piano pieces

nonet, any combination of 9 instruments or voices; composition for 9 instruments

notation, 458

note values, 459

notturno, see nocturne

Oboe, woodwind instrument with double reed mouthpiece, 449

oboe d'amore (It.), oboe with narrow bore which produces a muted tone

octave (Lat.), eight. Interval, compass of 8 notes, 458

octet, any combination of 8 instruments or voices; composition for 8 instruments

Offertorium (Lat.), Offertory, section of Mass

opera, 27

oratorio, 27, 31 ff., (Handel) 63

orchestra, arrangement of, 453 ff.

orchestra, make-up of, 445 ff.

orchestral suite, suite for orchestra (Bach), 33

organ-point (point d'orgue), a harmonic pedal, see pedal-point

ornaments, 464

ostinato (It.), persistent, dim. of basso ostinato, 18

overture, musical introduction (concert overture), 20, 22

p, piano (It.), soft

pp, pianissimo (It.), very soft

ppp, pianissimo possibile (It.), as soft as possible

paraphrase, metrical psalm in Presbyterian church

parody, in the style of some previous work

part, part of score played by a particular instrument or voice

passacaglia, 18

passage, passage work, 464

passepied (old Fr.), dance in triple time

passing note, 467

Passion, Passion of Our Lord set to music: chorales, motets, in form of oratorio

passionato, appassionato (It.), passionately

pastorale, old dance in 6/8 time (Siciliano) (suite), 20; pastoral play (Handel), 63; name of Beethoven's 6th Symphony, 139

pause, see General Pause

pavane (Fr.), slow, stately dance in quadruple (or duple) time, (suite), 21

pedal-point, note sustained in bass under the other changing parts, 21

pentatonic scale, scale of only 5 notes, 463

percussion instruments, 451 ff.

perfect interval, 461

period, usually 8 bars long (two 4-bar phrases), 13

perpetuum mobile (Lat.), perpetually in motion; quick instrumental composition of notes of same value

phrase, 470

phrasing, 470

piano concerto, concerto for solo piano and orchestra

pianoforte, 447, 453

piano trio, piano and two other instruments playing parts of equal importance

piano, p (It.), soft

pianissimo, pp (It.), very soft

piccolo, small flute with shrill tone, 449

piston, valve on brass instrument

più (It.), more, e.g. più mosso, more movement, faster

pizzicato, plucking string of string instrument

plainsong, see Gregorian chant

poco a poco (It.), little by little, e.g. poco a poco accelerando, getting gradually quicker

polka, Bohemian dance in 2/4 time

polonaise, polacca (suite), 21

INDEX OF NAMES AND WORKS